A SECRET COUNTRY

John Pilger was born and educated in Sydney, Australia. He has been a war correspondent, film-maker and playwright. Based in London, he has written from many countries and has twice won British journalism's highest award, that of Journalist of the Year, for his work in Vietnam and Cambodia. He has been International Reporter of the Year, and winner of the United Nations Association Media Peace Prize. His documentary films have won Academy Awards in the United States and Britain.

This is a patriotic book in the best sense, written in the belief that Australia deserves not old bromides and stereotypes, but the respect of critical appraisal. With *The Fatal Shore* by Robert Hughes it is an essential text for anyone wishing to understand the real Australia obscured by the advertising industry's image of a nation of 'white Anglo-Saxon Crocodile Dundees with the wit of the cast of Neighbours'. It is also a necessary book for those of us who believe in the redeeming power of truth.

Daily Telegraph, London

What the Hawke Government's cronies and the comfortable critics cannot forgive is that John Pilger has told the world of our most shameful secrets — about the Aborigines, about poverty, about the workings of power. He has done so with passion, with eloquence, and not at all negatively.

Sun-Herald, Sydney

John Pilger — like those other ratbags, Robert Hughes and Germaine Greer — cannot rid himself of a conviction that Australians are too good for what is happening to them. Australians are naturally democratic, naturally unpretentious, and instinctively fair-minded, so how can they have evolved into a society with the highest suicide rate for teenage boys ever recorded anywhere?

Germaine Greer

John Pilger's true genius is to break beyond the limitations of journalism. He showed us in his previous book, *Heroes* and even more in his latest, *A Secret Country*, in which he reveals a hidden Australia at once more ugly and more heroic than the official history. *A Secret Country* is vintage Pilger. Combining investigative journalism with whimsical anecdote, it's a powerful critique of Australian society and a bloody good read.

Australian Tribune

Pilger's Australia is so different from the image conveyed abroad by films and TV soap operas, so different indeed from the way many Australians see themselves, as to be another country . . . Australia is now run by a conspiracy of Mates, the 'Silver Bodgie' (Prime Minister Bob Hawke), 'the Dirty Digger' (Rupert Murdoch), 'the Goanna' (Kerry Packer) and others . . . A higher proportion of Australian children live in poverty than do in Britain, West Germany, Canada, Sweden, Norway and Switzerland. This is Pilger's secret country. But none of it alters one starkly apparent fact – he still loves the place. Pilger wants Australia to break free from its imperial past. He is a republican and an internationalist, and he has written a powerful anthem for his cause.

Sunday Express, London

John Pilger

A SECRET COUNTRY

V

VINTAGE

This edition first published by Vintage 1992

5 7 9 10 8 6

© John Pilger 1989, 1992

First published by Jonathan Cape Ltd 1989
Vintage edition 1990

VINTAGE
Random House, 20 Vauxhall Bridge Road, London SW1V 2SA

Random House Australia (Pty) Limited
16 Dalmore Drive, Scoresby, Victoria 3179, Australia

Random House New Zealand Limited
18 Poland Road, Glenfield
Auckland 10, New Zealand

Random House South Africa (Pty) Limited
Endulini, 5a Jubilee Road, Parktown 2193, South Africa

Random House UK Limited Reg. No. 954009

A CIP catalogue record for this book
is available from the British Library

Papers used by Random House UK Limited
are natural, recyclable products made from wood grown in
sustainable forests. The manufacturing processes conform to
the environmental regulations of the country of origin

ISBN 0 09 915231 2

Set in 10½/12 Sabon by Rowland Phototypesetting Ltd,
Bury St Edmunds, Suffolk
Printed and bound in Great Britain by
Cox & Wyman Ltd, Reading, Berkshire

To the memory of my great-great grandparents, Francis McCarthy and Mary Palmer, who came to Australia in chains, and to the Aboriginal people who fought back.

CONTENTS

Acknowledgments xiv

Introduction 1

1 On the Beach 7

2 A Whispering in Our Hearts 21

3 Heroes Unsung 87

4 The Struggle for Independence 139

5 The *Coup* 185

6 Mates 239

7 Battlers 327

8 Breaking Free 353

Notes 375

Index 399

ILLUSTRATIONS

1. Aboriginal fathers and sons who fought in the Second World War
2. Eddie Murray, who was killed in police custody, Wee Waa, 1981
3. Aboriginal artist, Albert Namatjira
4. Joyce Hall, Northern Territory, 1982
5. Alice Springs, 1987
6. Freda Glynn, Chairperson of Imparja Television
7. Clara Inkamala explains how to catch and cook a goanna
8-9. Denis O'Hoy in Bendigo, 1946; and in 1987
10. Maria and Carlo Calcagno's wedding, Sicily, 1954
11. The Calcagnos in Sydney, 1955
12. The Atlas football team, Sydney, 1940
13. Tom Stratton, with Greek 'New Australians', Athens, 1958
14-15. The author's parents: Elsie Pilger née Marheine in 1907; Claude Pilger in 1947
16. Valentina Makeev and her pet kangaroo, Snowy Mountains, 1940s
17. 'The Basher Gang' used by the New South Wales Government in the 1930s to break the coal-miners' strikes
18. The miners' last stand at Rothbury colliery, 1929
19. Robert Menzies when he was Prime Minister
20. A symbol of all that remains at the Maralinga test site, 1987

21. Vietnam veterans' 'welcome home' parade, Sydney, 1987
22. Harold Holt welcomes President Lyndon Johnson to Australia, 1966
23-4. Brian Day in the late 1950s; and with fellow Vietnam veteran and 'Agent Orange' victim Barry Wright, Blue Mountains, 1987
25. Christopher Boyce, who described CIA operations in Australia
26. The Governor-General of Australia, Sir John Kerr, who dismissed the Whitlam Government in 1975
27-9. Alan Bond with Neville Wran; Bondy with Bob Hawke; Hawke with Kerry Packer
30. Sir Peter Abeles
31. Tom Domican
32. Paul Keating
33. Rupert Murdoch
34. 'How the Rich Live'
35. Mates. George Shultz and Bob Hawke, 1987
36. The top-secret American base at Nurrungar, South Australia
37. Jack Platt, the Bondi Beach shark catcher, 1952
38. 'The Sunbaker'
39. Bronte Beach, Sydney, 1985
40. Thelma Thompson, nurse, Broken Hill, 1920
41. Harry King, wheat farmer, Mollerin, 1987
42. Working at home on poverty rates, Melbourne, 1987
43. King's Cross, Sydney, 1986
44-5. The 'new suburbia', western Sydney, 1987
46. John Pilger with the parrot that won't drink Bondy's XXXX beer
47. John and Sam Pilger, Ayers Rock, 1987

FIGURES

'The John Pilger version'   i
The Dead Heart   56
The Compact   84

ILLUSTRATIONS

Mary Palmer's conditional pardon, 1838   97
Francis McCarthy and Mary Palmer's petition to the
        Governor of New South Wales   98
Repelling the 'Asiatic Hordes'   120
A typical caricature of the 'yellow peril'   122
The Melbourne *Age*, February 23, 1988   238
'But . . . that's what friends are for . . .'   245
'No one could be more Australian than I . . .'   284
'There I was innocently driving home . . .'   324
'Whaddawewant'   357

ACKNOWLEDGMENTS

I wish to pay tribute to my father, Claude Pilger, who died as I wrote this. The son of a German sailor and an Australian pioneer, he grew up in coal-mining towns in the Hunter Valley, New South Wales. He was a miner at the age of fifteen, then an 'artisan in training', but was otherwise self taught, beginning at the Mechanics Institute library in Sydney, where he became a socialist. He remained a craftsman all his life, working meticulously with wood; and he loved Ellice, his wife, his sons, his friends, music, tennis, the writing of O. Henry, a bet and Australia. He spent some of his happiest days travelling in the Australian bush. Although having unresolved doubts about the nature of my chosen craft, he was proud of me and encouraged and stood by me unfailingly. I miss him and thank him.

I would like to express my appreciation to all those who have directly and indirectly helped me with this book. Without their knowledge and skill it would not have been written. I am grateful to Mark Aarons, Franca Arena, Steve Arnold, Faith Bandler, Paul Barry, Deborah Bick, David Bowman, Geraldine Briggs, Mike Broderick, Clyde Cameron, Paul and Rita Cauchi, Paul Chadwick, Preston Clothier, Frances Coady, John Cody, Jock Collins, Tim Comerford, Bill Cope, John Corker, Jenny Cottom, Liz Cowen, Joan Coxsedge, Ian Craig, Rachel Cugnoni, Peter Cullen, Allan Davies, Brian Day, David Day, Pat Dodson, Don Dunstan, Max Dupain, Peter Dyer, Ross Fitzgerald, Gerrit Fokkema, Denis Freney, Rosemary Gillespie, Sue Griffin, Colin Griffiths, Janice and

ACKNOWLEDGMENTS

Michelle Hartree, June Henman, Dorothy Hewett, Tony Hewett, Jane Hill, Joanne Hill, Donald Horne, Deborah Inman, Mary Kalantzis, Kevin Kearney, Rachael Kerr, Harry and Kath King, Jo Kolowski, Jacqueline Korn, Nick Lockett, Alan Lowery, Gavan McCormack, Ian Macphee, Isobel McLean, Valentina and Michael Makeev, Ken Marheine, Patsy Metchick, Robert Milliken, Bill Mitchell, Mon Mohan, Alan Moir, David Moore, Alec Morgan, Paul Murphy, Lorraine Nelson, Denis O'Hoy, Andrew Olle, June Peacock, Bruce Phillips, the late William Pinwill, the late Elsie Pilger, Sam Pilger, the Quagliata family, Henry Reynolds, Brian Robbins, Geoffrey Robertson, Glyn Rutherford, Colleen Ryan, Michael Sexton, Carole Sklan, Robert Stapelfeldt, Tom Stratton, Brian Toohey, Dimity Torbett, Joseph Trento, Frank Walker senior and junior, Sarah Westcott, Ted Wheelwright, Evan Whitton, Graham Williams, Joy Williams, Andre'e Wright and Barry Wright.

PICTURE CREDITS

I would like to thank the following for permission to reproduce photographs: Associated Press for no. 25; Kevin Berry for no. 31; Martin Brannan for no. 26; John Fairfax & Sons for nos 1, 3, 32 and 43; Gerrit Fokkema for nos 4–5, 9, 19 –20, 24, 39, 42 and 44–7; John Garrett for the author's photograph on the jacket; Phillip Lock for no. 30; Nick Lockett for nos 6 and 7; Brenden Mead for no. 21; David Moore for no. 22; News Ltd for no. 27; Peter Solness for no. 29; Rick Stevens for no. 35; Greg White for no. 36.

I would also like to thank the following for permission to reproduce the figures: the Melbourne *Age* for fig. 7; Bill Mitchell for the frontispiece; Allan Moir for figs 1, 2, 8, 9, 10 and 11.

INTRODUCTION

AS A YOUNG reporter on the Sydney *Daily Telegraph*, assigned to cover the wharves and the airport, I was obliged to ask 'visiting celebrities' what they thought of Australia. Although they might have seen only those unique Australian officials who spray arriving passengers with disinfectant, they were expected to play a game and make a statement affirming all that was good and sublime about 'Godzone'. Exhausted by a seemingly endless journey, and broiling or shivering in the corrugated iron sheds that stood at the nation's gates, they were prompted about the delights of 'our beer, beaches and way of life'. Compliance ensured them generous space in the next day's papers; resistance risked public opprobrium. When the actress Elizabeth Taylor loudly and accurately described the question as 'dumb as shit', the size of the bags under her eyes was reported and it was noted that her latest husband was 'dwarf-like and grizzled'.

At other times the question would be welcomed, as in the case of Henry Wiley Fancher, a wealthy Texas rancher. Arriving to do business with the Premier of the State of Queensland, Sir Johannes Bjelke-Petersen, Fancher described Australia as 'truly wunnerful' because he liked 'a nigra in a nigra's place' and in Australia his son would not be 'seduced by coloured girls'. When told there were Aborigines in Queensland, he said, 'I've heard you treat them like our injuns. You've put them on reservations and they're no problem. Is that so?' It was so.

The game was not confined to the rich and famous. When a newly arrived Turkish immigrant was asked what he thought of Australia, his response was, 'Where the hell am

1

I?' 'He wants to know', said an interpreter, 'why it took so long to get to Austria.' According to one version of this story, the Turkish Government, anxious to be rid of large numbers of unemployed and politically troublesome young men, blurred the distinction between prospects for 'guest work' in Austria and Australia. Like so many others who have come to Australia by accident, against their will or seeking refuge, the Turk chose to stay. Perhaps a society which began with no grand design, except as a 'living hell' for those sent to it in 'penal servitude', whose expectations are entirely those of ordinary people and which has developed, by default, a cultural diversity greater than almost anywhere else, has an abiding strength denied to others, even if this at times is expressed as insecurity.

I have long regarded my own country as secret, as a land half-won, its story half-told. It was as if the past was another country, mysterious and unexplained. 'Australian history' either was not taught or was not required for 'higher learning'. Contemporary history was unheard of. Black history was ridiculed. Historians and politicians, more concerned with imperial propriety than truth, covered up and distorted. Wars were fought against invading British armies, whole Aboriginal nations were wiped out and their land stolen, but no mention was made of them. The evidence was available; but as Henry Reynolds, one of the leading new-wave historians, has pointed out, 'Black cries of anger and anguish were out of place in works that celebrated national achievement or catalogued peaceful progress in a quiet continent . . .' In *The Fatal Shore* Robert Hughes described 'a national pact of silence'; and although there have since been many changes, the ideology of the 'pact' and of its stereotypes remains.

During the 1988 'celebration' of the two-hundredth anniversary of Britain's bloody dispossession of the Aboriginal people, the Australian Government and advertising industry strove to conjure a nation of white Anglo-Saxon Crocodile Dundees with the wit of the cast of *Neighbours*. One highlight of this endeavour was the spectacle of a number of fashionably dressed white people leaping up and down in front of the Aboriginal sacred site at Ayers Rock, singing 'Celebration of a Nation'. But such illusions failed to disturb a nightmare and its secrets. 'In the past', wrote Woli Saunders, an Aborigine, 'we died from ball and shot, poisoned flour, strychnined water-holes and smallpox. Today we are still dying. When will it stop?' Black Australians have died in police and prison cells on average every fourteen days, a rate higher than that of the death of black people in South Africa.

A Secret Country follows my book *Heroes* and a trilogy of documentary films, *The Last Dream*, which I made with Alan Lowery, Alec Morgan and others and were shown in a number of countries in the Bicentenary year. With the films as a starting point, I wrote this book so that it might be read dispassionately in the wake of the 1988 'celebrations'. It is not in any way definitive, but it is written in the belief – shared, I know, with many Australians – that our country deserves not old bromides and stereotypes, but the respect of critical appraisal and access to the widest range of views on its progress thus far.

At the beginning of their remarkable work, *A People's History of Australia*, Verity Burgmann and Jenny Lee explain that their aim was 'not merely to compensate for past neglect, but to assert that we can only understand Australia's history by analysing the lives of the oppressed'. That has been my guide, too. A nation founded on the bloodshed and suffering of others eventually must make its peace with that one historical truth. Otherwise the best of what has been achieved is undermined and, as many Australians now say, 'something is missing'.

This book is not just about Australia. What is happening today in Australia is no more than a warning that liberal societies are being returned to passivity, obedience and secrecy and that the subjugation of people's minds and pockets has a new set of managers and a new vocabulary. Chapter 6, 'Mates', is about this new world of the 'transnational economy' and 'rational economics', of which Australia is a microcosm. With its banks and much of its industry de-regulated and its currency 'floated', Australia is now compelled to sell off its resources and rely on tourism and the vagaries of the international money markets. The result is a Two-Thirds Society, a model for the deepening recession of the 1990s, with a majority embracing the 'good life' by getting deeper into debt and a large minority excluded and effectively disenfranchised. In 1992 unemployment in Australia stood at more than ten per cent, the highest since the Great Depression of the 1930s.

One of our distinctions as Australians was that, unlike Britons with their walls of class and Americans with their vast disparities of wealth, we had struck a fine balance between the needs of the community and the individual. We measured social progress, it was said, not so much in terms of productivity and 'consumption' as by the well-being of the producers – all the producers, especially the providers of labour. In 1920 the silver and zinc miners of Broken Hill won the world's first 35-hour week, half a century ahead of Europe and the United States. Long before most of the world, Australia had a minimum wage, child benefits, pensions and the vote for women. The secret ballot was invented in Australia. By the 1960s we Australians could boast that we had the most equitable spread of personal income in the world. Twenty years later this has been lost in the most spectacular redistribution of wealth since the Second World War.

The new world economics order is represented in Australia by the Order of Mates, an arrangement of mutual benefit between leading politicians, notably of the Australian Labor Party, and their very rich and powerful patrons. This has spawned thousands of freshly minted millionaires, their fortunes built on easy borrowing, property deals, tax avoidance and, for some, Government contracts and laws tailored for them and laws set aside for them. Today this new breed of Australian 'entrepreneur' has a place in the 'free market' parthenon, remembered for their spectacular successes and spectacular failures. For most of the 1980s Alan Bond, a principal Mate, was almost everywhere, selling XXXX beer in Britain and mining gold in Chile. Bondy, whose worldwide empire has now collapsed, at one time had a debt that accounted for as much as 10 per cent of the Australian national debt. Along with other Mates, he is, at the time of writing, awaiting trial.

The new order has meant poverty and homelessness on a scale unknown for two generations. The Minister for Social Security in the Hawke Government has warned of a new Australian poor 'living in massive deprivation . . . like perhaps we've never seen . . . a time bomb'. On sublime Bondi Beach bonfires are lit for thousands of homeless children. In the letters columns of the *Sydney Morning Herald* a 17-year-old boy writes a lament for his friends who have died. Australia now can claim one of the highest suicide rates of teenage males in the world.

Futurists seeking an example of the 'global village' need look no further than Australia. Nowhere else has the 'communications revolution' had such a profound effect. 'If you're not big, you'll be swept aside,' pronounced the New York media analyst Ed Atorino, whose dictum applies precisely to recent, dramatic changes in the Australian media. With Government support, a few Mates have controlled most of the information Australians watch and read. One Mate, Rupert Murdoch, controls almost two-thirds of all newspaper circulation, as well as the means of distribution. In one city, Adelaide, he owns the only morning paper, the only Sunday paper, all the local papers and all the printing presses. The Brave New World imagined by Aldous Huxley has clear echoes in these developments in the pleasant, vulnerable land of Rupert, Bondy and the Silver Bodgie, where the illusion of 'saturation media' masks censorship by omission and a growing intolerance to rival ideas. The essence of this 'new democracy' is an old idea; it was described by Edward Bernays, the leading figure in 1920s American corporate propaganda, as the 'engineering of consent'. I hope *A Secret Country* will help to alert those whom this 'new democracy' betrays.

Above all, I have written this book with affection. As one who has lived and reported from many countries, I am constantly drawn back to the friendship, warmth and diamond light of my homeland. In one sense, to be an Australian is to be an outsider. My Irish great-great grandparents, who arrived in leg irons, were certainly outsiders. The millions of people who have come from all over the world – the 'displaced persons' from post-war Germany, 'Ten Pound Poms', confused Turks, Vietnamese 'boat people' – have come as true outsiders. And like all of us they will remain outsiders until nationhood is restored to the first Australians.

The American dissident Gore Vidal was once asked whether he still felt wholly American, spending most of his time in Europe as that other great American writer, Henry James, had done. He replied, 'Henry James did not really like the United States. I do. James was deeply ashamed of his native land. I am certainly not ashamed of it, just appalled by what our rulers do. James wanted to be a European. I don't . . . I feel more and more American as the years pass.' Change 'American' to 'Australian' and his sentiments are mine.

Having said that, I declare a loyalty to another country once described eloquently by the great English internationalist Bruce Kent. 'I have seen it', he wrote, 'while flying over the long red deserts of Australia, in the lakes and forests of northern Canada and in the night stars of Africa. I have known it in the tens of thousands of decent, caring, suffering, unpublicised people worldwide who struggle in their different ways toward a new kind of world community into which the old nationalisms do not fit. The framework for that new unity and the terms of our trusteeship we have yet to understand. But there is a new country . . .'

Many Australians already belong to this new country. This book is a salute to them.

John Pilger
March 1992

I

ON THE BEACH

After grey, wintry London Australia's colour and light intoxicated . . . We flew for hours over Martian landscapes, reached the cobalt ocean and were stunned by Sydney's brilliance. As thirsty men cannot help but gulp, so pale arrivals from the northern hemisphere revel and gorge in a surfeit of hot dazzle and fruit salad colours.

Trevor Fishlock, *Daily Telegraph*, London

Summer without the beach is like a love affair without the lover.

Meg Stewart, *Bondi*

This Drinking Fountain Must Be Used Only For That Purpose – Use The Toilet For Washing Feet!

Sign in the Bondi Beach Pavilion

THE 'HOT DAZZLE' casts a light of diamond incandescence, which has forged in the Australian face a permanent squint and lop-sided smile. This makes us look laconic when often we are not. Squinting, head at an angle, hands on hips: this is how we are on the beach.

Waking soon after dawn, lying in my teenage bunk in Moore Street, Bondi, I used eagerly to await this light, which announced summer Saturdays. It beamed into my room, refracted from Mrs Esme Cook's red iron roof next door; it lit every particle of dust that rose like a silver escalator from the Feltex floor covering; and it swept the wallpaper (circles on flowers) like a searchlight, highlighting a three-foot hair-oil stain, the consequence of a family 'discussion'.

The sounds that came with the light belonged to locusts and currawongs. The locusts provided a background of incessant, mad humming. When summer was over they would rise like a black squall of minor Biblical proportions and expire *en masse* over Bob's Gully, where their carcasses lay until March. The currawongs sat on Mrs Esme Cook's iron and tarpaper roof – you could hear them sliding on the corrugations – and they sang and called to each other ceaselessly. Currawongs are garrulous birds with voices like flutes and a range from shrill to almost bass; in full cry they sound like an ornithological Welsh chorus. Ebony black with white plumage, they are a sort of primeval crow whose genetic origins, like birds of paradise and so many Australian creatures, are little known.

Like most scavengers, currawongs are not universally

9

loved; they fix you with a gleaming yellow eye and they dive-bomb and raid nests and eat like goats. They decimated Moore Street's backyard fruit trees, making sorties from Mrs Esme Cook's and the roof of our dunny. 'Get those flamin' birds outta here!' Mrs Cook would say to Ted, her snowy haired husband. I liked those birds: I liked their song and their wickedness. They kicked over the traces with style.

There is a smell and taste that come with the diamond light. By December, when the king tides have arrived from across the south Pacific, the salt spray blows up from the beach. It stiffens the air, covers windows with a sticky mist, corrodes paint on cars and mortar between bricks, and tastes like Bondi and summer. I still run down to the beach with my heart thumping at the prospect; by the time I reach Hall Street and turn into Campbell Parade, which skirts the length of the beach, the spray has the texture of sand. If a 'southerly buster' is blowing, the sand is in my hair, nose, ears, on my tongue. Bondi is the site of one of Sydney's main sewerage outlets; in an enduring environmental atrocity raw sewage is pumped into the ocean just beyond the last line of breakers. If a hot westerly blows, the nostalgic cocktail is complete: salt, sand and shit.

The beach is Australia's true democracy. Such a notion will infuriate those who do not like the beach, who do not regard Bondi as Hindus regard the Ganges, who prefer to remain grey skeined with sweat rather than covered in carcinogenic rust.

I have a friend like that. He was, admittedly, born way out west, somewhere near the Great Sandy Desert, which his childhood imagination might have conjured as a vast beach without water. Certainly, whenever he has visited me in my Bondi 'office', as he calls the south end of the beach, in order to discuss matters so urgent he is obliged to fill his uncongenial shoes with sand and to wear zinc cream on his nose, his temper is foul, and our friendship is strained. Not even G-stringed sybarites, close at hand, leaven his mood. I have told him he is not a real Australian. He has retorted that I am 'just a bloody expatriate'. The last time I persuaded him to meet me on the beach his ankles turned the colour of freshly boiled beets. He has not forgiven me for this.

The truth is that we Australians did not derive our freedom from bewigged Georgian founding fathers and their tablets of good intentions. There was no antipodean Gettysburg. We are still finding our freedom among condoms on the sand and joggers on the dole, 'banana lizards' on parole and others on illicit business, ageing 'hot doggers' and gays eyeing lifesavers and mums with 'toddlers' and tourists from Osaka. In short, we have found our freedom by taking our clothes off and doing nothing of significance, and by over the years refining and elevating this state of idleness to a 'culture' now regarded highly in the world's most fashionable places.

This is not quite the vibrant image promoted by Paul Hogan. Paul and his people are rich and shiny, and have excellent teeth. We are not like that. Sydney, our greatest city, is only recently glamorised, its skyline only recently Man-hattanised, its vocabulary only recently Americanised ('lifts' into 'elevators', 'holidays' into 'vacations', 'I reckon' into 'I guess'), its heroes only recently transmuted from underdogs who struggled to the top to become corporate spivs and money launderers.

Not long ago Sydney was an impoverished city, whose working conditions were at times worse than the worst in England. The sweatshops of east Sydney, with their low wages, long night shifts and unsafe practices – unguarded machinery and floors so hot the soles peeled from your boots – produced an hypnotic routine from working lives. Smoke from industrial chimneys blotted blue skies and congealed winter afternoons into premature night; and the silhouettes that moved along ribbons of tenement houses in the inner city might have been painted by L. S. Lowry. The repossessors, the bailiffs, the Dickensian sharpies, the man who sold clothes-props, were from lives on the edge.

At Central Station the rural poor, white and black, spilled out of the overnight mail trains that come from 'out west', the northern rivers and the southern tablelands, and dragged their cardboard cases, tied with string, to the hostels and a cheap hotel known as the 'People's Palace'. Here there were army surplus stores and greasy spoon Chinese restaurants with newspaper tablecloths and tiled pubs from which people staggered or were thrown.

In Balmain, now gentrified with houses that sell for a million dollars and more, people went hungry. In Paddington – a slum just down the road from Bondi – owl-eyes peered from behind lace curtains and the streets were places for tramps and winos and kids with serge short pants and bloody knees. If you lived in Paddo you were a 'battler' and a loser. Here, too, houses once rented to battlers and losers sell for a million dollars and more.

Bondi was borderline. Bondi was alleys of litter and smashed beer bottles and fences of rusted corrugated iron, and faded art deco flats, with stairwells that smelt of cabbage, and 'Bondi semis' where the occupants never seemed to turn on the light. Bondi was Jewish refugees who were known as 'reffos' and others who were known as dagos, wogs, Eyties, Balts, Chinks and boongs; and Catholics who were known as tykes; and women who were known as sluts, nymphos, old fowls and 'very nice ladies'.

Bondi was men coughing up their innards in a rush-hour tram because an entire Australian division was mustard-gassed on the Western Front. Bondi was men weaving home on a Saturday night clutching bottles of 'Dinner Ale', shaped like ten-pins, and bottles of Shelley's lemonade for the kids and a chook for the missus: the chook having been 'acquired ', or won in a pub raffle. Bondi was domestic trench warfare, with bodies thudding against thin walls, and a woman in an apron led bleeding to an ambulance: street entertainment for the young. Bondi was the inexplicable kindness of shop-keepers; at Mack's Milk Bar and Nick the Fruitologist's they seemed to give away as much as they sold.

In Bondi, even the crankiest streets have a glimpse of the Pacific, if not of the beach itself. Whatever the state of life in the streets, the great sheet of dazzling blue-green is always there, framed between chimneys and dunnies. On weekdays my friend Pete and I would 'scale' a Bondi Beach tram if we spotted an old 'jumping jack' type, which had a peculiarly high suspension and could be bounced off the rails by a swarm of eleven-year-olds synchronising their efforts. And of course Len's apoplexy was part of the fun. Len was a famous Bondi tram conductor who liked his grog and consequently had a face like a crimson ant hill. '*Forcrissake youse kids, you'll gimme a never sprak tan!*'

All principal beaches in Australia are public places. This is not so in the United States and Europe, where the private possession of land and sea is rightly regarded by visiting Australians as a seriously uncivilised practice. Although private property is revered by many Australians, there are no proprietorial rights on an Australian beach. Instead, there is a shared assumption of tolerance for each other, and a spirit of equality which begins at the promenade steps. I ought not to make too much of this, though foreigners, Americans especially, admire it.

Perhaps the reason for this sense of ease is that many on the beach are there to elude and evade: in other words to 'lurk'. Lurking, an Australian pastime, can mean being somewhere you are not meant to be. When I worked in a postal sorting office in Sydney one summer, I would clock on, sort letters for an hour or two, then, with others, slip out through a hole in the back wall. We would then proceed to Bondi for a day of lurking. Indeed, the hole was known as the 'Bondi Hole'. I was told the bosses knew, but they did nothing about it. The attitude this represented was summed up by Jean Curlewis in her book, *Sydney Surfing*, published in 1924. 'Why toil to get rich,' she wrote 'to do exactly the same thing that you are doing now, not rich? Why get all hot and bothered over More Production when the thing you want is produced by the Pacific cost free? It is a philosophy that drives the American efficiency expert into a mental home.'[1]

Whatever racists and Jeremiahs may say, Australia, a society with a deeply racist past, has absorbed dozens of diverse cultures peacefully. The beach and the way of life it represents are central to this. A spectacle at Bondi in the 1950s – second only to the sight of thousands of bathers

beating their personal best whenever the shark bell rang –
was the arrival on the beach of the first post-war immigrants:
Geordies and Cockneys, Calabrians and Sicilians. Bolting
lemming-like into a deceptively light surf, they would be duly
rescued by lifesavers with a large trawling net. The ritual was
repeated as each national group arrived; Cypriots, Greeks,
Lebanese, Turks, Chileans, Mexicans and Chinese.

Today the sons and daughters of these people are often the
majority on Bondi Beach, where lifesavers have Italian, Greek
and Turkish names and board riders are Vietnamese. Walk
at dusk along the colonnade of the Bondi Beach Pavilion and
the laughter and banter and music belong to former dagos,
wogs, Balts and reffos. Call them that at your peril; the beach
is theirs now.

From an early age I was aware that what happened on and
around the beach posed a threat to the ubiquitous custodians
of civic virtue in Australia and was something called pleasure.
One such custodian, Eric Spooner, became infamous as the
'Minister for Public Taste'. Eric was responsible for a local
law which stated that 'to secure the observance of decency
swimming costumes must: (1) have legs at least three
inches long; (2) cover the front of the trunk down to the legs;
(3) have shoulder straps or other support; and (4) include
half a skirt if worn by a bather over the age of twenty
years'.[2]

Eric did not understand that grey, tight-lipped Australia
ended at the beach promenade, where the nation's lascivious,
hedonistic *alter ego* took over. The beach was our secret life.
The beach was where most of us would discover sex, no
matter that the price was being stung on the arse by a blue-
bottle at midnight, or the arrival of a large, uniformed beer
gut and damning torchlight. The writer Meg Stewart recalled
her 'first time' one New Year's Eve at Bondi when 'after a
succession of hopeless parties, a photographer friend and I
finally fell into each other's arms at the last party, drove to
Bondi, swam naked in the surf, the most magic New Year ever

14

. . . Walking out of the water was not so magical. Headlights blazed, horns blared.'[3]

Perhaps Australian beach life is healthier and freer sexually than anywhere outside the Trobriand Islands. Certainly the dilemma has always been whether to surf or perv. You can do both, of course; but serious surfing and serious perving are almost sectarian pursuits that do not necessarily mix. The south end of Bondi, where clothes have always been unpopular, is best for the latter. It was to the south end that I took Fiona. Fiona was a 1934 Austin Ten, a car for midgets, a coupé with running boards and a 'dicky seat' also known as a 'rumble seat'. It was a model described as 'the original gutless winder'; and named by the previous owner after her mother. Fiona had mechanical brakes which operated with a cable stretched the length of the chassis. This often snapped.

The first time I took my girlfriend to the south end of Bondi the cable snapped and we ended up jammed in the entrance to a barber's shop, with the radiator hissing steam at the barber and a man with lather on his face. When the barber and the man with lather on his face helped us to push Fiona back on the road, the front bumper bar fell off. My girlfriend put it in the dicky seat.

The second time Fiona's brakes snapped, she was parked. It was after midnight and the crescent of beach was spread before us with the sky reflected in its gentle breakers. The hand brake went limp, and with my girlfriend and I otherwise engaged, Fiona proceeded downhill towards a fifty-foot drop on to the rocks below. We awaited our fate. Inexplicably Fiona altered course and rolled instead into the radiator grill of a parked Hupmobile, more a tank than a car. In the back seat of the Hupmobile was a naked, entwined couple. Upon alighting from a seriously concertinaed Fiona, my girlfriend, who was not retiring, put her head through the window of the Hupmobile and said immortally, 'Gidday, howzitgoin'?'

There was another side to this. The few chemists who sold contraceptives kept them under the counter and unavailable to teenagers. (Wearing a towelling hat, stubble and a falsetto voice sometimes worked.) When girlfriends fell pregnant, which happened frequently, their fear was justified. Few of us told our parents and many took the deafening train across the Harbour Bridge to a notorious chemist who was our tormentor. For weeks he would string the girls along with brightly coloured pills, which of course were fake, while reassuring us that they would 'work'. When the appropriate time had passed, he would make 'the arrangements' with a backyard abortionist for a fee of up to £A200, a huge amount then, especially to impecunious teenagers. Naturally he had a time-payment scheme with interest at 20 per cent. With Fiona on a parking meter outside a dry cleaner's, I waited in dread a day and a night for the 'doctor' to do his job.

Of course our spirit of freedom was not extended to gays. Almost all were in the closet then: a remarkable fact set against the current estimate that a quarter of Sydney's population is homosexual. They hung about the public lavatories, where they were duly set upon by thugs and cops; the Sydney Vice Squad was then run by a detective-sergeant called 'Bumper' Farrell, who had distinguished himself on the Rugby League field by biting an opponent's ear off.

At the southern end of the beach stand Bondi Ocean Baths, dominated by the Bondi Icebergs' Club. Since 1929 the Icebergs have swum through the winter season, from the first Sunday in May to the last Sunday in September. To qualify for membership a prospective Iceberg must swim at least three out of four Sundays 'irrespective of the weather and with good humour . . . for five years'. There is a 90 per cent dropout rate and the club is for men only.[4]

Reg Clark was a Bondi Iceberg who swam through storms. His skin might have been the product of a tannery. Reg said little; his extraordinary power and grace in the water expressed all that he seemed to want to say. I was eight when Reg taught me to swim seriously. Unsparingly he drove me to his standard, for which I am grateful. With the sun barely up over Bondi Baths, and waves crashing against and over the sea wall, I swam lap upon lap with Reg walking along the wall beside me. He was mostly silent; then a familiar intonation would enter my sodden brain: 'Face down ... neck down ... reach out ... reach out ... reach out ... Go!' I was a loyal member of Bondi Swimming Club and raced every Saturday over 50, 100 and 200 yards. Reg would sometimes be there, not speaking but moving his lips: 'Reach out ... reach out.' When I came second to Murray Rose, who went on to win an Olympic gold medal, Reg was waiting at the finish. 'Wherejageto?' he said, almost smiling.

When the races were over my friend Pete and I would defy Big Norm, who blew the whistle of authority at the baths, and dive from the wall into the ocean. Waiting for a wave to cover the rocks below, plunging into it as it recedes, then grabbing a safety rope slung between the wall and rocks, is a perilous ritual practised by generations of Bondi kids. I missed the rope once, was picked up by the undertow and despatched downward, spinning like a top. I re-emerged with the ocean in my head and gut and blood pouring from 'barnacle rash'. 'Get outta there with that blood,' bellowed Big Norm, 'or the sharks'll have yer!'

Sharks came on overcast days, when the ocean was still and sullen. Pete and I comforted ourselves with talk about sharks being 'blind as bats': a myth that expired one Sunday morning when a shark bit the shank of a boy called Sandy. On the same day Jack Platt, the official Bondi shark catcher, landed a fourteen-foot tiger shark after struggling for an hour and a half in his dinghy. MANEATER! said the front page of the Sydney *Sun* the next day.

A woman called Bea Miles, whom Elsie, my mother, knew as a student, used to dive off Ben Buckler rocks with a large knife in her mouth and look for sharks. Bea had performed brilliantly at university, then 'something snapped', said Elsie, and Bea 'went potty'. For years she was Sydney's most famous 'bag lady', whose speciality was tearing the doors off taxis that refused to pick her up. She often slept on Bondi Beach, like a caravan resting at an oasis, a variety of animals tethered to her button-up boots. Once she arrived on Bondi with a sheep and when the beach inspector told her to take it away, she pointed to a sign that mentioned only dogs and ball games and said nothing about sheep. 'Everyone used to say', said Jack Platt, 'that she was over-educated.'[5]

The great swells, known as bomboras, that sweep around Ben Buckler rocks deliver not the biggest but among the truest bodysurfing waves in Australia. You scout for the swell and watch it build inexorably, while assessing its power and whether it will 'dump'. A 'dumper' begins as a wall of unbroken water and is to be avoided; a 'roller' is an inviting pyramid. Reaching the top of the pyramid before it breaks requires strength, but also a style of swimming that has you skimming the water like a ski. Then, when the wave breaks and you feel the surge and know you are on it, you move your arms to your sides and dip your head; and you are suddenly free and moving down the face of the wave. And then you can raise your head; your torso protrudes from the bank of the wave, like a ship's figurehead. Using your feet as rudder, you can ride all the way to the kids building sandcastles.

Surfboards then were long, hollow, heavy and water-logged. As they picked up speed, rather like my brother's pre-war eight-cylinder Dodge, you needed exceptional strength to control them. Once on course, pity the board rider who failed to keep the bow of the board high and clear of the water. And once the nose dipped, explained Michael Blakemore, in his fine film, *A Personal History of the Australian Surf*, 'the board dived straight to the bottom where caught in the slingshot of its own buoyancy, it catapulted back into the air like a missile leaving a silo. When that happened you leapt as far clear as you could and stayed submerged until you heard the thump of splashdown. If you lost the board on a wave you were safe, but innocent inshore bathers were in mortal danger.'[6]

Lightweight Malibu boards, made from balsa, were introduced during the 1950s; and bodysurfing lost many of its faithful to the 'hot doggers' of the surf and what was said to be 'high-density stimulation'. There was also a new masonic way of life, not unlike that of the bikers. You rubbed lemon juice or Ajax sink cleaner into your hair to bleach it; you drove an old Volkswagen and you were never satisfied with the surf of one beach only. Alas, I was never a committed hot dogger. I love swimming and bodysurfing too much. Striking out for a wave, then touching the beach at the demise of a perfect 'boomer', seems incomparable; no vehicle is necessary. Or perhaps the real joy is walking the long way back up the beach, legs unsteady, chest rising and falling, and then lying face down on the hot white sand and listening to the rhythm of your heart and feeling the hot dazzle on your back. There is a photograph taken in 1937 by the celebrated Australian photographer Max Dupain, entitled 'The Sunbaker', which appears on the cover of this book. It is of a man of indeterminate age lying on his front on the summer sand. His arms are folded; his head rests sideways on a forearm. There are drops of the ocean on him, and a salt streak across his shoulders. His eyes are closed; I imagine he is me.

For most Australians, who live in congested coastal cities, the foreshore, the beach, is the one link with our ancient continent, about which we know little, whose surface we have grievously disrupted and whose original people we have banished and killed. We see and understand little beyond the last of the urban red-tiled roofs, but many of us understand well the rhythm of water on sand, of wind on current. A Bondi child will know the feel of a westerly, a nor'easterly and a 'southerly buster'. There is a grace about this life. 'The dolphins and the whales used to come in but we didn't worry about them,' said Jack Platt, the Bondi shark catcher. 'They'd come and knock the barnacles off their backs against the rocks. The porpoises still come in when they're mating . . . hundreds of them. They come in with the westerlies, they all pick their partners and dance [and] go up in the air. It's the most glorious thing to watch . . . just like the surfers, they ride the waves and everything. A real picture.'[7]

Bondi's secret is hidden beneath Campbell Parade on the ocean front. It was here that the first Australians built a network of workshops and armouries in which they fashioned the weapons and tools – axes, spear points and knives – by which they lived and with which they endeavoured to defend their homeland against the white-skinned invaders who landed not far from Bondi. Some of the artefacts of their beach civilisation were found early this century, but most were thereafter buried beneath tarmac and concrete. All but a few of the original people of Bondi died from diseases brought by the invaders; or they were shot or poisoned.

The first Aborigine I ever saw used to play Country and Western songs on a battered twelve-string guitar in the great urinals that were the public bars of Billy the Pig's at Bondi Junction and the Royal on Bondi Road. As a newspaper boy I was allowed in during the 'Six o'Clock Swill', when the pubs closed. I noticed that the drinkers seemed kind to the Aborigine, and threw coins into his hat. 'The boong's worth a zac [sixpence],' they'd say, 'give him a fair go.' In return he was obsequious in his appreciation, but his eyes were opaque and not at all grateful. He was called Jackie, as all blacks were called; no one would have known him by his real name. I last saw him swigging a bottle of sherry, slumped in one of the deckchairs that faced the music bowl at the back of the Bondi Pavilion. Jazz and *La Traviata* were performed there, admission free. On this occasion a Salvation Army band was playing 'All Things Bright and Beautiful' to an audience of a dozen or so, including an amorous couple unconcerned about the sabbath, while the rest of us seriously considered the sun.

A WHISPERING IN OUR HEARTS

At the white man's school, what are our children
   taught?
Are they told of the battles our people fought,
Are they told of how our people died?
Are they told why our people cried?
Australia's true history is never read,
But the blackman keeps it in his head.

Bill Day, from *Bunji*, December 1971

LA PEROUSE, 1951. It was one of those moments in child-hood when you stand outside yourself, outside 'normal' experience. The silhouettes related to no one. They were not meant to exist. They were meant to have 'died off'. Certainly few adults spoke of them as if they existed and, anyway, they were not counted, unlike the nation's sheep.

But they were not invisible.

I would go to La Perouse and stand on the sand hills and look at them. I was not supposed to do this, although no one had said so; it was assumed. It was not that these non-existent people, who lived in fruit-box houses, were dangerous, although no one could be sure. They were simply part of the collective 'menace' of vagrants and alcoholics who came here for refuge and truants and teenagers for 'no good', such as sex, and occasionally to drown in a surf that boiled and spat. There was also rusted iron and broken glass that made the sand scabrous and slashed your feet.

My friends and I – especially Pete who came all the way from Bondi with me – would dare ourselves to walk down the sweep of the sand towards the fruit boxes. The silhouettes then would become faces and eyes which stared. The houses, or shanties, had wire-mesh doors to keep out the squadrons of flies which came over from dumped garbage; 'Dump it at La Perouse' was an expression. Behind each wire door there seemed to be a woman, watching and still.

The flies were stuck on the children's eyelids; and this was fascinating to us. Some of the children kept one eye closed. Perhaps because everybody in Australia squinted, this did not

23

seem odd. That some could barely see at all was not known to us. Almost all of them had what I later heard described as 'the Abo H': permanent lines of mucus from the nose to the upper lip. This was confirmation that they were 'dirty'. That they were racked by preventable infection we did not know.

The boys of my age wore ragged 'army disposal' shorts with multiple buckles. The girls wore dresses made from sugar bags. We would gape at each other as if through an impenetrable wall of glass. The only exchange I can recall was when Pete was told by one of them to 'get rooted'. The only time I saw them laugh was when they were diving for pennies. A large white man, who used to sell boomerangs made into ink stands, would bring people to watch the diving. These 'tourists' would throw the pennies.

Men would appear from time to time, mostly from behind the houses and often with a bottle. They wore 'cowboy clothes', and whenever they caught sight of us they would go back behind the house. Shouting abuse at them was acceptable behaviour.

Some of the men would collect behind La Perouse Cable Station, which was built in the last century to link Australia and New Zealand by telephone. There they had a large, old pram, from which came the clinking noise of bottles. They would argue with each other. Once one of them smashed a bottle and put it in another's face. This had just happened when I got off the La Perouse tram, and it was exciting to run and see the pools of blood in the grass and a cop shouting, 'What d'yer think yer doin', yer black bastards?'

La Perouse was one of the few Sydney beaches not given an Aboriginal name. Nearby there were Bondi, Tamarama, Coogee and Maroubra. But Count Jean-François Gallup de La Perouse was remembered here, on the headland to Botany Bay. In one of history's coincidences, he had appeared with two ships in Botany Bay on January 26, 1788, just after the arrival of Britain's 'First Fleet' under the command of Captain Arthur Phillip.

At school we were invited to sympathise with the Count. Had he arrived a few days earlier he could have 'claimed'

Australia for France, and we would be speaking French now. We would try to imagine being French, and there was general agreement that we were fortunate to have been spared this unfathomable alternative to the higher calling of being British. No one seriously considered that Australia already belonged to people who had been there for millennia, who represented hundreds of 'nations' speaking their own languages and living in their own countries.

When the British invaded, they declared Australia 'Terra Nullius', empty land, and for the purpose of historiography, those who inhabited this 'empty land' did not exist. And not only was such a denial of reality and logic exclusive to the Georgian mind; subsequent generations accepted the nuance that in this 'empty land' the original people were 'dying off'.

From 1952, when I entered high school, a standard history textbook was *Man Makes History: World History from the Earliest Times to the Renaissance* by Russel Ward. It sold more than 200,000 copies. This is an extract:

Boys and girls often ask, 'What's the use of history?'

Answer: There are still living today in Arnhem Land people who know almost no history. They are Aboriginal tribesmen who live in practically the same way as their forefathers and ours did, tens of thousands of years ago . . . We are civilised today and they are not. History helps us to understand why this is so.[1]

Similarly, the standard Australian atlas in circulation from 1939 to 1966 described white 'exploration' of Australia as 'the curtain of darkness . . . being slowly rolled back'. 'Explored' Australia was represented as white oases in an otherwise dark continent.[2]

One explanation for the notion of 'empty land' was that the people living in it did not count because they were not really human. They were part of the fauna. The *Encyclopaedia Britannica* appeared to be in no doubt about this:

> Man in Australia is an animal of prey. More ferocious than the lynx, the leopard, or the hyena, he devours his own species.[3]

One of the most widely read textbooks in Queensland schools was *Triumph in the Tropics*. Commissioned in 1959 for the State's Centenary celebrations, it was the work of Sir Raphael Cilento and Clem Lack. The latter was public relations adviser to the Premier of Queensland. In Part Two, entitled 'Queensland's Expanding Frontiers: the Story of a Century of Progress', there is a chapter on the Aborigines. This is an extract:

> Like his own half-wild dogs, the black could be frozen into shivering immobility or put to frenzied flight by people or things that provoked impressions of terror; or moved to yelps of delight or to racing round, or striking grotesque poses, or to expressing frantic excitement by any sort of clowning when what might have been menace proved, instead, amusing or brilliantly productive. In his bushland home he lived in such insecurity that his immediate response to any situation of surprise was almost a conditioned reflex – instantaneous: to strike, to leap aside, to fall and roll. Like his dogs, too, he could be cowed by direct and confident stare into a wary armed truce, but would probably attack with fury if an opponent showed signs of fear, or ran away, or fell disabled. These are primitive reactions common to many feral jungle creatures.[4]

And as animals they possessed no rights, nor any claim to morality. A 1970 reprint of *The Squatting Age in Australia* by Professor Stephen Roberts concluded that:

> It was quite useless to treat them [the Aborigines] fairly, since they were completely amoral and usually incapable of sincere and prolonged gratitude.[5]

This was a departure for Roberts, whose *History of Australian Land Settlement*, regarded as a classic account, included not a single reference to Aborigines. When a chair of anthropology was endowed by the Australian Government at Sydney University, it was for research into the origins of the indigenous people of New Guinea, not the indigenous people of Australia, who had been banished into a silent absence. Indeed the first Australians suffered double dispossession: territorial and linguistic. The *Australian National Dictionary* refers to 'black gentleman', a term of irony. The verb 'to civilise', when used of Aborigines, meant to domesticate, that is to enslave. 'Dispersal' was a euphemism for mass extermination.[6]

'They are people who know almost no history ... We are civilised and they are not.' Lake Mungo is far from La Perouse, deep in the Australian continent. The hills of sand rise here like breaking waves petrified. Down their line pink cockatoos fall and ascend. These are the Walls of China which have marked the desert bed of Lake Mungo since the end of the Ice Age 15,000 years ago. Before that, there was an inland sea and glaciers on snowy mountains; and it was perilously cold. The first Australians lived here and survived the convulsions of these changes. At first they collected mussels at the lake's shore and fished for golden perch with woven bar-

rier nets. When the heat came and the lake vanished, they adapted to seed; and they endured.

When I went there in 1967, Lake Mungo was part of the Gol Gol Sheep Station, of which little remained. There was the cavernous woolshed, built in 1869 by Chinese labourers who had come to find gold, and there was a picture of an old Scottish church, St Mungo, which had hung in the original homestead. The distinction of Gol Gol, I was told, was that 50,000 sheep were shorn here every season. That it was one of the places where the world's oldest civilisation had begun was known only to the legatees of this civilisation, who then did not officially exist.

In 1969 the first discovery was made. It was a human skeleton remarkably similar to that of a contemporary person, and it was of a young woman who had been cremated in what appeared to be a religious ceremony 26,000 years ago. The most recent previous discovery was of the skeleton of a very tall man, who lived perhaps 30,000 years ago. The upper part of his body had been covered with ochre, its earliest known use, which indicated religious ritual and the cultural investments of art, dance and song that maintain Aboriginal civilisation today.[7]

Until recently white Australians knew little about this.[8] Guided by a profound sense of racial superiority and colonial insecurity, the white nation denied itself the knowledge that something unique had been sustained in its adopted land. In northern Australia, a great rock, the Obiri, gave up its secrets to white researchers only in the 1960s. Standing where the East Alligator River flows along the escarpment of Arnhemland, the Obiri is a cathedral of the Gagadju and Kunwinjku peoples, whose galleries of paintings are here. The significance of these paintings has been compared with the deciphering of the Rosetta Stone, with which the secrets of ancient Egypt were unlocked.

The Obiri paintings predate the pharaohs by 20,000 years. They are more sophisticated than the cave drawings at Lascaux in France, by which the European tribes have measured their civilisation. Unlike paintings at the European pre-glacial sites, the Australian pictures are dynamic portrayals of life as it was lived; and their line extends unbroken to strange stick figures in broad-brimmed hats, the British 'settlers' of the nineteenth century. Now included belatedly in the World Heritage List, the Obiri's galleries of paintings are said to be 'perhaps the oldest and most significant expression of human creativity . . . the longest record of any group of people'.[9]

During their long journey, which may have begun as immigrants from Asia 120,000 years ago, the first Australians evolved a civilisation whose sophistication is barely acknowledged by a white society still tied to stereotypes of its own invention. Far from being 'primitive', the first Australians demonstrated skills and mores in contrast with the rigid ways of the first Europeans. They learned languages better than whites. They displayed an intimacy with their environment that produced knowledge and skills of which the whites had no concept. They used fire to manage agriculture without threatening the environment, allowing them not only to increase food production but to create a mosaic, with each section at a different stage of regeneration. Their 'dreaming tracks' created a means of communication between people living great distances apart, which is only now matched by satellites. Moreover, they lived lives whose intrinsic value, whose 'Aboriginality', took for granted qualities of generosity and reciprocity and could not conceive of extremes of wealth and poverty.

The wellspring of this was Aboriginal reverence for the land of Australia, which they equated with life itself. They were the guardians of the land, and the land was critical to the sustenance of all human identity. 'The land is *us*; it is our mother,' a Walpiri man of northern Australia told me. 'To know the land, to know and love where you come from, and never to go out and destroy it, is being right . . . is being civilised.' Shortly before she died, the Aboriginal author Hyllus Maris wrote:

I am a child of the dreamtime people,
Part of this land like the gnarled gum tree,
I am the river softly singing,
Chanting our Songs on the way to the sea.
My spirit is the dust devils,
Mirages that dance on the plains,
I'm the snow, the wind and the falling rain,
I'm part of the rocks and the red desert earth,
Red as the blood that flows in my veins,
I am eagle, crow and the snake that glides,
Through the rain forests that cling to the
    mountainside.
I awakened here when the earth was new . . .
There was emu, wombat, kangaroo.
No other man of a different hue!
I am this land and this land is me.
I am Australia.

The Australian story, centred upon the original Australians, remains white Australia's secret. Fragments are known, of course, even taught in schools, and their legacies command headlines in newspapers and the attention of official commissions of enquiry. Some Australians claim to know more, but their confidence is frequently found to be unjustified. For these people, perhaps for the majority, the link between events in the uncharted past and today remains elusive or, as the historian Henry Reynolds has described it, 'a whispering in our hearts'.

'The barriers which for so long kept Aboriginal experience out of our history books', wrote Reynolds in his modern classic, *The Other Side of the Frontier*, 'were not principally those of source material', which had been 'available to scholars for a century or more. But black cries of anger and anguish were out of place in works that celebrated national achievement or catalogued peaceful progress in a quiet continent, while deft scholarly feet avoided the embarrassment of bloodied billabongs.'[10]

With the Aborigines written out, the Australian story seems apolitical, a faintly heroic tale of white man against Nature, of 'national achievement' devoid of blacks, women and other complicating factors. With the Aborigines in it, the story is completely different. It is a story of theft, dispossession and warfare, of massacre and resistance. It is a story every bit as rapacious as that of the United States, Spanish America, and colonial Africa and Asia. It is, above all, a political story.

Aborigines have been telling this political story for much of the past two hundred years. But few outsiders have seemed able to comprehend the enormity of what was done and is still being done. Australia was far from Europe and the Aborigines were relatively few in number. Unlike other indigenous peoples – the Indians of North America, the Maoris of New Zealand – they had no pact that acknowledged their rights as human beings. And although the anti-slavery movement showed interest in them, and an Aborigines Protection Society was formed in London, Aborigines appeared only fleetingly in the chronicles of the day. Few seemed to care that within days of the English landing in Australia the Aboriginal dreamtime ended and a nightmare began.

William Dampier, the first English navigator and explorer to 'discover' Australia, shot dead an Aborigine as he came ashore.[11] When the invasion began in earnest on January 26, 1788, the invaders were unlike anything the Aborigines had experienced. The Australians had enjoyed close trading relations with the Macassarmen of Indonesia; but the English showed no interest in trade or friendship.[12] They brought men and women in chains, whose crimes were related to poverty and politics, and they were led by Christian gentlemen imbued with a sense of racial superiority and imperial mission. This transplanted society of masters and slaves puzzled the first Australians, who had not known servility. They were bemused by the beardless, frock-coated Englishmen and even wondered what sex they were. They were curious, not hostile; they led the strangers to water and waited patiently for them to leave.

But they did not leave, and they brought death; and decimation was swift. Aboriginal blood carried no resistance to common European diseases, such as measles and colds. Within two years a smallpox epidemic had killed half the Aborigines living around Botany Bay and the coastal area north of what is now Sydney. Lieutenant Bradley, Royal Marines, reported in 1789, that 'from the great number of dead natives found in every part of the harbour, it appears that the smallpox has made dreadful havoc among them'.[13]

By 1795 Aboriginal guerrilla resistance was growing. Open warfare had broken out along the great river north of Sydney, known to the Aborigines as Deerubbin and re-named the Hawkesbury by the English. Troops were sent along its banks 'with instructions to destroy as many [Aborigines] as they could meet . . . and, in hope of striking terror, to erect gibbets in different places, whereupon the bodies of all they might kill were to be hung'.[14]

The Hawkesbury is as wide as the Mississippi in places, and is today a lush resource for the people of Sydney and the towns around Broken Bay. During the 1930s my father built a weekend house on the bay at Patonga, where the forest grows at the water's edge. We did not know then that our retreat had been a place of bloodshed, one of several battle-fields on which an epic war had raged for twenty-two years between the English and the Dharug people. Governor Lach-lan Macquarie, whose 'civilising influence' is emphasised in Australian textbooks, proclaimed that any unarmed group of Aborigines of more than six in number could be shot legally, and that this would also apply to any Aborigine found within a mile of white habitation. Women and children were not excluded.[15] The Dharug fought like lions; but they had no guns, and were defeated. The survivors were held in concen-tration camps near the town of Windsor, their children sent to 'special schools' to learn the way of the invaders.

A pattern of genocide and guerrilla warfare was now established. Neither the degree of slaughter, nor the flair and bravery with which the first Australians fought back, was acknowledged until recent years. By the 1820s troops had orders to wipe out the resistance with a strategy similar to that of 'pacification' and 'body count' deployed by the Americans in Vietnam. A rare court record of 1838 refers to twenty-eight Aborigines taken from the hut of a friendly white stockman, tied up and slaughtered. On December 14, 1838 the *Sydney Monitor* reported that 'it was resolved to exterminate the whole race of blacks in that quarter'.[16]

In the island state of Tasmania, the bloodletting continued for more than half a century. On May 3, 1804 the 102nd Regiment shot dead fifty people at Risdon Cove, including women and children. The Tasmanians had approached unarmed and with green boughs in their hands, a sign of peace. The commanding officer remarked afterwards that he did not 'apprehend' that these people would have been 'any use' to the English.[17] In 1830 martial law was declared in Tasmania and the 'Black War' was said to be a final solution, with 5,000 Europeans assembled to drive the remaining 2,000 Aborigines into the Tasman peninsula. Twenty years later the fabric of Tasmanian Aboriginal life had all but unravelled; and only a few survived.

Where the army could not defeat the Australians, chemicals were used. The *Sydney Monitor* commented that mass poisoning by strychnine, phosphorus and arsenic 'is much safer'.[18] A Queensland Government report described the effect: 'The niggers [were given] ... something really startling to keep them quiet ... the rations contained about as much strychnine as anything and not one of the mob escaped ... more than a hundred blacks were stretched out by this ruse of the owner of Long Lagoon.'[19]

The principal killing fields were in Queensland, where a specially formed colonial army, the Native Mounted Cavalry, used Snider rifles whose wide bore tore people apart. This force operated as 'extermination squads of 6–12 personnel sent in to "pacify"'.[20] Historian Andrew Markus has likened them to Hitler's *Einsatzgruppen*, the elite stormtroopers assigned to exterminate Jews in the invaded areas.[21]

The Kalkadoons were a tall Queensland people with exceptional warrior skills who managed to secure much of the Cloncurry region against encircling troops. But the cost to them was high. In 1884, after most of their women, children and old people were trapped and slaughtered in Skull Gorge, the Kalkadoons heroically faced gunfire with spears and axes. Eventually they were reduced by disease and dislocation to a few. Although statistics of the period are unreliable, it has been estimated that more Australians died on the Queensland battlefields than were killed in the wars in Korea and Vietnam.

Indeed, in a land strewn with cenotaphs which honour the memory of Australian servicemen who have died in almost every corner of the earth, not one stands for those who fought and fell in defence of their own country.

You fought here for your country.
Where are your monuments?
You resisted the invader as best you knew how.
Where are your songs of those days?
When you were captured you were not prisoners-of-war.
That would have been awkward.
You had the misfortune of occupying 'unoccupied land'.
You had to correct your gross error.
There was a pioneer tradition waiting to be unfolded.
Tales resilient as ironbark.
Your share in them was minimal and negative.
You were rather slow to understand this.
The bush and the stone and the stream.
The tree. The plain.
The special green. The faded calico blue,
They were your last line of resistance.
You fought here for your country.
Where are your monuments?
The difficulties we have in belonging
– these, these are your cenotaph.

Bruce Dawe, 'For the Other Fallen'

At the 1988 Remembrance Day service in Sydney an Aboriginal man attempted to place flowers on the Cenotaph during the playing of the Last Post. He was stopped and led away. 'I have a right to lay a wreath for my people,' he said. 'I represent the Aborigines who died defending their land, our land.'

During the 1960s, I spent much time travelling in the Americas, Africa, India and the Pacific. I began to set the experience of these societies against my own, and this was something of a revelation. In Africa I had seen sufferers of the ancient eye disease, trachoma, which, if left untreated, scars the eyelids and causes ulcers and eventual blindness. Trachoma is found only in the impoverished, overcrowded conditions of the 'developing world', with one exception: Australia. A United Nations doctor in Malawi told me this. We were standing in a camp full of children sent blind from trachoma. Here, I saw again the 'squinting' children of La Perouse.

In South Africa I was greeted warmly by white people, mostly of English origin, who spoke about 'good old Aussie' and cricket and beer drinking. They alluded cautiously, wistfully, to a land without blacks. What they meant was a land with 'perfect blacks' – blacks who were there but who were reckoned not to be there.

These English South Africans believed themselves to be liberal people, proud of their distinction from the 'uncivilised' Afrikaners on the veld, bullwhips behind their backs. Most of these liberal people had not seen, or had not wished to see, the fringes of their towns and cities, where people lived in cardboard houses without running water and behind barbed wire and watchtowers.

I took the train to Soweto, and saw the urban dust bowl which ran to caramel in the rain, and the red eyes and yellow teeth, melon bellies and stick legs, and the aura of decay and despair. Back in Johannesburg and Capetown, I told the liberal people what I had seen, and they stood around the barbecue and listened respectfully, shaking their heads. They might well have been on the other side of the Indian Ocean. I had glimpsed my own country in theirs.

I was banned from South Africa in 1967 and shortly afterwards returned to Australia. The day of my return, a national referendum was held, producing a remarkable result. More than 90 per cent of the Australian electorate voted to give the Australian Government the constitutional right to legislate justice for the Aboriginal people. No referendum anywhere in modern times had produced such an overwhelming, positive result. Aborigines were then at the mercy of State governments and institutions, which had much in common with their counterparts in Pretoria and Alabama. Now the Federal Government had an 'historic mandate' to intervene. This made Australia *appear* different from South Africa, and newspaper editorials underlined this point with pride.

The flight to Alice Springs had plenty of empty seats. In 1967 outback Australia was a land without conga-line tourism. When the plane had refuelled and headed back to Sydney, the airport fell silent. At the tea and coffee bar stood silent men wearing shorts and long socks and carrying attaché cases. On the counter lace covered a jug of milk. The lace was covered with flies. On the wall a display of tea-towels with Aboriginal motifs was black with flies. The hands of the men wearing shorts and long socks moved like windscreen wipers against a storm of flies. Silence and flies: then, with dusk, a light that burnished the earth.

Everything in the 'red centre' of Australia is imbued with this light. The walls of the Macdonnell Ranges, which stand behind Alice Springs like an amphitheatre, glow with it, as if the source is within the stone itself. The ghost gums that rivet heaven and earth glisten with it. Shadows seem only fleeting. The horizon is a line of fire, which is snuffed and consumed by a deep night with stars like ice. This is a place of artists.

The Papunya people now survive by their art, whose complex abstract dot design is recognised in the world as a unique form. For many years they kept it secret; it was said to be the expression of black paganism or it was dismissed as 'ashtray art'.

Albert Namatjira's art, on the other hand, followed a European form and was not suppressed. But the artist died.

Above the reception desk of my hotel in Alice Springs was a print of a Namatjira watercolour, 'Jay Creek Country'. That the artist was accepted was indicated by the beer mats thoughtfully tacked around its frame: an expression of the local culture. According to one estimate, people living in the Northern Territory are the third greatest consumers of alcohol in the world and are said to drink twenty-one litres of pure alcohol per person every year.[22]

Waiting at the hotel reception, I became aware that my shoes were sinking into a carpet sodden with beer and disinfectant. In the public bar, through plastic curtains, white buddhas in shorts and 'flip flops' (rubber sandals) consumed glasses, cans and jugs of beer. A face appeared through the curtains and said, 'Sign yourself in, mate. We're renovating. Put down what grog you want after hours.' Around the corner was another bar, where everyone was black. On the floor was an unconscious man. Outside, on the bonnet of a car, a woman was retching.

The next morning the Namatjira painting was different. The deep blue of the mountains had softened. The rocks had lost their burnish. The ghost gum had yellowed. Later in the day the painting seemed to change again, as if the shadows in it had receded.

Oscar Namatjira sat in the shade of a shed at a camp site a few miles from town. Oscar was the second son of Albert and Rubina, who had seven children. He was around fifty years old, a lean version of his father, with the same craggy forehead, the same melancholy eyes. With his two brothers, Oscar had followed his father and become a watercolourist. When I met him, he was completing a painting similar to one of Albert's most famous landscapes, 'Palm Valley'. Palm

Valley was a place beloved by the Namatjiras. 'That's our country,' said Oscar. 'We should be living out there, not in a place like this.'

The conditions imposed upon the family of one of Australia's most celebrated artists were typical of what most Aborigines could expect. There was one trickling water tap and no 'ablution block'. Children sat in the brown dirt, with the infamous 'squint' and 'H', several of them coughing incessantly. This coughing, which is more like hacking, is caused by respiratory illnesses that plague the Aboriginal young. A few years earlier one of the first demographic studies of the Northern Territory found that in central Australia 'the registered infant mortality rate was 208 per 1,000 live births, which must be among the highest infant mortality rates in the world'.[23]

The children sat alongside dogs, picking beer cans from newly acquired garbage. The eldest flattened each can with a blunt tomahawk, missing once and hitting a dog, which squealed but did not move. The flattened cans, explained Oscar, would be an additional wall for the shed, which was open to all weathers.

In 1951, at the peak of his fame, Albert Namatjira had tried to buy a block of land in Alice Springs, in the heartland of where his people, the Aranda, had lived for 35,000 years. The sale was denied him because he was an Aborigine. He then took his family to nearby Morris Soak, which had no facilities and soon became a slum.

When 'development' was planned there, the Namatjiras were moved on, and on again. After Albert died, they found a place overlooking a green valley; but it was not long before the new white suburbs of Alice Springs reached this valley, and there were complaints. They were moved on again, now into the dry bed of the Todd River, a place of boozing and violence.

'There was a war between whites and blacks a long time ago,' said Oscar, 'and the whites won. And I suppose the blacks, you know, just have to accept they lost. What I don't get is the whites wanting the war to go on.' Albert Namatjira was a victim of that one-sided war. He was born and grew up at a Lutheran mission, Hermannsburg. Baptised a Christian, he carried the wounds of a man torn between two lives. And when the white world, which embraced his talent, then betrayed him, he was defenceless.

Albert had only two months' tuition in watercolour technique. As a 'camel boy' in 1936, he met and travelled with a white watercolourist, Rex Battarbee, whose work he watched intently. Within two years he had held his own exhibition of some forty watercolours, all of which were sold. The public appreciated his work, although many critics did not and some expressed disdain. Perhaps they did not see, or want to see, the changing light in a Namatjira landscape, which was its 'Aboriginality'.

During the Second World War, with paper in short supply, Albert used panels of beanwood joined together. More exhibitions and acclaim followed. He was visited in the bush by the Governor-General and his wife, the English Duke and Duchess of Gloucester. He met the Queen in Canberra and was given the 'Coronation Medal'. His portrait won for its white artist prestige and prize money. To the Anglocentric establishment, he was the model of their 'assimilationist' policies, in which Aborigines who embraced white idioms were encouraged and elevated, while others who tried and failed, continued not to exist.

Albert Namatjira also failed. Far from his patrons in Sydney and Melbourne, he remained 'just another Abo', unwelcome in the white enclaves of the Northern Territory. Not only was he refused permission to build a house in Alice Springs, he was denied a grazing lease, and a court dismissed his appeal. In his Aboriginal world, it was taken for granted that the money he received from his paintings would be shared, as everything material was shared. Money of the kind he could earn had never been seen before. People signing themselves 'Namatjira' painted for the white trade. The taxation authorities took an interest and demanded large sums. Albert, who had never touched alcohol, began to drink. But it was illegal for an Aborigine to drink and he was arrested and spent a night in Alice Springs gaol, from where he emerged in despair.

In 1957, after a campaign by his white supporters, Albert Namatjira was made a citizen of Australia. Politicians and editorial writers rejoiced in the wisdom of this 'ultimate accolade'. Unlike the rest of his people, he now would be counted in the census and allowed to vote. Unlike the rest of his people, he could move about Australia without official permission; and he could buy and drink alcohol. A letter from the Governor-General, representing the Queen, ordained him a free man. His wife, Rubina, was also made a citizen. But their children were not. There were limits.

In 1958, a woman was killed by her husband at the Namatjira camp at Selly Oak. The man had been drinking heavily and Albert was named as the source of the booze. He was taken to Alice Springs and charged with supplying alcohol to an Aborigine; and the monstrous irony of that failed to deter a magistrate from handing down a gaol sentence of six months. His appeal to the Supreme Court was dismissed. The Federal Minister for the Territories intervened, not to free him but to send him to a 'native settlement': an Aboriginal concentration camp with a reputedly benign regime, where his sentence was shortened to two months 'for good behaviour'.

During this period of 'good behaviour', Albert Namatjira lost his will to paint and to live. He never painted again. Shortly after his release in August 1959 he suffered a heart attack and died.[24]

In 1969 I returned to Alice Springs. The print of Albert Namatjira's 'Jay Creek Country' was missing from above the hotel's reception desk. The decorative beer mats now framed an out-of-focus colour photograph of crumpled faces at a New Year's Eve party. The sodden carpet had been replaced by vinyl. The smell of beer and disinfectant remained.

I hired a Ford Falcon and, with Charlie Perkins and his mother Hetti, headed for Jay Creek. Hetti, whom Charlie described as a queen of the Aranda people, gave birth to him on a table in the Alice Springs Telegraph Office in 1934. As a 'half caste' Charlie was 'protected' by the authorities from 'full bloods', so that he might be 'assimilated'. He remembers his grandmother only as a face behind the wire of the 'native settlement' in which she was effectively interned. His brother killed himself. Charlie was sent to a mission school in Adelaide and thereafter to Sydney, where he distinguished himself as Australia's first Aboriginal university graduate. In 1965 he and white students, emulating the 'freedom riders' of the civil rights movement in the United States, descended upon towns in New South Wales demanding an end to segregation.

In the 1960s Moree, New South Wales, might have been Selma, Alabama. Life was divided racially at virtually every level. At the public swimming pool, where black children were banned, Perkins and his freedom riders were confronted by an angry white crowd. 'I thought we'd had it,' he said. 'Then this black woman stepped forward and made a courageous speech in which she pointed to a white man who had gone secretly with black women and had fathered black children. "Tell your wives what you've been doing, you bludgers," she said. "Go on, they're just over there: tell 'em!" That evening black children were allowed into the pool for the first time.'

We drove to the Santa Teresa Mission and filled our water bags, which we clipped to the front bumper. The carcass of a truck marked the turn off to Jay Creek. Mulga grew along the wire fence and a large yellow sign sanctified by the 'Commonwealth Government, Department of the Interior' warned that written permission was required before entering the 'reserve' and 'trespassers *WILL* be prosecuted'. There was one ragged gate, held by a wire loop. Charlie and Hetti, whose people had been here longer than the Department of the Interior, agreed that it made no sense to drive back to Alice to await a permit which might not come. So I reversed the Falcon, revved it and drove it at the gate, which exploded in a zephyr of rust. 'Cripes,' chuckled Hetti, whose large black hat came off in the process.

About three hundred Aboriginal people lived in the camp, in dead cars and under shelters of leaves and newspapers stiff

41

with flies and what flies had left. The white administrator had complete authority over their lives. He could divide families by sending 'trouble makers' into the bush and children to 'homes' in the cities from which they would never return. As punishment he could withhold food and water and confiscate money and personal possessions. Here Aborigines were being 'phased into society' by way of an iron shed, a prototype of which was on display behind the garbage dump. 'They'll be house-broken in that,' said the administrator, adding ruefully that no one wanted to live in it because it was either too hot or too cold. The next stage of 'phasing' would be an improvement: a 'modern structure with all mod cons', including floors of concrete and running water. The plans for that had yet to arrive. Whatever they were, said the administrator, 'it'll be done on the cheap'.

On the way back to Alice Springs we stopped at the Palms. Against the skyline it looked like a village built entirely of lavatories. Charlie described it as an Aboriginal 'pensioners' camp'. The nearest store was four miles away, to which the old people had to walk for tea and sugar and tins of Tom Piper's Irish stew. The store was leased by a white man known as the Pig, who swatted flies in the half-light and charged exorbitant prices and was rude whenever people approached him. 'Mind you,' said Hetti, 'the bastard might be deaf.'

In 1837 a House of Commons Select Committee completed hearings about the conditions of native peoples in the British colonies. Only one people was found to have been denied absolutely the right of prior ownership of their land: the Australian Aborigines. The Select Committee's Report demonstrated that *terra nullius*, empty land, was an absurdity, a legal fiction. The first Australians had 'an incontrovertible right to their own soil, a plain and sacred right, however, which seems not to have been understood . . . The land has been taken from them without the assertion of any other title other than that of superior force.'[25]

The modern Aboriginal land rights movement began in

1966 when the Gurindji people went on strike at the world's biggest cattle station at Wave Hill, north of Alice Springs. They were protesting against subsistence wages and poor conditions. Instead of returning to work, as expected, they camped on what they regarded as their land and in defiance of their employers, the English pastoral conglomerate headed by Lord Vestey.

It came as something of an embarrassment to white trade unions, proud of their legal, minimum wage, to learn that highly skilled stockmen were paid a few dollars a week, plus a few sacks of flour, sugar and tea, and suffered living conditions no better than those provided for the station's dogs. A national campaign formed behind the Gurindji; but Vestey's refused to acknowledge their grievances. As the strike wore on, Aboriginal demands changed radically, so that the call was no longer for improved pay and working conditions but for land rights and self-determination.[26]

The Gurindji's stand had a chain reaction. The Yirrkala people instructed lawyers to challenge the British common law interpretation of *terra nullius*. It failed; but Aboriginal activism now grew quickly. In 1972 Aborigines set up a 'tent embassy' outside Parliament House in Canberra and flew a flag of red, yellow and black denoting earth, sun and people. For the first time world attention was drawn to a cause few outside Australia had known about. Gough Whitlam, then leader of the opposition Labor Party, was invited into the tent by Aboriginal representatives and joined them in an historic meeting to negotiate terms for national land rights and human rights.

Shortly after he became Prime Minister in December of that year, Whitlam commissioned a land rights enquiry by a judge, Justice A. E. Woodward. The Woodward Commission recommended legislation to give back to Aboriginal people those parts of Australia where they now lived and had traditionally lived and which for them had spiritual importance. None of these rights was to be taken away without consent, and mining and other development should not take place on Aboriginal land without permission of the Aboriginal owners.[27]

In 1975 an Aboriginal Land Rights Act was drafted by the Whitlam Government. It was to be applied at first in the Northern Territory, which did not have statehood and was run directly by the Federal Government. In August that year Whitlam took a handful of soil and slowly poured the grains into the hands of Vincent Lingiari, a leader of the Gurindji people. The Government gave back to the Gurindji some 1,250 square miles. 'The people of Australia', said Whitlam, 'are finally restoring this land to you and your children for ever.'[28]

Three months later the Governor-General, Sir John Kerr, dismissed the Whitlam Government in sensational circumstances, which are dealt with in Chapter 5. The following year a conservative coalition Government,* led by Malcolm Fraser, introduced a version of Labor's land rights legislation. The Act gave freehold, 'inalienable' title to the land to Aboriginal communities living on 'reserves' in the Northern Territory, and to traditional owners the right to withhold consent for mining and development and to negotiate the terms and conditions of entry. Aboriginal land councils were set up to act on behalf of their new owners. A Supreme Court judge was appointed as Land Commissioner to hear Aboriginal claims for land.[29] Together with similar laws enacted by the State Labor Government in South Australia, it was a beginning.

But there was a catch. Virtually all the 'inalienable' land handed back was arid wilderness. The richest, most productive land, amounting to more than half the land of the Northern Territory, was leased to cattle owners, who represent 0·1 per cent of the population.

By the mid-1970s world tourism had found Alice Springs. Muzak-contaminated hotels and shopping malls were built. An 'international beerfest' was proclaimed. An ordinance

---

* There is no Conservative Party in Australia. I have used 'conservative' throughout to describe the Liberal/National (formerly Country) Party coalition.

banning the drinking of alcohol within two kilometres of 'licensed premises' ensured that blacks filled the police cells as they drank mostly in the open. The only Aborigines many tourists were likely to see on Fridays and Saturdays were those represented in fibreglass in a 'tourist complex', built like a McDonald's hamburger concession and announcing itself as 'the world's biggest dreamtime . . . an experience not to be missed'.

No tourists were taken to the Palms, where many of the old people continued to defy their life expectancy of forty-eight years: an age beyond which most Aborigines do not survive and which is twenty-five years less than the life expectancy of whites. When I saw the Palms a second time, it was flooded and the mud lay in the lavatory-style shelters, almost up to the level of the beds. However, the sheds had been painted bright pink, a benefit arising from emancipation.

A cousin of Albert Namatjira told me that most of Albert's seven sons and daughters had died 'from the usual business', which meant respiratory and intestinal infection, but that Oscar was still alive. When one of her daughters died, Rubina, Albert's widow, had 'sung' herself to death. I went to Alice Springs cemetery, hoping to take a photograph of her grave; but it was unmarked.

In the State of Queensland, officially a 'tourist paradise', the Aboriginal cemeteries are widespread, yet difficult to find. The cemetery on Palm Island is a case in point. Palm is one of the most beautiful islands on the Great Barrier Reef, yet few outsiders take the short flight from Townsville. Established in 1918 as a detention camp for Aboriginal men, women and children convicted of such 'crimes' as homelessness, rebelliousness and drunkenness, Palm Island has changed on the surface. While people are free to come and go, overcrowding, malnutrition, alcoholism and a plethora of other diseases remain. When I first went to Palm Island in 1980 an epidemic of gastro-enteritis had hospitalised 130 people. Two years later two researchers discovered in the records of the Queensland Health Department that Aboriginal deaths from common, infectious diseases were up to 300 times higher than the white average and among the highest in the world.[30] In Palm Island's cemetery, overlooking waves breaking gently on the Barrier Reef, many of the headstones bear the names of children.

Sir Johannes Bjelke-Petersen retired as Premier of Queensland in 1987, having ruled the State for more years than many Queenslanders can or care to remember. He did this largely by gerrymandering, by moving electoral boundaries; and he did it with cronies, many of whom controlled Queensland's business life. When the American rights campaigner Ralph Nader visited Queensland, he found laws restricting public protest so repressive that he said they would not be tolerated in Alabama.[31] Indeed, Sir Johannes was to Australian blacks what George Wallace had been to American blacks in Alabama. He offered them the destruction of their lands by mining companies, and unemployment, child poverty and disease. In 1977 he personally stopped an anti-trachoma programme in Queensland when he learned that the medical teams were explaining to Aborigines their political rights.

Under a State law passed in 1984 many Aborigines in Queensland are banned from voting for the local government in which their 'reserve' is situated.[32] Just as the American southern Governors represented themselves as champions of 'State rights', the code words for keeping the blacks in their place, so Bjelke-Petersen pursued a similar strategy and dared the Federal Government to challenge the sovereignty of his domain. And therein lay an Australian tragedy.

The 1967 referendum had given the Federal Government unfettered power to legislate justice for Aboriginal people wherever they lived; and more than a quarter of the Aboriginal population lived in Queensland. Since Whitlam's dismissal in 1975, no national Government had met Bjelke-Petersen's challenge. This was to change in 1983 when Labor was returned to power. The new Minister for Aboriginal Affairs, Clyde Holding, a close friend of Prime Minister Hawke, compared white Australia's crimes against the indigenous people with Hitler's persecution of the Jews. 'What we've got to face as a nation and we haven't faced yet', he said, 'is that the occupation of this vast island continent was a pretty brutal and genocidal occupation.' A national land rights policy, one which applied equal justice to every State, was the 'only restitution'.[33] In 1984 the Labor Party adopted a land rights programme which 'solemnly pledges' to finish that which the Whitlam Government began. Aborigines were to have a veto over all exploitation of land handed back to them. Australia was not South Africa. The first and third worlds would be reconciled in Australia.

Almost immediately the mining companies launched a multi-million dollar spoiling campaign centred in Western Australia, the 'Texas of Australia', a State rich in minerals and dominated by a few transnational companies: a State with the longest record of brutality towards Aborigines. A television and newspaper campaign appealed directly to white racism. A black wall was depicted dividing the State, and the message was clear enough: the small suburban plot of 'the ordinary Aussie' was threatened by Aboriginal land claims. This was false; only 'inalienable' and Crown land would be subject to land claims. What was threatened was the mining companies' power to exploit virtually all the land they wanted and to accrue and expatriate huge profits.

An election was due in Western Australia. The mining lobby made clear to the State Labor Government that a national land rights policy would present a serious obstacle to its own re-election. The Premier, Brian Burke, listened, then phoned Bob Hawke, who had just called a federal election for the following December.

On October 18, Burke met Hawke in Perth and told him that not only the State Government but several Labor Senate seats were vulnerable to the anti-land rights campaign. Hawke acted. In announcing that the Federal Government would not insist on an Aboriginal having a veto over mining, he withdrew the most fundamental right laid down in the proposed land rights legislation: security of tenure. He then fell silent. Not once during his re-election campaign did he or his Minister address the racial shibboleths and lies spread successfully by the mining companies.

The mining lobby's most persuasive propaganda had centred upon the 'fact' that land rights legislation in the Northern Territory had so seriously impeded mining exploration that the national interest was threatened. The evidence for this was one astonishing statistic: in 1983–4 money spent on exploration was down by no less than 60 per cent on the previous year. In using this figure, the former Director of the Australian Mining Industry Council, James Strong, said, 'The terms upon which large areas of land in the Northern Territory have been granted to Aboriginal ownership ... have had a severe and harmful effect on the industry which constitutes one of the largest revenue earners for the Northern Territory.'[34]

The figure was incorrect. The mining companies had supplied misleading information to the Australian Bureau of Statistics, which had released it without verifying it. In fact, exploration was down by an insignificant 5 per cent. When the Bureau admitted its error in March 1985, only *Australian Society*, a monthly, published the correction.[35]

Hawke was re-elected; and contrary to his Party's commitment and the constitutional responsibilities conferred on his Government by the 1967 referendum, he effectively returned the rights of most Aboriginal people to the State governments. This meant that in Western Australia and Queensland Aborigines remained bound to life-destroying 'reserves' and in New South Wales dispossessed on the fringes of towns and in Tasmania without recognition that they existed at all.

The betrayal was exemplified by a meeting between the Aboriginal Affairs Minister, Clyde Holding, and the newly appointed Minister for Resources and Energy, Gareth Evans. The *National Times* reported:

Evans put [to Holding] what he described as 'the three s's', the issues which had to be accepted.

These were that exploration and mining should not be

stopped on Aboriginal land, that explorers and miners should not be unreasonably '*stuffed around*' by poor administrative procedures for dealing with applications to explore for and develop mineral projects and that miners should not be '*screwed*' by unreasonable claims for compensation and royalty payments to Aboriginal communities.[36]

That the first Australians were once again being 'stuffed around' and 'screwed' was not now of political concern. Aborigines, Ministers would say to their friends in the parliamentary press gallery, were 'off the agenda'. And this was an agenda set not by the demands of the mining lobby, but by 'the wishes of the Australian people'. According to Hawke, the blame for the reversal of policy belonged with 'society' which was 'less compassionate' than it used to be. He regretted this, but legislating national land rights would amount to 'jumping miles in front of the populace'.[37]

Hawke did not say how this lack of compassion had been measured. Shortly after it had endorsed the mining companies' position on land rights, the Government commissioned an extensive and confidential survey, the result of which was never officially released. A copy of the 64-page report was leaked to Rupert Murdoch's *Australian*. Murdoch strongly opposes land rights.

Beneath a front-page headline, FEW SUPPORT ABORIGINAL LAND RIGHTS, the *Australian* reported that the study had found that fewer than one in five Australians supported land rights. The paper's 'scoop' was given wide media coverage and quoted by Opposition politicians and by the Minister himself, who appeared to substantiate the published version. 'It was found', said Clyde Holding, 'that many saw Aborigines as a privileged group and that less than 20 per cent had strong feelings of support for Aboriginal people and their aspirations.'[38] The implication was clear: the Hawke Government had popular backing for its abandonment of an electoral promise to implement land rights legislation. 'White backlash' quickly entered the political and media vocabulary.

None of this was true. The *Australian* story was false. The real significance of the Government's poll and the *Australian*'s misrepresentation of it was revealed much later, in May 1986, when a copy of the National Opinion Poll's report was obtained by Eve Fesl, Director of the Aboriginal Research Centre at Monash University and Andrew Markus, lecturer in Australian history at Monash. They wrote:

> The *Australian* chose not to report, and to our knowledge it has not previously been disclosed, that 56 per cent of the respondents *agreed* with the proposition that 'land rights will help Aborigines keep their culture and help the survival of the race', and 52 per cent *agreed* that 'Aborigines should get land rights because it's important to their way of life'.[39]

In other words, the message that the Minister and the Prime Minister received was the opposite of that which the *Australian* reported and Holding publicly lamented. And although the Australian Press Council subsequently upheld a complaint that the *Australian* had misled its readers, the Government made no attempt to disassociate itself from such a specious and negative interpretation of its own enquiry, thus helping to create a self-fulfilling atmosphere of distrust, 'backlash' and, above all, rejection of Aboriginal rights.

We white Australians sometimes grow up affecting the role of innocent bystanders in our own country. The past and its price have nothing to do with us. This is understandable when the efforts to suppress our history are taken into account. Consider the Embarrassment of Bingara.

In 1965 an adventurous Apex club in the small town of Bingara, New South Wales, proposed putting up a monument at the site of the massacre of twenty-eight Aborigines at Myall Creek in 1838. The 'Myall Creek massacre' represented the only time whites were convicted and hanged for the murder of blacks. The usual cover-up would have been arranged had it not been for the work of an extraordinary journalist, Edward Smith Hall, editor of the *Sydney Monitor*. Hall described in his columns how eleven whites had rounded up a group of peaceful Aborigines led by an old man called Daddy. '[He was] a man of giant-like structure', wrote Hall, 'and probably brave as he was magnificent in his form, the tears rolling down his aged cheeks.'

> At the place chosen for the catastrophe, the slaughter began. All, however, we can glean from the evidence is that two shots were fired. The sword, it would seem, did the rest without noise, except the cries of the victims. Decapitation appears to have been considered the readiest way of despatching them, from the great number of skulls afterwards found.[40]

When all the accused were acquitted, Hall, who had little respect for the laws of libel, wrote that their 'deeds' had no parallel 'for cold-blooded ferocity, even in the history of Cortez and the Mexicans, or of Pizarro and the Peruvians'.[41] An issue of the *Monitor* seldom passed without Hall's fire being aimed at the judge, the jury, the 'aristocracy' and the 'oligarchy', whose silence on this matter he considered a conspiracy. Finally, a second trial was ordered by the Governor. With the colony in a state of shock, seven of the eleven were hanged.

Bingara Apex Club's proposal that these events be acknowledged in stone had something of the spirit of Edward

Smith Hall about it. Equally, the response of much of the town, described in the *Bingara Gazette* as 'fast approaching apoplexy', was not dissimilar from the outrage directed against a 'treacherous' Hall. In a letter to the *Advocate*, one J. T. Wearne expressed a peculiarly Australian view of history.

> The whole idea is ill-conceived, unconsidered and mischievous and an insult to the Bingara people. Why should we carry the stigma of an event which occurred 130 years ago and for which not one of us could be held responsible ... The pity of it is that the Myall Creek massacre was practically forgotten and the great bulk of the people had never even heard of it![42]

Today there is no monument, and the site of the massacre is secured behind a locked gate.

Drive west from Cooktown in northern Queensland and more of secret Australia unfolds. The bush here is wilder than almost anywhere on the continent: dense tropical vegetation implanted on desert earth. The roads are barely passable, the tracks flooded or blown away, marked by miniature skyscrapers built by ants. It is spine-gutting terrain. As I travelled hundreds of miles across it in 1987, I saw Australia as an Andean society whose historical skeletons were enclosed both by an impenetrable landscape and an impenetrable state of mind. An Aborigine called Sonny Flynn once described the latter as 'the cult of forgetfulness'.[43]

'Matchstick' Matthews was camped with his son and son-in-law near Caulfield's Lagoon on the Palmer river. Matchstick is a spacious man beneath a spacious hat. He has a middle tooth and a middle finger missing and a brace of shotguns in the back of his truck. 'This place is running with crocs,' he said. 'You're not supposed to shoot the bastards, but what do you do . . . invite them over for a beer?'

Matchstick and his small clan are from a sepia image of the nineteenth century. In the life they lead and the work they do – clearing the land – they are not much different from the pioneers. There is, however, the difference of a satellite dish, which, says Matchstick, has brought disillusionment.

'All you get out here is the bloody ABC and Pommy stuff,' he lamented. '*Rumpole of the Bailey* and bloody *EastEnders*. I hate that *EastEnders*, mate. But I watch it. That's what gets me. I hate it and I watch it!'

I asked Matchstick about Caulfield's Lagoon. 'Murdering Lagoon is its name,' he said, 'that's what we call it. Everybody's known for years what went on over there. But you don't say about it. You don't say a word.'

I asked why. 'I dunno. You just don't, mate. People get shitty if you talk about it . . . not a way to make mates. The boys and me pulled a bus load of Japs out of the mud over there a few weeks ago. Christ knows where they'd come from. Japs and a bus! . . . Can you believe it? I'm not pulling the next one out, mate. They should leave this place, just leave us.'

At sunrise on November 6, 1873 a posse of Government officials and gold miners hunted between 80 and 150 Aborigines along the Palmer river. They shot them all and left the bodies floating in Caulfield's Lagoon. Voices were raised in protest; but no one was punished. Nor did white scholarship 'confirm' what had happened until 1984 when a postgraduate student researching a thesis about the Palmer river gold fields came upon information previously overlooked, or ignored.[44] Throughout Australia other killing fields await 'confirmation'.

The truth is that only when whites get to know Aboriginal people, and win their confidence, do they learn something about the scale and consistency of violence inflicted upon their black compatriots. An Aboriginal friend remembers his mother being tied to a veranda post, awaiting the visits of a white man who abused her and his sister repeatedly. No one was punished. Another friend, a lawyer, remembers an uncle shot dead by a policeman in a railway yard. No one was punished. Another described the decimation of his grandparents' family for 'cattle stealing', and the murder of an aunt at her front door. I know of other such stories; the most common is of violent death while in police custody.

White silence is the other component. How many white policemen, lawyers, magistrates and ordinary citizens knew about these atrocities and did nothing? How many reporters knew and wrote nothing? How many editors had an unwritten policy on 'Abos' and would publish nothing that cast doubt on the racial and moral superiority of the majority? The press, I often heard it argued, could not publish 'rumours'.

Today these stories are no longer rumours. Aboriginal deaths in police custody have become a public issue in Australia; and what is finally done about it will say much about the development of Australian civilisation. In 1989 a Royal Commission was enquiring into at least 105 unexplained deaths in police and prison cells; and every few weeks yet another death was added to the list. If white people were dying in a similar ratio, the death toll would be 8,000 in eight years.[45] As Australian governments of the 1980s have claimed the moral right to censure South Africa, the rate of imprisonment of blacks in Australia has risen to at least as high a level as in South Africa and the rate of deaths in custody is thirteen times higher than in South Africa.[46]

In 1987 the London-based Anti-Slavery Society, a leader of the emancipation movement since 1839, published a report about Australia. It was written by Dr Julian Burger, a world authority on the struggles of indigenous peoples. Aboriginal deaths in police custody, wrote Dr Burger, occurred mostly in lock-ups in small country towns where 'the atmosphere is closer to that of the USA's Deep South with its history of slavery, than to the Canberra-promoted image of a multicultural society', and 'victimisation at the hands of the police is not the result of one or two individual policemen but an apparent policy aimed at terrorising the Aboriginal community'.[47] The report gave the following examples.

One-third of all Aborigines in South Australia were arrested during a six-month period. Every Aboriginal man, woman and child in the town of Roebourne, Western Australia, experiences arrest at the rate of three a year. Moreover, this is part of a national pattern.[48]

In northern Queensland the lock-ups are known as 'hell holes'. At Wujal Wujal up to twenty-seven Aborigines have been forced into a space eight feet by four feet, without light, water, bedding or a lavatory. On March 29, 1987, a young black stockman was found hanging by a pair of football socks from a bar in the cell window. When no more prisoners can be jammed into the cell, they are locked in a small yellow police van called 'the monkey cage'.[49]

Few white Australians can comprehend the anxiety of a black person living in a small country town. Young blacks are stopped and searched by police, and their names taken, as a matter of almost daily routine. If Aboriginal organisations arrange a social event, the police are likely to turn up and make arrests on any pretext. A youth worker with the Department of Community Development in Alice Springs found that up to 85 per cent of black children he had seen in the courts had been 'bashed' by police. Complaints by Aborigines, including children, against the police have been largely ignored. Only in one State, Victoria, is there an independent police complaints authority.[50]

Eddie Murray was twenty-one when he was last arrested. Eddie lived in Wee Waa, New South Wales, where his family was well respected in the black community. His father, Arthur, was a member of the Aboriginal Advancement Council, and in 1981 Eddie was selected to tour New Zealand as a star player with the Redfern All Blacks Rugby team. He was, said Arthur, 'a spirited, happy-go-lucky boy with everything to live for'.[51] Eddie's 'spirit' guaranteed that he saw a lot of the police.

The imposing police station at Wee Waa, known to locals as the 'Opera House', was built in the early 1970s when large numbers of Aborigines migrated to Wee Waa seeking work in the cotton fields. 'There was a nine o'clock curfew for

THE DEAD HEART...

blacks then,' one of them recalled, 'and the whites used to sell blacks metho [methylated spirits] on ice in the liquor store.'[52]

On June 21, 1981 Eddie Murray was drinking under a tree with his cousin Donny and some friends. (Steel pegs were embedded in the tree, which Aborigines used to shin up to see if the police were coming.) Eddie was arrested at 1.45 p.m. and taken to Wee Waa police station. He was held under the Intoxicated Persons Act, a law used overwhelmingly against Aborigines. Within the hour he was dead, strangled with a blanket in his cell, his feet on the ground.

At the inquest five months later the police claimed Eddie had killed himself by hanging, even though his blood alcohol level at the time of death was 0·3 per cent. Under cross-examination, the police agreed that Eddie was 'so drunk he couldn't scratch himself'. Yet according to them, Eddie had managed to tear a strip off a thick prison blanket, deftly fold it, thread it through the bars of the ventilation window, tie two knots, fashion a noose and hang himself without his feet leaving the ground.

One policeman gave evidence that he had been off duty that day, then admitted he had lied when four Aboriginal witnesses identified him as one of those in the police van that took Eddie away. The inquest was also told about serious discrepancies in police notebooks, with dates appearing out of sequence and an absence of records altogether, except for a highly detailed record of events of June 21: the day of Eddie's arrest and death. The coroner found that Eddie Murray had died 'at the hands of person or persons unknown'. He said there was no evidence that Eddie had taken his own life and he strongly criticised the police. And that was that.

When I met Arthur and Leila Murray, it was six years to the day since Eddie's death. Arthur gripped a wedge of documents, including his many requests for the case of his son's unexplained death to be re-opened. He produced letters from three New South Wales Attorney-Generals, who either passed him on to another official or expressed no dissatisfaction with the public enquiry.[53]

'You know how it all began?' said Arthur. 'Eddie's sister was trying to give back some rotten food to a take-away shop. That's what they do to us all the time, you know. There was an argument and her husband was arrested by the police. Well, Eddie witnessed this and gave evidence for them, and they were acquitted . . .'

When the Murrays went to the morgue to identify their son's body, they could not find any of the clothing he had on that day. 'Those clothes were never found,' said Arthur Murray, 'I wrote again and again to get them from the hospital. There could have been evidence on them that Eddie was killed, then taken to the police station and strung up. We haven't got an answer to these questions yet. We want an answer . . .'

Leila interrupted, 'They're killing Aboriginal people . . . just killing them.'[54]

After Eddie's death, and his parents' attempts to find

answers, many in the Wee Waa black community took fright. The Murrays were 'trouble makers'. Arthur was voted off the Aboriginal Advancement Council. 'It bloody hurt us', said Arthur, 'and it's still hurtin' us today. The up-town niggers thought we were causing trouble. Up-town niggers are black but they're white. The whites and Aboriginal people thought we had stirred up trouble and wanted us out of town. Whites would come to the front of our home with guns. They threatened my wife and other members of our family.

'If I was caught in the street after dark, I would get a hidin', which I got on a number of occasions, by the whites and up-town niggers. I've still got photos of me afterwards. The kids were hassled at the school by white kids.

'In March 1983, we left Wee Waa and settled in Dubbo. A barrister who was involved in Eddie's inquest told us that it would be best if we left because of all the problems, the worry and the threats. I thought the day before we left that maybe we were running away, giving up.

'It took about three weeks for my wife to pack our things. We were ready to come over to Dubbo and the police came and stood outside the front of the house on the day before we left. They were looking for some stolen goods. We don't know what was stolen but they [the police] were informed that we had something we shouldn't and they knew that we were movin' . . . They pulled out all of the crockery and stuff that my wife had packed, clothing and different private property that we own. They ransacked it and when they couldn't find the things they were looking for, they called on some extra police officers to come and look.

'I drink a lot now. I couldn't drink after Eddie's death because I was on medication, which kept me drowsy and I couldn't think about anything like meetings with land councils — just Eddie's death. I was just drugged out. I was just walkin' around like a zombie . . . I drink more now when I think about how we lost him.'[55]

Shortly after they moved away from Wee Waa, the Murrays' eldest daughter was brought home in the back of a police van. She was bleeding and had been assaulted. In 1987 their youngest daughter, aged seventeen, was arrested and imprisoned without her parents being told. In August 1988 their eldest son was placed on a kidney machine after two policemen had assaulted him.[56]

John Pat, aged seventeen, died in 1983 in Broome, Western Australia. He had gone to the aid of a friend who was involved in a fight with five off-duty policemen. Witnesses at the inquest said they had seen him kicked in the head after he had lost consciousness, 'like a dog'. Other witnesses, who lived overlooking the lock-up, said the police repeatedly assaulted John Pat after pulling him unconscious from the van. He was left in a cell and no doctor was called. He died from extensive head wounds; and he had broken ribs and a tear in his aorta, the main blood vessel leading from the heart.

The five policemen were sent to trial for murder, but the charge was later changed to manslaughter. They were acquitted and reinstated to the police force. The Aborigines arrested with John Pat were convicted of aggravated assault against the police and sent to prison. They are scarred from their beatings.

When the news got around Brewarrina, New South Wales, that Lloyd Boney had been found hanging by a sock in the police lock-up, the Aboriginal community rose up. Lloyd Boney's friends described him as 'paralytic' with drink when he was arrested and, like Eddie Murray, incapable of killing himself; and with no motive to do so.

On the morning of August 16, 1987 Lloyd Boney, aged twenty-eight, was buried in Brewarrina Cemetery, with his football team forming a guard of honour. He was the sixteenth Aborigine to die in police custody within eight months. His aunt, Priscilla, who had looked after him since he was an infant, had to be carried away from the graveside. They had lived in a tiny house beside the river, which had walls of asbestos and a tin roof, with tyres and bricks on it to secure it during a big wind. Despite this, and the lack of sanitation, it was neat and clean and there was a small garden in front.

That evening there were few whites on the streets of Brewarrina. Up from the river marched Aborigines to the

Brewarrina Hotel, which, they said, refused to serve blacks. They hurled beer kegs and bottles, smashing windows. Riot police were called and at first were beaten back. The New South Wales Police Minister said on television that violence by blacks 'will only cause more harm to their cause'. The local National Party candidate, who was also town coroner, accused the Sydney media of causing 'racial disharmony' and 'stirring up' the Aboriginal community.[57]

In the crowd was Arthur Murray, who happened to be in Brewarrina visiting his dying mother. He had attended the funeral of Lloyd Boney who, like his son Eddie, had died violently in police custody. Arthur was charged with assaulting a policeman. At his trial a Sydney journalist, Tony Hewett, gave evidence that Arthur had been well away from the incident. An all white jury found him guilty and sentenced him to 18 months' prison. I was one of Arthur's character witnesses. I wrote to the court that I had known him to be a kind and decent man, indeed courageous in the terrible circumstances of his life, a man who mediated rather than initiated conflict. At the time of writing, Arthur's appeal to the Supreme Court in Sydney is pending.

As Brewarrina was about to erupt, the Hawke Government appointed a Royal Commission of Enquiry into Aboriginal deaths in custody. Four years had passed since the Government was first pressed to do something. In December 1988 the Commission published an interim report in which it recommended that police investigating the death of Aborigines in custody should presume homicide, not suicide, that public drunkenness should be abolished as an offence and police and prison officer recruits should be vetted to eliminate racists. And yet the Commission studiously ignored the likelihood that a considerable number of Aborigines were murdered by police and prison officers.

The Federal Justice Minister replied that most of the recommendations were the responsibility of State governments. The Queensland Government immediately denied its police force was racist. The Western Australian Government said that it would support a challenge by its police to the validity of the Commission itself. These two States have the worst reputations for brutality against Aborigines.

In April, 1991 – three weeks after Arthur Murray was sent away – the Royal Commission delivered its final report. There was a familiar echo in the remarks of the Chief Commissioner, Elliott Johnston. 'I had no conception', he said, 'of the degree of pin-pricking domination, abuse of personal power, utter paternalism, open contempt and total indifference with which so many Aboriginal people were visited on a day-to-day basis'.[58]

So spoke, once again, the Innocent Bystander. The Royal Commission made 339 recommendations, such as that arrest ought to be 'the sanction of last resort' and that the police should 'exercise greater impartiality'. There was no call for criminal charges and not a single conclusion of foul play in cases that went back nine years. The Commission did not address itself to widespread police cover-ups. It referred in passing to the critical importance of land rights, as did another Royal Commission 16 years earlier.

Once again, said Paul Coe, chairman of the National Aboriginal and Islander Legal Service Secretariat, 'Aboriginal people will feel they have been betrayed'. He pointed out that the Commission had merely recommended that the changes in policing, education and poverty should be left with 'those same state governments that have been the main oppressors of Aboriginal people'.[59]

The Commission found that John Pat – whose death had become for Aboriginal people a symbol of injustice and oppression had died as a result of a head injury he had suffered during a fight started by the 'ill-advised, unprofessional and provocative' actions of an off-duty police officer. Referring to Pat's suspicious fall from a police van, Commissioner Johnston said, 'I do not accept as necessarily true much of the evidence of the officers relating to this incident'.[60] He recommended no action.

The Australian Government, said Prime Minister Hawke, 'has committed itself to ensuring that there is a co-ordinated and comprehensive national response to the Royal Commission's final report'.[61] Five months later it was disclosed that the number of Aborigines in New South Wales prisons had risen by 72 per cent.[62] There have since been other similar revelations. So far, as a result of the Commission's findings, only one person has been charged and convicted. A prison officer in western Australia was found guilty of a breach of prison regulations. He was fined $A50 and returned to work.[63] Black Australians continue to die in custody on average about one death every fourteen days.

These deaths have discomfited many Australians. It is not widely appreciated that they are not a new phenomenon, but the latest in a litany of physical, political and cultural brutality which has continued, uninterrupted, since January 26, 1788.

In the winter of 1987 I returned to Alice Springs with film makers Alan Lowery and Alec Morgan. We looked for the family of Albert Namatjira and found them living beside an abattoir, two miles from the land Albert had not been permitted to buy. They were there under sufferance of the Northern Territory Lands Department, in tenuous possession of one tree and four tin outhouses. It was terribly cold. When the wind kicked up the red dirt, it stung those at ground level. Reg, son of Oscar and grandson of Albert, wore his woollen hat almost down to his neck as he sat cross-legged and painted.

Then an ambulance arrived. Two white nurses, in crisp white uniforms, lifted out a frail old black man and led him to a place on the dirt between Reg and the dogs. One of the nurses patted the old man on the head and said, 'See you Tuesday.' They had delivered Oscar 'home' for a few days. The night before they had found him climbing out of the window of a nursing home, trying to make his way back to the camp. Now he squatted and nodded approval when Reg repeated his words of twenty years before: 'How long do you reckon we'll have to wait for a bit of a decent place to live?'

Son and grandson of the great Albert remain in abject poverty – as do some 5,000 Aboriginal artists in the Northern

Territory, even though their art has an estimated market value of $A5 million. In 1988, with Australia fashionable in the United States, the owner of a Los Angeles gallery visited the Northern Territory and took away Aboriginal art worth $A52,600 for a special exhibition. She also commissioned a series of bark paintings, but later cancelled the order, complaining that the artists' prices, between $A60 and $A750 an item, were too high. When the Los Angeles exhibition opened, its prices amounted to $A650,000. Aboriginal artists like Reg Namatjira earn an average of $A700 a year, on which subsistence is not possible.[64]

I drove west from Alice to the former mission at Hermannsburg. 'Blessed are they that hear the word of God and keep it,' warned an inscription, dated September 21, 1896, on the small sandstone church. Although few Aborigines were thus blessed, the remains of the settlement, with the bones of a 'T' Model Ford at its centre, offer a testimonial to the stoicism of the Lutherans. Here, encased in woollen suits and high collars, they performed such fated tasks as translating the New Testament into the language of the Aranda, a people whose own God predated Jesus Christ by thousands of years and require no such manual: only land.

Since the Northern Territory Land Rights Act in 1976, Hermannsburg has been owned by its 700 former residents. Three-quarters of the people, mostly stockmen, have set up 'outstations' – cattle ranches – where they are self-supporting and can lead a modified traditional life, free from the dependencies of alcohol and 'the welfare'.

Wallace Rockhole outstation is run by Barry Abbott, his cousin Mark, and their relatives. They broke even in 1987 and could afford to hire a helicopter for the muster. They wear checked shirts, wide hats and Western boots and drive Toyota trucks, which discharge at full volume the plaints of Glen Campbell and Dolly Parton. Theirs is a familiar style and swagger. It is one of Australia's hidden ironies that its finest cowboys are black.

The confidence of people in the outstation movement represents something new and profound in the Aboriginal world: renaissance. Aboriginal population figures reflect this indirectly. Between 1982 and 1987 the number of Aborigines increased from 160,000 to more than 227,000, an astonishing rise of more than 42 per cent. Although the black birth rate is twice that of the white, this alone does not account for the increase. The truth is that many Australians are now proud to declare themselves Aborigines.

Whites have grown used to drawing patronising distinctions between full-blooded Aborigines and those of mixed parentage. 'Half caste' and 'quarter caste' are terms of derision. Although there are important differences between, say, the urban young and the more conservative tribal Aborigines, *all* Aborigines, regardless of their background and shade of skin, consider themselves one people with a common culture and struggle for survival.[65] In recent years this long-suppressed sense of nationhood has found, against the odds, renewed and vibrant expression. With the establishment in the 1970s of the first Aboriginal medical and legal services, and land councils based on the traditional structure of the clans and linguistic groups, Aboriginal unity and self assertion have grown steadily.

On a frosty autumn morning in 1985 hundreds of tribal Aborigines converged on Canberra to join up with their paler cousins from the cities. Such a momentous event had never happened before. Stewart Harris was one of the few white journalists who reported it. Moved by what he saw, he wrote:

As I stood with them at their rally last Monday and then walked to Parlt House for their emotional meeting on its steps, I sensed that an Aboriginal nation was being born. The tribes and clans of the people who owned Australia before 1788 have become united in the past decade as never before.

Their growing unity has been the result of a common experience of frustrated expectation. There is, for the first time, a political awareness which is broadly based

. . . For the first time I saw tribal elders and old women from the Centre and the North confidently using hand microphones to speak their minds in their own languages and also in English. They were sharing the opportunity with Aborigines from the south and east, whom they used to call 'yeller fellers'. It was very moving to see the evidence of this and, for all Australians, the whole week should have been instructive.[66]

The Australian Broadcasting Corporation thought otherwise and ignored it on television. Apart from Stewart Harris's reporting, there was little opportunity for public understanding of such a momentous meeting.

The renaissance has not needed white backing or white approval. It has come from within, from the notion and spirit of 'Aboriginality' and has had a momentum of its own. It is also intensely political. Since Victor Lingiari and the Gurindji made their stand, and Charlie Perkins set out with the freedom riders, Aboriginal Australians have produced some of the most sophisticated political activists anywhere. Among them are Paul Coe, founder of the Aboriginal Legal Services, who has put the Aboriginal case before the United Nations; Marcia Langton of the Central Lands Council, who has argued that land and human rights are indivisible; Galarrwuy Yunupingu, who at the age of fifteen helped his father draft the first major land claim, written on bark and sent to Parliament, and twenty years later negotiated uranium rights for his people; Bob Riley, like many Aborigines stolen from his mother at the age of twelve, who became the eloquent chairperson of the National Aboriginal Conference; Michael Mansell from Tasmania, whose intellect and flair have unnerved politicians; Helen Corbett, chairperson of the Committee to Defend Black Rights, who has fought for justice for the families of those killed in police custody; Mick Miller, a Queensland teacher who has conducted an often lonely political struggle in Australia's 'deep north'; Gary Foley, whose understanding of the common strands between urban black Australians and those in the bush has made him an enduring, effective voice of his people. And many more. Such a list must be arbitrary.

One man who personifies the renaissance is Pat Dodson, whose quiet anger and generosity, issuing from his fine, bushy head, leave few unmoved. A descendant of the Yaoro people in the Kimberley region of Western Australia, Pat was one of seven children who were orphaned when he was ten years old. Sent to a Catholic missionary school, he was ordained, at the age of twenty-seven, the first Aboriginal Catholic priest. But, as so often happened, his Aboriginality conflicted with his Christianity, specifically with the hierarchy of the Catholic Church. Put in charge of a mission south of Darwin, he was criticised for introducing reforms which restored Aboriginal ceremonials and placed them within a Christian context. He left the priesthood in 1981 and joined the land rights movement as national co-ordinator of the Federation of Land Councils.

When I met Pat Dodson in Alice Springs in 1987, I asked him to explain 'Aboriginality'. 'Well, it means the sense of *belonging*,' he said, ... 'to family, to where you've come from, and of knowing what your spirit is, that has given you life, and knowing the tradition that relates to the area of country you come from. [It's] a bond between people from one part of Australia and people from another . . . a sense of rapport, a sense of understanding and of brotherhood . . . a sense not just brought about by common suffering and oppression, but the fact that we are the unique survivors.

'You see, after years of holocaust . . . there is a certain genius not extinguished within us, despite what has happened to us. [It's] not a genius in the sense of being highly intellectual, but in the sense of something special in us that needs to be nurtured and cultivated and brought more and more into the light.'

I said I was puzzled by the apparent lack of bitterness among Aborigines. 'I can recall', he said, 'being very angry at one point and frustrated . . . simply not knowing which direction to go, of being up against all kinds of forces. But then I listened to an older person like my grandfather, who talks in terms of the spirits that give life to the winds and the trees, and the sun and the sea, and that no one controlled that spirit; and that despite the inhumanity and injustice, mankind must be seen in this broader context. And this was a man who had suffered at the ends of the whips of pastoralists. He was not speaking from a sense of stoicism. He was saying that the total human experience includes an ability to try to see what is in another human being.'[67]

Geraldine Briggs is a renaissance woman. She is eighty years old, an elder of the Yorta Yorta tribe and a teacher at Worowa School in Victoria. Worowa is the State's only all-Aboriginal school and was established by Geraldine's daughter, Hyllus Maris, the acclaimed author of *Women of the Sun*, who died in 1983. With her ability to speak a range of Aboriginal languages, Geraldine traces the kinship and tribal links of the children and is able to give those of mixed parentage a sense of who they are and where they come from.

As a young girl Geraldine Briggs lived on a mission near Deniliquin, New South Wales. It was from here that her three older sisters were taken away by police and sent to work for white women. Only minutes before a policeman arrived to snatch Geraldine from her mother, an uncle bundled her into a buggy and drove her to the safety of another reserve. She was five at the time. Today her grandmotherly appearance belies her flint; her eyes say, '*I have survived.*' To the children at Worowa School, she is Aunty Gerry.

'Worowa means eagle,' she said. 'These children will be eagles. They'll learn their own culture and language and then they will understand the white ways from a position of strength. In the white schools they wouldn't find this confidence, because the system as it is reinforces prejudices and makes our kids compete on white terms. They soon lose their way and their identity. They become truants and crisis rules their lives. Here they are eagles.'[68]

For Aborigines, the past is always present. Next to the school is Coranderrk Cemetery where the spirits of Baby

Nelly, Old Harry, Pretty Boy and King Billy reside. They and hundreds of others died from pulmonary diseases following a Government edict ordering the removal of all 'half castes' from the district. This divided every family and decimated many. Today there is a monument to the memory of Barak, an elder of the Yarra Yarra people, who was one of the last to die. The monument was erected in 1934 by the Healesville Bread and Cheese Club.

The personal odysseys of those like Geraldine Briggs, and their efforts to break the long silence and to repair the damage done to others, are at the heart of the renaissance. Few white Australians are aware of the Aborigines Protection Act and its demonic child, the Aborigines Protection Board. Black oral history has long described the inhuman practices, the suffering and division caused; white scholarship is only now offering 'confirmation'. In New South Wales between 1901 and 1940 thousands of Aboriginal children of mixed parentage were torn from their families, and used virtually as slave labour. According to the Act, the children had to be 'bound by indenture' and apprenticed to 'any master'. Moreover, 'any such child so apprenticed [was] liable to be proceeded against and punished for absconding'.[69]

Police were used to find and steal the children. They had orders not to tell the children or their parents where they were being taken. This is a report from the *Sydney Morning Herald* of January 10, 1925:

ABORIGINALS
Children Removed from Parents' Control
Heartrending Scene

Grafton, Thursday. The circumstances under which four aboriginal children, whose ages ranged from four to 13 years, were separated from their parents have aroused much indignation locally.

The separation occurred just before Christmas . . . It

appeared that the [police] officer's instructions were to meet the parents at the ferry, and thither [the children] went accompanied by their parents, who did not know that their little ones were to be taken away from them.

The scene at the parting was heartrending, but the children were taken, despite protests and tears, and conveyed to Kempsey. The children had been properly fed and clothed by the parents. It was a nice Christmas box to give to the parents of the children. The parents were in a terrible state about it ... It is understood that the action originated with the Aborigines Board in Sydney.[70]

The boys were taken to the Kinchella Home for Aboriginal Boys, where they were given rudimentary training as farm labourers. They were then sent to sheep and cattle stations where they were 'indentured' and paid in rations and pennies. The girls, who were the majority, were sent to the Cootamundra Training Home for Aboriginal Girls, where they were made into domestic servants, then 'indentured' to 'masters' in white middle-class homes.

There is an historic parallel with the use of black slave girls as domestics in the American southern states before emancipation. While books, plays and laments were written about the dispossession and suffering of black Americans, there was no such outpouring in Australia. At best there was the belief that the children were being 'saved' from the horrors of a 'primitive' upbringing. Not until Alec Morgan's searing documentary film, *Lousy Little Sixpence*, made in the early 1980s, was there the beginning of a popular understanding of the real meaning of 'protection'.

Indeed, where massacre and disease had failed to destroy Aboriginal life and culture, the Protection Board would provide a final, quieter solution. In 1988 the Aboriginal writer Roberta Sykes was given an official list from 1938 which, she wrote, 'contained dozens of names and ages of children taken, and the age at which they died'.

I felt faint as I read through and found I had in my hand perhaps the earliest list of black deaths in custody ... Girl taken, aged 13, died three years later, aged 16; girl taken, aged 8, died four years later, aged 12; girl aged 13, died aged 14; taken 13, died 18; taken 13, died 17; taken aged 7, died aged 12 ... and so on.[71]

This was known, among imperial historians, as 'smoothing the pillow on the black man's death bed'. Once removed from their families, the children who survived would never be allowed to return home. The Aboriginal elders would die off. The reserves would be sold as farm land, and the Aboriginal race would be an anthropological memory, its pale-skinned 'remnants' secreted in the lower reaches of the white working class.

Joy Williams is another woman of the renaissance. Joy never accepted the status of 'remnant' and has spent a lifetime searching for a childhood stolen from her. Joy was taken from her mother when she was a baby in the 1940s and sent to an Aboriginal children's home near Nowra, New South Wales. There her real name, Eileen, was changed to Joy, because 'there was already one Eileen at the home'. 'I was one of the fortunate few', she said, 'allowed to keep my real birthday.' At the age of five she was removed to a white children's home near Sydney. The application form for her admission, submitted by the Aborigines Welfare Board, reads:

Q: Why is admission sought?
A: To take the child from association of Aborigines as
   she is a fair-skinned child.

I met Joy in 1987 in Wollongong, the steel city south of
Sydney. She is an attractive, wistful woman, with a humour
as dry as dust and a slightly wicked laugh; and she is fragile.
'My mother herself was stolen,' she said. 'My grandparents
lived in Cowra, New South Wales, and they were told that if
they went through a Christian wedding, their girls would not
be taken away. So they did it, but the Board came and took
them anyway and my mum was sent to the Cootamundra
training home.

'People would hide their kids. A truck would pull up outside and the officers would get out a bag of boiled lollies, give
the kids one, then snatch them. It was kidnapping. I knew
one woman who was waiting for her son to come back from
the dentist. He'd be fifty-three years old now, and they
snatched him when he was nine on the way back from the
dentist; and he never saw his mother again.

'Mum was sent straight from the institution to domestic
service in Watson's Bay, Sydney, looking after white kids,
cleaning the house, that sort of thing. She was seventeen and
got two shillings and sixpence a week. But she never saw the
two shillings. That was put away for her, for new clothes.
But the Board provided clothes from their stores. So it was
practically slavery.

'Not long afterwards I came along. As soon as she'd had
me, she was given a hysterectomy at the age of eighteen, and
it was involuntary. She didn't know anything about it, and
when I finally met Mum she told me she used to wonder why
she didn't have any more children.'

'Was that unusual?' I asked.

'For Aboriginal women? No . . . for example, Western Australia was notorious for it.'

'When did you begin to think about your mother?'

71

'All the other kids in the institution used to get visitors every first Saturday of the month, and I didn't get visitors. You know how kids fantasise ... I just thought I was an orphan. When I was told, it was a hell of a shock.

'I suppose I started looking for Mum when I was about eleven. That was after an episode when I ran away from the home and they caught me and rushed me to the hospital to see if I was still a virgin ... God, which I was! ... that was the same day I had to write out 500 times "God is love". I should get eye strain compensation for all the Bible verses I had to write ... and that's when they told me I had mud in my veins, that I'd end up as bad as my mother. But hang on, what mother? And what did "bad" mean? When I asked, they said my mother didn't want me.

'Well, when I found her all those years later, she was living in what I thought was a dreadful little tin hut down on the south coast. It was a terrible moment, because the first thing she did was hit me. Afterwards I found out that she'd come to visit me at the home and they'd reassured her I would be coming back to her. But they were lying; it wasn't true; and she blamed me for not coming back to her.'

Joy had a daughter, Julie-Ann, who was adopted while she was in hospital. 'I was sedated on that day,' she said. 'I wasn't aware I was signing adoption papers. The baby was taken to a Catholic children's home and, as far as I know, she went to an Italian hairdresser and his family, because she was the right colouring. I found out last year she was married. Not a day passes when I don't think about her.'

I asked if she had ever tried to get in touch with her daughter.

'The law in New South Wales says you have to write to the adopting parents to get their permission to see the child, even if the "child" is an adult. I've written twice and I haven't had any answers.'

'Do you think she knows she is Aboriginal?'

'I don't think so. In the white world it's a stigma, it's not normal.'

In 1989 Joy completed a BA degree in English and History

at the University of Wollongong. 'I never thought I would go to university as I didn't think someone with my background could do it,' she said. 'In the first year I did Europe in the twentieth century ... needless to say, I failed miserably. I mean, who cares about Ataturk, Mussolini and Hitler when one's own country has a rich "history" of invasion, dictatorship, genocide and inhumanity? ... I felt it was a cop-out by the History Faculty and a whitewash of what had happened in Australia.'

Joy now advises in schools and colleges about the Aboriginal experience, anxious that young whites understand that the Australian past is welded to the present. She identifies racist and stereotypical books in school libraries and advises white teachers on their methods. 'I am finding', she said, 'that perhaps ignorance is one of the bases for racism. However, I refuse to whitewash racism with that knowledge. After all, the white man says that "ignorance is no excuse for breaking the law": *their* law, that is.'[72]

Joy's energy and achievements, both as an Aboriginal woman and in the white world, are typical of a growing number of teachers, historians, broadcasters, writers, artists and playwrights from similar backgrounds. Their work is often precise and unsentimental. For example: Ruth Waller's 1988 oil painting 'Death in Custody', with its great black swan of Western Australia and its hanging black human; and Kevin Gilbert's book, *Because a White Man'll Never Do It*, in which the author courageously presents the degradation of Aboriginal Man: 'He bowed to the fact of his women having to prostitute themselves for the food that would allow the children to survive, or for the alcohol that would yield the oblivion that was so much more desirable than the daily reality.'[73]

In 1989 the Aboriginal National Theatre Trust staged its second conference of Aboriginal playwrights, actors, writers, dancers, technicians and directors. The playwright Justine Saunders said, 'It's about telling our stories our way, without white interpretations.' The actress Rhoda Roberts said, 'The beauty of it is that most black writers don't write with bitterness.'[74] One of Australia's most commercially successful record albums in 1989 is *Building Bridges*, which proclaims on its cover, 'Australia has a black history,' and includes black and white acts calling passionately for a just settlement between all Australians.

In 1985 an all-Aboriginal radio station, 8KIN, began broadcasting in stereo from a former convent, the Little Sisters of Jesus, at the foot of the Macdonnell Ranges near Alice Springs. Freda Glynn, the manager, told me of the reaction of the old people the first day on the air. 'I showed them how to find the station on the dial,' she said. 'They began to cry. They were overwhelmed to hear their language on the radio.' Within four years Freda and her colleagues had extended radio to television, winning the licence for the first direct satellite service to central Australia. Her company, Imparja Television, is wholly owned by Aboriginal organisations such as the land councils and, although established with Federal Government money, has to operate almost entirely on advertising revenue.

When the Australian Broadcasting Tribunal announced that Imparja had won the licence, an editorial in the Darwin newspaper, the *Sunday Territorian*, attacked the decision as 'a cynical exercise' and said that it was 'of such simple-minded imbecility that it almost defies description or understanding'.[75] The Northern Territory Government appealed against the decision all the way to the Federal Court, and lost. Only a week before Imparja was due to go on the air, the Northern Territory administration reneged on a guarantee to buy $A2 million worth of services from the new licence holder. With only three days to go, the opposing Northern Territory television station in Darwin, owned by the billionaire Kerry Packer and the lawyer Malcolm Turnbull, asked the Broadcasting Tribunal to review Imparja's licence and to enquire into its resources.

In spite of this, they went on the air on schedule. In less than eight months they hired and trained staff, equipped studios, assembled the technology, bought programmes, decided schedules and found advertisers. With the help of white technicians and administrators, an Aboriginal television service now broadcast to a third of the Australian continent, an area the size of Europe. The audience is about 85,000 and it is growing. Imparja's charter – to nurture the Aboriginal culture and provide material appropriate for a majority white audience – is undoubtedly an historic advance in race relations. But its major achievement is its very existence as a source of Aboriginal images of pride and self respect. The first Aboriginal current affairs programme, *Urrepeye* – the messenger – is broadcast in six languages with ten interpreters providing English subtitles.

But there is a price. Aboriginal linguist Eve Fesl has described the effects of television as 'like cultural nerve gas'. 'You sit and watch it, you feel good while you watch it and all the while it's destroying your culture and you don't realise it,' she said. 'It's especially devastating if Aboriginal children have no input but English programmes all day.'[76] With only enough resources to make a few programmes of its own, and the need to survive on advertising revenue alone, Imparja has little choice but to show re-runs of *Dallas*, *Dynasty* and *Sale of the Century*. Like white parents, black parents are concerned about the influence of commercial television on their young. Some Aboriginal communities have rejected it; Maryvale, a community of 250 which has never known broadcast television, has installed a satellite dish on the understanding that the only sets will be kept in the school. Other communities have set up their own production units, making videos for local viewing. Freda Glynn is understandably angry that the Federal Government has forced Imparja into commercial competition, while underwriting a television network that promotes the language and culture of Australia's immigrant communities.

In its search for funds Imparja, after much agonising, accepted alcohol commercials, while at the same time running a campaign called 'Beat the Grog', aimed at the most virulent disease among Aboriginal people. When the expected revenue did not materialise, a commercial decision was taken to drop the alcohol advertisements.

Still, what Freda Glynn remembers as 'a foolish racial ideal' has brought entertainment and information to thousands of isolated people. 8KIN's *Radio Bushfire* series, aimed at schoolchildren, has delivered full school attendances on the one day of the week it is on the air.[77] In Alice Springs there is a three-year training scheme to put black people into television jobs, and where local programmes are made 70 per cent of the people are Aboriginals. They include men in big hats and big boots and women who laugh easily with each other. There are no grey suits, not yet. For those of us who remember Jay Creek and the Palms, their achievement is a marvel.

On January 26, 1988 white Australia celebrated the 200th anniversary of the British invasion. It was midsummer. From on board a yacht in Sydney Harbour the wine and food correspondent of the *Sydney Morning Herald* sent this report of the 'ultimate party':

Nothing I've seen, not Churchill's funeral, not *Aida* at Luxor, nothing, no sight in 52 years can match this. A thousand masts, kilometres of rigging disposed across the junction of sky and sea like a giant's set of fiddlesticks . . . There are polite luncheon parties, dainty teas in some of the posher silvertail residences. But the real people are assembled in euphoric proximity . . . cheering each passing vessel, exulting in the spectacle . . .

To hell with the knockers. If they don't understand that any nation needs its rituals, its ceremonials, its opportunities to show how well-behaved it can be when given the chance and the stimulus . . . then there is no hope for it.[78]

The 'knockers', most of whom were the original people of Australia, had not assembled in 'euphoric proximity' to the 'real people'. They were well used to being told to go to hell. They were pleased, of course, that the 'real people' were 'well behaved', as this had not always been the case.

They came from Pilbara in the north-west, Alice Springs in the centre and Tasmania in the far south, from Perth on the Indian Ocean and Townsville on the Pacific. They travelled in convoys of 'freedom buses' painted red, black and gold, and in cattle trucks and old Toyotas. At Tennant Creek in the Northern Territory, John Christopherson, the deputy chairman of the Northern Lands Council, addressed a roadside meeting of his people. 'This is serious business,' he said. 'People from all over Australia will be watching us. You mob are taking stories, and if you're going to take a story, it should be a sober one. If you take a drunken one, you might as well leave it at home.'[79]

The temperature reached 110°F. Radiators blocked, head gaskets cracked. Eight buses stopped, but only one was abandoned. The hum of the didgeridoo and the resonance of clapping sticks generated energy; but the old people, who had insisted upon going, were tested severely. One of them died on the road to Adelaide, and the convoy faltered, consumed with grief. Normally Aboriginal people go back home to mourn; but Frank Chulung, Chairman of the Kimberley Land Council, said they would go on to Sydney 'because this trip means so much to us and to all Aboriginal people in this country'.[80]

The old men coming from Menindee, New South Wales, remembered well the previous anniversary of white conquest, known as the 'sesqui-centenary'. This was 'celebrated' on January 26, 1938 with a re-enactment of Captain Arthur Phillip's landing at Sydney. A commentator of the Australian newsreel company, Cinesound, described the scene:

> History flames into life as the dramatic scenes of the first landing at Circular Quay are re-enacted at Farm Cove

... We see the natives gathering ... to ward off the invaders just as they then did. Before Captain Phillip lands, Lieutenant Ball takes a boat-load of marines ashore to keep the natives in check.

In the face of menacing savages, the white men advance up the shore of a new land ...

(*Voices*) 'Is there any likelihood of an ambush?'

'See that none of them remain skulking about.'

Now Phillip himself lands. So a handful of Englishmen took possession of a continent! A vast unknown primeval land.

It is now fitting that we should turn our minds to the purpose underlying this enterprise ... which is to plant a fresh sprig of Empire in this new and vast land. It may be that this country will become the most valuable acquisition Britain has ever made![81]

Twenty-five Aborigines were brought from a reserve in Menindee to play the role of 'menacing savages'. They were held overnight in a police compound next to dog kennels and relatives were not allowed to see them. They were told that if they did not co-operate their food rations would be stopped. The 'celebrations' attracted tens of thousands of people, and only cursory reference was made to the original inhabitants. The *Sydney Mail* described their fate as a 'sorry tale' and noted that 'it could not have been otherwise. They are not very alert in modern business methods.'[82]

The pity might have been spared; for on that day, unbeknown to the majority, black Australians were making history. The Aborigines Progressive Association, which was the creation of Bill Ferguson, a shearer, and Jack Patten, a writer, convened the first national conference of Aborigines and declared a Day of Mourning. Addressing the white nation before an audience of both blacks and whites, Jack Patten said:

You have almost exterminated our people, but there are enough of us remaining to expose the humbug of your claim, as White Australians, to be a civilised, progressive, kindly and humane nation. By your cruelty towards the Aborigines, you stand condemned in the eyes of the civilised world.[83]

In contrast to the propaganda of the day, his words have survived with dignity. Half a century later, as the 'freedom buses' entered Sydney, an elder held aloft Jack Patten's manifesto and a younger man helped him read it to others, who listened in silence and tears.

Thirty thousand Aboriginal Australians marched through Sydney on the Bicentenary day. The police halved that number, of course, and commentators with nothing else to say about it said incessantly that the march was peaceful. Only they had implied that it might be otherwise.

Out on the harbour a sailing ship, which was meant to represent one of the 'First Fleet', was emblazoned with an advertisement for Coca Cola. On the quayside the Prince of Wales made a gentle speech alluding to the truth that a nation is judged as civilised by how *all* its people are regarded. The Prime Minister, Bob Hawke, made no such accommodation. 'In Australia', he said stridently, there must be 'no privilege of origin'.[84] The people from the buses, the 'knockers', knew what he meant. As he spoke, families of those who have died in police custody threw flowers into Botany Bay.

Many of Australia's secrets did not survive the Bicentenary year. People around the world became interested in the struggle of a people about whom they had known little. To them, the resurgence of the first Australians seemed a twentieth-century phenomenon and the real point of the Bicentenary. The Anti-Slavery Society, which in 1970 published a report noting that 'many Aborigines live in dependent poverty which is extreme by world standards', reported in 1988 that 'these observations remain valid'.[85] A United

Nations study found that Aborigines lived in 'poverty, misery and extreme frustration' and condemned the Australian Government for being 'in violation of her human rights obligations'.[86] Most hurtful of all, Australia was compared openly with South Africa.

One reflex response to this was to deny the past. After my series of documentary films, *The Last Dream*, was shown on Australian television early in 1988, in which I made reference to the deaths of more than half a million Aborigines, voices of the Established Truth fulminated that such a suggestion risked a 'big backlash' as 'the most scholarly estimates' put the Aboriginal population in 1788 as low as 215,000.[87]

Suppression of Aboriginal population figures has been a feature of the imperial record. This is understandable. If history was to show large numbers of people inhabiting the 'empty land' at the time of the invasion, the deduction would have to be made that genocide was on an even more appalling scale than previously assessed.

Indeed, on the eve of the Bicentenary year a sensational 'discovery' was made by the anthropologist Dr Peter White and Australia's most celebrated pre-historian, Professor D. J. Mulvaney. They reported that the Aboriginal population in 1788 was 750,000, or three times the previous estimate. They concluded that more than 600,000 people had died in the years following the invasion. News of this was published on page sixteen of the *Sydney Morning Herald* under the byline of the paper's 'Environment Writer'.[88]

The Mulvaney/White disclosure is not isolated. The Aboriginal renaissance has been helped by a group of white Australian historians whose work has had a striking effect whenever it has found popular expression. Henry Reynolds's books, *The Other Side of the Frontier*, *Frontier* and *The Law of the Land* are outstanding examples. Similarly, the work of Noel Butlin, Ross Fitzgerald and others has broken the silence, though not without incurring the wrath of some of their compatriots, from racists to their academic peers.

In journalism, in the face of indifference and at times hostility, the same recurring names have distinguished their craft

1. *Above:* Fathers and sons among Aboriginal soldiers who fought in the Second World War. From Left: Con and Ron Edwards, Cyril and James Scott

2. *Left:* Eddie Murray, who was killed in police custody, Wee Waa, 1981

3. *Above:* Aboriginal artist Albert Namatjira, fêted by Melbourne 'society' 1951, gaoled and died, 1959

4. *Right:* Joyce Hall, Northern Territory, 1982

5. Alice Springs, 1987

6. *Right:* Freda Glynn,
chairperson of Imparja
Television, Alice Springs,
owned by Aboriginal
Australians

7. *Below:* Clara Inkamala
explains how to catch and
cook a goanna

8. *Above:* China in Australia: Denis O'Hoy, right, with his brothers and sisters, Bendigo, 1946

9. *Left:* Denis in 1987, overseen by his grandparents

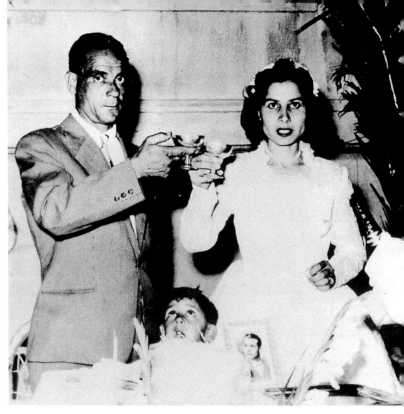

10. *Above:* The wedding
of Maria and Carlo
Calcagno, Sicily, 1954 -
with the groom missing.
Carlo was represented by
his brother-in-law and in a
picture on the cake

11. *Right:* The couple on
the day Maria landed in
Sydney in 1955

12. The Atlas football team, Sydney, 1940. The players all originate from the Greek island of Castellorizia, whose people have emigrated to Australia since 1916

13. Tom Stratton, immigration officer, with Greek 'New Australians', Athens, 1958

14. *Left:* The author's parents: five-year-old Elsie Marheine, later Elsie Pilger, in the middle of her two sisters, Kurri Kurri, 1907

15. *Below left:* Claude Pilger, Sydney, 1947

16. *Below:* Valentina Makeev, a 'displaced person', and her pet kangaroo Richard, Snowy Mountains, 1940s

by reporting events that once were 'non events'. They are Tony Hewett, Jan Mayman, Stewart Harris, Jan Roberts, Graham Williams, Michael Cordell, Robert Haupt, Matt Peacock and the journalists of the ABC current affairs programme, *Four Corners*. In his column, Peter Cullen, Editor of the *Illawarra Mercury* in New South Wales, described graphically the difficulties most of them have had to face:

There are times when journalists become totally ashamed of their profession and some of the people who practise it.

I have experienced that sense of shame for reasons many and varied. But by far the worst case I encountered was back in 1978 when I became interested in the plight of south coast Aborigines, their health and living conditions.

Some people had phoned the *Illawarra Mercury* to complain that Aborigines in Nowra and on a mission known as Wallaga Lake were living in squalor and exposed to disease.

With a trusty photographer, I headed south. For the next few days I was to see degrading things: young Aborigine mothers and their babies living in car wrecks, families in humpies, widespread sickness and disease, teenage alcoholics, hopelessness and despair.

I wrote about the demoralisation of the South Coast Aborigines in a special series for the *Illawarra Mercury*. The stories were no sooner on the streets when a long-time South Coast journalist phoned me to express his astonishment.

'Are you serious about those stories?' he asked.

I told him I had never been more serious in my life.

This scribe then proceeded to lambast me for some minutes for having the gall to write the stories and then lay some claim to them as exclusive pieces of journalism.

'I've known about the Abos and their conditions for years,' he said.

I was becoming angry by this time. 'Then why in hell have you not written about it?' I inquired.

And his reply made me ashamed of the profession I had chosen to pursue. He said: 'I have never bothered for two reasons:

'Firstly, they are only coons and live like animals anyway.

'And secondly, nobody gives a damn.'

I had no desire to continue the conversation and hung up. But over the next few weeks I encountered sneers and jibes. People even stopped me in the street with the typically insulting comment: 'Nothing else to write about, mate?'[89]

Among large sections of the Australian people common slurs against Aborigines now meet with revulsion. This was demonstrated following an extraordinary article in the *Sydney Morning Herald* by the English gossip writer Auberon Waugh, who described Aborigines as 'warring, nomadic packs' with a 'non-existent' wisdom and an art that 'must be judged the merest piffle by any civilised standards'.[90] So outraged was the response that the letters editor of the *Herald* appealed to readers to stop writing. 'We don't have to listen to every mealy-mouthed racist who deigns to visit from the "mother country",' wrote one reader. 'A carefully fabricated persona', wrote another, 'cannot conceal the ersatz base of his gratuitous and tiresome insults.'[91]

So it was not surprising that when the 'freedom buses' converged on Sydney on Bicentenary day, January 26, and drove to Belmore Park, traditionally a resting place for Sydney's homeless, they were joined by thousands of white Australians, young and old, in that universal solidarity that transcends nation, language and race.

Flying across the sweep of Australia the wounds below become apparent. They are erosion as deep as valleys, and they are plains of petrified forests. For hundreds of miles the land does not move: the wildlife shot, stunned and beaten into handbags in Osaka and pet food in Chicago. In Alice Springs Pat Dodson lamented this destruction. 'Trees and wetlands have gone,' he said. 'The country has become a large chequerboard of fences, with little hedgerow bushes that are an imitation of Britain's countryside. None of this has anything to do with the spirit of Australia. A human being has to be in resonance, in harmony with his country, and he lives from that strength. Our efforts to regain land are simply part of our effort to regain life; and if we can't regain our land, our life is virtually lost. This is not a vote-catching cause. It requires moral fortitude and commitment, which is politically inconvenient.'[92]

In 1987 Bob Hawke was re-elected with an increased majority and, for a Labor Prime Minister, an unprecedented third term. At the start of his re-election campaign Hawke appeared in a front-page picture smiling at the camera after he had sung his campaign's jingle, 'Let's stick together'. The jingle was the result of a \$A2·7 million contract with an advertising agency run by John Singleton, whose other accounts included the Pope's visit to Australia and a liquor chain known as 'Buck Off Bill' ('If ya' don't buy from Bill, then buck off!')

Directly beneath the Hawke picture was a headline, 'Hepatitis B hits NSW Aboriginal children'. The report said that 90 per cent of Aboriginal children in the western part of the State had suffered from Hepatitis B before they turned sixteen, and nearly one-third had been infected before their first birthday. The disease 'caused chronic liver problems, which can lead to premature death'.[93]

During only his second visit to an Aboriginal community in more than four years as Prime Minister, Hawke said that his Government wanted a 'compact' with black Australians. When asked what this meant, he refused to say. One year later, with international interest in the treatment of Aborigines at its peak, Hawke said he hoped a 'treaty' would be possible by 1990. When asked what this meant, he gave only scant detail. He made no mention of land rights. Almost half way through 1990 enquiries to the Government about the progress of the 'treaty' were met with a 'no comment'. On the day he ceased to be Prime Minister, in December 1991, Hawke unveiled an Aboriginal bark painting in Parliament House and called on his 'followers' to work for a 'reconciliation document'. He then cried. 'It was not clear', reported the *Independent*, 'if yesterday's tears were a product of being carried away by his abrupt loss of power or the wider losses of Australia's indigenous people'[94]

In any case, the Opposition promised to repeal any such 'document' or 'compact' or 'treaty', thus threatening the security of the present land rights legislation laws in the Northern Territory without which, as Pat Dodson said, 'our life is virtually lost'.

In the wake of the 'ultimate party', no leading Australian politician has yet summoned the courage and wit to explain

THE COMPACT

adequately to the majority that Aborigines are not seeking unmerited privileges, merely basic human rights and justice; that support for land rights ought not to be the product of guilt, rather of an understanding that Australian society is debased by what has happened; and that until we white Australians give back to black Australians their nationhood, we can never claim our own.

3

HEROES UNSUNG

As the lot of a slave depends upon the character of its [*sic*] master, so the convict depends upon the temper and disposition of the settler to whom he is assigned.

House of Commons Select Committee report, 1838

We have 25 years at most to populate this country before the yellow races are down upon us.

Arthur Calwell, Minister for Immigration, 1947

I think inevitably we'll become predominantly a Eurasian country. I'm talking about twenty-five years' time perhaps . . . that is a process which is under way.

Bill Hayden, Minister for Foreign Affairs, 1984

WHEN I WAS a boy, I used to ask my relatives how our forebears came to a place as remote as Australia. The story on my father's side was straightforward enough. His father was a German clipper sailor, for whom Newcastle, New South Wales, was a port of call; there he met my grandmother, the daughter of an English surgeon who had been granted land by the Crown.

My mother's story, however, never seemed complete. Her mother was of 'yeoman stock', and as proof of this welcome distinction there was a replica of a memorial tablet to a cousin much-removed who had been 'with' the Duke of Wellington at Waterloo. Her father's grandfather was said to be of such elevated breeding that he had been a pillar of the Australian colony: 'an early landowner' who was 'well to do' and 'nicely connected'. Indeed, so much was made by certain members of my mother's family of the social pre-eminence of my great-great grandfather that I guessed something was afoot. According to one aunt, he 'even knew the Governor' and enjoyed the privilege of 'delivering milk to Government House' from his farm on 'elegant Brickfield Hill'.

Elsie, my mother, used to take me to Brickfield Hill, which in the 1950s was occupied by the grand Sydney department store, Anthony Hordens. This made any suggestion of prior ownership equivalent to a claim upon Harrods or Bloomingdales. It was a cavernous 'emporium' of mail-order mustiness, of bolts of cloth and regiments of blue serge suits and tea chests of imported 'kitchenware', and had a magnificent art deco tea-room. I would imagine that I was standing on the very spot where great-great grandfather oversaw his dairy herd; and Elsie and I would try to estimate the cost of the land today. 'It must be worth *thousands*,' we would agree, but what had happened to these 'thousands' was not mentioned.

Nor was great-great grandfather's wife mentioned, except that she was 'tiny' by comparison with her husband, who was a tall man for the period. A photograph existed of them both, taken in the 1880s. The aunt in possession of this photograph refused to show it to me or to anyone else, which of course deepened the mystery.

One Christmas Day, with all my mother's siblings assembled (there were nine offspring), I decided to force the issue and ask out loud about my great-great grandparents. The aunt in possession of the photograph almost swallowed her teeth. 'Oh, we shouldn't talk about *them*,' she twittered. An aunt I liked leaned across and whispered, 'Yer see love, they were Irish *and* they had the Stain . . .' Elsie had not told me this before and nodded mischievous affirmation. 'I'll tell you later,' she said. The aunt in possession of the photograph said, 'Oh, leave them dead and buried, Elsie!' And the matter was left there, to the relief of all but me.

Of course, the truth was that 'the Stain' was upon us. 'The Stain' was a term deployed most commonly when discussing the 'suspect' origins of one's neighbours and enemies. It meant convict ancestry; and it was almost never spoken of in the first person, as this was bound to induce embarrassment in others or, at worst, mockery. Moreover, research into these genealogical shadows was discouraged or condemned as downright subversive, or dismissed as worthless and 'all talk'.

There was a serious sociological purpose behind this cover-up, which was widespread. (I cannot recall anyone of my age who was aware of or would admit to convict background.) Among the theorists of the origin of character and intelligence who came to prominence during the early Victorian years were those who concluded that criminality was congenital and especially prevalent among the poor. This assessment covered almost all the Irish, adding legitimacy to a belief already popular among the 'criminal classes' themselves. Bilge of this kind ran deep in Australia where, not surprisingly, people felt the need to speak defensively and often about the 'good stock' they had come from.

My own family used this word, 'stock', a great deal; the milkman or a local fruit and vegetable merchant would be categorised by his apparent 'good' or 'bad' stock. During the First World War the casual behaviour of Australian volunteers, and especially their lack of respect towards English officers, whom they rarely saluted, was put down to their 'inferior' convict and Irish breeding. During the Second World War Winston Churchill railed against an Australian Labor Government, which wanted to give priority to the defence of its homeland, not Britain, as coming from 'bad stock'.[1] My aunts, who loved Churchill, were keenly aware of our congenital flaw; therefore secrecy was crucial.

Unfortunately, unbeknown to the keepers of this secret, sensational evidence was to hand in St Mary's Roman Catholic Cathedral, Sydney. Every Thursday, in a vestry, a nun would turn the page of a register of Catholic, mostly Irish convicts. Their crime, sentence, the ship they came on and their physical characteristics were listed. Francis McCarthy and Mary Palmer were two among the names; and enquiries at public record offices in London, Dublin and Sydney have provided portraits, as yet unfinished, of two members of a luckless tribe who attended the birth of white Australia and were my great-great grandparents.

Francis McCarthy could not have been more different from the accredited version. He was a farm labourer from County Roscommon, from an area where people lived in the bog in caves of mud, and worked the land for absentee Englishmen under constant threat of death by disease or, if the crops failed, of bloody eviction and arrest.

Like many Irishmen of the time, McCarthy was neither led nor organised. He simply objected to an imposed way of life, and was arrested and convicted of 'uttering unlawful oaths' and 'insurrection'. These were political crimes, also described in the English courts as 'taking part in seditious conspiracy'. He was sentenced to fourteen years' penal servitude in New

South Wales. Whatever he did, it must have been considered a threat to the prevailing order, as the Tolpuddle Martyrs received only half this sentence for forming a trade union.

He was taken to Cork harbour and fitted with four-pound leg irons, which were standard. He was then 'stored' on a hulk left over from the Napoleonic wars, where convicts slept six to a berth, chained together, and rats scampered and defecated. Far from being the colonial gentleman my aunt had conjured, McCarthy belonged to what Queen Victoria called 'the inflammable matter of Ireland' and Jeremy Bentham inveighed against as 'the *animae viles*, a sort of excrementitious mass that could be projected, and accordingly was projected . . . as far out of sight as possible'.[2]

Shit, that is. And shit to be disposed of along with the 'swinish multitude'[3] of the English lower orders whom Georgian Britannica was sending to its antipodean Siberia, just as Soviet Russia would despatch its political dissenters and Nazi Germany its ethnic and sexual deviants.

The year was 1821. McCarthy was twenty-six years old, standing five feet nine inches with sandy hair and a red bushy beard. In the early hours of June 13, 1821 he was taken by barge to the *John Barry*, a 520-ton barque, being readied for departure to Botany Bay, wherever that might be.

The voyage of the *John Barry* took five days short of five months. It was likely to have been no different from most such voyages: a purgatory of dysentery, pneumonia and scurvy, with the 180 convicts wallowing in each other's vomit and filth in the ship's hold – although the ship's surgeon, John McNamara, appears to have been a kind man, concerned about the convicts' health.

One of my favourite places in Australia is Manly on the ocean front at Sydney, with its Norfolk pines bent like reeds against the wind and spray. At one end of the bay is North Head, where the surf bucks against vertical cliffs. This is one of the towering gateposts to Sydney Harbour. I have often walked along the paths winding around North Head, which is not much changed since the *John Barry* hove to in the swell below. Facing the greatest expanse of water on earth, the

Pacific, I have tried to imagine McCarthy's thoughts on the day he caught sight of his new prison, Australia. The convicts had been told that the Aborigines feasted on white flesh, and they must have glimpsed these 'savages' standing on jagged rocks protruding at the water's edge like monstrous teeth and on the creamy sand of perfect beaches. Or perhaps their fear had long since been overtaken by the relief of reaching somewhere, anywhere.

'Shout out your trade!' McCarthy and the other Irishmen were ordered, having been brought ashore in a long boat, still in leg irons and wearing their yellow prisoners' uniform. He had no trade and was 'assigned' to labour for a Mr Robertson, by all accounts a benevolent man not unlike the patrician slave owners in the American Deep South. It was Mr Robertson who lived on 'elegant Brickfield Hill'. In her version my aunt had neatly swapped master and slave.

On October 24 of that year, while McCarthy was at sea in the *John Barry*, an Irish scullery maid from a London house stood in the dock of the small court attached to Middlesex Gaol and heard her sentence: 'Transportation for the term of your natural life to New South Wales.'

Her name was Mary Palmer. She was sixteen, with brown hair, hazel eyes and skin described in a church register as 'pitted from the smallpox'. I cannot find record of what she did to deserve such a punishment, but it was almost certainly a crime against property. She had originally been sentenced to death; but this was commuted, thanks, according to a family source, to her pregnancy.[4] She sailed one year and a day later, manacled in the hold of the *Lord Sidmouth*. She was my great-great grandmother.

Robert Hughes described vividly in *The Fatal Shore* the scene when a ship bearing female convicts anchored in Sydney:

its upper deck became a slave-market, as randy colonists came swarming over the bulwarks, grinning and ogling and chumming up to the captain with a bottle of rum, while the female convicts – washed for the occasion and dressed in the remnants of their English finery – were mustered before them, trying as hard 'to set themselves off to the best advantage'. Military officers got the first pick, then non-commissioned officers, then privates, and lastly such ex-convict settlers as seemed 'respectable'.[5]

The first white women of Australia thus were regarded as little better than prostitutes. On the voyage out seamen were given 'free access' to the convict women or allowed to cohabit with those of their choice; gang rape was not uncommon. On arrival women were 'assigned' as 'house servants', which usually carried an obligation to service sexually the predominantly male population. This fact was generally suppressed by Australia's imperial historians.

Mary Palmer arrived emaciated and ill, although the nature of her illness is not recorded. So it is unlikely she was of use to anyone. As was the practice with the sick, she was lifted with planks on to the dockside. And she and those like her, described by Hughes as 'the rejects from the "market", the poor, the ugly, the mad, the old, the wizened' were sent to the Female Factory, twenty miles west of Sydney at Parramatta.[6]

I remember the Female Factory as the Parramatta Lunatic Asylum, which it became in the 1870s. It was the object of schoolboy banter. 'You ought to be in Parramatta,' was an insult. I did not know then my family's story in Australia had begun behind the same sandstone walls. My mother remembers passing the clock tower on her wedding day and hearing the wails emanating from what was called the 'imbeciles' yard' and hoping it was not a bad omen. She did not know that 'tiny Mary' had been incarcerated there; no one had mentioned it.

When it opened, the Female Factory was known as the Centre of Labour Supply and Punishment, a name that conjured the Georgian Siberia. The *Cumberland Pilgrim* described it as 'appallingly hideous . . . the recreation ground reminds one of the Valley of the Shadow of Death'.[7] Arriving at night, Mary Palmer had nothing to sleep on, only boards and crushed stone and some straw and filthy wool full of ticks and spiders. She was put to work spinning and carding cloth the texture of hessian, which was worn by the male convicts and called 'Parramatta cloth'. There was no division by age or crime: the strong and the weak, known as the 'intractables' and those 'knuckling under', were thrown together.

All the women underwent solitary confinement. Their heads were shaved and they were placed in total darkness without food and with mosquitoes and spiders. 'Penology' was then flourishing in England, as prisons increasingly were used as depositories for the 'criminal classes'. Penal experts of the day saw the antipodean colony as a testing ground for their exciting new theories. Thus, the 'modern' treadwheel was introduced into the Female Factory in 1823, the year Mary was there. The treadwheel, a device of torture, was a revolving cylinder in which the prisoner had to keep stepping upwards in order to keep the cylinder moving and not to fall out. Few of the women escaped it.

However, this did not always have the intended effect of quelling the 'intractables' and breaking the women's spirit. The New South Wales Attorney-General, Roger Terry, described, with a mixture of horror and admiration, how the women of the Factory had driven back 'with a volley of stones and staves' soldiers who had been sent to put down a rebellion during which the women (not the soldiers!) had used 'excessive violence'.[8] Missionaries sent from England to repair the souls of the women were given similar shrift; one of them reported, with a deep sense of failure, that at Parramatta 'the bad soon became the worse'.[9]

Nevertheless, the Factory provided a high point in the life of the colony when its marriage market was held every third Monday. This was known coyly as 'courting day'. The 1838 House of Commons Select Committee on Transportation described what happened:

The convict goes up and looks at the women and if he sees a lady that takes his fancy, he makes a motion to her and she steps to one side. Some will not do this, but stand still, and have no wish to be married, but that is very rare. They then have, of course, some conversation and the ceremony goes on with two or three more.[10]

Some of the women found 'finery' for the occasion; others wore the coarse sacking of their uniform. Some primped urgently, as if any inspecting male might provide the only way out of their predicament; others turned their backs if the aspiring husband was elderly, a 'stringybark' down from the bush. During all this the matron would bellow the 'good points' of each woman, which were said to be a revelation to all.

In this way Francis McCarthy chose Mary Palmer. On November 9, 1823, in company with four other convict couples, they were married at St Mary's Church (later Cathedral). Within eight years both were given their 'ticket of leave'. Unions made at the Factory were not known to last, but theirs was a notable exception. When her tenth child was due in 1839, Mary was pardoned, but as she would have had to pay a fee, she did not bother to collect a splendid document, of which I have a copy. It bore the royal seal of George III, in whose name:

I, Colonel Snodgrass, Captain-General and Governor-in-Chief of Her Majesty's said Territory of New South Wales and its Dependencies, and Vice-Admiral of the same, taking into consideration the good conduct of Mary Palmer, who arrived in this Colony in the ship *Lord Sidmouth* . . . under sentence of Transportation for Life, . . . do hereby Conditionally Remit the remainder of the Term or Time which is yet to come and unexpired of the Original Sentence or Order of Transportation passed on the aforesaid Mary Palmer, at Middlesex Gaol.

CONDITIONAL PARDON.

No. *39/262*

WHEREAS His late Most Excellent Majesty KING GEORGE THE THIRD, by a Commission under the *Great Seal of Great Britain* bearing Date the Eighth Day of November, in the Thirty-first Year of His Majesty's Reign, was graciously pleased to Give and Grant full Power and Authority to the GOVERNOR (or, in case of his death or absence, the LIEUTENANT GOVERNOR) for the time being of His Majesty's Territory of the *Eastern Coast of New South Wales* and the Islands thereunto adjacent, by an Instrument or Instruments in Writing under the Seal of the Government of the said Territory, or as *He* or *They* respectively should think fit and convenient for His Majesty's Service, to Remit either Absolutely or Conditionally the Whole or any Part of the Term or Time for which Persons convicted of Felony, Misdemeanor, or other Offences, amenable to the Laws of Great Britain, should have been, or should thereafter be respectively conveyed or Transported to New South Wales, or the Islands thereunto adjacent.

By Virtue of such Power and Authority so vested as aforesaid, I *Colonel Snodgrass C B Barker* Captain-General and Governor-in-Chief of Her Majesty's said Territory of New South Wales and its Dependencies, and Vice-Admiral of the same, taking into consideration the good conduct of *Mary Palmer,* who arrived in this Colony in the ship *Sir C Sidmouth Kis Fenix* Master, in the Year One thousand eight hundred and *twenty three* under sentence of Transportation for *Life* and whose Description is on the back hereof Do hereby Conditionally Remit the remainder of the Term or Time which is yet to come and unexpired of the Original Sentence or Order of Transportation passed on the aforesaid *Mary Palmer,* , at *Middlesex Gaol Delivery,* on the *Twenty fourth* Day of *October* One thousand eight hundred and *twenty one,*

Provided Always, and on Condition, that the said *Mary Palmer,* continue to reside within the limits of this Government for and during the space of *her* original Sentence or Order of Transportation :—Otherwise, the said *Mary Palmer,* shall be subject to all the Pains and Penalties of Re-appearing in Great Britain and Ireland, for and during the Term of *her* original Sentence or Order of Transportation ; or, as if this Remission had never been granted.

GIVEN under my Hand and the Seal of the Territory, at Government House, Sydney, in NEW SOUTH WALES, this *First* Day of *February* in the Year of Our Lord One thousand eight hundred and *thirty eight*

(L.S.)   (SIGNED) *K Snodgrass*

By His Excellency's Command.

Mary Palmer's conditional pardon, 1838

This was His Majesty's Pardon of an Exile, which Mary was granted almost fifteen years to the day after she was brought ashore. It was conditional, however, on her not 're-appearing in Great Britain and Ireland, for and during the Term of her Original Sentence'.

She never 're-appeared' in England or Ireland. Nor did Francis, who, having served his sentence, received his Certificate of Freedom. He lived a considerable life, becoming a miller, then a horseman rising to overseer in a 'Horse and Buggy Bazaar' in Sydney. Both he and Mary died in old age, remembered by their children and grandchildren with love and respect. Only later generations disclaimed them and sought to erase their memory and devalue the heroic dimension of their lives. When I learned who and what they really were, and spread the word with pride, my estrangement from the keepers of 'our secret' was complete. The irony of this is that droves of convict skeletons have been recently liberated from Australian closets, having found themselves the objects of an inverted snobbery which none of us would have dreamt possible in our previous lives.

Francis McCarthy and Mary Palmer's petition to the Governor of New South Wales to be married as Roman Catholics, October 21, 1823.

More than 160,000 men, women and children were shipped to Australia in chains. Although slavery was abolished throughout the British Empire by the Emancipation Act of 1834, it lasted in Australia for another forty years, in spite of a public campaign during which the House of Commons Select Committee compared the suffering of a convict with 'the lot of a slave'. It also lasted long enough for the sons of the English landed class, who became known as 'squatters', to claim large tracts of Australia and make fortunes on the backs of their convict labourers.

Imperial historians did not use the term 'white slavery', no doubt out of respect for the sensibilities that preferred 'Government man' to 'convict'. The contrivance of respectability in order to obliterate 'the Stain' became the mission of historians and a large section of the population. This respectability required, apart from money, certain sub-Thatcherite poses. Among them was the affecting of an accent in which nasal inflexion was eliminated, if not completely, then in certain company. (One of my aunts, a sixth-generation Australian, would say, 'Oh she speaks so *Australian*.') There was also the embrace of all things British and, for some, the adoption of what were understood, often incorrectly, to be 'English ways'; and obligatory xenophobia towards all non-British elements, such as 'tykes', 'yids' and 'Abos' (not necessarily in that order); and, above all, the establishment of a precise suburban existence, with manicured English flower-beds, garden gnomes and/or piccaninnies, stained glass in the front door, rooms that admitted little of the southern light and containing a row of *Encyclopaedia Britannica*, unopened and guarded by pieces of china commemorating the festivities and funerals of the English royal family.

It is not possible to understand present-day Australian society without appreciating the indelibility of the 'Stain' and its heritage. It is such a potent part of our psyche that its appanage is passed to newcomers who are not from Anglo-Celtic backgrounds. It touches the way we are with each other, our language and humour; where else but in Australia is the vocabulary of irony, even perversity, such everyday currency? When the Royal Theatre opened in Sydney in 1796, the following lines were spoken from the stage by the Irish convict George Barrington. They were seed to our language.

Through distant climes, O'er widespread seas we come,
Though not with much eclat, or beat of drum.
True patriots all, for it be understood,
We left our country for our country's good.[11]

In their flirtation with Australia as the 'last frontier', many Americans believe we are similar peoples, hewn from the same, simple pioneer background. Australians have encouraged and exploited this view. I remember as a teenager seriously discussing with my friends the hope that we Australians might one day be regarded as 'honorary Americans', so that our isolated society might shed its dullness and insignificance. There was even something called 'The Fifty-first State Movement'. Hollywood was omnipresent; the United States filled the vacuum of our own experience, past and present, for which there was no popular mirror. Our own story, its rapaciousness and struggle, remained secret. American mythology was very different from ours, but we did not care to admit the difference: that unlike the first white Americans, who imagined themselves on a mission from God, the first white Australians *knew* they were Godforsaken.

Even the image of ourselves which *Crocodile Dundee* personifies, that of the outrageous, yet sceptical 'larrikin' who rejects all convention and authority, is mostly wrong. True, generations of us were encouraged to distrust, even despise the police: a bequest of our convict past, it was said. But we made only anti-authoritarian noises behind authority's back and, in the end, we did as we were told, with some of us going so far as to adopt the peculiar deference that 'lags' have for their 'screws'. Consider that within a few years of the abolition of white slavery in Australia, those who had survived King George's concentration camps were rushing to help the Crown put down popular resistance in China, New Zealand and South Africa, and that during the imperial slaughter-fest of 1914–18 their sons volunteered a vassal's army and stoically sustained more casualties, proportionately, than the British or anyone else.

Our history travelled from convicts to trench fodder with hardly a demur; and when, in 1975, an imperial Viceroy sacked an elected Australian Government there was, wrote an American reporter, 'a strange silence over this country'. This was not altogether true, but much of the popular reaction was that of impotence and of those concerned with 'restoring order'. The truth is that no nation was born under as cruel a star as Australia; and if there is ever to be an Australian 'identity', rooted in an independent Australia free of the multifarious ties that bind, it will not be due to events set in train by the establishment of a penal colony in 1788, but in spite of them.

Today the 'sails' of the Sydney Opera House rise above the botanical gardens and the ferry wharves of Circular Quay. The postcard scene is the quintessence of the new Australia: confident, dynamic, futuristic. Yet it was here that Francis and Mary and the other convicts of their period were brought ashore. To my knowledge, the Japanese and Americans stepping from their tour buses to be addressed by their guide, are not told this.

I remember this place when it was Bennelong Point, named after the Aborigine Bennelong, who was captured in 1789 and sent to England to meet George III, while his people died from smallpox introduced by the King's men. It was here that the launch run by the Stannard Brothers would pick me up shortly after dawn and chug through the mist and the first shafts of light to the ships waiting just inside Sydney Heads. The ships were the *Oronsay*, *Orion* and *Orsova*, the *Southern Cross* and *Northern Star*, the *Fairsky* and *Fairsea*. It seemed they lined up according to parentage: the dowagers of the Orient Line ahead of those of Greek registration and uncertain birthplace. On some days there would be three or four of them: 4,000 people in one day, up to 30,000 a month, every month.

It was 1959. I was a young journalist working as a shipping reporter on the Sydney *Daily Telegraph*, a position I now realise was one of great privilege because it made me a witness to an epic human migration from one end of the earth to the other. Only the unique beginning of white Australia is comparable with the story of those who came in their millions following the Second World War. Within my lifetime they have converted Australia from a whites-only fortress, a second-hand England, to a refuge for more than 100 nationalities, the second most culturally diverse society in the world after Israel. And it has happened peacefully. This is a remarkable achievement by any measure of human decency and progress.

If I had to choose an Australian anniversary to celebrate, I would choose July 21. On that day in 1947 a man, who spoke out of the corner of his mouth and always wore a black tie, signed for Australia an agreement to take a nation of people from the refugee camps in Europe. It is difficult to know what to make of Arthur Calwell, Minister of Immigration in the post-war Labor Government. Perhaps in time he will be regarded as a visionary, a true reflection of the fears, paradoxes and strengths of his people. The man who once said that 'no red-blooded Australian' would want to see 'the creation of a chocolate-coloured Australia' conceived and implemented an immigration programme that, despite his own prejudices, has led Australia inexorably towards its future as a Eurasian society.[12] What is astonishing about the upheaval Calwell planned is that it has succeeded virtually by default. In 1947 most Australians did not want diversity, or 'multiculturalism'; but few actively opposed it. Equally, most Australians were touched by racial and ethnic prejudice, but few generated communal conflict.

A glimpse of Australia as it was begins to explain why. At the close of the Second World War, with a land mass roughly equal to that of the United States, Australia had a population of around seven million. On maps it appeared suspended between two great oceans, at the southern tip of Asia, 'alone and vulnerable', as school textbooks used to say. Japanese attacks against Darwin and Sydney had convinced most Australians that the Yellow Peril was intent on having its way with the Great White Virgin of the South. This did not happen, but it might have happened; and when Calwell launched his post-war immigration policy with the slogan, POPULATE OR PERISH, he exploited brilliantly the nation's deepest fear. 'We have twenty-five years at most to populate this country', he declared, 'before the yellow races are down upon us.' With these words he set in train a process which, to some, was to justify his own warning.

If Calwell had undisclosed motives, his own background put him beyond suspicion. During the 1930s he had opposed the admission of immigrants from anywhere, even refugees from Europe. In so doing, he had reflected dutifully the wishes of the Australian labour movement, which regarded 'aliens' as those who took a decent man's job and worked for less pay. Chinese were barred from trade unions. The world's first labour Government, formed in Queensland in 1899, saw as its 'historic task' the protection of white workers' jobs from the 'threat' posed by bonded sugar-cane workers, the 'Kanakas', whom the plantation owners had shipped from the islands of the south-western Pacific. The federation of the Australian States in 1901 was founded on racial exclusion and included legislation which prohibited permanent settlement by non-Europeans. This was enforced by a bizarre dictation test, not in English but in a language deliberately chosen to ensure the applicant's failure. Japanese war brides of Australian servicemen were to be 'tested' in Gaelic and lawfully denied entry. Not surprisingly, such a device originated in South Africa.

'It is my hope', said Calwell, even before the Japanese surrender in 1945, 'that for every foreign migrant there will be ten people from the United Kingdom.'[13] The hope was illusory, as Calwell must have known. There were not enough ships to bring that number of British people to Australia. At the same time he appeared to be preparing Australians to think of themselves as belonging to a 'new America'. He extolled the 'splendid specimens of American manhood walking the streets of Australian cities' during the war and said that when he recalled that:

America has been, for more than a generation, a melting pot for European nations, I am satisfied with the result of the amalgamation. We should lose nothing by adopting a similar policy. It would be far better for us to have in Australia 20 million or 30 million people of 100 per cent white extraction than to continue the narrow policy of having a population of 7 million people who are 98 per cent British.[14]

The fact that the United States was an 'amalgamation' of many cultures other than European was conveniently suppressed.

On July 21, 1947 Calwell signed the historic agreement for unlimited numbers of 'displaced persons'. Prime Minister Ben Chifley and his Cabinet undoubtedly knew what this meant. The Australian people did not know, and were not told.

On December 7, 1947 the first shipload of 'DPs' arrived in Melbourne and Calwell's great ruse was unveiled. The passengers had been carefully chosen. They were all from the northern Baltic states and they were all young and single. None was a Jew. The press, radio and newsreel recorded the arrival of this smiling, waving group, among whom there just happened to be fluent English speakers who were delighted to effuse for the cameras on the 'Australian way of life'. A young blonde woman was recorded for posterity proclaiming her appreciation of 'your kookaburras, your lovely kookaburras'. Twenty-five years later Calwell remembered fondly his 'beautiful Balts'. There were, he said, 'a number of platinum blondes of both sexes. The men were handsome and the women beautiful. It was not hard to sell immigration to the Australian people once the press published photographs of that group.'[15]

Having manipulated the media and, he hoped, public opinion, Calwell ensured that 'less desirable' categories followed quickly, almost stealthily – although the 400 Australian immigration officers sent to Europe were instructed to favour 'European races'; Jews especially had to be 'exceptionally good cases'.[16]

Tom Stratton was one of the 400 directed, as he put it, 'to find an entire population'. Having helped to select the shipload of 'beautiful Balts', he served in eastern Europe, Greece and Britain. A genial, kindly man from a traditional Sydney working-class background, he is retired and lives overlooking the Pacific at Manly. He described to me 'an amazing period when all the excitement and guilt were part of the same dream ... it was like standing at the gates, arbitrarily stopping one or two in a crowd that surged past you.'

I asked him what was meant by the White Australia Policy.

'Well, there never was one,' he replied. 'What we had was something verbal called a Non-European Policy under which a person had to be 60 per cent European in appearance and outlook.'

'What did that mean?' I asked.

'Mate,' he replied, 'Christ only knows ... 'scuse my French.'

'Did it mean, say, people with dark hair, dark eyes, dark complexion?'

'Maybe it did. Nobody ever told me. So you played God. I still have regrets about people I turned down. There was this bloke I can never get out of my mind. I was on the Hungarian/Yugoslav border, where we were dealing with Hungarian refugees. Well, as you may know, Hungarians are normally fairish people or of fair appearance colourwise ... you know what I mean ... well, this bloke was a Hungarian gipsy and he was dark ... very, very dark ... and I rejected him. And he used to stand outside my open-door office for days on end and I'd look at him and think, "I've got to give him a go." But then I'd think of the effect on him when he got to Australia.'

'The effect on *him*?'

'Yes, you see I visualised him walking down Martin Place in Sydney, and in 1956 if somebody coloured walked down Martin Place, he would be at the centre of all attention. So I rejected him for two reasons ... one, for Australia's sake and the other for himself . . . so he wouldn't be embarrassed and treated badly when he got there.'

I asked how he assessed a potential immigrant's 'outlook'.

'A tricky one, outlook. Say, if you were working in Lebanon and a fellow turned up on a camel . . . and now I'm not joking, this happened . . . and shall we say he was wearing pantaloons, a fez and a big droopy moustache, etcetera. Well, here again you have to visualise him riding down Martin Place.'

'That's assuming he brought his camel with him.'

'Correct. But camel or not, he had to be rejected. He just wasn't right.'

I asked Tom about the propaganda of the time, which depicted Australia as an immigrants' paradise.

'A paradise . . . that's right. I suppose in the early days we did present a rosy picture, particularly in Britain. We wanted the British, you see. Now you may recall the whingeing Poms going back home, saying they had been brought out under a misapprehension . . .'

'Who were the whingeing Poms?'

'Well, most of the whingeing Poms – and I hate using that expression – stemmed from the wife who missed home and her mother. That was the basis for the whingeing Poms. And to stop whingeing Poms coming here, I was sent to Brighton in England in 1966. Well, in came this couple, and the husband was a typical fop . . .'

'A typical . . . fop?'

'Correct. Anyway, this fop had inherited a hundred thousand pounds from his father. The wife was an overbearing, domineering woman who said to me, "Oh yes, we'll go out to Australia, we'll show them."

'I thought, "You're going nowhere, lady." Reject!'

'So their outlook was wrong?'

'Definitely correct. No one would have spoken to the woman because of her overbearing attitude and, anyway, some Australian conman would have got his hands on the hundred thousand pounds within a month.'

I asked Tom about the regrets he had. 'In many ways it

106

was a sad time,' he replied. 'The displaced persons were sad people. The poor devils would come to you with no papers, no background. They were doctors who couldn't prove they were doctors. And these people weren't popular simply because they couldn't speak English. I tell you, I didn't boast that I worked for the Department of Immigration because even my mother-in-law said, "What are you doing, bringing those reffos out here?"'

The 'poor devils' and 'reffos' had to work where they were sent for up to two years. Australia wanted mostly labourers, so immigrants with skills had to lie and say they had none. The former New South Wales Labor leader, Jack Lang, called it 'slave labour under the guise of immigration'.[17] The newcomers were bonded to 'dirty jobs' which Australians would not do. 'DPS TO HAVE ONLY UNATTRACTIVE JOBS', said a headline in the *Sydney Morning Herald* and the story had a reassuring tone. The unnamed source was Arthur Calwell. Fear not, it said, doctors were to dig roads, engineers were to scrub public lavatories, musicians were to collect garbage and nurses were to work on assembly lines; and their qualifications would not be recognised. They were to work unsocial hours and if redundancies were required, they were to be the first to be dismissed. And if they objected, the unions would not protect them. Indeed, the unions had insisted on these conditions. That was the good news.[18]

The suffering of the 'DPs', or 'Balts', was generally kept secret. It was not known that people lived in fear of petty, often punitive officials, who controlled their lives and told them little; that mental breakdowns were common; that children grew up not knowing parents who were forced to work the night shift at some distant factory.

The policy then was 'assimilation'. For the immigrants it was Catch 22. It meant that they were expected to become indistinguishable from the Australian-born population as quickly as possible, but that helping them to achieve this was anathema to the ideology of 'sameness'. Hence the tortured logic that nothing was to be explained to people in a language other than English and that interpreter services and special programmes were 'counter-productive'. The Government had invented a perfect foil against demands that it should meet the needs of people it had sponsored and labelled 'New Australians'.[19]

Apart from the departure home of a flock of 'whingeing Poms', or a shoot-out involving 'gangs' of ethnic origins, immigrants were not news. Like Aborigines, they were declared invisible; in this way traditional Australian life could proceed without its devotees being aware of or discomfited by the trials of the 'New Australians' and of the prospective seismic changes in their own society.

Perhaps the seeds of future 'acceptance by default' lay in this almighty ignorance; for the majority, becalmed in indifference, perceived no threat. It is not surprising that some 'old' Australians today cannot grasp that those who now represent almost half the population bore their hardships and sometimes broke their dreams, unseen and unacknowledged, and are the nation's modern heroes.

In those days, had the term 'Third World' existed, much of Australia would have qualified. The population lived 'off the sheep's back'; the industrial and manufacturing base was tiny. Public works were often regarded as a national joke. Huge, unattended holes were left for so long that no one could remember why they were dug in the first place. In Sydney I grew up near a mysterious cavern that was said to mark an underground railway station. Similarly, the word 'pot-holes' became part of the Australian lexicon, denoting the state of the nation's main roads which regularly disappeared from the map, beneath dust, mud and water.

The arrival of the 'New Australians' changed that. One of the engineering wonders of the twentieth century is a monument to them. Begun in 1949, the Snowy Mountains Scheme grew to a massive complex of tunnels, dams, bridges and power stations that turned the great east-flowing rivers of New South Wales away from the ocean and into the outback, realising the pioneer dream of irrigation in two States and enough electricity for Sydney and Melbourne. The builders of this were of sixty nationalities, an international brigade who fought on a subterranean battlefield, digging in, blasting, moving forward, looking out for each other, dying. For every dam they built, for every mile of tunnel they dug, at least one man would die. In Cooma, in the Snowy Mountains, there are many flags and a cenotaph with lists of 'reffo' names: Larchowski, Nagy, Sevegnano, Pizol, Sledowski . . .

In 1949 Michael and Valentina Makeev were 'DPs' indentured to work on 'the Snowy'. Michael's parents were white Russian who had fled from Germany after the First World War. His wife, Valentina, also a Russian, lived in Yugoslavia but ended up in Germany where she met Michael in a displaced persons' camp. 'We could have applied for America,' said Michael, 'but Australia was interesting because we knew nothing about it, except that it had a lot of sheep. For us, coming from war, that sounded so wonderfully uncomplicated!'

I met the Makeevs in the Snowy Mountains, which they never left. At No. 2 Alkoomi Place, Cooma, past beds of sweet-pea flowers and behind frilly curtains, they live surrounded by photographs of their forty-year odyssey as 'New Australians'. In one photograph Valentina, a striking young woman in a finely tailored jacket, skirt and high heels, her hair in the fashionable braided style of the 1940s, poses, beaming, with a kangaroo against a landscape of bleached, ragged bushland.

'In the camp in Germany', said Valentina, 'we sat across a table from this Australian official who didn't say much, only that we'd have to be indentured. We didn't know what this meant. And he said we'd have to be separated. Michael would have to go to the Snowy and me to a domestic job somewhere. This was terrible! I pleaded against it, but the man said, "Where will you live with him, Madam? There are no houses, just tents." I thought, "Mister, I'm not being separated from my man. You wait and bloody see!"'

Michael: 'On the day we arrived in Sydney it was very hot. We were put on a train and sent west to Bathurst migrant camp, where there were sheets of ice on the ground. What sort of a crazy country was this? At Bathurst we lived in a camp of round tin huts; we waited; we didn't know what was happening to us. Then someone came and said the train to the Snowy left in an hour and I'd better be on it.'

Valentina: 'We clung to each other. I didn't mind a bloody tent!'

A tent it was. Pitched on frosty ground on the rim of a valley near the Snowy Scheme camp at Jindabyne, it did not always withstand the wind that scythed down from the mountains. There was no running water, and power was one hurricane lamp. Valentina was alone for weeks at a time while Michael worked in the tunnels and slept at the base camp. She could speak only a few words of English. There was no transport and the weather often enclosed her.

'I didn't sit like a stupid woman,' she said. 'I was a dressmaker, so I went out and found sewing and I did it under a hurricane lamp; I guessed a lot where the stitches went. I was lonely, yes, but it was my life, my decision . . . I had one *big* complaint, though . . .'

Michael: 'My God, here it comes.'

Valentina: '*Cows!* I am afraid of cows. I think I have cow phobia. I have nightmares about cows. Once upon a time a cow chased me in Yugoslavia and I can't forget it. So you just imagine what it was like: every time I left the tent to get food, this cow would come up and stare at me, and I'd be terrified. I even learned to say, "Get lost, mate", or something Australian like that to the cow . . . but no good . . . So I bought a cow.'

'You were afraid of cows and you bought a cow?'

'Yes. When you have one of these big fears, you should confront it; and it was better for me to be frightened of my own cow, than by somebody else's cow. Anyway, we needed the milk.'

The Makeevs progressed to a shack and put in a wood stove. The shack was next to a river where they bathed and washed their clothes, even in winter when it snowed. Still terrified of her own cow tethered outside, Valentina shared the shack with a kangaroo. 'Someone shot his mum,' she said. 'His name was Richard and he sat between me and Michael and had everything we ate. He loved boiled eggs. He loved wine. We tried to drink a lot of wine, and so did Richard. He also had a schnitzel once.'

'Did he like it?'

'*Loved* it.'

'With wine?'

'Of course.'

Michael shared a cabin on the site with two other men whom he seldom saw and who spoke languages he did not know. They would nod in the shadows at a change of shift, using the *lingua franca* of 'Howyagoinorite?' Each man worked a different eight-hour shift, so that work never ceased, except when a man was killed, usually crushed by a rockfall or machinery. Then all shifts would go into Cooma and drink through the day and night. 'It was a ritual,' said Michael. 'The only time we ever got to know one another was when there was a death. It was like war.'

Valentina: 'We have never resented those bonded years. We wanted to forget Europe and be left alone. And Australia is where people leave you alone. No one ever called me a "reffo".'

The Displaced Persons Programme created almost 200,000 new citizens. But this was not enough. Australian officials now began to look south and east. The Korean War, in which Australia was an early and eager participant, reinforced the fear implicit in 'Populate or Perish'. Although the Labor Party had lost power in 1949, Calwell's policies were pursued by the conservative Government of Prime Minister Robert Menzies. So anxious was Australia for people, millions of people, white people, or as white as possible, that officials scoured the world for more ships that would bring waiting immigrants from Britain, Germany, Holland, Austria, Yugoslavia, Hungary, Czechoslovakia, Italy, Greece, Malta and Cyprus.

Under the Assisted Passage Scheme, immigrants paid a nominal £10 and agreed to stay for two years. The British, known as 'Ten Pound Poms', emigrated with such enthusiasm that a labour shortage threatened the home market. The

111

Mediterranean countries sent mostly young men, and not for reasons of national altruism. Conservative and social democratic Governments in Greece and Italy, fearing the rise of left-wing movements, promoted the emigration of young men of voting age. This had happened during the 1920s when large numbers of antifascist Italians were encouraged to find work in the sugar plantations of Queensland.

There was, at the very least, an ambivalence towards southern Europeans, and only a minority received assisted passages. A Government report half a century earlier had described southern Italians as 'the Chinese of Europe . . . scum and refuse', while the lighter-skinned northerners were 'thriving, highly paid and long-headed . . . the Scotchmen of Italy' and much to be preferred.[20] When they arrived in the 1950s, young Italians and Greeks were told they would be settled into a job after a brief 'transit period' in a camp. The reality was quite different. One of them, Giovanni Sgro, described his new life in 1952 in Bonegilla migrant camp, whose ribbons of huts stretched into the bushland of northern Victoria.[21]

'We reached Bonegilla about four o'clock in the morning', he said, 'and got off the train on a railway track, not a proper station. At the camp we found thousands of other migrants waiting . . . Before we left Italy we understood that within seven days of our arrival we were entitled to a job . . . But seven days passed, two weeks, three, one month, two, no work. Bonegilla had been a prison camp . . . the huts had been built by Italian prisoners of war from Africa. They had tin ceilings and walls and in the day they were boiling hot, in the night freezing cold. The food . . . the poor bloody rabbits had no chance. We used to dig up their holes and kill them with sticks, and ask the cooks to prepare them.

'After two and a half months, the ships kept bringing people. In the camp the Italians, all single men, were separated by a road from the families. We were not allowed to mix with them, not allowed to cross that road. Why? No one ever explained to us. Some of us used to cross illegally at night and visit because some of the Yugoslavs had been in Italian camps and spoke good Italian and it was good to be in the family atmosphere again ... Some young men hanged themselves because they were demoralised being in a foreign country, in a camp without family, without money.

'We organised a rally and a protest march to the authorities to ask for a job or be sent back to Italy. The camp manager told us there was no work and he couldn't send us back because he had no authority ... We started to revolt. We burned two or three huts and set fire to the church, not because we didn't like the church, but because the Italian priest there used to say, "Have patience, God is on your side," and we were fed up with him.

'We marched towards the main office, then we saw four tanks with machine-guns on top in front of us. Some of us ran. I was one of them. I never saw a tank in my life. Soon after, the Italian Consul arrived and the first thing he said was, "You are fortunate to be in a country like Australia." No sooner he finished those words than people rush on the stage and nearly killed him ...

'I remember a farmer who came to get a worker. He wanted only one and there were thousands unemployed. I don't know why they do it, picking one name out of thousands. Perhaps they look in the book to find a single name, and I was the only Sgro, so they thought they call me. I was away from the centre in those hills hunting rabbits but they had loudspeakers and I heard my name called, "Giovanni Sgro, come to the office," and I think I broke all records I run so fast.

'When I got there I saw this big farmer, and the farmer shook his head and said something to the interpreter, but the interpreter would not tell me. Then they told me he didn't want me because he realised I was dark, I came from the south and he wanted a northern Italian. So I taste Australia with the tanks and the farmer ...'

For his part in the Bonegilla uprising Giovanni was refused Australian citizenship. He has been unable to return to Italy, fearful that he will be refused a re-entry visa to Australia. He was finally 'freed' from Bonegilla when a priest offered a job painting a nearby church and working on his 'chook farm'.

'The first time the priest took me to his chook farm', he said, 'I couldn't speak a word of English, just "Good morning, good night". At teatime we had roast beef, which was very nice, then we had a sort of creamy sweet, which to look at was revolting, yellow goo, like we used to stick paper on walls. I was polite, I eat it, I thought. His sister ask me if I like it and I said "yes". So she fill up the plate again. I gulp the thing down, then I go outside and vomit. I know now what it was. Custard! I never had it in my life before.'

The ships now brought whole communities: streets and villages and islands. The village of San Fele went to Drummoyne in Sydney; the village of Canneti to nearby Five Dock; the Sicilian village of Vizzini to Melbourne. The Greek island of Castellorizia, a barren rocky outcrop four miles long and two miles wide, had long sent its men to Australia, the United States and Brazil, and now almost everybody else set out for Sydney and settled in five streets in the suburb of Kingsford.

By the late 1950s immigration officials realised that the preoccupation with numbers was making a nation of men without women. Outback communities such as the Snowy Scheme, where men had been directed to work on public works, were entirely without women. Australian officials were despatched to 'encourage the immigration of suitable females of similar cultural background'.

One result of their efforts was the 'bride ships', whose spectacular arrival I covered as a reporter and will never forget. On a spring morning in 1959 I climbed up the side of the *Fairsky*, an Italian ship of the Sitmar line, as it lay at Sydney Heads. On board were hundreds of teenage girls married by proxy to men they had never met or could barely remember from their childhood. As the ship berthed at Pyrmont, each girl held a photograph of her husband, her only means of identifying the man she was meant to spend the rest of her life with. Down on the wharf young men in best shiny suits and winkle-picker shoes held aloft their own verities. I recall one girl sobbing at the sight of a small, fat, balding man to whom the image in her hand bore no relation. Still, she handed over her dowry of lira notes and they left on the night train to Narrabri. She had little choice.

Maria Calcagno was on the *Fairsky* on another of its bride deliveries, and Carlo, her proxy husband, was at Pyrmont with a box of chocolates, a bouquet of flowers and a determination to claim his beloved at the earliest opportunity. He remembers the moment as one of '*Terrore!*' Maria and Carlo both came from neighbouring villages in Sicily. Their families worked in the local marble factory. Maria worked as a seamstress near Carlo's house; they had seen each other, but according to custom, had never spoken, though their families were friends.

Carlo arrived in Sydney in 1951 and worked in factories and vineyards. He wanted a wife, so he wrote to his sister, who suggested Maria. But Maria was preparing to emigrate to the United States. Carlo moved quickly. He wrote to her parents asking permission to marry their daughter. Permission arrived, said Carlo, 'by the early post'; and Maria and Carlo exchanged letters and photographs.

They were married in 1954 by proxy. Maria had a splendid church wedding with almost everybody from the two villages there, except Carlo, who was represented by the bride's brother and a grave-looking photograph of himself pinned to the wedding cake.

'Funny feeling I had,' said Maria. 'I come into the church. Nice wedding, I think. But where is the husband? In Australia, of course! But funny feeling all the same.' After Carlo had managed to save for her fare, Maria sailed for Australia one year later with a family friend as chaperone.

I took Maria and Carlo back to the wooden wharf at Pyrmont where they met and which now stands rotting and silent. It is the equivalent of Ellis Island in New York, the immigrants' gateway to the United States and a national monument. As at Bennelong Point, nothing at Pyrmont records that a nation began here.

I asked Maria what it was like to be one of a consignment of young women who had never met their husbands. 'Funny!' she said. 'All the time they speak about *him* . . . is he a young

one still? Or is he an old one with wrinkles? Worry, worry
. . . that's what they do. We couldn't dance, because we had
old women look after us. All we do is play bingo . . . bingo,
bingo.'

Carlo: 'Listen, these old women were necessary. There were
men on that ship.'

Maria: 'Trouble, yeah . . . one month on that ship and
some of the girls are forgetting *everything*!'

For Maria's arrival in Australia Carlo had rented a room,
where friends crushed to greet them and they had the wedding
party he missed. There is a photograph of the two of them at
that party, sitting on the edge of a bed; both have the whimsical, fragile look of happiness almost acquired. It is a glimpse
of the universal heart of immigrants.

Many of the proxy marriages did not last; Maria's and
Carlo's was an exception. Their laughter with and care for
each other is infectious. In 1958 they opened an espresso bar
in Sydney and introduced, claims Carlo, the first 'real gelato'
to Australia. Like so many of their compatriots they thought
nothing of working fifteen hours a day, seven days a week,
year after year. The role of immigrants in small business in
Australia has never been adequately appreciated. Maria
brought up five children, and also cooked and served in the
café. Carlo says he owes 'everything to my wife'. Neither
bears a likeness to the two people in the photograph on the
edge of the bed; the hardship of their lives has extinguished
that.

In 1969 they took their children to Sicily and were greeted
as 'the Australians', as if they had been reincarnated. They
were surprised to find Italy had developed and the standard
of living was at least as high as in Australia. 'Maybe', said
Carlo, 'my life would have been easier if I had stayed . . .
maybe, maybe. My children are Australians. I am here now.'

There is another side to such a story. Beneath Australia's
multi-cultural sheen there are other Marias. They can be
glimpsed standing on inner city doorsteps pleading in broken
English for more than a few dollars from a middle man who
employs them in conditions little better than Dickensian.

Sonja Abarcia was like that. I met her in Wollongong, the steel city south of Sydney. She and her family had arrived from Chile in 1974, refugees from the Pinochet regime. Her husband was seriously injured in his first job and much of the burden of the family's provision fell on her. For ten years she worked in a tin hut little bigger than herself at the bottom of her garden, at first for less than a dollar an hour. As a result, she is handicapped with arthritis.

'I started at seven in the morning and I finished eight or nine at night,' she said. 'I did this all week, sometimes with Sundays off. In the summer the temperature in the shed got up to 40 degrees, and in the winter it was so cold I had an electric radiator on all the time. When it rained I was scared, because the rain was coming in and you know what happens when these electrical industrial machines get wet.

'A typical job would be to make up ladies' trousers from about thirty-six pieces. It took me two days and I was paid five dollars ninety-five cents. I went up to Sydney once and saw the same trousers in a very nice shop in the Centrepoint arcades. They were charging two hundred dollars for them. That made me sad.'

Gina came from Italy in 1973. She says that if her correct name is published, she will not work again. She is a qualified nurse, but her qualifications are not recognised in Australia. Only after fourteen years of applications was she granted an interview. 'The nursing sister was amazed at the extent of my experience,' she said, 'but it was too late, as my health had been damaged by years of work in the leather clothing industry.'

Gina paid several thousand dollars for her own leather-binding machine. She worked at home, beginning, like Sonja, before her children awoke. Leather work is extremely arduous as the leather first must be beaten with a hammer before it will fit into a machine. She was paid eight dollars an hour, and is now disabled in her back, shoulders, hands, arms and right leg.

Sonja and Gina are typical of thousands of Australian immigrant women known as 'outworkers'. A report by the

New South Wales Women's Directorate found that some 30,000 outworkers in the State were getting as little as eighty cents an hour; and that the majority, like Gina, were justifiably afraid of complaining, as 'unco-operative' workers were inevitably replaced.[22] Similarly, a confidential report by the New South Wales Government, following a two-year investigation, described as Dickensian the working conditions of 60,000 mostly immigrant women in clothing sweatshops. Less than 3 per cent received normal allowances such as sick pay.[23]

Rukiye Savigil, a young Turkish woman, used to work in one of these sweatshops, in Collingwood in Melbourne. 'No one told me how to do the job,' she said. 'The bosses use computers to evaluate our working rate. They are counting the minutes we spend on each piece of garment. The foremen are physically standing over us and timing our rate. Sometimes they bring in people from outside to time us. Sometimes they time us secretly. Almost no one can complete the quota, which equals 495 minutes in one day. There are only 480 minutes in a working day!

'We are not allowed to talk or ask questions. The bosses are always punishing us and then they reward us with a piece of material. They never say, "Good morning." We brought transistors so that we could listen to our 3EA (Turkish) language programmes, but the bosses stopped us and instead put in a loudspeaker which plays only English music.

'We have a ten-minute tea-break a day. There is no first aid or rest room. Workers who injure their hands are forced to keep working. If we get pregnant we have to tell the bosses and expect to get sacked at different stages of pregnancy. I got sacked because I didn't finish my quota. I have since been unemployed. This is hard, because my husband was injured at work. I used to get a hundred and forty-three dollars a week. I miss it.'[24]

In 1987 the Australian Arbitration Commission, in an historic ruling, extended trade-union protection to outworkers, whose treatment was described as 'a serious affront to the moral and social conscience of the community'.[25] Out-

workers are now entitled to union agreed wages, sick, over-
time and holiday pay and pensions.

We were in a cemetery near Bendigo, left by the gold rush
beyond a façade of Victorian architecture in the bush. Denis
O'Hoy was preparing joss sticks, incense and rice. 'I am very
lonely coming here on my own,' he said. 'As a child, there
would be two buses full and a dozen cars. Now it's just
my sister and me, paying respect to our ancestors. I'm even
questioning now why I do it; the tradition is dying because
we are one of the oldest Australian communities, and my
sons, well, they are indifferent.

'Last time I was here I saw a group of orthodox Jews . . .
the Jews and the Chinese are buried together in Bendigo . . .
and they were doing virtually the same thing, saying prayers
and venerating those to whom we owe our existence. We
looked at each other and they raised their black hats and gave
a little bow. I bowed, too, or saluted or something. Jews and
Chinese . . . I appreciate a courtesy of that kind when you
consider everything else that has gone before.'

The cemetery contains the remains mostly of Chinese gold
diggers who fell upon hard luck and could not get home.
Most of the Chinese who came after the discovery of gold in
1851 had no intention of staying. To them Australia was
'Tsin Chin Shan', the 'New Gold Mountain'. To the Australian diggers and much of the population, the Chinese were
the Yellow Peril incarnate, plotting to seize and enslave the
nation. It was a corrupt and rapacious period, which saw the
transfer of much of the colonists' bigotry and violence from
the Aborigines, whom they had effectively subdued, to the
Chinese who, in the 1860s, represented one in nine of the
male population.

The Chinese were in the classic double bind. Despite abund-
ant evidence to the contrary, they were viewed as liars, thieves
and ruffians. Whenever their good behaviour was conceded,
it was argued that only 'weakness keeps them quiet'.[26] When
they became numerically powerful enough to form organisa-

The Bulletin

Registered at the General Post Office, Sydney, for Transmission as a Newspaper.

SATURDAY, SEPTEMBER 28, 1901.

AUSTRALIA'S LIE FOR BRITAIN'S SAKE

Repelling the 'Asiatic hordes', Sydney *Bulletin*, September 28, 1901

tions not unlike trade unions, it was said they were showing their 'true colours' as 'the most immoral, lying and thievish people in the world'.[27] And if that was not enough, the Sydney *Bulletin* declared that 'the European's dislike of the Chinaman is not a matter of taste, but a healthy racial instinct ... in the case of the chinkies, this out-of-date instinctive dislike has lasted long enough to be useful again as a protection against a race that is more dangerous to civilisation than a savage with a club is to a fellow savage'.[28]

This 'healthy racial instinct' was translated into savagery at Lambing Flat in New South Wales. By 1861 some 15,000 diggers had been attracted to the Lambing Flat field, where gold lay just below the surface. About 2,000 were Chinese, described by the local paper as 'a swarm of Mongolian locusts' and 'moon-faced barbarians'. Although the discovery was the richest yet in the State, it came at the end of a long period of disappointments for the diggers, as individuals were replaced progressively by mining companies. The miners looked upon Lambing Flat as a 'last resting place' where they would make a stand against the 'swarming' Chinese.

The miners rallied at Tipperary Gully and marched the four miles to Lambing Flat, picking up men along the way. A Union Jack fluttered at their head, with a banner proclaiming 'Roll up! Roll up!' and a band played 'Rule Britannia', although many were Irish, German and American. They set upon several hundred Chinese, brandishing their Bowie knives and beating them with pick handles and the butt ends of whips. Tents were rifled for gold, then set on fire. 'I noticed one man', the *Sydney Morning Herald* correspondent reported, 'with eight pigtails attached to a flag and he glorying in the work that had been done. I also saw one pigtail with part of a scalp the size of a man's hand attached, that had literally been cut from some unfortunate creature.'

Eleven rioters were brought to trial, only to be acquitted by sympathetic juries. One judge argued that, since all Australians looked the same to Chinese, the Chinese could not possible identify their attackers! The Chinese remained in hiding, or dispersed to other diggings and occupations, their community now aware that, together with the Aborigines, they had become the colony's scapegoats.[29] Later, the poet Henry Lawson offered recompense with his line: 'Some of my best friends are Chinks!' Today in the town of Young, which stands at Lambing Flat, the scene of the riots is a tourist attraction, and the flag the miners marched behind is exhibited in a museum. There is no reference, however, to the hatred and the scalping.

'We were blamed for everything,' said Denis O'Hoy. 'We polluted the water and we brought disease and we coveted the European women . . . we were *voracious*! There wasn't a racial stereotype that was not applied to us. But even in those days large numbers of whites and Chinese began to find their own peaceful common ground; and I always had the impression that my own family enjoyed the respect of all kinds in Bendigo.'

A typical caricature of the 'yellow peril' from the Sydney *Bulletin*, near 1900

The Mongolian Octopus - His Grip on Australia.

During the gold rush Bendigo had a Chinese population estimated at 4,000. Denis's grandfather, Louey O'Hoy, arrived in Australia on a junk and established himself as a merchant. (He had reduced the honorific in his name, giving it an Irish sound.) His son, Que O'Hoy, had two wives, which was customary, and Denis was born to the second in 1938 in Bendigo.

Denis drives the town's splendid collection of vintage trams, and acts as local historian, guiding academics and others to the small, plain headstones of the White Hills cemetery, overlooking the diggings. With an uncertain pride, and guilt, Bendigo takes its Chinese heritage seriously. The preciously restored joss house, painted traditional red, stands among ceremonial trees beside a lotus pool. The Dai Gum San collection of imperial Chinese figures in wax looks incongruous in Australia, though no more than the Doric columns of Castlemaine Marketplace. And the dragon in the 'Sun Loong' procession at the Easter Fair is one of the longest in the world. Denis believes that the transformation of this still isolated town, from a cassine of white exiles besieged by oriental phantoms and phobia to a state of tolerance and civilisation, is the journey of Australia itself.

When, on April 25, 1976, a wooden fishing boat, the *Kien Giang*, dropped anchor off a suburb of Darwin, for many people an Australia imagined only in fear and caricature was inaugurated. The five Vietnamese on board the *Kien Giang* were not the first Indo-Chinese refugees to arrive in Australia; but they were the first of many to navigate all the way to Australia's shores. 'A country whose immigration policy was built on the rock of Asian exclusion', wrote Jock Collins, in his *Migrant Hands in a Distant Land*, 'was to take in large numbers of Asians for the first time since the Gold Rush of the 1850s.'[30]

The Labor Government of Gough Whitlam was in power when the Vietnam War ended in 1975 and the exodus of 'boat people' began. Labor, which had opposed the war, was unfriendly towards the refugees from American-sponsored South Vietnam. Whitlam himself was quoted as saying that 'Vietnamese sob stories don't wring my withers.'[31] What seemed significant was that politics, not race, was at the centre of a national debate about how Australia should meet its responsibilities towards its former allies. The first refugees may well have been mostly military officers and others associated with the Saigon regime, but they and their families suffered and often died terribly trying to reach a safe haven. When the conservatives under Malcolm Fraser succeeded Labor, the political colouring of the boat people was acceptable; and in the years since the war Australia has given refuge to more people from Indo-China than any country except the United States. In the late 1980s almost half of all newcomers to Australia were from Asia. And there has been no 'earthquake'. A campaign to exploit the confused and bitter feelings held by many Australians about their divisive war in Vietnam failed perceptibly. Tabloid headlines such as VIETNAM WAR IN THE SUBURBS warned of racial warfare, but there was none.

Moreover, those who have since tried to raise false alarms and to inflame continue to fail. In 1984 the historian Geoffrey Blainey attracted considerable publicity when he described the arrival of the Asians as 'the new surrender policy'.[32] Blainey claimed that a pro-Asian and anti-British conspiracy was being imposed on the Australian people by an 'alliance of academics and ethnics', trade unions and Civil Servants, who met in a 'secret room' at the Department of Immigration. He described 'front-line' suburbs in the cities and said he spoke for ordinary Australians whose dissent was confined to 'graffiti on the café lavatory'. He quoted complaints about immigrants 'who spit everywhere and spread germs' and 'cook on their verandas, so the sky is filled with greasy smoke and the smell of goats' milk', and 'fly around in flash cars while I have to walk all the time' and dry 'noodles on the clothes line in the backyard'.[33]

The reactions to Blainey's outbursts were more revealing than what he said. An historian who had enjoyed considerable respect for his work in popularising the Australian past, Blainey found himself isolated among his academic colleagues and in demand by that section of the media which favoured and saw currency in his views. (He went on to become a columnist with Rupert Murdoch's *Australian*.) His political support, according to Jock Collins, 'was, embarrassingly for him, relegated to the far right fringe. National Action and the League of Rights carry the torch of anti-immigrant and anti-Asian abuse. Their graffiti on subway tunnels and toilet walls give an inflated impression of their influence in Australia: both groups have minimal membership and negligible public support.'[34]

Curiously for such a scholar, Blainey offered virtually no data in support of his warning that racial diversity was causing serious disquiet among 'large sections of Australians'. He must have known of the abundance of studies that refuted his views. In 1986 the Department of Immigration and Ethnic Affairs published the results of one of the most comprehensive surveys of attitudes among Australians and Asians living side by side. The great majority of Australians interviewed expressed positive views about their Asian neighbours, whom they no longer regarded in terms of pre-conceived stereotypes. There was no evidence of 'ghetto formation' among Asians, a majority of whom reported that they 'had an Australian neighbour whom they regarded as a casual friend'.[35] The litmus test is, of course, discrimination. In 1989 research by the Australian National University (the ANU) found that 'most native Australians did not discriminate against migrants generally, and did not believe migrants should suffer discrimination . . . A typical employer was more likely to give a Vietnamese migrant an even chance than discriminate against him or her.'[36]

Reading the best Australian newspapers, especially the Melbourne *Age* and the *Sydney Morning Herald*, I am struck by the number of feature articles and supplements which both celebrate 'multi-culturalism' and provide examples of harmony among 'old' and 'new' Australians. The headlines say 'Across the Culture Gap to be Best of Neighbours and

Friends' and 'Harmony on the Street Where the Races Meet', and the stories report the common ground between people. In this, they represent the press at its best, for it is honest and honourable journalism that dismantles stereotypes and attempts to reflect society in all its diversity – a society where almost half the schoolchildren have at least one parent born in another country and a third of the populations of the two principal cities were born outside Australia.

In Sydney's far western suburb of Cabramatta, the Cousins and the Kooks speak little of each other's language, but together they celebrate Chinese New Year and exchange Christmas gifts. Leila Cousins, who looks out for the Kooks' children when the Kooks are at work, said, 'We have been here since the 1940s and we have seen them all: Pommies, the Italians and now the Vietnamese. I think it makes our life interesting.'

Agar Street, in the old working district of Marrickville, has a different nationality represented at almost every address: Greek, Italian, Portuguese, Indonesian and Australian-born. More important, the people of Agar Street are prepared to talk generously about living together and to have their photograph taken, apparently with much hilarity. The photograph was published across page three of the *Sydney Morning Herald*: a mirror held up to a vibrant reality. This kind of reporting is largely extinct in Britain, where multi-racialism is invariably represented as a problem, or a disease.

Westbridge Migrant Hostel at Villawood in Sydney could not be more different from the old 'silver cities' of tin Nissen huts, one of which stands preserved in glistening green paint. The surroundings are landscaped and peaceful, and in several visits I saw none of the nonplussed and obdurate officials who presided at the birth of mass immigration. I watched a group of Vietnamese arrive under the Family Reunion Programme – that most humane component of any immigration policy. The health services and the education possibilities for their children were explained with care and patience and in their own language. Lynne McElroy of the Australian Red Cross said, 'They're a bit nervy and you've got to second-guess their feelings and be cautious and sensitive. If you're not, the best-thought-out programmes will collapse. The reward is watching people shed their burdens and relax.'

Those like Lynne McElroy understand, for example, why Khmer parents will not leave their children in a crèche. Having endured the horror of the Pol Pot years, they trust no one with their children: not yet.

This understanding of *difference* is part of an attitude and a commitment I have found reflected widely. It is in the work of the assiduous human rights organisations and the Anti-Discrimination Board of New South Wales, whose internationally renowned programmes seek to resolve conflict and injustices at the earliest sign. It is in many of the multi-racial schools which foster pride in ethnic background rather than a denial of it; it is in the energy of teachers at these schools and in specialists committed to breaking down stereotypes: people like Mary Kalantzis and Bill Cope, whose radical 'social literacy' programmes have helped teachers identify hidden racism and take multi-culturalism beyond what they call 'the spaghetti and polka' stage. And it is in the many innovative and often poorly funded teaching aid programmes, such as the Materials Production Project in Sydney, which gives expression to those immigrant children with a longing in their hearts. This poem, for example, is by an anonymous Vietnamese boy:

The miles which separate me from my parents
And my loved one are many;
Only memories remain;
Another world from old school yards and
    honoured teachers
From the streets I played in
The village I lived in.
My hopes of today are empty;

127

In a strange land I live,
In a strange school I study.
The school yard is full of animation
With voices from many lands;
The school yard shines with bright futures
Our hopes of one day returning to our homelands.[37]

This 'reaching out' by a substantial group of 'old' Australians is reciprocated in the constant *celebration* of diversity by immigrants themselves: in the carnivals and festivals and impromptu events that are now part of the quality and confidence of Australian street life.

On a Saturday morning in the west of Sydney, a traditional Lao wedding procession makes its way through streets where, less than a generation past, you were careful not to speak your language let alone sing and laugh and make mockery of a bridegroom who has mislaid thirty-two important bodily spirits. At the bride's house pleas are made over a picket fence to let the poor fellow in. He is, after all, decked out in the *pha hang ngao*, which is a glittering costume with gold buttons, and his matronly bodyguards have offered a handsome bribe of a litre of Johnnie Walker Red Label, to which the bride's representative replies drily, 'Have you also brought the servants and horses?'

Communities who on their home ground are at war – the Muslims and Christians of Lebanon, for example – are generally at peace here. A Turk who arrived in Australia fifteen years ago, believing he had signed up for a spell of 'guest work' in Austria ('I tell you, it was a bloody long flight for a country next door') remains ambivalent about the charms of his adopted country – except one. 'I have been in the States and it's the difference between here and there,' he said. 'Over there immigrants take their fights with them. Australia is where you leave all that behind. Don't ask me why.'[38]

None of this is to suggest that the old ways have gone. In 1991 the Human Rights and Equal Opportunity Commission reported that the ethnic community lived with verbal abuse, police harassment and violence – some of it racist.[39] And many who pass through Westbridge hostel are, like the Displaced Persons of the 1940s, prevented from using their skills. An immigrant from Afghanistan, Zalmai Haildary, has a master's degree in archeology and ancient Indian history and culture and is one of the authors of a UNESCO history of archeology. He has applied for jobs at universities and museums, yet has been refused even an interview. He has been told that his decade of study is equal to 'two years of tertiary study in Australia' and the best Australia can offer him is uncertain work as an interpreter – just as the best Australia can offer an architectural draughtsman from Chile, Peter Llana, is work as a ditch digger and cleaner. There are thousands of these cases and they may represent a majority among small ethnic groups. The Australian professional groups remain Anglocentric, tradition-bound and discriminatory.[40] The test given to immigrant doctors is said to be so hard that recently graduated Australian doctors would not be able to pass it.

There is also an oddly Australian fear of 'summoning up the devil' of racism by speaking his name. When two Government commissioned researchers uncovered discrimination in the Department of Community Services and Health, their report was placed in the National Library in Canberra and no one was told about it; the authors cannot even discuss their findings in public.[41] At times this 'ostrich' approach has allowed the voices of racism free rein. A Sydney radio 'personality', Ron Casey, used his popular programme on Station 2KY to make racist jibes. He described Asians as 'slopy-headed slanty-eyed, bow-legged little bastards' and incited others to get 'a dozen or so of your footballing mates together and have a night [in Chinatown] and sort these little bastards right out'.[42] Casey skilfully used the publicity to represent himself as the 'underdog' and to justify his behaviour. He was suspended, then sacked only after considerable pressure. A few months later he was given his job back, although the Australian Broadcasting Tribunal subsequently ordered 2KY to broadcast a reprimand that amounted to an apology.

In 1988 a major enquiry into immigration commissioned by the Hawke Government and chaired by a former Ambassador to China, Dr Stephen FitzGerald, proposed that 'the voice of opposition to multi-culturalism be taken seriously, not dismissed as simply the voice of extremism or racism'. The Fitz-Gerald Report offered no evidence of the existence of this reasonable and moderate opposition, yet it recommended changes in the Family Reunion Programme which would affect mostly Asians. It proposed that only a naturalised citizen should have welfare rights. If adopted, the proposed measures would emulate Britain and divide immigrants into citizens and non-citizens, creating a structural division on which to accelerate racism. In its respectable guise, the Fitz-Gerald Report put race back on the Australian political agenda for the first time in twenty years.

Reaction was unusually swift. Prime Minister Hawke stood up at a citizenship ceremony in his own electorate and in reaffirming his Government's commitment to its immigration policies seemed to be rejecting FitzGerald's proposals.[43] But Hawke's words belied the less than public actions of his own officials. Two days before the release of the FitzGerald Report, changes were made to the system of points which governs immigration quotas, in order to place more emphasis on skills and less on family reunions. In addition, the application charge all immigrants must pay was trebled to $A200, a sum out of reach of most Asian and Third World applicants.

Still, it is difficult to imagine a British Prime Minister feeling the need to defend publicly and passionately the principles of a multi-racial society, as Hawke did; and he is nothing if not a politician, whose instinct is to react to what he perceives as the public mood. And however varied that mood, and however deep the fear of Asia in the heart of white Australia, the truth is that since Arthur Calwell's ship of 'Beautiful Balts' and Tom Stratton's *angst* over whether a man in pantaloons should be seen on the streets of Sydney, two generations of Australians have been educated to understand that immigration is 'good' for everybody – gastronomically, culturally and politically.

Here again, the contrast with Britain is striking. In 1983 the Thatcher Government introduced a Nationality Act which institutionalised racism by removing the automatic right to citizenship of all British-born children of immigrants. These non-citizens cannot vote and are excluded from welfare benefits. Family reunion has been virtually eliminated, and an atmosphere of racism begets violence every day. With justification the immigrant community regards the police and much of authority as its enemy. Similarly, Governments in Western Europe have tried to repatriate 'guest workers' and to reduce family reunions. Police harassment of minorities and racist attacks are now commonplace. Fascist parties, such as the National Front in France and the National Democrats in Germany, are able to exploit the 'new xenophobia' while ethnic communities are increasingly marginalised.

Little of this is true of Australia, where immigrants are *encouraged* to take out Australian citizenship and anti-immigrant groups are treated with public contempt. There is racism, deep and historic, but in everyday life the worst, perhaps, is indifference. 'Most employers have neutral feelings,' said the ANU study, 'neither actively liking nor disliking immigrants.'[44] One explanation for this is a consensus of support for immigration that has spanned the political landscape. In the 1960s the statements of Geoffrey Blainey and Ron Casey would have been unexceptional and might even have been regarded as the view of the 'Silent Majority'. In the late 1980s they create 'controversy' and draw immediate fire. John Elliott, when he was the outspoken president of the Liberal (conservative) Party and chairman of Elder's IXL (Foster's Lager), publicly expressed his enthusiasm for immigration as a vital stimulant to the economy. These are not surprising conservative positions; the last conservative Government, headed by Malcolm Fraser, was considerably more 'liberal' in its refugee policy than the Hawke Labor Government, not simply because most of the refugees were 'fleeing communism', but because immigration is 'good for business'. Since the end of the Second World War the phases in Australia's immigration policy have brought economic boom. First-generation immigrants provide the flow of labour that is capitalism's 'reserve army'. They have no choice but to be pliant and controlled and to work at the bottom of the pile. Second-generation immigrants, having moved up the pile, provide a ready-made 'consumer' society.

Tragically immigration is now an ideological issue. The coalition leader in 1988, John Howard, having watched as the so-called 'middle ground' was taken from him by the right-wing policies of the Hawke Government, searched for an issue that could be his alone. He found it in the Bicentenary year. In August 1988 he announced that a future Government led by him would pursue a 'One Australia Policy'. This meant, in effect, the White Australia Policy brought up to date.

Howard argued that this was necessary because the present level of Asian immigration was 'imposing social tension and a lack of social cohesion'. Like Blainey and FitzGerald, he offered no hard evidence and made no acknowledgment of the racial peace in Australia since the adoption of non-racist immigration policies. All politicians stoop for power: the degree of stoop being a matter of personal conscience and taste. It is difficult to recall a contemporary politician who has sought his ends by such potentially destructive and wholly contemptible means.

At first Howard's statement was rejected by his own party's immigration committee and spokesman. Former Prime Minister Fraser reminded Howard that the issues of race and multi-culturalism represented 'fundamental values' for the conservatives. The Chief Minister of the Northern Territory, Marshall Perron, a leading conservative, responded by calling for a 'massive boost' in immigration from Asia as well as from Europe. Asia, he said, was 'an immense human resource which can play an integral part in the settlement and development of northern Australia'.[45]

Howard's opportunism, it was clear, was bad for business. Worried by the results of a confidential survey that showed that most businessmen in Singapore and Malaysia now believed there were strong anti-Asian feelings in Australia, Foreign Minister Gareth Evans said, 'There may be billions of dollars at risk.'[46] A Sydney headline asked, WILL WE BECOME THE POOR WHITE TRASH OF ASIA?, and beneath it a leading commentator on economics, Max Walsh, worried that a discriminatory immigration policy would close Australian capital out of Asia.[47] A racist reputation, as white South Africans have learned, is extremely bad for business. That racism is, above all, bad for humanity is seldom mentioned by the 'pragmatists'. In a vivid demonstration of this pragmatism, the Hawke Government, while pouring scorn on Howard, set out to implement much of what the FitzGerald Report proposed. In December 1988 the Government announced the biggest changes in immigration for twenty years, cutting the number of reunions of parents with their immigrant children by 40 per cent. This affected mostly people from Asia. In 1992 the Government was under increasing internal pressure to cut immigration drastically, with proposed arrivals of less than 50,000, or less than half the present annual immigration. The Opposition, led by John Hewson, is also believed to favour this. Ironically, the severity of the Australian recession has undoubtedly caused a record number of immigrants to return home; in 1991 there were 31,000 permanent departures.[48] The politicians appear not to have noticed this phenomenon; or they see advantage in not noticing it.

So the 'debate' has continued, if debate it is. Geoffrey Blainey (who like Enoch Powell in Britain protests he is no racist) has questioned the loyalty of Asian Australians during a future war. The radio 'personality' Casey fulminated and smashed a glass in order to make his point on television – and has since exchanged punches during a television debate about republicanism. The Opposition has published a document claiming there has been a 'loss of a sense of unified motherhood' in Australian society. And the letter pages of newspapers reflect almost daily the anxieties of Asian and Arab Australians. My own view is that in the long term the Blaineys miscalculate. They miscalculate the strength of an attitude I have already outlined: that of good will and sensitivity at many levels of Australian society; and they miscalculate the depth of change now in everyday evidence. That Howard is no longer conservative leader is a striking example of this.

In 1984, when he was Minister for Foreign Affairs, Bill Hayden spelt out the meaning of this change. 'I think inevitably we'll become predominantly a Eurasian country,' he said. 'I'm talking about twenty years' time perhaps. That is a process which is under way ... the very fact that I've been able to say this so often without the flood of letters one used to receive for expressing views critical of the White Australia Policy in the 1960s is an indication that [Australia] is already in that process.'[49]

Hayden's prediction is supported by the conclusion of a study by Dr Charles Price, the leading Australian authority on ethnic populations. Dr Price has calculated that in one or two generations' time 90 per cent of the Asian population in Australia will 'marry out' of their community. Asked what he thought the members of the Australian team would look like when they paraded at the Olympic Games in 2052, Dr Price said, 'I think you would see a great variety of racial types. There will be some northern European types with fair hair, some Middle East types, some Asian types, some southern European types, but there will also be a sizeable number of mixtures and of these many will be Asian.'[50]

For those Australians seeking international acknowledgment of their country's achievements and its place in the civilised world, the bonus of multi-culturalism is that it removes the old, occasionally stigmatic comparison with South Africa, which, until recently, could not play cricket with anybody. Of course, the flaw and brutal irony in this is the continued mistreatment of the Aboriginal people. Here the parallels with unreconstructed South Africa today are uncomfortably close.

There is another barrier to self-congratulation. About a million immigrants have not chosen to become Australian citizens. That represents almost a quarter of all those who have arrived since the Second World War. Politicians refer with caution to this 'sleeping million', whose enfranchisement could dramatically change voting patterns. For many, their grievance is the oath of allegiance to an English Queen which all new citizens must swear. When Hawke sought to address this, he said the oath was 'not to the Queen of Great Britain, but to the Queen of Australia, the Head of State of a mature and independent nation'.[51] This is sophistry, and Australians whose names are not Bruce and Smith, but Mohammed, Wilensky and Wong, know it. The imperial connection is not merely antiquated; it divides Australia as surely as trenches of class divide Britain.

My friend Franca Arena understands well this divide. Franca, born in Genoa, is a Labor member of the New South Wales Parliament and one of Australia's few non-Anglo-Celtic politicians. In 1980 she became the first elected woman of non-English speaking background. She emigrated as a young girl, alone, in 1959 and graduated from the tin sheds of the former prison camp at Bonegilla. Eloquent and passionate, she can be heard on Sydney talkback radio, switching from English to Italian, cajoling, persuading on behalf of immigrants and Aborigines. 'Listen, mite,' she will say to an obstreperous caller, 'we are *all* different, but our rights are the same, OK?'

She has done much for her adopted country, which she loves. In the Bicentenary year she was asked to write her vision of Australia for the journal of the Australian Bicentenary Authority. She wrote that 'true Australian nationhood will be retarded so long as there is a psychological dependence on the symbols and traditions of another country; when national subservience is inculcated by clinging to colonial and imperial ties'.[52]

This displeased the chairman of the Bicentenary Authority, Jim Kirk, a retired oil company executive who describes himself as 'just an Aussie dag' ('dag' = ordinary person). Kirk banned Franca's article, and at the same time withdrew funding for a documentary film which would have made light of the Queen's endless tours of Australia.

'Every time the Queen or one of her family comes here',

said Franca, 'the Government worries. Where will the *big* crowds come from? So what do they do? Children are given a half-day holiday and bussed to where she is, and so are pensioners; and it all looks fine on TV. We have to live with this ridiculous illusion. Tell me what other self-respecting nation has to borrow its Head of State from another country.

'Becoming a citizen was a big problem for me. I could not swear allegiance to the English queen, her heirs and successors, because I had no loyalty to her. So I asked the local council if I could have a ceremony of my own. I just couldn't do it in public. I felt so ashamed on that day . . . I don't want to be buried here if we're still a semi-colony, as we are now. If we decide to become a republic, then I want my ashes thrown from the Sydney Harbour Bridge. I've already made my will!

'I think I am typical of many. I love this place not because of some stupid jingoism. I tell you why. Some say it's not possible for people of diverse cultures, regions and races to live peacefully together. I think we can show it can happen in Australia. We have 120 different ethnic groups, we speak 90 different languages and practise over 60 religions. The point is if we fail in Australia . . . we, a nation of only 16 million people, a country of such big open spaces . . . if we fail to live together there is really hardly any hope for the rest.'

Tourists wishing to glimpse something of the 'real Australia' are well ad'ised to skip the 'koala parks' and drop in on a citizenship ceremony. Every week there is one somewhere in Australia. They are advertised in the local paper. The last one I went to was in Ashfield, an old part of Sydney where the streets are narrow, the houses small with verandas of dark Federation brick and roofs of red and green tiles. Inside, the voices are Arabic, Vietnamese, Farsi, Spanish; in the streets, the children call to each other in Australian English. It was here that Carlo brought his proxy bride, Maria, on the day she landed.

At Ashfield Town Hall I was directed to an auditorium, where I sat bemused as to why those about to be 'naturalised' as citizens had shaven their heads and dressed in orange. Was this a new attempt by the authorities at assimilation? When the God Krishna was invoked, I left and was re-directed upstairs, where the oath-taking, though equally abstruse, had a more familiar ring.

'OK', said Mayor Lew Herman in robes and gold chain, 'I won't dilly any longer. I'll ask Mr Bob Gander if he would like to call out the first batch of names and then I'll take you through the proceedings as we go along. Thank you very much and over to you, Bob.'

Bob Gander produced his list and intoned names in a manner marking them unrecognisable to all but students of Australian *pidgin*. They belonged to Argentines, Filipinos, Poles, Vietnamese, Turks, Jordanians, Fijians, Koreans, Chileans, Taiwanese, Britons, Italians, Sri Lankans, Chinese, Lebanese, Singaporeans, Thais, Yugoslavs, Iranians and an Irishwoman.

'Rightee-o everybody,' said Lew, 'here we go. I won't rush it. Now you mob just say after me . . . I swear by almighty God . . .'

'*I swear by almighty God . . .*'

'that I will remain faithful . . .'

'*that I will remain faithful . . .*'

'and bear true allegiance . . .'

'*and bear . . .*'

At that point there was a noise like glass breaking. It was Lew's gold chain disintegrating in slow motion.

'. . . true allegiance . . . to Her Majesty . . . (*whispers* – Hey Bob, get me a paper clip, will you?) Elizabeth the Second . . . (Come on, do something somebody. Jeez, I'm coming apart).'

A paper clip was produced and the gold chain was salvaged. Oath completed, Lew handed out certificates of citizenship. Said he as he passed along the ranks of recipients: 'Gidday and congratulations . . . good luck . . . What a *lovely* smile you've got . . . Hang on, is this the right certificate? . . . Now, what's your name? Is it Moon or Moonska? . . . Here we go . . . Gidday and congratulations . . . I'm really proud, too . . .

Right, thanks everybody for coming. Now how about a big round of applause for these folk?'

The expressions borne by the multi-cultural assembly were of delight tinged with incredulity. The latter intensified as the Sweet Adelines Ladies' Barber Shop Group advanced on them, dressed in baby blue and cooing the refrain from the musical *Oliver!*, 'Consider yourself our mate.'

This was followed by tea, cup-cakes and photographs with Lew, the mayoral chain and paper clip. The oath of allegiance to distant royalty was patently ridiculous; but there was none of the joyless chauvinism that requires people to renounce their backgrounds and join some closed order, some non-existent 'melting pot'. The only speech, apart from Lew's 'few words', was by a Mrs Choong, a Chinese-Australian who made the most stirring call for internationalism I have ever heard. 'Australia is the only continent at peace', she said, 'because we are re-making a history founded on fear and rejection, and because the world is now here.'

Mrs Choong left few eyes dry. That the world is here is irrevocable.

4

THE STRUGGLE FOR INDEPENDENCE

A sick feeling of repugnance grows in me as I near Australia.

> Robert Menzies, Prime Minister of Australia, 1941

Wherever the United States is resisting aggression . . . we will go a-waltzing Matilda with you.

> John Gorton, Prime Minister of Australia, 1969

President Lyndon B. Johnson always thought that Australia was the next large rectangular state beyond El Paso and treated it accordingly.

> Marshall Green, US Ambassador to Australia, 1973–5

NEW YEAR'S DAY, 1901, was the day of Federation. The six Australian colonies came together as one nation, 'a Commonwealth . . . independent and proud' proclaimed the headlines. Rain deluged down in Sydney's Centennial Park, where the Earl of Hopetoun, a hitherto unheard-of member of the British aristocracy, struggled to cope with dysentery (known then as the 'antipodean scourge') as he declared himself the nation's first Governor-General.

'The whole performance', wrote the historian Manning Clark, 'stank in the nostrils. Australians had once again grovelled before the English. There were Fatman politicians who hungered for a foreign title just as their wives hungered after a smile of recognition from the Governor-General's wife, who was said to be a most accomplished snubber, having trained her eyes to brush the cheek of those who were desperate for a smile, no matter how watery, from an English noblewoman.'[1]

Most Australians did not want independence. They wanted extravagant assurances of imperial fidelity. They wanted Mother England to be more protective of her most distant colony which, they pleaded, was threatened by a host of evil spirits: the 'Asiatic hordes' and the Tsar's navy and the Hun's navy and the Emperor of Japan's navy. Few heard what the new Head of State had to say. His sodden plumes and uncertain knees seemed to symbolise the day.

Australia still has not gained true independence, as the historical record shows. We Australians remain one of the most profoundly colonised of peoples and Australian sovereignty

141

the goal of dreamers: a goal which other, usually poorer, countries have achieved after struggle and bloodshed. It is a melancholy irony that Australians, proportionate to their numbers, have shed more battlefield blood than most, and that so much of this sacrifice has not been in the cause of independence, but in the service of an imperial master.

The Australian tradition is to fight other people's wars, against those with whom Australians have no quarrel and who offer no threat of invasion. Australians fought in China during the Boxer Rebellion so that British mercantile interests could continue trading in opium; in New Zealand so that British interests could exploit that country and destroy the resistance of its Maori people; in South Africa so that the same British interests could subdue the Boers and dominate the Cape of Good Hope; and in Europe during the 'Great War' of mass slaughter, which was generated by a family squabble between Kaiser Wilhelm II and his cousin, George Saxe-Coburg; the latter, in the course of events, wisely changing his name to Windsor.

Until recently, the Australian national day was not the anniversary of the arrival of the British 'First Fleet' in 1788, nor the federation of the colonies, but Anzac Day, April 25, which commemorated the landing in 1915 of Australian and New Zealand troops on the Gallipoli Peninsula and their rout by Turks dug into the cliff face. For every 500 yards gained, at least a thousand Australians were lost. The bodies were piled four feet deep. The wounded lay in their blood and filth with little water and rancid rations; 'Casualties?' said the British General, Hunter Weston, 'What do I care about casualties?'

These matters were not mentioned in the first news despatches which arrived almost two weeks later. Instead, the Melbourne *Argus* announced that Australia had 'in one moment stepped into the worldwide arena in the full stature of great manhood'. Australia now had 'a place among nations . . . on the anvil of Gallipoli was hammered out the fabric of what is destined to be our most enduring national tradition'.[2] Thus the Australian 'legend' was cast; by emphasising the willingness, dash and bravery of the Anzacs, imperial chroniclers were able to obscure the scandalous truth of Gallipoli, whose victims were exploited as shock troops, in an engagement of no military or strategic worth and the folly of which was repeated many times over on the Western Front in France.

In 1987 I spent Anzac Day in the village of Villers-Bretonneux in France. It was here that Australian troops broke through the German advance in April and May 1918. On the brow of the hill, overlooking the town and its surrounding fields wild with mustard flower, stands the Australian war memorial, white and clean, its lawns manicured and headstones paraded in perfect symmetry. There are only 772 headstones; the rest, 11,000 in all, have no known grave. In the 'Great War' men tended to be blown to small pieces.

Seen from afar, a phantom image runs across these fields, regardless of seventy years' ploughing; it is the jagged line of the trenches in which the men were slaughtered. Here I found a 'bully beef' can, a strand of barbed wire, pieces of shrapnel; in each scoop of earth cupped in my hands there were fragments of bone, the remains of those whose names are inscribed on the memorial wall. It was late afternoon and lightning arched over the fields as it began to rain heavily; the white fragments washed into a culvert. I ran for cover in the village.

'Are you Australian?' said a man outside the church, where an Anzac ceremony would be held that evening.

'Yes.'

'I am a teacher. We owe a debt to the diggers; it wasn't their war and it wasn't their cause. My father used to ask: why did they come?'

He produced a brown paper package, carefully wrapped with string, which was a sepia photograph of two diggers in their poncho capes (digger being the Australian word for soldier), the rain coursing down their 'slouch hats' with the brims turned down all round, as the Australian General John Monash insisted of his 'elite' Third Division. Both men were beaming, one with his single tooth and large freckled forehead, the other with his bony arms on his hips, the way

Australians stand. 'My grandfather took this picture the day they came,' said the teacher. 'He was so pleased to see them, but he *never* knew why they came.'

When the war was over, Australian money rebuilt Villers-Bretonneux and children from the State of Victoria donated the money which raised a new school; among them were those whose fathers had fallen here. On the wall of every classroom are the words, *N'oublions Jamais l'Australie* – We Never Forget Australia. On the day I was at the school children sang 'Waltzing Matilda' and displayed drawings of kangaroos and the Sydney Opera House, as well as a Toohey's beer poster and ancient water colours entitled 'Herbert River ring-tailed possum' and 'Pont sur le Yarra à Melbourne'.

That evening French veterans (mostly of the Second World War) filled the church with their vast unit banners. A contingent of serving diggers presented the usual spruce faces of the career military, so unlike those in the sepia photograph. One of them whispered tired jokes about the quality of French soldiering. A small French girl spoke movingly about her country's gratitude; the daughter of an Australian diplomat chirped a warm response. Hymns and anthems were then sung and the 'Last Post' was played by candlelight outside, its lament drifting over the fields of white fragments.

> The dead at Villers-Bretonneux
> rise gently on a slope towards
> the sky. The land is trim – skylines
>
> of ploughed earth and steeples; unfallen
> rain still hanging in the air;
> confusion smoothed away
>
> and everything put back – the village
> too (red brick/white sills) in nineteen
> twenty, unchanged since. Headstones

speak a dry consensus. Just one
breaks free: 'Lives Lost, Hearts Broken –

And For What?'[3]

During the First World War, Australia, with a population
of fewer than five million people, lost 59,342 young men and
sustained 152,171 wounded. As a percentage, more Australians died than Americans in both that war and in all the
years of the Vietnam War. Australian battle casualties represented more than 64 per cent of troops in the field; only the
French figure was higher. No army was as decimated as that
which came from farthest away. And all were volunteers.
The Australian Prime Minister overseeing this carnage was
the famous imperial warlord, Billy Hughes, also known as
'the little digger'. Although Hughes himself never fought in
any war, he loved the British Empire and made his reputation
by calling it to arms. 'War', said Hughes with relish, '. . . war
prevents Australians from becoming flabby. War has purged
us from moral and physical decay!'

At the height of the war the British demanded more Australians, and so did Hughes. With the confidence of one whose
oratory had been acclaimed in Britain, he announced a
national referendum on conscription. If the 'yes' failed, he
warned, Australians at home 'will be like sheep before [the
German] Butcher'. The same year, 1916, also saw the Easter
Uprising in Ireland; and Irish Australians were in no mood
to die for King and Country. Nor were those in the Australian
labour movement, who remained unmoved by Hughes's desperate invocation of the 'threat' of the 'Yellow Peril' – 'This
lonely outpost of the white man's civilisation will be deprived
of its scanty garrison and left open to cheap Asiatics, reduced
to the social and economic level of Paraguay or some other
barbarian country.'[4]

Above all, and in marked contrast to the campaigns of
women's organisations in Britain, it was women who

mounted the successful 1916 campaign against conscription, which started the modern phase of Australians' struggle for independence. Led by the Women's Peace Army, their propaganda was brilliant. A famous poster, declared illegal in several States, was headed 'The Blood Vote' and showed an anxious woman placing her vote in the ballot-box above the verse:

> Why is your face so white, Mother?
> Why do you choke for breath?
> Oh, I have dreamt in the night, my son,
> That I doomed a man to death.

On polling day all but one of Australia's political leaders urged a 'yes' vote. They lost. A majority followed the women, and in a second referendum called by Hughes the following year the nation again voted 'no'. The writer and historian Donald Horne has described the result 'not as a protest against the war, but as an affirmation that the war was to be fought in the Australian manner' — with volunteers.[5]

That was true of the way the 'no vote' campaign was run; but its success had deeper roots. Such a poll would have been unthinkable during the Second World War, when Australia was in real danger of invasion. My mother, Elsie, a fine oral historian, was a student during the First World War. In 1983 she recalled the 'great unease' ordinary people felt about the war, Protestants and Irish Catholics alike. 'We were conditioned to being part of the Empire, we couldn't see straight in front of us,' she said, 'but we knew in our hearts we were being used and conned and that what we should be fighting for was not in Europe, but right here at home. The anticonscription vote was pretty close, but when you think of all the gush Hughes was giving us, the result was really an act of national rebellion. *And* it was led by women – who, I might add, didn't give up knitting socks for the poor beggars in the trenches.'

For many Australians, there was no historical record of this. When I was at school in the 1950s 'history' ended at 1914. I was assured that there had not been enough time to develop 'a proper perspective'. As for 'contemporary history', it did not exist. In the ancient books we read, imported from England or reprinted from the English originals, there were merely asides or footnotes about the Anzacs.

The Returned Soldiers and Sailors Imperial League, a lobby which became almost as powerful as the Catholic Church, had called for 'the prohibition of war books which defame the soldiers of the Empire' and demanded that 'all war books should be censored by the official war historian'. The New South Wales Government complied, banning among others the classic novel *All Quiet on the Western Front*.[6] The First World War was to be remembered as a war without horror, as we could see in George Coates's famous painting, 'Arrival of the First Australian Wounded from Gallipoli at Wandsworth Hospital, London', in which the wounded were treated with dignity, and George Lambert's 'The Landing at Anzac', in which all was manly, romantic and admirable.

My mother and father grew up in the same mining town, Kurri Kurri, in the Hunter Valley of New South Wales. The main street of Kurri Kurri was almost as wide as a paddock, with hitching posts on either side. The shops were shaded by great awnings of corrugated iron and the cavernous pub had balconies of fine wrought iron. The mines were worked according to nationality: a pit for the Scots, one for the Welsh, another for the Australian born. There was a brass band and a pipe band, a WEA (Workers' Educational Association), a Miners' Institute, a School of Arts, a well-used library and an annual eisteddfod.

My mother's father had taken his expanding family there in 1906, by train and bullock dray. They lived in Hopetoun Street, named, like so many streets, after the Earl of Hopetoun, the Viceroy who had presided at Federation. Their house was made of slab weatherboard in the 1860s and dragged on wooden wheels to Kurri Kurri. At that time it was the only solid structure in Hopetoun Street; the rest were 'bag humpies', frames of branches covered with hessian, not unlike the traditional Aboriginal shelter. When I found the house still standing in 1987, the occupant, a lady of my mother's vintage, said, 'Of course I remember that family! How could you forget them? They ended up with a dozen kids, didn't they? [nine actually] . . . lots of girls, all beautifully turned out every Sunday in frills and bows, *and* in the dust or mud! . . . Yes, I remember that Elsie. She had curls and was always reading. You're not Elsie's boy, are you? Are you, dinkum? *Good God!*'

My father's father, Richard, was a German seafarer whose ship, the fully rigged *Maréchal Suchet*, had put into the nearby port of Newcastle in 1896. 'I was at the rail with the mate looking down upon the crowd of sightseers who had gathered around the ship under a canopy of waving parasols', he wrote, 'when I found myself gazing into the eyes of a most attractive woman.'[7] This was my grandmother, Alice, who was to wave goodbye many times during the years she bore him five children.

When he finally 'came ashore' and worked in the mines, Richard Pilger became one of Australia's first naturalised citizens. He believed Australia to be a 'special place' and took his new citizenship seriously: so much so that he enlisted in the Australian army when war broke out in 1914 and offered himself for service against the land of his birth. But Germans then were 'baby-devouring Boche' and German agents were said to be 'rife' among the 33,000 German-Australians, who soon became the 'enemy within' and a 'nest of traitors'. South Australia, the State with the strongest German heritage, prohibited the teaching of German. The town of Hamburg became Haig; German Creek became Empire Vale; Mount Bismarck became Mount Kitchener.

Incipient violence entered the lives of my grandfather and his family after a smear campaign against them. The English,

Scots and Welsh in the pits refused to work with Richard. Desperate to feed his family, he was forced to drift from one miserably paid job to another, until the inevitable accusation – 'German, out!' A quarter of a century later, during another war, my brother Graham was stoned at school for his German name. Such events tend to happen in an immigrant society, especially one that fights other people's wars.

Captain Jim Throssell took the stand in a large public rally at Northam's Peace Day Celebrations in Western Australia in 1919. He seemed to many to be the logical choice. A champion athlete and the son of a conservative politician, he had been wounded at Gallipoli and awarded the Victoria Cross.

He took his position on the stand next to the West Australian Premier, receiving loud applause from those in attendance. But the enthusiasm turned to an uncomfortable embarrassment. For Captain Throssell did not give the usual platitudes about King and Empire, his address was Why The War Made Me A Socialist.

He explained how the war had lost its glory for him when his brother disappeared at the second battle of Gaza, and he spent all night searching in vain through trenches full of the dead and dismembered. He believed that the war was not only futile, it was an imperialist venture.

His wife was in the audience, Katharine Susannah Prichard, then a struggling author, later to become one of Australia's greatest writers. Katharine recorded, 'You could have heard a pin drop. Jim himself was ghastly, his face all torn with emotion. It was terrible – but magnificent.'[8]

John 'Togs' Tognolini, 'Red Anzacs'

When Kurri Kurri welcomed home its survivors from the 'Great War', the miners' stadium was draped with banners such as 'Home is Jock the Brave'. The bands paraded and the men marched; but tears of pride hardly disguised the poverty. The diggers had not come home to the jobs the pit owners had promised to keep for them. A general strike in 1917 had closed the mines and now the woolclip remained on the docks. Riots spread as the diggers contemplated their 'glory'.

In the Hunter Valley the miners fought on the issue of safety. With some shafts almost vertical and so confined that a man had to shovel coal over his shoulder, the coalfields around Kurri Kurri were among the most dangerous in the world. First-aid stations and training were unknown. The owners were intransigent and brought prosecutions against miners' lodges under the Master and Servant Act; strikers were sent to prison as felons and scabs went to work in shafts where men had died. 'Tin-kettling was the battle cry,' recalled Elsie. 'Women and children would appear on verandas, in doorways, each with a kettle and a spoon. When the scabs were sighted, they'd beat to a rhythm that made your blood curdle. It was a terrible sound; we'd dread to hear when the shifts changed.'

By 1929 the New South Wales coalfields were in a state of open rebellion. A new Federal Labor Government, elected on a promise to support the miners, allowed a conservative New South Wales Government to nationalise the mines in order to run them with scab labour. In what they called an 'historic compromise', the mine owners demanded a cut in wages and the right to dismiss at will; notices were sent immediately to 10,000 men. In an accompanying press campaign the miners' resistance was described as 'treacherous to our British way of life'. Many of the miners had fought for Britain.

Rothbury mine was the first to open with non-union labour. On December 16 a column of miners, intent on turning back the scabs, set out from Kurri Kurri behind a pipe band. They were met by a paramilitary force known as the 'Basher Gang', who drew their revolvers and fired. Scores were wounded and Norman Brown of New Greta Lodge was killed. Jim Comerford, then a sixteen-year-old miner, was there. At the age of seventy-four, he described to me 'a revolutionary atmosphere':

There were three lines of foot police, then behind them the mounted police, then another line of foot police with revolvers drawn. When they started firing, Thomas, my mate, fell down screaming beside me, 'I've been hit.' I could see a kid of my own age with two bullets under the loose skin under his jaw. A lot of the young blokes went down to collect the wounded, and the police let them. The men then tried to get to the pit railway to pull it up, and you could hear the bullets hitting the water tank. No one knew how many had been hit. There was a woman nearby who tore up all her bed sheets to make bandages. I pushed through a crowd, and a white-faced Rothbury miner said, 'You can't go there, son. It's young Norman. He's done for.' I didn't see him, but by Jesus I heard him. I'll never want to hear that awful sound again . . . and we were beaten.[9]

Insurrection became a presence in the streets of dust and small prim houses of weatherboard and iron. On January 7, 1930 a meeting of 400 ex-servicemen at Kurri Kurri established a Labour Defence Army, the first of its kind in the English-speaking world. The first parade of the 'people's army' was held in the centre of nearby Cessnock, where more than a thousand miners were drilled by former soldiers and cheered on by the townspeople.

A week later, at a second parade in Kurri Kurri, the army's strength had doubled and was gathering support from beyond the coalfields. It was a hot, grey day with squalls threatening. Suddenly the Basher Gang reappeared, driving motorcycles through the spectators, clubbing women and children, dragging others from shops and doorsteps and beating them. People fought back; barricades went up; the police withdrew. On January 17 the Labor Senator J. C. Eldridge warned of 'impending civil war'. The historian A. G. L. Shaw wrote that in the early 1930s New South Wales 'was on the brink of serious disorder, to say the least'.

The election of Jack ('the Big Fella') Lang as State Premier of New South Wales in 1925 had given the miners hope. Lang had enacted legislation which helped the miners establish employers' liability for injury or death. This was followed by the Mines Rescue Act, which brought rescue stations and the training of rescue squads. The Lang Government introduced the world's first child benefits legislation, as well as widows' pensions and the forty-four hour week. Lang believed the source of poverty and social distress in Australia lay in the imperial connection. Certainly Australia's economy, based on wool and wheat, depended on loans from London banks and on the capriciousness of the London money market.[10]

Indeed, the Great Depression was first felt in Australia not with the crash of Wall Street but with the failure of two Australian loans in London early in 1929. The exchange rate was devalued by private English banks; the Government of Australia had no say. The upheaval that followed struck Australia harder than Britain or the United States. By 1933 a third of breadwinners were out of work. Communities of unemployed sprang up on the outskirts of the cities. Vistas of squalor became known as 'happy valleys': such is the Australian exigence for irony.

In August 1930 Sir Otto Niemeyer arrived from London, sent by the Bank of England 'to advise on economic policy'. To many Australians, Niemeyer was an imperial bailiff inspecting the assets. The British Government, at the behest of the London banks, was demanding payment of interest on loans at the rate of £10 million a year. Without reference to the national misery, Niemeyer pronounced that Australians were living 'luxuriously' and that the interest would have to be paid and wages would have to come down. Most Australian politicians accepted this; the Federal and State Governments agreed to increase taxes and to cut wages and pensions by 20 per cent.

Lang decided to fight Niemeyer, and in the election campaign of October 1930 he placed Australian independence in the political arena. Lang's manifesto was uncompromising: a forty-four hour week, no cuts in public service wages, a public works programme for the unemployed financed by loans and, provocatively, interest payments to London to be repudiated if necessary. Once in power Lang demanded at a State Premiers' conference that no further interest should be paid to the British bond holders and called on the Federal Labor Government to abandon the London gold standard 'and to finally set us free'. For a time interest rates repudiated by Lang were met by the Federal Government, which eventually issued a writ for their recovery from Lang's New South Wales Treasury.

The Labor Party split between the right wing and those who proclaimed 'Lang is right'. The New Guard, a fascist organisation run by former army officers, emerged to meet the 'threat' of Lang and his 'revolutionaries'. In 1932 the newly elected Federal Coalition Government moved quickly to deal with 'the Big Fella', who was now isolated and condemned on all sides as an egocentric and a demagogue. Under attack Lang agreed to some wage cuts; then in defiance he withdrew public money from the New South Wales banks and barricaded the State Treasury against Federal officers.[11]

In May 1932 Sir Philip Game, Governor of New South Wales and an appointed British Viceroy acting in the name of the King of England, sacked Jack Lang. To the dismay of many of his supporters, Lang accepted this. The miners were pressed by Federal Labor politicians to make an 'orderly retreat' and to accept the owners' conditions. With Lang's demise, they had no choice. And independence again was lost.

Australia marches with Britain! From her fighting men to her army in overalls. Land of plenty, land of untold resources: all placed gladly, willingly, at the feet of Mother England. Wool blankets the world, helps to win wars and the greatest wool-producing nation in the world backs Britain to the last men, the last shilling, the last sheep!

Such was the commentary of a film entitled *Australia Marches with Britain!*, which exemplified Government propaganda at the start of the Second World War.[12] On September 3, 1939 the conservative Prime Minister, Robert Menzies, announced that it was his 'melancholy duty' to inform the Australian people that since Britain had declared war on Germany, Australia also was at war. By pursuing Britain into war, once again without questioning their role, Australians under Menzies were left in confusion. 'Other British Dominions', wrote Malcolm Booker, 'insisted on the right to make their decision, but the Australian Government and people were happy for it to be made in London.'[13]

Menzies, an anglophile *ad absurdum*, had difficulty in finding his own direction. Less than a year before war broke out he took the line shared by many British Tories that 'it was a great thing for Germany to have arms'.[14] Even with the war under way he expressed his 'great admiration for the Nazi organisation of Germany ... There is a case for Germany against Czechoslovakia. We must not destroy Hitlerism, or talk about shooting Hitler.'[15] During the first two years of the war Menzies saw little of Australia, preferring his beloved London, where he devoted himself to jockeying for a place of influence close to Churchill, even imagining himself taking over from Churchill. Returning home in April 1941 he wrote in his diary, 'A sick feeling of repugnance and apprehension grows in me as I near Australia.'[16]

So we Australians were led by a man who apparently disliked us, who may well have despised us and who evidently had little comprehension of where the real threat to his country lay. In 1939 Menzies had gained the nickname 'Pig-

Iron Bob' after forcing dockers to end their ban on loading pig-iron for Japan. Menzies accused the men of 'inciting a provocative act against a friendly power'. At that time the 'friendly power' was busily conquering China and spreading its 'Co-Prosperity Sphere' closer to Australia.

As if blind to these developments in his own region, Menzies despatched the Australian army to join the British in the Middle East, the Australian air force to the skies above Europe and the most modern Australian warships to serve the Royal Navy. When the Japanese struck at Pearl Harbor in 1941, then at Australia in 1942, destroying Darwin in fifty-nine bombing raids, Australia's defence forces were elsewhere, fighting somebody else's war.

A Second World War myth, still alive in Australia, is that the Japanese were able to conquer southern Asia because of their superior numbers. This complied with the national nightmare of 'Asiatic hordes' and the 'Yellow Peril'. In reality, the Japanese invaders of Malaya and the Philippines were at a serious numerical disadvantage, numbering only 15,000 compared with the Allies' 120,000. They succeeded in the Philippines mainly because General Douglas MacArthur slipped away to Australia and left them to it. Had there been Australian forces strategically placed in the region, the Japanese advance might have been stopped, at least before the disastrous capture of the Dutch East Indies (Indonesia) and New Guinea to the immediate north of Australia. Although Australia was spared a land invasion, its defencelessness during the six months from December 1941 to June 1942, argues Malcolm Booker, 'caused more subtle long-term damage [and] created a psychology of dependence on the United States which continued long after the war and still lingers on. Moreover, our Government's panic-stricken appeals for help induced a degree of contempt in American government circles which still lingers on.'[17] Such an astute observation comes from one of the very few Australian diplomats who have understood the nature of Australian indebtedness to the United States since the Second World War.

With Menzies defeated at the polls in 1941, the Labor

leader John Curtin stood waiting to welcome General MacArthur, who had not bothered to tell the Australian Government he had landed in their country. Australia's imperial capital had moved to Washington and the bond between the two countries, as MacArthur explained when he addressed the Australian Parliament in 1942, 'is that indescribable consanguinity of race which causes us to have the same aspirations, the same ideals and the same dreams of future destiny'.[18]

Australia's imperial historians have described this shift away from Britain and the new relationship with the United States as 'the dawning of independence', as if it is possible to measure independence within the confinement of dependency. Australian politicians are still credited as 'statesmen' when they successfully serve foreign interests.

This pattern of acquiescence and failure was briefly interrupted by Dr Herbert Vere Evatt, who was both a nationalist anxious about his country's honour in the world and an internationalist who sought to establish the community of nations. A shy man of intellect and dignity, 'Bert' Evatt was a central figure in every civil rights struggle in Australia for a generation and the youngest judge to sit in the High Court, where his opinions established universal precedents of freedom. During the Second World War, as Minister for External Affairs in the Labor Government of John Curtin, Evatt may well have done more than any individual to save his country from invasion when he secured from Churchill and Roosevelt the reversal of a secret policy known as 'expendable Australia' or 'Germany first'. This was little better than a conspiracy, enshrined in a top secret document 'WW1'. Britain and the United States had agreed to 'allow' the Japanese to take Australia while they 'dealt with Germany'. The Australian Government knew nothing about this; and, as David Day has written, the secret agreement reflected Churchill's contempt for a nation he once described as coming from 'bad stock' (convicts and Irish) and whom his wartime High Commissioner dismissed as 'inferior people'.[19] When Evatt found out, he was furious and told Churchill what he thought of him, and determined to end forever his country's servility to Britain.

Immediately after the war Evatt proclaimed Australian independence as his goal: a policy he called 'the New World'. Australia was to be in the southern hemisphere as Sweden was in the north: libertarian, non-aligned, prosperous, envied and, above all, at peace. At San Francisco in 1946 Evatt was a dominating figure in the framing of the United Nations Charter and, as first President of the United Nations, it was he who announced the Declaration of Human Rights. This was one of the highest points in white Australia's history, for which Evatt was to pay dearly.

Evatt sought independence for Australia at a time when the American empire was claiming the economic and strategic dependency of much of Asia, with Japan as the principal link to the rest of America's global network. In Washington Australia's allegiance to this new order was assumed. For Australians to 'stand alone', free of new imperial ties, they needed leaders of strength and courage. Evatt was such a leader; so too was Ben Chifley, who had become Prime Minister on Curtin's death. Chifley had little formal education; yet his management of Labor's war economy distinguished Australia as the only Allied nation to emerge from the Second World War with a favourable balance of credit under the US Lend-Lease Scheme. Chifley believed in full employment, and under his Government full employment was achieved. He believed in public works which gave universal benefit, and under his Government the great Snowy Mountains Scheme was conceived and begun, eventually turning rivers away from the sea and into the interior. The Chifley Government was also Anglo-centric and racist in its conduct of the White Australia Policy; yet paradoxically it was the Chifley Government that initiated an immigration programme which was to put an end to an exclusively white Australia.

To Australians, it was Chifley himself who embodied the ethos and mythology of Australianism. 'Chif' was an unprepossessing, fair-minded man who believed that a system of 'them' and 'us' was an absurdity in Australia. My parents loved him for this. When he was not at home in Bathurst, in western New South Wales, he lived in room 205 of the Kurrajong Hotel in Canberra, with a tea kettle and a pile of 'westerns'; the lavatory and bath were down the corridor. The cost to the taxpayer was six shillings a day.[20]

Many Australians regarded the 'New World' policies with ambivalence. As the historian Humphrey McQueen has pointed out, 'The trauma of near invasion froze all critical responses [to American policies] for a generation.'[21] The United States had 'saved' Australia and there public debate foundered. Washington understood this and took advantage of it. During the Second World War the Curtin Government had puzzled over an American request from Washington for a US Air Force plane to fly on what seemed to be a reconnaissance of the entire Australian continent. A 'top-level US military team' would be on board. The request was granted and discreet enquiries revealed that the 'military men' were mining geologists and businessmen. This 'aerial prospecting' was standard practice wherever the US military went, and allowed US corporations to assess the availability of energy resources and 'strategic materials'. Australia is rich in minerals, and has a third of the world's known uranium reserves.[22]

In 1946 the Truman administration demanded swift Australian acquiescence to a draft 'Treaty of Friendship, Commerce and Navigation', which would give the United States effective control over Australia's natural resources and much of the Australian economy through the World Bank, the International Monetary Fund and the US Import-Export Bank, all of them dominated by Washington. The force of American pressure took the Government and bureaucracy by surprise; for two years it was unrelenting. Senior officials of the Treasury and the Commonwealth Bank expressed alarm about the effects of granting 'special privileges' to US dollar-projects in foreign investment and of surrendering exchange control. Dr John Burton, Secretary of the Department of External Affairs, who shared Evatt's vision of independence, played a significant part in what began as a bemused, slightly stubborn

Australian resistance and developed into a struggle for sovereignty. Advising extreme caution to the Australian side, Burton ensured that the negotiations dragged on and that the treaty eventually was abandoned.[23]

Evatt was becoming a serious problem for the Americans. Not only had he opposed the 'Treaty of Friendship', but he refused to see world events in Cold War terms; and, as President of the United Nations' General Assembly, his voice was heard beyond Australia by those seeking independence in the 'emerging nations'. 'We have all been troubled by the Australian attitude of attempting on various issues to find a middle ground,' complained the US Representative at the United Nations, Hayden Raynor, in a memorandum to Washington. The memorandum is one of a batch of Government documents declassified by the Whitlam Government in the 1970s which reveal the degree of American concern about the 'threat' of Australia pursuing a 'middle ground'. This concern had risen to the level of panic in 1948 when Washington declared the Australian Government a 'security risk' and began to undermine it: a process that was to become known as 'de-stabilisation'.

To Washington the 'security risk' was that of communist influence in Australia and the Australian Government's 'unwillingness' to deal with it. US Embassy despatches from Australia at the time included a 73-page top secret report which listed 'leading Australian communists and fellow travellers'. The official who compiled the list, Webster Powell, was an intelligence agent, like most US 'labour attachés' in Australia or elsewhere. Webster classified people as 'alleged communist' or 'communistically inclined' or 'recanted communist'. (The latter category remained 'suspect'.) He cautioned that 'care should be taken in the use of this list, although it is believed to be reasonably accurate'.

American spying in Canberra became so rife that, according to John Burton, 'I could never send a message from my office to Dr Evatt's office without the American Ambassador having precise details within minutes ... the Ambassador used to drop little hints to let me know that he knew what I knew.'[24]

It was during the visit of a Soviet delegation that the Government began to think it should have its own intelligence sources, and the Australian Security and Intelligence Organisation, ASIO, was established. According to Burton, this was 'a most reluctant' decision by Chifley, and 'the organisation developed step by step away from the British model, on which it was based, toward the American type'.[25]

Under a treaty with Britain and the United States, Australia (with Canada and New Zealand) became a junior partner in an 'exchange of intelligence'. This was the UKUSA Co-operative Intelligence Agreement, the precise terms of which are still secret. It meant that both British and American intelligence could operate freely within Australia. Burton described how 'a small group of people were "initiated" by a special oath of secrecy over and above the normal and adequate oath taken by public servants. Certain matters of direct concern to foreign and defence policy were to be known to these persons and these only'; and yet these officials were 'taking part in an intelligence organisation with which other countries were associated'.[26] It was this 'association' which, argues Dennis Phillips in his *Cold War Two and Australia*, 'fixed Australia firmly in an American-dominated defence and intelligence web'.[27]

The election year of 1949 saw huge amounts of American and British capital transferred to Australia, much of it passed secretly to an anti-Labor election fund. British interests with Australian investments gave £100,000 – an unheard of political donation in those days – to finance a propaganda campaign that was a model for the McCarthy era to come. Chifley was likened to Mussolini, Hitler and Stalin. The *Women's Weekly*, owned by the arch-conservative Frank Packer, published a series of advertisements in which the Government was depicted as aiding an enemy within. One had a full-page picture of a young woman putting a gun in her handbag and the caption: 'No need to pack a pistol in *your* handbag' because the 'sinister forces' overseas which were threatening Australia were being kept at bay as long as Australia remained 'strong'. The message was 'Don't take risks.' Put Labor out of office. Labor was associated with 'broken homes' and worse, 'no shopping choice for women!'[28]

Labor might have won had Chifley matched the conservatives' promise to end petrol rationing and had he not been committed to nationalise private banks. He refused to compromise, remembering as a child the social effects of the failure of two-thirds of Australia's private banks in 1892. He also remembered, as a politician during the Depression in 1931, how the chairman of the Commonwealth Bank, a public servant, had refused to co-operate with a job creation plan because the private bankers did not approve. The 'banks issue' gave the opposition the opportunity to depict Labor as 'dictators of socialism'. On December 10, 1949 Robert Gordon Menzies was reinstated as Prime Minister.

I belong to the Menzies generation. Sir Robert Menzies, as he became, Knight of the Thistle, Companion of Honour, Fellow of the Royal Society, Knight of the Order of Australia, Lord Warden of the Cinque Ports, President of Kent County Cricket Club, reigned during the 1950s and most of the 1960s, the longest-serving Prime Minister of the Commonwealth of Australia. It was he who shipped the Queen of England and members of her family to the Antipodes more times than they can probably remember; and it was he who caused the Queen to splutter with embarrassment when he turned to her and intoned, 'In the words of the old seventeenth-century poet who wrote these famous words, "I did but see her passing by and yet I love her till I die".'

It was partly Menzies's comic sycophancy to the upper reaches of the English class system that qualified him as Our Better, the kind of inflated authoritarian figure many Australians admired, and still do. Menzies not only found us 'repugnant', as he wrote in his diaries, he also fooled those of us who confused his verbal flatulence with oratory and regarded the measured affectation of his voice as 'correct', and his arrogance as knowledge. One of my aunts claimed 'Bob' could be relied upon not to pick his nose in the company of

Her Majesty, whereas Labor politicians were said to pick their noses and to adjust their groins with impunity.

The Australia over which Menzies ruled was deeply unsure of itself. 'The Stain' of the convict experience occupied the Australian psyche. Like religion and sex, it was seldom spoken about in public. 'We were lags and screws set down on the edge of the earth,' said the poet Dorothy Hewett. 'There was no love for the country. And when the free settlers came, they came because they were younger sons and there was nothing for them to do in England. So there was neither love nor understanding of the country. I'm sure if most of them were given the choice they would have got up and gone back home to England as quickly as they could. It took such a long time even to make sense of the place.'[29]

Certainly no place is more different from Britain than Australia. The land is ancient and harsh, the colours muted and the leaves turn the wrong way to the sun. The heat is intense. In this country an illusion was created; English counties were conjured and prim gardens landscaped, and early nineteenth-century Australian writers described their country as 'a great parkland' and Australian painters banished the heat and flies and vastness and saw green fields and hedgerows that did not exist. 'To me', said Menzies in 1950, 'the British Empire means a cottage in the wheat lands of the north-west of the state of Victoria, with the Bible and Henry Drummond and Jerome K. Jerome and the "Scottish Chiefs" and Burns on the shelf.'

My generation glued cottonwool to its Christmas cards, sang imperial hymns, celebrated 'Empire Day' and memorised a catalogue of mostly murderous regal events on the other side of the world; this was known as 'history'. With honourable exceptions, our teachers made plain that there was 'no real point' to the learning of Australian history, for the sound, practical reason that it contributed nothing to the passing of any important examination and was therefore worthless in the pursuit of 'higher education'.

I went to Sydney High School, a 'selective' state school whose students were chosen on the basis of their successful completion of a jigsaw puzzle and a game of building blocks. This was known as an 'intelligence test'. At Sydney High I learned about Egyptian pharaohs, Shakespeare and the 'law' of supply and demand, most of which I quickly forgot. Sydney High was the only state school in an organisation known as the 'Great Public Schools'; private schools are sometimes known in Australia, as in Britain, as 'public schools'. This brought me into contact with the heirs of the 'squatters', who owned tracts of Australia, and of the mercantile families who had prospered behind imperial tariff barriers. Here was another Australia, even more Anglo-centric than the lower drawer from which I had come.

This other Australia assumed a gentility and snobbery which, I was later to discover, originated in the Home Counties of England. This other Australia even affected another accent, although this endeavour was usually unsuccessful; Australian vowels have a resilience all their own. The boys I would meet at the annual rowing regatta and at rugby matches went to schools with names like Sydney Church of England Grammar School ('Shore'), and The King's School. 'King's boys' wore a Ruritanian uniform reminiscent of the Crimean and Boer wars and which gave the impression of pyjamas. The Englishness of these people was a manifestation of their power; they were Menzies People. My mother once tried to explain the difference between them and us. 'They're not better,' she said, 'just better off.'

Menzies's return to power ended the hope and ambiguity of the 'New World' years. Evatt's commitment to internationalism had remained at odds with a perceived need to maintain a 'special relationship' with the United States, the great power that had 'saved' Australia. Australian policy towards Korea had exemplified this. The Labor Government had argued at the United Nations for elections throughout Korea and had criticised the American military Government's support for the extreme right and its police force, which tortured and murdered political enemies. Australia had voted against separate elections in the south; yet the UN resolution of approval for the American conceived Republic of (South)

Korea was drafted by the Australian delegate, James Plimsoll.

Under Menzies the policy was now clear: the goal of assisting small countries like Korea was to come a poor second to unqualified support for the policies of the United States. 'Australia', said the Minister for the Interior, Wilfred Kent Hughes, in 1950, 'must become the 49th state of America.'[30] And this was effectively Australia's relationship with the United States during the Korean War. When, in 1950, the United States created a 'United Nations Command' without the concurring vote of the Soviet Union, as required under Article 27 of the Charter, Washington had one immediate and supine ally in the Menzies Government. The Australian Minister for External Affairs, Percy Spender, heard that Britain had decided to send land troops to Korea. Anxious not to be beaten at 'the US loyalty stakes', Spender announced that Australian troops were all but on their way; he had not thought it necessary to consult Menzies.[31]

Menzies represented the Korean War to the Australian people, not as the revolutionary civil war it was, but as a struggle against 'Asiatic communists' backed by Moscow, who were 'sweeping down' on to a 'plucky democracy' in the south. The South Korean regime's record of murder and torture, which had been documented by Australia's own UN observers, was not an issue. Echoing the US Secretary of State, John Foster Dulles, Menzies blamed the Soviet Union's manipulation of events in Korea: Stalin's 'world communist plot' was behind the war. Few now believe this. In November 1950 even General MacArthur told James Plimsoll that he had found 'no evidence of any close connection between the Soviet Union and the North Korean aggression'.[32]

In what the journalist James Cameron later called a 'dress rehearsal for Vietnam' three to four million people were killed, millions more became refugees and not one substantial building was left standing in the north. Australian propaganda concentrated on exciting racist fears of the 'Asiatic hordes'. 'Look at those dirty Reds run,' said the commentator on Cinesound newsreel. 'Look at that scum of the East.'

As the United States rebuilt Japan, the Menzies Government and its bureaucracy took fright. They had little understanding of the region, except in colonial terms. For example, Australia had supported the return of Indo-China to the humiliated French *colons*. Our imperial education system had done its work. Oxford degrees were plentiful; the head of the Department of External Affairs and the head of the Pacific Division were both Rhodes scholars, and the Minister himself, Lord Casey, was an experienced servant of Empire, almost as 'English' as Menzies. To them, Asia was the 'Far East' from which protection had to be sought. Thus, Australia pleaded with the United States for a 'security pact'. The Australian Ambassador in Washington, Percy Spender, proposed a NATO type agreement under which attack on one signatory constituted an attack on another. Alas, all the Americans would give him was the ANZUS Pact, which, with these words, guaranteed nothing: 'The Parties will consult together whenever, in the opinion of any one of them, the territorial integrity, political independence or security of any of the Parties is threatened in the Pacific.'

The Americans saw the 'pact' as relatively unimportant, an expression of Australian support for its anti-communist crusade around the world. As Dennis Phillips has pointed out, it was Dulles who, fearing political opposition at home, 'made certain that the ANZUS pact did *not* commit the United States to intervene if Australia was attacked'.[33] In Australia, the pact was trumpeted as a 'landmark for diplomacy' when all it really demonstrated was that 'Australia could best prove her independence by deciding upon whom she chose to become dependent'.[34] In return for an illusion, Australia had committed itself to side with Washington whenever the Americans chose to impose their will in Australia's part of the world.

However, the Australian independence movement had not died overnight. On the contrary, as the nuclear arms race accelerated, the Australian peace movement grew proportionately to become one of the largest in the world. In 1950 a quarter of the population signed the petition to ban nuclear weapons. There were mass demonstrations against the Korean War, including a riot that stopped the centre of Sydney.

In 1951 Menzies called a national referendum in which people were required to vote for or against the banning of the Communist Party of Australia. At the age of eleven I stood outside Mac's Milk Bar on the corner of Bondi Road and Wellington Street, handing out 'Vote No' cards for the Labor Party. I understood clearly the issue, and I recall the opinion of many people that 'Ming' (Menzies) had 'gone too far': that the right to be a communist was as good as any other right. The 'no' votes won. It was a salutary moment of which Australians could be proud.

Having despatched young men to die for the Americans in Korea and the British in Malaya, and having failed to proscribe an 'enemy within', Menzies now immersed Australia in a McCarthyism almost as virulent as the American original. People stopped calling themselves socialists in public for fear of being 'named' and losing their job. The Australian Security Intelligence Organisation, ASIO, took full advantage of its constituted powers as a secret police force, passports were confiscated, politicians were watched, phone tapping was common and official car drivers were encouraged to report on public servants.

My friend, the novelist Faith Bandler, lost her passport. She remembers 'how difficult it was to function as a free person if you refused to accept the terms of the Cold War. I had a telephone in my house and I'd go out to a public booth. You had a lot to lose. You could lose your job and I knew of hundreds of professional people who lost their jobs under Menzies. It was a rule of terror and I think it had a very lasting effect on Australians.'[35]

When Ben Chifley died in 1951, Bert Evatt became Opposition Leader. Evatt lacked Menzies's political guile and parliamentary bombast, but he fought steadfastly for the principles he had espoused during the 1940s. In an election called for May 1954, he looked a winner. Menzies's refrain about a Soviet 'fifth column' in Australia was no longer believable, even by many of those who wanted to believe it. Not a single spy had been produced.

On April 13, with six weeks to go to the election, Menzies had his 'spy'. On the second to last day of the parliamentary session, with Evatt absent, Menzies announced that Vladimir Petrov, Third Secretary of the Soviet Embassy in Canberra, had defected to ASIO, and that a Royal Commission would enquire into 'espionage activities' in Australia. Ten days before the election the three Royal Commissioners sat in a concert hall in Canberra attended by maximum publicity and rumours about 'nests of communists close to Evatt'.

The 'Petrov affair' consumed the rest of the election campaign. Menzies's conservative coalition won the House of Representatives by just seven seats, although Labor won a clear majority of the votes cast. Not one criminal charge resulted from the Petrov Commission. Petrov, a drunk, was never seen in public. Smear upon smear was heaped upon Evatt, whose health began to fail. The Labor Party disintegrated under the weight of McCarthyism; and the spoiling tactics of an extreme right-wing splinter group, the Democratic Labor Party, kept the conservatives in power for the next eighteen years. For his part in the Petrov affair, Menzies was credited with a 'masterful piece of political contrivance'.[36] Welcomed in the United States soon afterwards, he was given the honour of addressing the joint houses of the United States Congress. 'May all that you stand for and we stand for', he told the Congressmen, 'be preserved under the providence of God for the happiness of Mankind.' A Republican Congressman, Lawrence H. Smith, later wrote that an Evatt victory in the 1954 election would have made Australia 'the Poland of the Southern Hemisphere'. Had Petrov not defected, 'Australia today might be Iron Curtain territory . . . freedom had a close call Down Under.'[37]

In Australia's secret heartland monoliths stand where the ice receded, and fine white sand drifts over the red earth, through spinifex and dead trees rising like black needles in mist. From a distance this is no more than desert, but look closer and the simplicity is really a rich mosaic of acacias, cassias, emu bushes, honey myrtles, grasses, even daisies, binding the sand. Through the skeins of sand-mist, out on the plain, a red kangaroo comes into sight, a species once almost extinct.

Rain has just fallen: barely a cloudburst, but enough for plants to throw out new shoots and seeds in the earth to germinate. Some of these plants are able to fit their whole life-cycle into four weeks, providing green feed for the red kangaroo's body chemistry. Hormones then switch on the female's breeding mechanism, stimulating a tiny ball of four-day-old cells – the future embryo – that has lain dormant on the uterus wall for as long as there has been drought. Now the cells begin to divide and grow into the young kangaroo. Almost a month later, the mother cleans out her pouch, a sign of impending birth. She places her tail forward and sits back on her rump; and presently a movement is seen. The blind, pink, bean-sized offspring is born and begins its unaided three-minute journey over the fur to the pouch, where it attaches to a nipple, to remain there for 190 days. Shortly afterwards, when the ride becomes too rough, it leaves for good. And the mother can mate again.[38]

It was here, between 1952 and 1958, that Australia gained the distinction of becoming the only country in the world to have supplied uranium for nuclear bombs which its Prime Minister allowed to be dropped by a foreign power on his own people without adequate warning.

On September 16, 1950 the British Prime Minister Clement Attlee sent Prime Minister Menzies a top-secret cable asking for permission to test British nuclear weapons in Australia. According to James McClelland, the Australian judge who presided over the Royal Commission of Enquiry into the effects of the tests, 'Attlee asked Menzies if Menzies could lend him his country for the atomic tests. Menzies didn't even consult anybody in his Cabinet. He just said yes. With anything that came from the British it was ask and you shall receive, as if they were God's anointed.'[39]

Menzies took only three days to reply. It was not only his Cabinet who remained unaware of his momentous commitment; the Australian people knew nothing of the decision for eighteen months. On February 19, 1952 they were told in a one-paragraph announcement that 'an atomic weapon' would be tested in Australia 'in conditions that will ensure that there will be no danger to the health of the people or animals'.

If the well-being of his fellow Australians was of concern to Menzies, it is not apparent in the documentation now available. What concerned him was that the British might change their minds. As Joan Smith has written:

The one thing Menzies seems to have feared is that Britain would change her mind and go elsewhere. In 1954, a rumour went round that Britain was again thinking of conducting some of her atom tests in Canada. Menzies was beside himself, and had to be placated by the British High Commissioner in Canberra. A cable to London outlined the High Commission's efforts at smoothing over troubled waters: 'I felt it best to use discretion . . . and scotch any suggestion that we had been thinking of Canada as an alternative'.[40]

The attitude shared by the British Government and Menzies was similar to that of the first colonisers of Australia in the late eighteenth century: that this was an 'empty land' and expendable. When one Australian official attempted to speak up for the Aboriginal people who lived within the test area, whose country this was, he was warned that he was 'apparently placing the affairs of a handful of natives above the affairs of the British Commonwealth of Nations [and] the sooner he realises his loyalty is to the department which employs him the sooner his state of mind will be clarified'.[41]

It was dawn when I left the Sheraton Hotel at Ayers Rock. The specials of the day were already posted: 'flambé Pernod prawns' and 'kangaroo sirloin, the taste of Australia'. Chauffeured Mercedes awaited Japanese chairmen-of-the-board, who would view the Rock from behind tinted glass. Japanese love the Rock. Japanese golfers climb to the summit and declare it a driving range. One golfer attempted to return to earth by parachute; another threw his clubs, one after the other, down the rock face. Another erected a shrine to his Buddhist prophet and chanted his devotion through a loud-hailer.

The Rock's mystery unfailingly touches outsiders, including white Australians who regard the interior of their continent as another country. Only two peoples properly understand it: the Pitjantjatjara and Yankuntjatjara people, the traditional owners of *Uluru*, their name for the Rock which means 'meeting place'. Their culture is called *Tjukurpa*, of which 'dreaming' and 'dreamtime' are broad and inadequate translations. *Tjukurpa* is not dreaming in the conventional Western sense, nor is it a collection of stories and fables; it is existence itself: in the past, present and future. It is also the explanation of existence and the law which governs behaviour. For the Aboriginal people, this is expressed in themselves – in their actions of hunting, marrying, ceremony and daily life. And it is in the land: in the creeks, hills, claypans, rockholes, soaks, mountains and red plains that stretch beyond *Uluru*.[42]

The previous day I had climbed the Rock with my son Sam and a friend, Gerrit Fokkema, who took some of the pictures in this book. A wintry wind forced us irresistibly to the edge; and when there was no longer link chain to hold or white arrows to follow, we descended to all fours. Sprawled on the Rock, I looked across to the Olgas, a range of huge stones known by the Pitjantjatjara as *Katajuta*, or 'many heads'. Rising out of the plain they appeared as mammoth figures that had died in each other's arms at the moment a cataclysm had enveloped them. The next morning I flew in a small aircraft between the Rock and the Olgas towards the atomic desert at Maralinga.

After two hours in the air the waves and ripples of the great red earth-ocean below stopped. Now there were few trees and no sign of desert life. No tracks in the sand; no red kangaroo. Only coils of the indestructible spinifex rolled along empty concrete highways, which had not been used for more than thirty years. The roads formed a series of baseball diamonds. At the centre of each stood an obelisk. This was Ground Zero, the point of the bomb's explosion. There were obelisks to the horizon. Then a town appeared, decapitated. The buildings had been torn out, leaving only the foundations and a water tank. We began to land on one of the longest airstrips in the world, now deserted.

Two Federal policemen were waiting outside a tin shed. I had permission, but they were theatrically suspicious. 'What are the *real* reasons for your visit?' said the senior officer. 'Is there something you haven't revealed to us? ... You must not speak to anyone. There must be no interviews.' In the tin hut where the policemen lived three months at a stretch were 1950s murals, a picture of the Swiss Alps, a poster of Samantha Fox and a depressing collection of paperbacks and videos, including the four *Death Wish* movies. Food and water were shipped in; the little that grew could not be eaten. Each man wore a radiation tag on his trousers. 'Mine lights up', said the junior one, 'when it hits the ground. Now don't you fellas pick anything up; don't you touch anything; and when we're driving out to Ground Zero, keep the windows wound up tight. Remember, the wind is your enemy.'

We drove through two lines of fences, each marking the degeneration of the land. Past the first fence there were petrified trees of haunting ugliness, as if the leaves had been frightened off them. Past the second fence, with the gate locked behind us, we drove into the equivalent of a nuclear battlefield, the size of Wales and Ireland combined. The ground was coated with a grey stubble, like a permanent frost. Nothing grew. Nothing moved. Standing in the midst of this nothingness was a concrete base with a lavatory bowl in it, an Australian joke, an appropriate symbol.

We had arrived at Taranaki Ground Zero, with its crater and obelisk, on which is inscribed, 'A British atomic weapon was test exploded here on 9 October 1957.' On the rim of the crater was this sign:

WARNING: RADIATION HAZARD

Radiation levels for a few hundred metres
around this point may be above those
considered safe for permanent occupation.

The sign was in English, Italian, Greek, French, Spanish and Arabic. The only people who might have seen the sign were Aborigines, for whom there was no warning.

From one side of the crater it was possible to see across the wilderness dotted with obelisks, each marking a nuclear explosion. In silhouette they appeared as gravestones. When someone in our group picked up a stone, the senior policeman commanded, 'Put that down!' Raw plutonium lay all about, scattered like talcum powder; a speck of plutonium contains more radioactivity than it was safe for a person to ingest over a year. When the first of our two vehicles left the vicinity, the second waited until the dust had settled. With the second fence now behind us, the senior policeman said, 'Well mate, you're now back in Australia.'

During the tests there were thirteen Aboriginal settlements within 200 miles of the Maralinga range. An Australian safety committee belatedly set up in 1955 to advise the British knew that Maralinga was a highly unsuitable place to continue testing. But the chief British scientist, Sir William Penney, denied to the McClelland Royal Commission that he had been told about the Aborigines.

For years Aboriginal people tried to tell the world what the British had done in Australia. Few listened. It was only when British and Australian servicemen and others who had worked on the tests began to suffer and die from cancers that the horror of the bombs began to emerge. Dr Hedley Marston, the scientist who researched the fall-out patterns, disclosed that 'extensive areas of Australia have been contaminated'.[43] Patrick Connolly, who served in the RAF at Maralinga, was threatened with prosecution by the security services after he had revealed that 'during the two and a half years I was there I would have seen 400 to 500 Aborigines in contaminated areas. Occasionally, we would bring them in for decontamination. Other times we just shooed them off like rabbits.'[44]

When an extended Aboriginal family, the Milpuddies, were found in the test area, a cover-up was instigated. The journalist Robert Milliken described it:

> the men working on the Maralinga range were called together and told to keep quiet about the Milpuddie affair. One of them was John Hutton, a 19-year-old soldier in the Australian army [who] recalled the men being mustered together and addressed by a colonel who told them they had not seen the Milpuddie incident because the British and Australian governments had poured a lot of money into the atomic tests and if it got out to the newspapers the money would have been wasted. The colonel reminded them, said Hutton, that they were bound by the Official Secrets Act, and they could be shot or sent to jail for 30 years if they were found guilty.[45]

The McClelland Royal Commission found that, despite the British claim to have cleared up the ranges of Maralinga and Emu, the test site was left 'heavily contaminated' and that there was a 'significant hazard' to Aborigines in the area.[46] The Commission urged immediate action and, as James McClelland later wrote, 'the British – who, after all, had befouled the area lent to them by their admirer Bob Menzies, without consulting even his Cabinet – should pay for the clean-up . . . What's the position today? (1991) The plutonium is still out there . . . and the British are refusing to pay up'.[47]

Today the people of Maralinga live at Oak Valley, some

forty miles to the north of the test site. At any time there are between sixty and 300 of them, depending upon the season and their travels. Since 1984, when they drew all their people together and made a triumphant return, they have received freehold title to land promised to them twenty-two years earlier by the South Australian Government. It is a harsh life, particularly for those of the young men who are not as spiritually rooted there as the elders; and water has to be trucked in at twenty cents a gallon. But the community is strong and its council employs specialist advisers, teachers and a nurse, and alcoholism has been kept at bay. Such is their resilience.

Shortly before I flew to Maralinga I read that an official of the Australian Atomic Energy Commission, Des Davey, wanted the Oak Valley community 'to help' by wearing plutonium monitors and by subjecting themselves to an anthropological survey. Davey insisted there were no health dangers. 'The people understand very well', he said, 'what vegetation areas they should stay away from and it is a characteristic of plutonium that there is very little danger from eating contaminated animals.'[48] He did not say precisely what he meant by 'very little danger'. Plutonium is so dangerous that a third of a milligram gives a 50 per cent chance of cancer.

Two weeks later it was reported that plutonium had been found in the Oak Valley camp and that scientists were 'puzzled at the appearance of the radioactive material [which] was unexpected'. The Australian Radiation Laboratory subsequently announced that the plutonium levels 'are clearly well below acceptable safety levels'.[49] More than thirty years earlier scientists had given the same assurance. Indeed, Menzies himself had said that injury as a result of the atomic tests was 'inconceivable'.

During the 1950s Australian newspapers seldom published analyses of events in their own region by knowledgeable Australians. Commentators were more often than not British and American, whose columns were bought as part of cheap syndication deals. Thus, the American sage Walter Lippmann could wax eloquent to his Australian readers about US policy in their part of the world without ever mentioning Australia, let alone Australia's special interests. To the Australian press this was a natural state of affairs, just as *I Love Lucy*, the *Reader's Digest* and Ronald Reagan B-movies were adopted as 'ours' by default of the Australian film and television industry. I suspect that much of my generation's perception of Asia was shaped by the sub-human stereotypes John Wayne would see off single-handed at a Saturday afternoon matinée. So it was not surprising that events then unfolding in Indo-China were not understood in Australia.

In 1956 President Eisenhower endorsed the sabotage of democratic elections in Vietnam – elections which had been agreed at a United Nations conference in 1954 and which Eisenhower later conceded would have been won by Ho Chi Minh 'with eighty per cent of the vote'.[50] The result was the artificial division of Vietnam and the invention of a South Vietnamese 'ally' by the United States. A State terror apparatus was set up and run by the CIA and was so successful that at one point it accounted for half of all the world's torture cases registered by Amnesty International. The CIA even provided a ready-made Prime Minister, Ngo Dinh Diem, whose 'triumphant return' to his homeland from the United States was the work of one Colonel Edward Landsdale. Diem described himself as 'the George Washington of Asia'. News of these machinations rarely reached Australia.

The election of John Kennedy in 1960 was regarded as a 'new beginning' for American-Australian relations. President Kennedy, a liberal, began by announcing that the United States had a 'mission' in the world. In far-off Vietnam, this 'mission' was translated into extensive bombing, the introduction of death squads and the spraying of forests and crops with toxic herbicides. The aim and effect of this was to drive several million people off their land and into concentration camps known as 'strategic hamlets', where they were 'protected' from those of their compatriots resisting the foreign attack.

The resistance to American terror was described by the liberal thinker, Adlai Stevenson, as 'internal aggression'. The Australian response was, as ever, a call to arms on the side of the invader. In May 1962 the Australian people were told that an 'Army Training Team' was going to Vietnam, at the 'request' of an embattled people. This was false. A memorandum, from the head of the South-East Asian Division of the Department of External Affairs, Gordon Jockel, declared, 'Although we have stressed the fact publicly that our assistance was given in response to an invitation from the Government of [South] Vietnam, our offer was in fact made following a request from the United States Government.'[51]

The Australians would be 'advisers' providing 'instruction in jungle warfare' and 'village defence'. It all sounded proper, and there was no fuss; Vietnam then was a footnote. For their part, the Australian public remained ignorant of the truth that many of their soldiers in Vietnam were to run assassination squads, which would torture and murder civilians. The Australians would take orders from the CIA and write reports which would be kept from the Australian army and the Australian Government. They would enlist mercenaries and dress in the uniform of the enemy. Once again, they would be fighting somebody else's war, only this war would be secret.

While Menzies and his Ministers spoke incessantly about the 'downward thrust of Chinese communism', even urging the United States to use nuclear weapons against China,[52] senior CIA officers in Vietnam knew that Chinese involvement was nominal. The National Liberation Front, NLF – whom the Americans called the Vietcong – was a *nationalist* resistance movement and any fraternalism with communist China belied the ancient and strategic differences between the two peoples. The famous American counter-insurgency adviser, John Paul Vann, wrote in a memorandum to Washington that the majority of the people in South Vietnam 'primarily identified' with the National Liberation Front and 'a popular base for the [American-propped] Government of South Vietnam does not now exist'.[53]

The Australians who worked for the CIA operated under

17. *Right:* 'The Basher Gang' used by the New South Wales Government in the 1930s to break the coal miners' strikes

18. *Below:* The miners' last stand at Rothbury colliery, 1929

HIGHEST NET SALES OF ANY NEWSPAPER IN THE CAPITAL CITIES — MORNING OR EVENING

THE NEWCASTLE SUN

NEWCASTLE, MONDAY, DECEMBER 16, 1929.   'Phone: 1730 (Seven Lines).

BLOODSHED — FIERCE RIOTS AT ROTHBURY

POLICE FIRE ON MOB

Loss of Life and Many Wounded Reported

BULLETS AND STONES

Fierce Fights at Rothbury Colliery Gates

ONE MAN KILLED: 45 WOUNDED

FOUR THOUSAND MINERS IN BUSH

Fierce rioting, in which there was loss of life, occurred at Rothbury this morning at intervals between miners and police.

ARRIVED SAFELY

Special Police Train

"THE CASE AGAINST SOCIALISM IS A *DEADLY* ONE"

"IT CONCERNS THE SPIRITUAL, MENTAL AND PHYSICAL FUTURE OF OUR FAMILIES"

(Mr. Menzies' Policy Speech)

SOCIALIST DOCTRINE HAS LOST ALL SPIRITUAL CONTENT:

It is, as Church leaders have pointed out, the lineal descendant of the gross materialism of Karl Marx.

SOCIALISM MUST MEAN THE REDUCTION OF HUMAN FREEDOM:

You cannot have a controlled economy without controlling human beings, who are still the greatest of all human factors.

19. Prime Minister Robert Menzies, the 'Queen's man', dominated conservative politics for a generation. In the 1950s Menzies allowed the British Government to drop atomic bombs on South Australia, where the land remains lifeless and highly contaminated

20. A symbol of all that remains at the Maralinga test site, 1987

21. Vietnam veterans' 'welcome home' parade, Sydney, 1987

22. Prime Minister Harold Holt welcomes President Lyndon Johnson to Australia, 1966

23. *Left:* Brian Day in the late 1950s

24. *Below:* With fellow Vietnam veteran and 'Agent Orange' victim Barry Wright, Blue Mountains, 1987

25. *Right:* American Christopher Boyce, convicted of espionage in 1977, described CIA operations in Australia aimed at bringing down the Whitlam Government

26. *Below:* The Governor-General of Australia, Sir John Kerr, who used his 'reserve powers' to dismiss the Whitlam Government in 1975

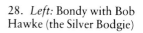

28. *Left:* Bondy with Bob Hawke (the Silver Bodgie)

27. *Below:* Alan Bond (Bondy) with Neville Wran (Nifty)

29. *Far Below:* Hawke with Kerry Packer (the Goanna)

30. *Above Left:* Sir Peter Abeles, owner of trucks, ships and airlines

31. *Above Right:* Tom Domican ('The Enforcer')

32. *Left:* Paul Keating, Australian Treasurer

Daily Mirror

Wednesday, December 3, 1986

MURDOCH HAS THEM ON RUN!

RUPERT Murdoch literally had reporters on the run today following yesterday's $800 million takeover bid for the Herald and Weekly Times group.

Mr Murdoch geared up for a big day with an early morning jog.

And the News Corporation chief executive looked in fine form when the Daily Mirror caught up with him at 7.30am jogging around Melbourne's Fitzroy Gardens.

Mr Murdoch said he had a good night's sleep, and only scanned the morning newspapers before setting out on his run.

He told the Daily Mirror: journalists should do this every day.

He said he was pleased with the morning newspapers which echoed headlines of his lightning move for Australia's biggest media company.

Despite some possible hurdles, Mr Murdoch was confident he would secure the HWT.

Trade Practices Commission chairman Bob McComas has indicated the takeover would appear to contravene the merger provisions of Section 20 of the Trade Practices Act.

But Mr Murdoch said: "It is not insurmountable problem."

FOOTNOTE: A HWT reporter and photographer were close on the heels of Mr Murdoch so that they, too, could snap the man who may soon be their boss.

$1.8 BIL OFFER ... THEN AN EARLY MORNING JOG

● Race for TV stations — p2

UP! UP! UP! BEER, SPIRITS PRICES TO SOAR: PAGE 3

ON THE MOVE: News Corp chief executive Rupert Murdoch in action early today

LATE FINAL EXTRA ● No 13,483 ● PHONE: 268 3000 ● TV: P 18 ● FINANCE: P 47 ● LOTTERY: Jackpot Lottery No 2916/2917 P 45,46 ● MOVIES: P 21

33.

a cover name, the Combined Studies Division, CSD, and it was this which appeared in official documents. It was not until 1984 that Ian McNeill, a former Australian army Major researching an official history, found an admission in US Congressional evidence that the CSD was part of the CIA.[54]

Some of the Australians were integrated into the American 'Phoenix Programme', which is credited with between 30,000 and 50,000 murders of Vietnamese, most of them civilians. The aim of Phoenix was to terrorise people who supported the NLF, that is the majority of the population. Names were supplied by corrupt village informers who were paid on a 'quota' basis. Civil servants, nurses, midwives, teachers and engineers were shot or had their throats slit at night. The first Commander of the Australian 'Training Team' in Vietnam, Colonel Ted Serong, later admitted, 'Yes, we did kill teachers and postmen. They were part of the Vietcong infrastructure. I wanted to make sure we won the battle.'[55] Serong was later seconded to the service of the US State Department in Vietnam. He was ordered not to wear an Australian uniform and to have as little as possible to do with Australian troops.[56] Defenders of the Phoenix Programme insist it was essential for 'intelligence gathering' and that murder was never the intention. An American CIA expert on 'counter terror', Barton Osborne, told a Congressional enquiry, 'I never knew in the course of all those operations any detainee to live through interrogation. There was never any reasonable proof that any one of those individuals was in fact co-operating with the Vietcong. But they all died.' He also said that 'by late 1968 . . . we were getting into a bad genocide program'.[57]

Brian Day, an Australian Warrant Officer, was in charge of a death squad, known as a 'hatchet team' and a 'black team'. He described its operational method:

The black team was usually given a mission of a target figure, a target figure being a person who was suspected

177

of selling out to the enemy or being a double agent, or someone who the province chief suspected of blackmarketing and therefore affecting the war effort. He would be numbered, he would be pinpointed and at an opportune time a black team would go out, usually dressed in the enemy's gear, carrying enemy equipment, and then of course the next day you'd read a report where the VC had annihilated a particular person.[58]

Today Brian Day is disabled from his war injuries and suffers an illness associated with the effects of dioxin, the poison in the herbicide spray, 'Agent Orange'. He now believes the war was a 'criminal act' and that Australians were merely used by a 'new political master':

I remember one night a very senior American officer, who was a close friend of mine, said he had nothing but praise for the expertise and discipline of the Australian soldier. He told me, 'We really like having you guys here,' and I said, 'Why's that?' and he said, 'You're very good, you've helped us a lot ... it's like the British having the Gurkhas, we have the Australians.'[59]

Brian Day's honesty is rare among his former superiors. Just as German political and military leaders at the end of the Second World War rushed to deny they knew about the crimes against the Jews, so Australia's leaders and top brass have denied complicity in the CIA's 'bad genocide programme'. In August 1987 the Australian edition of *Time* magazine described this ignorance as 'an extraordinary fact'. *Time* reported two former Chiefs of the General Staff as saying they knew 'nothing' about the murderous work of Australians in the Phoenix Programme. 'The whole show', said Lieutenant-General Sir Mervyn Brogan, 'was really in the hands of the US. We sent our troops up there. They did what they were told by the Americans . . . we were really on the tiger's back.'[60] Former Prime Minister John Gorton said he was 'never told' that Australian soldiers were fighting for the CIA and that he was 'quite sure' his predecessor Harold Holt did not know, and that he 'very much doubted' if Menzies knew. Colonel (now Brigadier) Ted Serong, who led the Australian 'Training Team', thought otherwise. 'There were other channels to Menzies than the military hierarchy', he said, 'and I had sufficient feedback through those channels from Menzies to cause me to believe that he knew.'[61]

So successful were the Australian 'advisers' that by 1963 the Americans wanted more. They also wanted supporting units to 'share in our combat casualties', as the US Ambassador to Saigon, Henry Cabot Lodge, put it.[62] More Australians meant 'putting out more flags' for the American cause in Vietnam. In May 1963, the Australian Minister in Washington, Alan Renouf, thought it would be 'admirable' if Australia could comply quickly. He explained why in a message to Canberra:

> Our objective should be . . . to achieve such an habitual closeness of relations with the US and sense of mutual alliance that in our time of need . . . the US would have little option but to respond as we would want. The problem of Vietnam is one . . . where we could without disproportionate expenditure pick up a lot of credit with the United States.[63]

Warrant Officer Conway was the first of 494 Australians to die. Thousands were maimed and otherwise scarred. For the Vietnamese, the 'disproportionate expenditure' amounted to at least 1,300,000 people killed, untold millions maimed and their once bountiful land devastated.

In April 1965 Menzies announced that Australians would be conscripted and sent to Vietnam. 'The takeover of South Vietnam [by the NLF]', he said, 'would be a direct military threat to Australia. It must be seen as part of a thrust by Communist China between the Indian and Pacific Oceans.'[64] There was no 'thrust' by China and no 'threat' to Australia. Young Australians were to be compelled to fight and die in a country whose people were resisting an invasion by a great power determined to enforce its regional dominance.

In seeking a pretext, Menzies did not confine himself to a 'thrusting' China. For several months before his announcement Australian officials in Saigon had badgered the South Vietnamese regime to 'request' Australian regular troops. They had failed. The regime in Saigon knew not only that the population would oppose the presence of foreign armies, but that this would be a gift of propaganda to the NLF and compound the difficulties of pursuing a 'Vietnamese peace'.

On the afternoon he had intended dramatically to inform Parliament of the South Vietnamese 'request' for Australian help, Menzies was in a fury. He had no confirmation, no piece of official paper to quote and wave. Moreover, 'some bastard in the Cabinet' had leaked the news that Australia was to send troops to Vietnam.[65] When Parliament returned after the dinner adjournment Menzies's luck was in; he was handed a letter from the South Vietnamese Prime Minister, Dr Phan Huy Quat, confirming the Saigon Government's 'acceptance of an *offer*' of Australian troops.

Menzies stood up and lied that a 'request' had been received. He made no mention of an 'offer'. The evidence of his duplicity was not tabled in Parliament for six years, until shortly before the last Australian soldier was withdrawn from Vietnam. That this episode should have passed into the public domain without serious challenge seems barely credible. Neither the Labor Opposition nor the bureaucracy nor the intelligentsia nor the media sought out the truth. Except for maverick voices, there was approval or there was silence. 'Throughout the war', wrote the peace campaigner Alex Carey, one who did speak out, 'our leaders punished or intimidated any Department of Foreign Affairs scholar or diplomat who dared to question the Vietnam commitment, or provide evidence against the myths by which it was justified.'[66]

In the mid-1960s, with reports of *coups* in Saigon on the front pages of American newspapers, President Johnson appeared to falter in his crusade to 'stem communist aggression' in south-east Asia. There was alarm in Canberra. Australian officials in Washington lobbied the administration almost every day. Why, they asked, had the President 'gone quiet' on the war? Surely now was the time to prosecute the war with renewed vigour and to bomb North Vietnam? Menzies wanted none of this to reach the Australian people. Although it is now known that Australia opposed and lobbied against peace negotiations with Hanoi, the only available record is a heavily censored American memorandum. A vital meeting between Menzies and Johnson at the White House went unrecorded because Menzies requested no minutes be taken and no third party be present.[67]

It is highly doubtful that Australian pressure precipitated the escalation of the war that followed. But the relief with which Australian Ministers and Labor opposition politicians alike greeted 'Rolling Thunder', the most sustained aerial bombing in history, gave President Johnson the comfort he clearly appreciated. Said he:

There's not a boy that wears the uniform yonder today that hasn't always known that when freedom is at stake and when honourable men stand in battle shoulder to shoulder that Australians will go all the way — not a third of the way, not part of the way, not three-fourths of the way, but all the way until liberty and freedom have won.[68]

Soon after the President made that ringing speech, Australia's Department of Foreign Affairs expressed diplomatic frustration about the lack of information received from Washington on the progress of the war. The British, it was said, were better informed than America's Australian comrades in arms. To which the Assistant Secretary of State, William Bundy, replied, 'We have to inform the British to keep them on side. You are with us, come what may.'[69] As the war dragged on, Australians stirred. Many opposed the war with consummate skill and courage and ensured that when President Johnson came to Australia he did not receive the acclaim he might have expected in a country he had once called 'the next large rectangular state beyond El Paso'.[70] Instead, he met confusion, anger and bitterness in the streets; blood-red paint was splashed over his limousine in Sydney and people threw themselves in front of his motorcade. In moratorium rallies hundreds of thousands filled the cities as never before.

A new generation, and others not used to speaking out, wanted an end to the war and to the demeaning status described by William Bundy. Like the developing peoples of their own region, they wanted to live lives beyond the terms of a 'protector'. They wanted the right to identify and defend their own causes, not to act as pawns or surrogates; and the right to examine their own national myths and to make their own mistakes. They wanted independence.

The 1960s saw an Australian awakening. Small events carried great significance: the establishment of the first Chair of Australian Literature at Sydney University, the opening of the Australian Ballet School, the rebirth of the Australian cinema and theatre, the publication of the first volume of Manning Clark's *History of Australia* and of Donald Horne's ironic and brave book *The Lucky Country*, both of which struck at imperium's distortion of the Australian past and present. *The Female Eunuch*, a book by an Australian woman, Germaine Greer, changed lives all over the world. In 1967, more than 90 per cent of the population voted to give the Federal Government the power to negotiate justice for the first Australians. It was, wrote Donald Horne, 'our time of hope'.

5

THE *COUP*

We have never interfered in Australian politics. And so, whatever the charges, the answer is no. We don't interfere in Australian politics period.

William Colby, ex-Director of the CIA, 1981

The CIA's aim in Australia was to get rid of a government they did not like and that was not co-operative ... it's a Chile, but [in] a much more sophisticated and subtle form.

Victor Marchetti, ex senior CIA officer, 1980

'DO YOU BELIEVE in miracles?' Prime Minister Menzies was asked when he retired in 1966. 'Well,' he replied, 'when I look back on the last seven federal elections, I *know* they happen!'[1]

In all the elections for the Australian House of Representatives during Menzies's reign – from 1949 to 1966 – support for his own misnamed Liberal Party was never more than 34 per cent of the popular vote, and for his conservative coalition 42 per cent. A divided Labor Party was one explanation for Menzies's sustained rule. The gerrymandering of electoral boundaries was another; vast rural electorates with more sheep than people greatly devalued the voting power of the crowded cities, where almost 90 per cent of the Australian people live.

When Menzies retired in 1966, he was succeeded by a series of conservative politicians of such minimal stature – the last, William McMahon, was described succinctly by the famous CIA man, Harry Goldberg, as a 'nincompoop' – that the system finally yielded. On December 2, 1972 the first Labor Government for twenty-three years was elected. The Prime Minister was Edward Gough Whitlam.

A tree of a man almost six and a half feet tall, Whitlam was a politician from the old middle classes, the son of the Deputy Crown Solicitor, a classicist, constitutionalist and a Queen's Counsel. Whereas Menzies, the son of a working man, was a contrived grandee, a figure of fearsome superficiality, Whitlam was entirely patrician. Indeed, Whitlam had never been identified with the left of the Labor Party and on several occasions had moved decisively against the left. He was and remains an individualist of maximum proportions: at once arrogant and generous, passionate and quixotic. When he is on form, he is a fine political orator: inspiring, withering, ironic and funny; when he is out of form, he raises his chin and goes on, and on.

In 1972 Whitlam was, above all, a leader of remarkable imagination and devout principle. Those who remind us that Whitlam was 'no radical' are right in a narrow sense; but they surely miss the point of true radicalism. That he understood so clearly what had to be done, and what could be done quickly and perhaps even irrevocably, was his enduring strength.

'Men and women of Australia,' he said on election night 1972, and went on to use the same words and phrases spoken by John Curtin, the wartime Labor Prime Minister. It was a time of high emotion. People laid siege to Whitlam's home in his electorate in working-class western Sydney. Throughout Australia similar streets stayed awake all night. The moment and thrill of Labor's victory are still recalled by millions of Australians, who believed that 'the chance' at last had been won.

For above all other descriptions, Australia is a 'nation of battlers', the colloquialism for the descendants of the 'lags' and 'screws' and the immigrants who have come in waves from almost everywhere. Most Australians are wage-earners; fewer than 20 per cent employ others or are self-employed. 'We are', wrote Joan Coxsedge, Gerry Harant and Ken Coldicutt, 'overwhelmingly working class, a fact that will not go away, in spite of the efforts of academics to promote workers to the middle class on the basis of home ownership or white collar employment or false political consciousness.'[2]

The events that followed rapidly Whitlam's election caught much of the world unaware; for nothing like it had happened in a modern democracy. Whitlam had a 'period of grace' before the Party caucus elected the Cabinet. Working only with his deputy, Lance Barnard, he began to honour his campaign promises in a series of edicts, many of which led to historic legislation.

Conscription was ended immediately and the last Australian troops were ordered home from Vietnam. Young men imprisoned for draft evasion were freed unconditionally. The Federal Government assumed responsibility for Aboriginal health, education and welfare and the first land rights legislation was drafted; the Aboriginal people were drawn into administration of their own affairs for the first time. Racially selected sporting teams were banned from entering Australia.

Equal pay for women was introduced. Wages, pensions and unemployment benefits rose. A national health service was established, open to all. Spending on education was doubled and university and college fees abolished. Censorship was ended and the divorce laws reformed, with the establishment of the world's first 'family courts'. Legal aid became a universal right. A range of cultural initiatives for Aborigines, women and immigrants were encouraged and funded; 'access' and ethnic radio networks were set up. The arts were elevated; and the already resuscitated film industry was given the flesh and blood of extensive Government funding. Creative Australians, driven overseas during the Menzies years, began to return home. Royal patronage was scrapped and, with it, imperial adornments such as knighthoods and 'honours' proclaiming such nonsense as 'Membership of the British Empire'. (These were retained by several States.) An Australian anthem replaced 'God Save the Queen'. The 'Commonwealth Government' was renamed the Australian Government.

An American observer wrote that no country has 'reversed its posture in international affairs so totally without first having passed through a domestic revolution'.[3] Not only did Australia finally withdraw from the Vietnam War, but Australian Ministers publicly condemned the American conduct of the war. The Nixon/Kissinger bombing of Hanoi during Christmas 1972 was called the work of 'maniacs' and 'mass murderers'. A senior Minister, Dr Jim Cairns, described the Nixon administration as 'corrupt' and called for public rallies to condemn the bombing and for boycotts on American goods. In response, Australian dockers refused to unload American ships. Whitlam himself warned the United States that he might draw Indonesia and Japan into protests against the bombing.

Australia moved towards the Non-aligned Movement, expressing support for the Indian Ocean Zone of Peace, which the United States opposed, and once again speaking up in the United Nations for small nations, as well as for the rights of the Palestinians. 'Pariahs' were given diplomatic recognition: China, Cuba, North Korea, East Germany. The French were condemned for testing nuclear weapons in the south Pacific, and refugees fleeing the Washington-inspired *coup* in Chile were welcomed into Australia: an irony later to be savoured by Whitlam.

On the day after his election, Whitlam announced that he did not want his staff members vetted or harassed by the security organisation, ASIO, because he knew and trusted them. Richard Hall, in his book *The Secret State*, reports that the next day he was told by an American Embassy political officer (CIA agent), 'Your Prime Minister has just cut off one of his options.'[4] That turned out to be a considerable understatement. Frank Snepp, a CIA officer stationed in Saigon at the time, said later, 'We were told that the Australians might as well be regarded as North Vietnamese collaborators.'[5]

Alarm in Washington rose to fury when, in the early hours of March 16, 1973, the Attorney-General, Lionel Murphy, led a posse of Federal police in a raid on the Melbourne offices of ASIO. Murphy and Whitlam wanted to know if ASIO had allowed local fascist Croatian groups to carry out terrorist acts both in Australia and against Yugoslav diplomats abroad.

Since its inception in 1949, ASIO had distinguished itself by not uncovering a single spy or traitor (this is still the case); yet it had become almost as powerful in Australia as the CIA was under William Casey during the Reagan years. ASIO's speciality was, and is, the pursuit of paranoia.

For example, in 1970 the South Australian Labor Premier Don Dunstan discovered that his State had a 'Special Branch' whose existence he had known nothing about, even though he had been the State's Attorney-General. Dunstan asked a judge to make enquiries and learned that ASIO had helped to set up and maintain a secret police organisation within his bureaucracy and had kept files on all Labor candidates and members, union leaders, members of the Council of Civil Liberties and anyone holding an opinion 'to the left of an arbitrary centre point fixed by someone in Special Branch ... with the assistance of ASIO ... Even prayer meetings for peace were watched and recorded.'[6]

A leaked ASIO file on Jim Cairns, Deputy Prime Minister under Gough Whitlam, was more to the point.[7] Cairns, as a leader of the anti-Vietnam War movement, echoed 'communist views' and his activities could lead 'to the fascist cult of the personality ... and to the destruction of the democratic system of government'.[8]

When Whitlam was elected, ASIO's real power derived from the spirit of the UKUSA Treaty, with its secret pact of loyalty to foreign intelligence organisations. To many in the ASIO bureaucracy, 'headquarters' was not in Canberra but in Langley, Virginia, home of the CIA. This was demonstrated dramatically when the *National Times* published extracts from tens of thousands of classified documents under the headline: 'How ASIO Betrayed Australia to the Americans'. Brian Toohey, the editor, wrote:

Members of the Australian Security Intelligence Organisation handed over potentially damaging information to American authorities about prominent Australian figures during secret visits to the US over many years, according to a super secret supplement to a Royal Commission report.

The Royal Commission, headed by Mr Justice Hope, found that the practice had been highly improper and definitely not in Australia's national interest. The practice had gone on for decades before it was uncovered by Hope, who had been appointed in the mid-

1970s to investigate Australia's intelligence services.

One problem with the handing over of the material is that it gave the recipient – the CIA – ammunition to use against Australian politicians and senior officials regarded unfavourably by ASIO . . . the information is understood to have ranged from accusations of subversive tendencies to concern about personal peccadilloes.

The information gave the CIA the opportunity to work against the people who had earned ASIO's disdain in ways which ranged from blackmail to efforts to block their careers.[9]

During his dawn raid on the ASIO offices, Attorney-General Murphy came to M in one file. Murphy turned to a senior ASIO official, who had been called from his bed, 'God help you if my name's in this.' It was not.[10] The CIA's public response to the Murphy raid came in an interview with James Jesus Angleton, for twenty years the head of CIA counter-intelligence. He said:

We . . . entrusted the highest secrets of counter-intelligence to Australian services and we saw the sanctity of that information being jeopardised by a bull in a china shop . . . How could we stand aside? You don't see the jewels of counter-intelligence being placed in jeopardy by a party that has extensive historical contacts in Eastern Europe, that was seeking a new way for Australia . . . seeking roads to Peking.

(At that time President Nixon was also 'seeking roads to Peking'.) Angleton went on to say that the CIA had been given 'assurances that the antics and cowboy tactics were not to be of concern to us, that the precious information would be held intact'.[11]

Who gave these 'assurances'? He did not say, but he gave the strongest clue in his answer to a question about CIA funding of Australian trade unions. 'I will put it this way very bluntly,' he said. 'No one in the agency would ever believe that I would subscribe to any activity that was *not co-ordinated with the chief of the Australian internal security*.'[12] (Emphasis added.)

While ASIO is run as an internal organisation, the Australian Secret Intelligence Service, ASIS, operates abroad and is less well known. Code-named MO9, its existence was acknowledged only after the Whitlam Government came to power in 1972. As Opposition Leader, Whitlam had never been briefed on ASIS, and knew nothing about it until told by the Malaysian Deputy Prime Minister, Tun Abdul Razak. The following extract from an ASIS top-secret document describes its activities:

Definition of Covert Action

Special Political Action

Clandestine action against another country designed to further the foreign policy aims of the Australian Government, primarily in the politico/economic field. Operations may be broadly classified as support, disruption and deception (examples are funding of political parties on one side or the other and the use of propaganda).

Special Operations

Clandestine action against another country in wartime or in a serious situation short of war. In this case, operations may involve the provision of arms, explosives and other equipment. An example would be the equipping and training of a local guerrilla movement. It goes without saying that operations in either category are deniable and, if discovered, should afford no proof of the instigation or even connivance of the Government.[13]

ASIS has played an important part in the implementation of American foreign policy and has participated in secret American operations against other countries. In two striking examples ASIS worked *against* Australian foreign policy.

After Cambodia's Prince Sihanouk broke off diplomatic relations with the United States in 1965, the CIA looked to ASIS to fill the breach. From 1966 to 1970 two ASIS officers acted as proxies for the banned CIA, even though Australian policy then was one of strict neutrality. When Sihanouk was overthrown in what was widely regarded as a CIA-inspired *coup*, US land forces invaded Cambodia and American bombing was intensified. The bombing laid waste much of the countryside and served as a catalyst for the accelerated rise of Pol Pot and his Khmer Rouge. Subsequently, at least one million people, perhaps many more, died.

Whitlam also discovered that ASIS agents were working for the CIA in Chile, 'de-stabilising' the democratically elected Government of Salvador Allende, which the Whitlam Government supported. Although he delayed his decision, Whitlam eventually ordered them home. However, one ASIS officer and an operational assistant remained in Chile, under Australian Embassy cover and without Whitlam's knowledge, until shortly before Allende was murdered and his Government destroyed. Whitlam later ordered the transfer of the head of ASIO, and dismissed the head of ASIS over secret ASIS involvement in East Timor. As events unfolded, it became clear that their removal had serious consequences for the survival of his own Government.

The most secretive Australian intelligence organisation is the Defence Signals Directorate, DSD, which is modelled on the American National Security Agency, NSA. The DSD's birth in 1947 is testimony to the extraordinary secrecy embodied in the UKUSA Agreement. According to Professor Desmond Ball:

No more than a handful of Australians have ever seen this Agreement; it was certainly never shown to any Labor Minister (including the Prime Minister) during the Whitlam period, and in fact may never have been shown to *any* Minister. Central to the UKUSA Agreement is the relationship between NSA and DSD, a relationship which, at least until recently, was never disclosed to the responsible Minister.[14]

The DSD is part of Washington's 'Naval Ocean Surveillance Information System'. This means that it spies for the Americans in the Indian Ocean, the south Pacific and southeast Asia. The principal DSD base was in Singapore, until Whitlam closed it down. It was then moved to Darwin, where it monitors communications within Australia and throughout Asia for the NSA. As many as fifty NSA officers have been based at the DSD's Melbourne headquarters.[15]

The list does not end there. There is also the Joint Intelligence Organisation, JIO, established in 1970 under the supervision of the CIA's analysis division; and the office of National Assessments, ONA, whose job is to co-ordinate and analyse Australia's wealth of spookery.

The question begs: why should a relatively small country find itself with such a plethora of spies and hi-tech dirty tricksters? Why should the CIA become so active in Australia that, at one point, the head of ASIS requested it to 'draw in its tentacles'?[16] The answer is surely that Australia is important to the United States and has become even more so since Washington was forced to abandon Indo-China. In 1973, as the last American regular troops were withdrawn from Vietnam, American planners sought to 'contain' the region by linking Japan, Australia and the American-supported Association of South-East Asian Nations, ASEAN. Of these, Australia was the only Western nation and 'traditional ally' with a record of 'political stability'. This stability was now crucial. What had been regarded by some US strategic planners as a backwater was now, in the words of one CIA executive, 'the big jewel of south-east Asia'. A major influence on this re-assessment was the discovery of vast deposits of uranium. Potentially Australia was the world's largest supplier of uranium: the ingredient of nuclear weapons.

On January 8, 1973 the American Ambassador in Canberra, Walter Rice, called on the new Prime Minister. His intention, after pleasantries, was to upbraid the US's 'traditional ally' for the unprecedented criticism by Government Ministers of American bombing of civilian populations in North Vietnam. There was also the question of a personal letter Whitlam had sent to Nixon. Whitlam believed his protest was 'moderately worded'. Former US ambassador Marshall Green, who was in the White House when Whitlam's letter arrived, told me that its effect on Nixon was to make him apoplectic.

According to minutes of the meeting with Ambassador Rice, Whitlam began by speaking 'virtually without interruption for 45 minutes'. The sum of his remarks was that 'the US should be in no doubt regarding [my] determination to do everything possible to end the war'. He told the Ambassador it would have been 'difficult to avoid words like atrocious and barbarous' at a press conference planned the next day had the United States not been prepared to return to the peace talks in Paris. The minutes recorded that:

Mr Whitlam said there had been a lot of speculation about US/Australian relations. There had been extravagant talk about a trade war and about the US 'doing a Cuba'. He did not imagine the US was about to do 'any more Cubas'.

On ANZUS he was aware of the institutional arrangements for the US bases in Australia and, as he understood it, they did not harm Australia and could help the US. He did not propose to change these arrangements. *But to be practical and realistic, if there were any*

*attempt, to use familiar jargon, 'to screw us or bounce
us' inevitably these arrangements would become a matter of contention.*[17] (Emphasis added.)

This was the first hint that America's top-secret installations in Australia, about which Australians knew so little
and which included the two most important American bases
outside the United States, were in jeopardy.

At seven o'clock every morning a convoy of two or three
buses with dark tinted windows moves through the streets of
suburban Gillen in Alice Springs, in the 'red centre' of Australia. Gillen, with its squat brick and tile houses, is where
most of the Americans live. The buses return at three in the
afternoon and at eleven at night.[18] These are the three shifts
worked at Pine Gap, officially an American-Australian 'Joint
Defence Space Research Facility'. The name is a cover; Pine
Gap is an American spy-satellite base, planned and set up by
the CIA and run by the CIA with the American NSA.

Pine Gap is fifteen miles from Alice Springs in the country
of the Aranda people, one of the world's oldest communities.
When I first went to Alice Springs in the 1960s there were
two giant silver radomes; now there are six. These are made
of Perspex and designed to protect the enclosed antennae
from the elements and from 'unfriendly' observation. In the
early evening, with the sun setting against the Macdonnell
Ranges, the light striking the domes has a laser effect and
they appear as stars fallen to earth.

Pine Gap has been described by the CIA's Victor Marchetti,
who helped to draft the Pine Gap treaty, as a 'giant vacuum
cleaner' which can pick up communications from almost anywhere. What the Russians do in Europe, Pine Gap is told
about by satellite directly overhead. Those who seek to justify
the base's presence in Australia say that it performs a necessary task in verifying the Soviet side of nuclear arms limita-

tions agreements, but this is debatable. According to Owen Wilkes, an authority on electronic espionage bases and arms control, 'only 0·37 per cent of Pine Gap's work is verification'.[19]

Pine Gap's primary function is the collection of data from CIA sources and transmitters, in order to track and target 'the enemy' and to prepare for nuclear warfare. According to James Jesus Angleton, Pine Gap's importance is such that 'unlike any similar installation that may be in any other place in the free world, it elevates Australia in terms of strategic matters'.[20] This means that Australia has been positioned in the front line of a prospective nuclear war on the other side of the world – a fact underlined by numerous Soviet statements that the bases are nuclear targets. In 1987 Washington belatedly offered Australia 'early warning' of Soviet 'retaliation' against the bases.[21] The CIA's attitude was straightforward. Robert Crowley, a former CIA 'special operations' executive, told me, 'We had so much in Britain, we couldn't fit anything more on there. So Australia was real attractive real estate.'[22]

The history of Pine Gap and of the other dozen American installations is one of secrecy, wilful official ignorance and official lying. Pine Gap was established by a secret treaty in 1966 drawn up by Richard Stallings, a CIA officer working under cover of the US Defense Department. Stallings later became Pine Gap's first commander. Victor Marchetti, who as Chief Executive Assistant to the Deputy Director of the CIA, helped Stallings write the Pine Gap agreement, told me, 'You know it was very funny. We were sitting there laughing, the two of us were just scribbling this thing out. Dick had found in this old law book something about a peppercorn arrangement . . . that in return for a peppercorn from Washington, Australians would allow us the use of the land and their facilities . . . it just broke me up.'

When I reminded him that Australian Governments have always denied that Pine Gap is anything but a joint facility, with an equal arrangement between the two countries, he laughed. 'Listen,' he said, 'the CIA runs it and the CIA denies it. I mean, that's the way things are done in our business.'[23]

Marchetti told me that the Australian Government did not question a line of the treaty he and Stallings drew up. This is hardly surprising as Australia was then in the hands of Menzies's successor and protegé, Harold Holt, who had become to the Americans what Menzies had been to the British. History remembers Holt for his statement on the White House lawn before a grinning Lyndon Johnson that, in its prosecution of the war in Vietnam, Australia was 'all the way with LBJ'. Holt's successors displayed similar faith. Prime Minister John Gorton said, 'I don't even know what Pine Gap is all about . . . I could have asked, but it didn't arise.'[24] Prime Minister William McMahon reflected on his 'increasing doubts' that Australian Governments knew 'the entire truth' about the bases.[25]

So secret were the plans for Pine Gap and the other principal base at Nurrungar in South Australia that it was not until 1969, shortly before Pine Gap became operational, that Parliament debated the purpose and value of the bases to Australia. The quality of the Government's contribution to this 'debate' can be judged by the remarks of the Minister of Defence, Alan Fairhall. 'I do not believe for a moment', he said, 'that the people of this country will not trust the judgement of their government.'[26] He was supported by a fellow conservative member, H. R. Holten, who said, 'It is my opinion that the average Australian must have faith in the people in authority in the United States and Australia who make responsible decisions which are in the best interests of the defence of this country.'[27] Here again, to borrow from the historian Greg Lockhart, was 'the sub-imperial reflex in its most exquisite form'.[28] The Pine Gap agreement was for ten years. Notice of renewal was to be given one year before expiry on December 9, 1975.

'The Australians', wrote an American observer, 'have accorded the [Pine Gap] facility remarkable hospitality. People and cargo routinely fly in and out, entering and exiting without the burden of customs or immigration checks. The place enjoys almost extra-territorial status.'[29] This was confirmed to me by a former senior US intelligence officer, William Corson, with much experience in south-east Asia. Corson told me in Washington in 1988 that the CIA ran between ten and fifteen 'black airfields' in Australia during the Vietnam War. 'Hot' CIA agents were flown from Vietnam for 'cooling off' and debriefing. In 1975, as South Vietnam crumbled, massive supplies of drugs which had been stashed in Vietnam were flown into the secret Australian airfields. The drugs 'did not stay in Australia', said Corson, but were redistributed to 'regional drug banks', thus providing the 'reserve currency' of international criminal activities associated with CIA covert action.[30]

Pine Gap is supplied direct by the US Air Force Military Command. It has its own water and power supply, luxury accommodation and enough food for at least a week. There is a seven-mile 'buffer zone' in the surrounding bushland, and air-traffic controllers at Alice Springs have standing orders not to allow aircraft to fly within a four-kilometre radius of the base. The notion of a 'joint facility' is an open fraud. According to P. L. Kealy, a former computer-programmer at Pine Gap:

What the Americans did was to make a huge list of all personnel at the base, including those in the unclassified area outside perimeters, who included housemaids for the motel units, cooks, gardeners. This allowed the Americans to satisfy the 50–50 relationship admirably, but leaving almost entirely all Americans in the Top Secret sector. [Pine Gap] is not a place where Australians can feel comfortable.[31]

The base at Nurrungar is even more secret. Opened in 1971 in an area of extreme isolation, its twin radomes have been seen by few outsiders. To my knowledge, only one press photograph exists of Nurrungar, and that is dominated by a sign offering trespassers seven years in prison. Nurrungar is linked to a ground station in Colorado. The two bases are part of the US 'Defense Support Program', which was set up to detect a Soviet attack on the United States and to contribute to nuclear war fighting strategies.

On the northern coast of Western Australia is North West Cape base, renamed in 1966 the 'US Naval Communication Station Harold E. Holt' after the Prime Minister who went all the way with LBJ. As Desmond Ball has pointed out, the Australian Government made 'a conscious decision not to inform the Australian public or Parliament as to the whole truth regarding the nature of the North West Cape facility'. The announcement by Menzies in May 1962 that the base was to provide 'radio communications' for American and Allied shipping was a deception. He made no mention of the nuclear-missile-carrying Polaris submarines whose battle orders would be transmitted through the Australian base.[32] It was left to an American magazine, the *Reporter*, to charge that 'the Australian Government deceived the public' over a base that was 'a priority target in any nuclear war'.[33] With Prime Minister Holt beaming at his side, American Ambassador Ed Clark – a Texan crony of President Johnson – inaugurated the base with these words:

> Now our friendly Australian landlords haven't yet demanded their rent, but we Americans will always be good tenants. We want you to know we pay our bills promptly. Here then, Mr Prime Minister, I want to present you with one peppercorn payment. In full for the first year's rent. I thank y'all.[34]

During the first months of the new Labor Government, in spite of Whitlam's implied threat to the bases if the Americans 'try to screw us or bounce us', the bases probably were as safe as they had been under the conservatives. Whitlam wanted to reform the alliance with the United States, not destroy it. On the second day of the new Parliament, Labor's Minister of Defence, Lance Barnard, seemed to go out of his way to reassure Washington. 'Although we are going to make changes [to the bases agreements]', he said, 'we are not making a fresh start . . . there is no doubt in our minds that the data being analysed and tested in the stations must be kept highly secret if the two installations are to continue to serve their objectives.'[35] In March 1973 Whitlam himself said, incredibly to some ears, that he would not reveal any of the secrets of Pine Gap or Nurrungar 'because they are not our secrets. [They are] other peoples' secrets.'[36]

Whitlam's tolerance of 'other peoples' secrets' was soon to be put to the test. Leaked Australian Defence Department documents disclosed that in 1972 high-frequency transmitters at North West Cape had helped the United States to mine Haiphong and other North Vietnamese harbours; and that satellites controlled from Pine Gap and Nurrungar were being used to pinpoint targets for the American bombing of Cambodia[37] – a bombing so intense that during one six-month period in 1973 American B52s dropped more bombs on the populated heartland of Cambodia than were dropped on Japan during the Second World War, the equivalent, in tons of bombs, of five Hiroshimas.[38] Both these actions were undertaken by the United States without the consent or knowledge of the Australian Government.

Then in October 1973, during the Middle East War, President Nixon put US forces on nuclear 'Level Three alert', through the base at North West Cape. When Whitlam found out, he was furious and said that the Third World War could have begun in Australia without the Government knowing. Australians had become involved in a war whose battlefield was half a world away. This of course was not unusual; the new dimension was the potential nature of this war. Shortly afterwards the US Defense Secretary, James Schlesinger, gave secret testimony to a Congressional committee that bases such as North West Cape would be 'the most likely targets' in a nuclear war.[39] On April 4, 1974 Whitlam told Parliament, 'The Australian government takes the attitude that there should not be foreign military bases, stations, installations in Australia. We honour agreements covering existing stations ... *but there will not be extensions or proliferations.*' (Emphasis added.) For Washington further proof of the 'instability' of the Australian Government was hardly needed. Yet further proof would be forthcoming.

Within six months of Whitlam's election a new American Ambassador was appointed to Australia. In marked contrast to his predecessors, Marshall Green was the most senior American career diplomat ever sent to Australia. Green was a top-level US policy planner for south-east Asia. He also had the distinction of having been involved in four countries where there had been *coups*, and he was known widely as 'the *coup*master'. A courtly, cultivated man, Green protested that he was nothing of the kind. However, as Ambassador to Indonesia from 1965 to 1969, Green had contributed to the decisive part the United States played in the events that led to the massacre of between 500,000 and a million Indonesian 'communists' and the overthrow of President Sukarno. Soon after he arrived in Australia to take up his post, Green was asked about this. He said, 'In 1965 I remember Indonesia was poised on the razor's edge. I remember people arguing from here that Indonesia wouldn't go communist. But when Sukarno announced in his August 17 speech that Indonesia would have a communist government within a year, then I was almost certain ... *what we did we had to do.*'[40] (Emphasis added.)

A senior Minister in the Whitlam Government, Clyde Cameron, reported a visit by Green to his office during which Green threatened that if the Labor Government handed control and ownership of US multi-national subsidiaries to the Australian people 'we would move in'.[41] When I met Green in Washington in 1987 I reminded him of his threat. He said he had been speaking in a 'half-humorous way' and that his words had been given 'the wrong implication'.

'Well, what did you say?' I asked.

'I said, "Well, you know in the old days, the Americans would probably send in the Marines. We don't do things like that any more." Just to be funny, I accompanied it with a laugh.'[42]

Another Whitlam Minister, Kep Enderby, who is now a judge, told a similar story about Green. In early 1974 Green addressed the Australian Institute of Directors. The following day Enderby received a call from a member of the Institute 'in a state of alarm'. He reported that the Ambassador's speech had amounted almost to 'an incitement to rise against the Australian Government' and that Green had gone on to say that Australian business leaders 'could expect help from the United States', which would be similar to the help 'given to South America'. (The CIA-orchestrated overthrow of Allende in Chile had happened only a few months earlier.) Marshall Green, now retired, returned to Australia in February 1985. At a reception at the American Consulate in Sydney, Judge Enderby confronted Green with the allegation of his 'incitement'. Green laughed and said he could not recall the speech.[43]

In April 1974 Labor was re-elected with a slightly reduced majority in the House of Representatives, with the balance held by two independents. Two months later Dr Jim Cairns was elected Deputy Prime Minister by his parliamentary colleagues. Cairns was the leader of Labor's left wing. He had been a highly effective opponent of the American war in Vietnam and believed in Australia's total independence from Super Power politics. Whitlam described 'American terror' at the thought that Cairns would have to be briefed on Pine Gap and the other 'joint facilities'; and although Cairns never asked to be briefed, the possibility was always there, in the words of one staff member, 'like some ulcer that could erupt any day'. For the Americans, the unthinkable was that Cairns might end up running the country.

The discrediting of Cairns became urgent. ASIO's leak of its 'Cairns file' to the *Bulletin* magazine in June 1974 was almost certainly timed to coincide with Cairns's election as Deputy Prime Minister. The headline read: 'CAIRNS:

ASIO'S STARTLING DOSSIER'.[44] But abuse of a popular man with an unblemished record is too crude. A few weeks later ASIO tried again, with a second file passed to journalist Peter Samuels, who frequently publishes CIA and other intelligence 'leaks'. Under the headline, 'The Pathway to Terrorism', Samuels wrote that ASIO's prime concern about Cairns was the 'terrorist' potential of his part in the anti-war movement.[45]

In the wake of the Middle East War the cost of energy rose as never before and the Australian economy fell into extreme difficulties. By the end of 1974 inflation and the money supply were rising at an alarming rate. The Whitlam Government, however, remained determined to honour one of its main election promises and to 'buy back the farm' – that is, to reclaim national ownership of minerals, oil refineries, the motor car and other industries which had been sold to mostly American transnational interests. In the 1970s a source of funds for a number of Western countries was the Arab world, which then had more petro-dollars than it knew what to do with, as well as potential investors wanting to diversify their new-found wealth. Whitlam instructed two of his Ministers to scour the Middle East for what would have been the largest loan in history: $A4 billion (later to be reduced to $A2 billion).

Enter Tirath Khemlani, a Pakistani 'commodities merchant' who, with others, succeeded in preparing a government for destruction.

When Khemlani met the Minister for Minerals and Energy, Rex Connor, in November 1974, he was working for the London brokers, Dalamal & Sons. Connor asked the London bullion firm, Johnson Matthey, for an opinion of Dalamal & Sons; he received an effusive reference and so saw no reason to doubt Khemlani. But there was every reason. He was a bankrupt; he had spent most of his career as a carpetbagger without an office or a telex machine; he consorted with criminals and was an arms dealer.

Khemlani was a con man, who had been sent to approach Connor by a Hong Kong arms firm closely associated with

Commerce International, a Brussels-based armaments company with widespread links with the CIA. Commerce International was set up as a front for Task Force 157, an intelligence-gathering arm of the US navy which had evolved into a highly secretive CIA covert action or 'dirty tricks' organisation.[46] *National Times* journalist Marian Wilkinson, who had established Commerce International's role as a CIA arms dealer, was told that if she continued her enquiries into the company she could end up having her head blown off.[47]

In March 1975, Jim Cairns, who was Federal Treasurer as well as Deputy Prime Minister, was introduced to a Melbourne businessman, George Harris, who had close connections in the Melbourne establishment; Sir Robert Menzies, no less, reportedly regarded him 'as a son'. Harris, a dentist by profession, had a reputation as a property developer. According to Cairns, Harris told him that a $A4 billion loan was available 'with a once-only brokerage fee of 2·5 per cent'. Harris showed Cairns a letter confirming the offer. The letter had come from the New York office of Commerce International. An intermediary between Cairns and Harris, Leslie Nagy, was also at the meeting. He later made a sworn statement that Cairns had described the terms as 'unbelievable' and the letter as a 'fairy-tale' and had rejected the deal.[48]

However, Cairns had agreed to give Harris two letters which said that the Government was interested in raising a loan, although otherwise he made no commitment. When they left the Minister's office, according to Nagy, Harris said, 'Let's get out of here,' and produced, to Nagy's surprise, a letter signed by Cairns, agreeing to the 'brokerage fee' of 2·5 per cent. Why and when did Cairns change his mind? Or more to the point: *did* he change his mind? Did he sign a number of letters without checking them, as Ministers often do? Or was there another explanation? Harris denied setting Cairns up. However, Cairns has steadfastly maintained he never agreed to or put his name to such an outrageous and incriminating letter.

Two months later Harris was seen with Phillip Lynch, Deputy Leader of the opposition Liberal Party. When Lynch raised the question of the brokerage fee in Parliament, Cairns denied any agreement existed. Within days, a letter with Cairns's signature was reproduced on the front pages of the nation's newspapers, and Cairns was forced to resign from the Ministry for 'misleading Parliament'. Neither Harris nor Khemlani raised a cent of the loan. The effect of their actions was to produce the kind of 'scandal' and relentless publicity that consumed the Whitlam Government.

For those who doubted that the CIA stood in the shadows, a side show offered further evidence. In July 1975 the Australian media reported that the Mercantile Bank and Trust Company, based in the Bahamas, had issued a letter seeking $US4,267,365,000 'for and on behalf of the Government of Australia'. The bank did not claim to be acting with the approval of the Australian Government; in Canberra Cabinet Ministers had never heard of it. But the implication was enough to fill newspapers with yet another 'scandal'. Moreover, the bank no one seemed to have heard of added on a figure of $US267 million as its 'proposed profit' from a deal no one had sought.[49]

Mercantile Bank and Trust was set up and owned by Colonel Paul Helliwell, who had worked for the CIA's predecessor, the OSS. Helliwell had been the CIA's paymaster for its abortive invasion of Cuba in 1961. He built up a network of banks, including the infamous Castle Bank, which collapsed after American tax investigators found it was 'laundering' millions of dollars for the Mafia. When US Justice Department officers moved to prosecute, they were warned off by the CIA; laying open the affairs of the bank, it was said, would 'endanger national security'.[50]

On July 3, 1975 the *National Intelligence Daily*, a top-secret CIA briefing document for the President, reported that Jim Cairns had been sacked 'even though some of the evidence had been fabricated'.[51] Much later an ASIO officer speculated publicly that 'some of the documents which helped discredit the Labor Government in its last year in office were forgeries planted by the CIA'.[52]

As the loans affair reached its climax in the spring of 1975, a 'blizzard' of documents, including copies of telexes, descended upon the Australian media from as far afield as the United States. Whitlam himself received a copy of a message found in an Hawaii hotel room. Handwritten, it was said to be the draft of a telex message sent to Malcolm Fraser, Leader of the Opposition. It gave detail of the 'chaos' which Khemlani was being 'funded' to cause, in an effort to bring about the 'capitulation' of the Government. The message included the instruction that it should be coded before transmission, by calling a Honolulu phone number. Brian Toohey called the number. It was the Hawaiian headquarters of the CIA.[53] Was this a forgery and more of the 'disinformation' so prevalent then? Quite likely, but it is impossible to know.

The height of farce was reached when Khemlani himself arrived in Australia weighed under by two bags bulging with more 'copies of telex messages' and more 'incriminating documentation'. He was accompanied by bodyguards provided by the Opposition parties, and all his expenses were paid. He made outrageous claims in the media: Labor Ministers were to receive commissions and 'kickbacks' from the loans; documents proving corruption were soon to be made public, and so on. None of his documents added up to or proved anything. Not a penny was paid by anyone to the Government, nor did any member of the Government profit from the affair.

In 1981 a CIA 'contract employee', Joseph Flynn, claimed he had forged some of the loans affair cables and had 'bugged' a hotel room where Gough Whitlam was staying. He said he had been paid by one Michael Hand, co-founder of the Nugan Hand Bank.[54]

In its short life, the Nugan Hand Bank was associated with serious crime on an international scale and with CIA 'covert' activities in Australia and around the world. It 'laundered' money and dealt in arms, drugs and blackmail. In so doing, it helped to undermine the political opponents of the United States.

Michael Hand was a former 'Green Beret' in the US Special Forces in Vietnam. He was assigned to Operation Phoenix, whose assassination and terror squads were responsible for the deaths of between 30,000 and 50,000 civilians. According to an American admiral who later became President of the Nugan Hand Bank, Hand was 'such a strong believer in the Christian Science religion that he did not smoke or even drink coffee [and] had a great love for children'.[55]

Hand settled in Sydney in the late 1960s after his discharge from the army. Sydney then was the most popular 'R & R' (rest and recreation) centre for American troops serving in Vietnam. One of Hand's closest friends was Bernie Houghton, a US Naval Intelligence officer who worked closely with the CIA. Houghton ran three night clubs in Sydney popular with GIs – the Texas Tavern, the Bourbon and Beefsteak and Harpoon Harry's. A large, expansive man, seldom without a bodyguard on either side, Houghton had a network which included John Walker, the CIA Station Chief in Canberra, senior ASIO officers and CIA agent Edwin Wilson, who worked with 'Task Force 157' (and who is today serving forty years in an American prison for 'freelance' arms dealing with Libya).

Frank Nugan was a Sydney businessman/spiv whose family ran a fruit-packing business near Griffith in southern New South Wales, a district famous for its marijuana crops and gang murders. Nugan and Hand set up their bank with the dubious claim of paid-up capital of a million dollars, which Nugan said he had acquired by trading in mineral shares. Bernie Houghton became the third partner.

It was not long before the bank was opening branches around the world, and in exotic places, such as Chiang Mai in Thailand, the centre of the 'Golden Triangle' drug trade. The former Nugan Hand manager in Chiang Mai, Neil Evans, later reported that he had seen millions of dollars smuggled through the branch, all of it 'CIA money'. He said that Michael Hand had told him that 'he'd been successful in arranging a contract with the CIA whereby the bank was to become its paymaster, for disimbursement of funds anywhere in the world on behalf of the CIA and also for the taking of money on behalf of the CIA'. Evans said he resigned because 'the CIA are the heaviest people on this earth'.[56]

One of Nugan Hand's distinctions was that its managers

had virtually no experience in banking. But they did have considerable expertise in other fields, and were described as 'of a calibre and number to run a small sized war'.[57] They included US Air Force General LeRoy Manor, Chief of Staff of the US Pacific Command and a specialist in counter-insurgency; army General Edwin Black, the Commander of US forces in Thailand; Rear-Admiral Earl Yates, former Chief of Staff for Policy and Plans of the US Pacific Command; and Patry Loomis, a CIA officer who helped Edwin Wilson recruit a team of Green Berets to train Libyans. There were numerous others who, in one guise or another, had worked for and were still working for the CIA. Notable among these was William Colby, who until 1976 had been Director of the CIA and previously had set up the CIA's Operation Phoenix pro-gramme of political assassinations in Vietnam.

'This thing is so big, it's bigger than you can imagine,' a former Nugan Hand executive told the Washington investi-gator, Nancy Grodin. The links between international crime and the intelligence services are, of course, not new. In its assault on Castro's Cuba, the CIA used Cuban exiles organ-ised by the Mafia. Nugan Hand's influence extended well beyond a hive of crooks. It was, in intelligence jargon, a 'conduit': an influence felt by Australian politicians, trade union officials and journalists, some of whom were unaware of the source of favours and of disinformation.

Former Nugan Hand principal Karl Schuller provided evi-dence that the CIA transferred a 'slush fund' of $A2,400,000 to the opposition parties in March 1973, four months after Whitlam's election. Schuller made this admission to South Australian Corporate Affairs investigating officers who were convinced he was telling the truth. Former CIA officer Victor Marchetti confirmed that the CIA had funded both opposition parties.[58] Schuller pointed the investigators to documented sources; but none could be found. This was not surprising, as thousands of documents were destroyed following the mys-terious 'suicide' of Frank Nugan himself.

At four o'clock in the morning of January 27, 1980, a police patrol car stopped beside a white Mercedes on the roadside near Lithgow, in western New South Wales. The body of Frank Nugan was slumped across the front seat with a bullet hole in the head. In his hands was a rifle he had bought two weeks earlier. The police took no photographs of the body or the car, nor were the gun and its magazine kept for fingerprints. The policeman who made the discovery determined that suicide was the cause of death and the coroner agreed. The business card of William Colby, the former head of the CIA, was found on the body. The Nugan Hand bank collapsed soon afterwards.

When Federal investigators examined the bank's offices in Sydney they found most of the company's books missing. At the time of Nugan's death 194 companies were banking with Nugan Hand, but no person or companies came forward with claims on the $US50 million owed by the bank. The bank's principals went into hiding. In response to Freedom of Information Act requests in Washington, the FBI released less than half of a 119-page file on the bank. Most of the pages were blacked out 'in the interests of national defence or foreign policy'.[59]

In 1982 the CIA issued an unprecedented statement prior to a visit to Australia by Vice-President George Bush, who had been CIA Director following Colby's retirement. 'The CIA has not engaged in operations against the Australian Government,' said the statement. '[The CIA] has no ties with Nugan Hand . . .'[60] This was not the conclusion drawn from an investigation by a special New South Wales police task force and the New South Wales Corporate Affairs Commission. In calling for criminal charges for 'drug, conspiracy, perjury and passport offences', the Commission's cautious report said that:

many links were found between individuals connected with [Nugan Hand] and individuals connected in very significant ways with US intelligence organisations, specifically the Central Intelligence Agency and the

Office of Naval Intelligence [Task Force 157] ... at times those links appear to have been an intrinsic part of the then ongoing activity and have the appearance of the direct involvement of the US intelligence community itself.[61]

One year after Frank Nugan's death, the Deputy Director of the CIA, Admiral Bobby Inman, was asked about the collapse of the Nugan Hand empire. He expressed deep concern that investigation of Nugan Hand would lead to disclosure of a range of 'dirty tricks' calculated to undermine the Whitlam Government.[62]

As the Watergate scandal spread during 1974, so did news of the part played by the Nixon administration and the CIA in the destruction of the Allende Government in Chile the previous year. On the first anniversary of Allende's murder, Gough Whitlam addressed the United Nations General Assembly. He warned against moves by states to bring about political or economic change in other countries by 'unconstitutional, clandestine, corrupt methods, by assassination or terrorism'.

Three months after Whitlam's speech, Christopher Boyce, the twenty-one-year-old son of a former FBI officer, was given a special job by TRW Incorporated, a Californian aerospace company where he worked as a cipher clerk. TRW is an important CIA contractor, and Boyce was to work in the black vault, the code room where top-secret messages were received and deciphered from American bases and satellites all over the world, including Pine Gap. Only eight people had clearance to enter the specially built vault, 'cocooned on three sides by special penetration-proof layers of concrete and on the fourth by a thick Mosler Safe door'. Here they received the CIA's 'deepest' background briefing, a process actually called 'indoctrination'.[63]

Shortly afterwards Boyce and a close friend, Andrew Daulton Lee, were discussing Watergate and the military *coup* in Chile. When Lee deplored the CIA role in Chile, he was told by Boyce, 'You think that's bad? You should hear what the CIA is doing to the Australians.'[64] This and a great deal more emerged in 1977 at the trial of Christopher Boyce who, with Lee, was convicted of passing secrets to the Soviet Union. Boyce's defence was that he opposed American foreign policy not only in Chile, but also in Australia, and that he had been blackmailed by Lee, a heroin addict and pusher.

Boyce was a young Christian idealist who almost certainly would not have got his sensitive job had his FBI father not vouched for him. In agreeing, as he said in his evidence, simply to circulate 'a statement concerning what I believed to be violations of law perpetuated [sic] against the Australians', Boyce had cast himself in the role of a dissident hero who would serve his country by exposing the illegalities of the CIA's Australian campaign, just as the Pentagon Papers had exposed the corruption of the United States' role in Vietnam.

Boyce maintained he had never intended the information about Australia to go to the Russians, that Lee had agreed to make it public through one of his father's influential friends in a way that would not immediately implicate Boyce. What-ever the truth of that, Lee flew to Mexico City, went to the Soviet Embassy and sold the document to the Russians, nam-ing Boyce as the source. The market value of national defence secrets is not something that is published in the *Wall Street Journal* and is subject to many unknown variables, but the Boyce case can be compared with that of a CIA officer found guilty of selling a top-secret manual about a spy satellite, a transaction described by the CIA as having 'seriously harmed' America's national security. For this the KGB paid $US76,000.[65]

In his evidence Boyce said that, during the briefing for his job in the black vault, he was told that most of the communi-cations would be coming from Pine Gap, and that although the United States had signed an Executive Agreement with Australia to share information from Pine Gap, the agreement was not being honoured and 'certain information' was to be concealed from Australia. He described the 'daily deception of an ally' and said that Pine Gap was being used to 'monitor' international telephone calls and telex messages to and from Australia of a political character. He said the CIA had campaigned to subvert Australian trade unions 'particularly in the transport industry' and had funded the opposition political parties. Later, in an interview for Australian television, Boyce said that Whitlam, 'by wanting to know what was going on [at Pine Gap] and publicising it, compromised the integrity of the project and made his Government "a threat"'.[66]

Boyce's disclosures caused a sensation in the United States. The prosecuting lawyers made no attempt to refute his allegations and successfully objected to any further evidence about Australia. Boyce's lawyer said that the judge had complied with a direct CIA request, and agreed that his client would not mention the 'Australia information' at his trial if, in return, the Government did not use it against him – such was its sensitivity. The *New York Times* report of the trial said that these machinations and Boyce's behaviour had convinced many observers in the courtroom that Boyce was telling the truth.

This view was reinforced when both Boyce and Lee were found guilty and Lee was given a life sentence and Boyce was sent for 'psychiatric observation' – indicating that he might be treated leniently. However, Boyce had made it consistently clear that he was so outraged at the 'betrayal' of Australia that he intended to talk. He was subsequently given forty years in Marion Federal Penitentiary in Illinois, the 'Alcatraz of the 1980s', where, with other 'unredeemable criminals', such as rapists and multiple murderers, he is kept in solitary confinement. Whenever he leaves his cell, he is manacled, handcuffed and accompanied by two guards. It is said that his only hope of freedom rests on his continued silence about what happened in Australia.

In an interview he gave to Australian journalist William Pinwill, Boyce made special mention of one name. He said, 'There were references to your Governor-General by the Central Intelligence [Agency] residents there at TRW,' and that once in the black vault Joe Harrison (the CIA chief) referred to Sir John Kerr as 'our man Kerr'.[67]

John Kerr, the son of a boilermaker, grew up in working-class Balmain, on Sydney's dockland, in the 1920s. Almost everything Kerr pursued in his career denied his roots: from his passion for imperial pomp and ritual to his conspicuous consumption of Laurent-Perrier vintage champagne. In his black top hat and 'Ruritanian flak jacket', Sir John Kerr, Knight Grand Cross of the Order of St Michael and St George, Grand Cross of the Royal Victorian Order, Knight of the Order of Australia, Knight of the Most Venerable Order of the Hospital of St John of Jerusalem and so on, rivalled Menzies as the embodiment of imperium in Australia.

After studying law, Kerr began his long association with political and military intelligence as a member of the top-secret 'Directorate of Research and Civil Affairs', whose job was to counter 'enemy elements' in Australia during the Second World War. He was sent to Washington, where he was seconded briefly to the Office of Strategic Services, the OSS, which became the CIA. After the war he continued his service in intelligence with the Government's School of Civil Affairs, where he helped to establish a national police force for New Guinea.

Although he joined the Australian Labor Party early in his career, Kerr has always been a conservative: a monarchist, an Anglocentric and a vigorous defender of the extreme right in the Australian labour movement in the 1950s. He was chief legal adviser to what became known as the 'Industrial Groups', which sought to dominate trade unionism and were linked to the Democratic Labor Party. The DLP was an extreme 'anti-communist' organisation whose split from the Labor Party and subsequent spoiler tactics kept Labor in opposition until Whitlam's election in 1972.

Kerr was an enthusiastic member of the Australian Association for Cultural Freedom, described by Jonathan Kwitny, in his book *The Crimes of Patriots*, as 'an elite, invitation-only group . . . which in 1967 was exposed in Congress as being founded, funded and generally run by the CIA'.[68] In researching his book, Kwitny, a senior journalist with the conservative *Wall Street Journal*, had unusual access to Kerr. He spoke twice to him, once to check the accuracy of what he had written about him. Kwitny wrote:

> In the 1960s Kerr helped organise and run (as founding President) the Law Association for Asia and the Western Pacific. He travelled to the United States to arrange financing for this body from a tax-free group known as the Asia Foundation; that, too, was exposed in Congress as a CIA-established conduit for money and influence. In fact, Victor Marchetti, the retired CIA officer says in his book with former Foreign Service Officer John Marks, that the 'Asia Foundation often served as a cover for clandestine operations', though 'its main purpose was to promote the spread of ideas which were anti-communist and pro-American'.[69]

'The CIA', Kwitny concluded, 'paid for Kerr's travel, built his prestige and even published his writings, through a subsidised magazine . . . Kerr continued to go to the CIA for money.'[70]

All this was on the record when in February 1974 Prime Minister Whitlam selected Kerr to succeed Sir Paul Hasluck as Governor-General of Australia. The Governor-General is, or ought to be, a living anachronism. He (never a she) represents the nominal Head of State, the English monarch, who is also 'King or Queen of Australia'. He is not elected; the job was once a sinecure, mostly for lesser breeds of the English aristocracy, and the duties are ceremonial; or so the Australian people believed.

Certainly Whitlam believed it. According to Richard Hall, Kerr's biographer, Whitlam saw Kerr's appointment as appeasing 'those who wanted a titled Governor-General and would accord with Labor principles against creating knighthoods'. Whitlam also believed Kerr had 'a good presence' for representing Australia overseas and 'as a lawyer, Kerr would be aware of the development of Constitutional Law and the principles of responsible government'.[71]

For a man who supposedly understood the nature of the forces ranged against a reformist Labor Government, Whitlam's naïveté in appointing Kerr was astonishing. Kerr's associations with the far right, with intelligence operations and the CIA were not at issue when the appointment was announced. I remember reading much about Kerr's membership of the Labor Party and his rise from 'battling poverty'. A friend of his was quoted as describing the future Governor-General as a 'pre-war Socialist'. The press made few enquiries of its own, reflecting both an idleness and general uninterest in the 'anachronism'.

Indeed, when Kerr was sworn in, he attracted headlines with his announcement that women were no longer required to curtsy to him. Like so much about the man, even this was not as it seemed. Those fortunate enough to be presented to the vice-regal personage were given the impression that they *should* curtsy. None the less, the women's section of the Sydney *Daily Mirror* gave him the 'yum' award for this vital reform.

Kerr occupied a world unimagined by his fellow Australians – 'a formidable little principality'. The Governor-General's Canberra residence, 'Yarralumla', was a sixty-room mansion surrounded by more than 130 lush acres. There were fifty staff, of whom thirty were classed as domestic servants. There was a Sydney residence, known as Admiralty House, set in three splendid acres overlooking the harbour. And there were twelve Rolls-Royces awaiting him throughout Australia.[72]

Among the guests at the vice-regal table were often those from the 'defence and intelligence community', who were deeply hostile to the Government. According to Richard Hall, Kerr 'ensured that the names of intelligence personnel were not included in the vice-regal guest lists'. He also 'asked for and was given codeword material, and once sought a special briefing from ASIO on Communism in Australia'.[73] In addition, he received briefings on 'international affairs' from the United States Ambassador, Marshall Green.[74] With this special access Kerr would have had an insider's knowledge of matters which were to dominate Australian national life during 1975: the 'loans affair', the 'supply crisis' and a succession of controversies involving the Australian intelligence organisations and the CIA.

On October 14, 1975 the loans affair appeared to be reaching its climax when Whitlam forced a second Minister to resign. Like Jim Cairns before him, Rex Connor, the Minister for Minerals and Energy, was accused of misleading Parliament. Connor had maintained contact with Khemlani after Khemlani's authority to negotiate a loan had been withdrawn. In his own defence Connor argued that only a massive overseas loan would give the Government the funds with which to resume control of Australia's vital industries. He continued to believe Khemlani could raise such a loan without the controls demanded by the International Monetary Fund. His ideals and judgment were poorly matched.

Connor's sacking had a disastrous effect on the Government's rating in the opinion polls. Malcolm Fraser called it a 'reprehensible circumstance' and made his move. The next day the Opposition used its slender Senate majority to defer a vote on the Budget Appropriation Bills, thus blocking money supply indefinitely. The clear implication was that when the money ran out essential public services would cease to function. In its seventy-four years, the Senate had never used its power in this way.

Fraser warned that the bills would not be passed until Whitlam had agreed to an early election – in spite of the fact that the Whitlam Government had won two elections in less than three years. Six of Australia's leading professors of law declared publicly the manoeuvre to be 'constitutionally improper'. Within two weeks the opinion polls showed a dramatic change; 70 per cent of the public disapproved of the Opposition tactic and substantial support was returned to the beleaguered Government. Why did the conservatives attempt such high-risk action when it was plain that all they had to do was wait for the Government to fall apart under the strain of the loans affair and an election within six months might well have seen them in power?

Six months was too long to wait; notice of the renewal of the Pine Gap treaty, which would determine the future of the CIA's most valuable overseas base, was due in less than two months, on December 9. Moreover, the uncertain future of the bases, and the 'instability' of the Australian Government, now obsessed the CIA. William Colby, the CIA Director, later wrote that the 'threat' posed by the Whitlam Government was one of the three 'world crises' of his career, comparable with the Middle East War in 1973, when the United States considered using nuclear weapons.

After Whitlam had threatened in private and in Parliament not to extend the lease of the bases, the CIA made a series of direct moves to get rid of him: that is, to persuade others with shared, vested interests to do the job. The information for this comes from the highest sources in US intelligence: up to the level of a former Deputy Director of the CIA, as well as Regional Director and Station Chief. They are not renegade officers. They agreed to speak only after being given guarantees of confidentiality, and they have provided detailed briefings on what happened to the Whitlam Government, why it happened and how it happened.[75]

During 1974 the CIA Station Chief in London, Dr John Proctor, got in touch with the British security organisation, MI6, and asked for help with 'the Whitlam problem'. Proctor was close to the British and had been Director of Strategic Research for the CIA. His speciality was satellites and, according to one source, 'he had a unique understanding of what could be lost if Pine Gap was shut down'. In early 1975 William Colby himself directly approached his opposite number, the head of MI6, Sir Maurice Oldfield. Later the CIA sought assistance from MI5 and MI6 liaison officers based in Washington. In all these contacts the CIA emphasised to the British that 'if this intelligence capability was lost, then the Alliance would be in danger ... the Alliance would be blinded strategically'. Australia, it was argued, was 'traditionally Britain's domain'.

British intelligence had a vested interest in the concern expressed by Washington. MI6 operates its own base at Kowandi, south of Darwin, where its highly secret activities are concealed from the Australian Government and people. They include widespread intervention in other people's communications and covert operations in Asia.[76] The Australian Secret Intelligence Service, ASIS, also operates from this base, and is so integrated with MI6 that London is still referred to as 'head office'.[77] In approaching MI6 about Whitlam, the Americans wanted to invoke the British/Australian old-boy network. Between 1974 and 1975 the number of calls from British intelligence to ASIS almost doubled.[78]

At the same time the infamous Peter Wright and his colleagues in British intelligence were busy destabilising the Labour Government of Harold Wilson. Wright was a close friend of James Jesus Angleton, the head of CIA counter-intelligence, and by all accounts a figure of fanatical tendencies. Between them, according to British journalist David Leigh, author of *The Wilson Plot*, Wright and Angleton 'targeted' three Western leaders they regarded as 'communist agents': Wilson, Whitlam and Willy Brandt in Germany. Leigh says the proof of a plot against Whitlam is in 'unpublished correspondence by Peter Wright either to other intelligence officers or that which he never thought would see the light of day'. Wright was personally bitter about Whitlam who, in removing the head of ASIO, Peter Barbour, had dashed Wright's plan to move to Australia as a 'counter-espionage consultant' with Barbour's approval. Wright's letters, says Leigh, 'show him conspiring with Angleton [who was] directly involved in the pursuit of Whitlam'.[79]

In the latter part of 1975 Whitlam began to grasp the precise nature of what was being done to him. He discovered that British intelligence had long been operating against his Government. 'The Brits were actually decoding secret messages coming into the Foreign Affairs office,' he said later, '. . . the reason they make such an assault on me is that they hope I will crack.'[80] Having already removed the heads of both ASIO and ASIS, Whitlam was now moving against the CIA. When he heard that a CIA officer, Richard Stallings, was a friend of the National Country Party leader, Doug Anthony, and had rented Anthony's Canberra home, Whitlam called for a list of all 'declared' CIA officers who had served in Australia during the previous ten years. Stallings's name was not on the list. He then learned that another, 'confidential' list of CIA officers was held by the Permanent Head of the Australian Defence Department, Sir Arthur Tange. He demanded to see this list and found Stallings's name on it.

Tange, a conservative 'mandarin', effectively ran Australian intelligence and was its principal contact with the CIA and MI6. He was enraged by Whitlam's outspokenness. On November 2, 1975 Whitlam accused the Opposition of being 'subsidised by the CIA'.[81] In Parliament Doug Anthony confirmed that Stallings was his friend and challenged Whitlam to provide evidence that Stallings belonged to the CIA. Whitlam prepared a reply which he intended to give when Parliament resumed on the following Tuesday, November 11. Tange was now frantic. Not only was the Prime Minister about to 'blow' the cover of the man who had set up Pine Gap, proving that the 'joint facility' was a CIA charade, but the future of the base itself was to be subjected to parliamentary debate.

On November 10 Whitlam was told that the acting Director of ASIO, Frank Mahoney (who had been appointed by Whitlam himself) had received a telex message from the ASIO station in Washington which required urgent attention. 'What's it about?' Whitlam asked a member of his staff. 'It's about you,' was the reply. The message said, in effect, that the Prime Minister of Australia was a security risk in his own country.[82]

The message had been virtually dictated by Theodore Shackley, head of the CIA's East Asia Division. Shackley is one of the most controversial figures the CIA has spawned. He made his name in 'covert action', first as head of the CIA's Miami-based operation against Castro, then as CIA Station Chief in Laos and Vietnam. He worked on the CIA campaign in Chile at the time of Allende, and since leaving the CIA he has been involved in Central America.

Shackley's message to ASIO bordered on the hysterical. He berated Whitlam for suggesting the CIA funded the Opposition, for threatening to name agents and, above all, for wanting to 'blow the lid off those installations in Australia, where the persons concerned [Stallings and other CIA officers] have been working and which are vital to both of our services and countries, particularly [Pine Gap]'. Shackley described his threat as 'an official *de'marche* on a service-to-service link', which meant that it was to bypass the Government and that ASIO was to continue to lie to Whitlam about the bases, and to pressure the Government into accepting CIA demands. If this was not done, Shackley threatened, the 'sharing' of secrets would be broken off. Brian Toohey, who first published the message, later met Shackley. He gained the clear impression that the threats had had the full authority of the Secretary of State, Henry Kissinger.[83]

According to the former Deputy Director of Intelligence for the CIA, Dr Ray Cline, the CIA passed information to Opposition politicians not only to discredit the Whitlam Government but also to put pressure on Australian civil servants, who in turn 'would have been pressuring the Governor-General'.[84] Another senior CIA source, who cannot be named, was more explicit. On the weekend of November 8–9, a top civil servant was directly in touch with Sir John Kerr to pass on the CIA's demands, as spelt out in the Shackley message.

Kerr's denials are interesting. 'I have never had any direct or indirect association with the CIA or with any British intelligence organisation,' he has said. 'In fact, I have never during my Governor-Generalship, or at all, had any intelligence contacts whatsoever.' He has also denied specifically having any contact with Australian intelligence. 'I didn't seek to know them,' he has said.[85] These are remarkable statements.

Kerr's intelligence career and his association with the CIA are matters of record. There is also the matter of his documented whereabouts on Sunday, November 9. On that day

Kerr travelled to the ultra-secret headquarters near Melbourne of Australia's most important spy organisation, the Defence Signals Directorate, DSD, where he was briefed on the 'security crisis'. He then asked for a telephone and spent twenty minutes in hushed conversation. According to the base's commanding officer, he demanded that the phone be 'secure'.[86] This fact alone represents an important discrepancy in the story of a man who not only denies having had 'any intelligence contacts whatsoever' but who emphasised that he 'didn't seek to know' Australian intelligence. Kerr has never explained this, or allowed himself to be subjected to public scrutiny on these or any other matters.

For the CIA, December 9 remained a critical date. The agency was certain Whitlam would announce the cancellation of the Pine Gap agreement on that day. If the conservative coalition was to be elected in time to 'protect the sanctity of the bases', an election would have to be held before the Christmas holiday period. And this would mean calling the election no later than the week of Remembrance Day, November 11.

If what was about to happen had not been planned, the indiscretions of one Andrew Peacock six weeks earlier would have amounted to an astonishing coincidence. Peacock, then a member of the Opposition and now its leader, was visiting Indonesia and briefed Government officials there on the current state of the Australian political crisis. He described in detail the events which were about to take the nation, and presumably himself and his conservative colleagues, by surprise. A record of the briefing was later read into Australian *Hansard*. This is an extract:

> Whitlam will not agree to hold an election ... the Governor-General would be forced to ask Malcolm Fraser to form a Cabinet. But this Cabinet would not be able to get a mandate to govern, because Parliament is controlled by the Labor Party ... Fraser is appointed

PM, a minute later he asks the Governor-General to dissolve Parliament, following which a general election is to be held.[87]

And that is what happened.

On November 11, the very day Whitlam was to inform Parliament fully about the CIA and American bases in Australia, he was summoned by Kerr from Parliament House and, without warning, sacked. Kerr's cunning was such that at the moment he was dismissing the Prime Minister, he had Malcolm Fraser hiding in another room. He had even seen to it that Fraser's official car was parked where Whitlam would not see it. With Whitlam off the premises, Fraser emerged and was made caretaker Prime Minister.

Whitlam did not return directly to Parliament, but went instead to The Lodge, his official residence, where over lunch he struggled to reconcile his shock and rising rage with the innate stoicism of one who believed, above all, in respect for the law and procedure – even though his dismissal was, at best, constitutionally dubious. Back on the floor of the House of Representatives he moved a motion 'that this House expresses its want of confidence in the Prime Minister and requests Mr Speaker forthwith to advise His Excellency the Governor-General to call on me to form a Government'. This vote of confidence in a twice-elected Prime Minister was approved by an overwhelming majority of the House of Representatives. Indeed, six motions proposed that day by the Government, including a motion censuring Malcolm Fraser, were passed by absolute majorities.

Parliament's clear message of confidence in the Whitlam Government was delivered personally to the Governor-General by the Speaker of the House. Kerr refused to accept it, although he did accept the Supply Bills, which were also passed *after* he had dismissed the Government. Thus, an unelected official made his arbitrary decision and the legitimate acts of a democracy amounted to nothing. In modern

Australia democracy had been usurped, said the Melbourne *Age*, by 'the right of Kings and Queens to unilaterally appoint Governments'.[88]

There are no Kings and Queens in Washington.

'The CIA's aim', said former CIA officer Victor Marchetti, 'was to get rid of a Government they did not like and that was not co-operative . . . it's a Chile, but in a much more sophisticated and subtle form'.[89] The sophistication and subtlety were described by the CIA's former Chief of Clandestine Services, Richard Bissell, in a secret speech. In this passage Bissell portrays the Agency's ideal foreign agents in 'destabilisation' operations:

> Covert intervention is usually designed to operate on the internal power balance . . . to achieve results within at most two or three years . . . The essence of such intervention is the identification of allies who can be rendered more effective, more powerful, and perhaps wiser through covert assistance. Typically these local allies know the source of the assistance but neither they nor the United States could afford to admit to its existence. Agents for fairly minor and low sensitivity interventions, for instance some covert propaganda and certain economic activities, can be recruited simply with money.
>
> But for the larger and more sensitive interventions, the allies must have their own motivation. On the whole the Agency has been remarkably successful in finding individuals and instrumentalities with which and through which it could work on this fashion.[90]

The Washington investigative journalist, Joseph Trento, interviewed former CIA officers who were among the Agency's 'top seven' in 1975. In an interview with the *Sydney Morning Herald* in 1988, he was quoted as saying,

Whitlam was set up. The action that Kerr took was so extreme that it would take far more than . . . a constitutional crisis to cause him to do what he did. There are other ways out. This is what I was told by a Deputy Director of the CIA. He told me, 'Kerr did what he was told to do.' [The Deputy Director] did not tell me – and I asked him – that Kerr worked for the CIA. He did not tell me that Kerr did any favours for the CIA, that there was any *quid pro quo*: simply that Kerr did what the British told him to do.[91]

Kerr – who died in 1991 – denied that anyone told him to act. The senior Government official who was directly in touch with Kerr – and 'directly in touch' was emphasised by the CIA source – was neither American nor British, but Australian. He was described by the CIA source as a man with whom he had regular contact, 'an honourable man'. He was the principal messenger, the 'conduit'. As the source cannot be named, neither unfortunately can the official.

During the first week of the *coup* the Australian army was recalled to barracks and there were reports that units were issued with live ammunition. Army brass insisted that their 'experts' ride in the engine cabs of trains in New South Wales 'to observe the condition of the tracks'. According to Whitlam, Kerr was prepared to call out the Army, of which, he had once boasted, he was the Commander in Chief.[92]

There were demonstrations throughout Australia; and people in working-class streets gathered through the hot night, as they had done on election night. Now the mood was incredulous and becoming embittered. 'Maintain your rage,' Whitlam had said on the steps of Parliament House that day. Many ordinary people, the losers, maintained it.

The unions began to mobilise and prepare for a general strike. But this required leadership, and there was none.

The President of the Australian Council of Trade Unions, Bob Hawke, summoned the press and delivered a stirring, almost tearful speech which effectively cancelled Whitlam's call to his supporters. Working people, said Hawke, 'must not be provoked . . . we have to show we are not going to allow this to snowball'.[93] Hawke's intervention was critical; an American reporter wrote that Australia 'is strangely quiet'.

An election was called for December 13. 'Whitlam and his colleagues', wrote Joan Coxsedge, Ken Coldicutt and Gerry Harant,

> had been deprived of the normal prerogative of a retiring Government of choosing the date and the issues for an election. The nature of their dismissal had placed them in the position of convicted criminals, lending credence to the continuing cries of scandal from anti-Labor forces. The former Government was even deprived of access to information that would otherwise have been available. For example, Treasury had revised its Budget forecasts, and believed that recovery would be under way in June . . . This would have allayed the fears of the middle class . . . In any event, it appeared as if the Labor leaders were dazed by the *coup* and were incapable of analysing how and why it occurred.[94]

During the election campaign three letter bombs were posted to Kerr, Fraser and the ultra-conservative Queensland Premier, Johannes Bjelke-Petersen. Most of the press, led by Rupert Murdoch's papers, concluded that the bombs were sent by left-wing extremists within the Labor Party. There was not a scrap of evidence to support this and no culprits were ever found. But the issue of 'terrorism' was used to effect by the Opposition.

This, and one final, bizarre episode, delivered the *coup de grace* to Whitlam's chances of re-election. Four days before the election, Bjelke-Petersen called a special session of the Queensland Parliament to hear 'dramatic revelations'. He claimed to be 'in possession of material' which made clear 'that two Ministers of the Whitlam Government . . . were due to receive staggering sums of money as a consequence of secret commissions and kickbacks'. At this, his Police Minister, Russ Hinze, interjected, 'Murphy [the former Attorney-General] will be a surfie by the time we're finished with him!'[95] Bjelke-Petersen moved quickly to gag any debate and to prevent the State Labor Opposition leader from calling before the bar of Parliament one Henry Wiley Fancher, the source of the 'revelations'. Fancher was an American rancher who had done foreign deals for the Queensland Government and had much in common with Bjelke-Petersen. He had settled in Queensland, he said, 'to avoid living near negroes'.[96]

The undisclosed 'revelations' made large headlines. No 'material' or evidence of any kind was ever produced. Whitlam lost the election.

Prime Minister Malcolm Fraser renewed the Pine Gap Treaty for another decade. He also offered Washington a naval base at Cockburn Sound, even though the Americans had not requested it. He began the mining of uranium, the 'strategic material' whose short supply in the United States had prompted a lawyer acting for Westinghouse Electric, a leading manufacturer of nuclear materials, to comment prophetically a few weeks earlier, 'If the Labor Government in Australia is kicked out within the next five weeks . . . we can get the uranium we thought we had.'[97] In his first budget, Fraser increased the size of ASIO and gave it more money, proportionately, than any other Government body. Kerr, too, was given an unequalled pay rise of 170 per cent and was promoted to 'Knight Grand Cross of the Order of St Michael and St George'.

Many people never forgave Kerr and saw to it that he

seldom had peace; they followed him and taunted him, almost until he died. He resented this, believing that he had not only preserved the friendship between the United States and Australia, but had saved the entire Western alliance. He drank heavily, and on one memorable occasion following Australia's principal horse race, the Melbourne Cup, he slurred abuse at a hostile crowd, his black top hat wobbling precariously on his snowy crown.

Inside his 'principality' in Canberra nothing changed; the booze was excise free, the fifty servants still awaited his word, as did the Royal Australian Air Force and the chauffeurs of his Rolls-Royces. One evening, when the Queen was visiting Australia, the Governor-General, wrote Richard Hall, was 'in an expansive mood'. He dropped next to her on a sofa, and with his considerable girth protruding, slid his arm behind her. Malcolm Fraser was horrified, and shortly afterwards announced the retirement of the man to whom he owed so much.

'He feels', said Fraser, 'that the events of 1975 and the association of his office with issues of state which arose at that time evoked partisan feeling in the Australian community which have now substantially subsided [but] which have left feelings which might be resolved more quickly if he now makes way for a successor.'[98]

Whitlam maintained his rage, but directed it at first against Kerr and Fraser and not the secret forces that stood behind them. When I interviewed him three months after the *coup*, he seemed almost stunned. He spoke at length about the anomalies of the Constitution, and deflected questions about the CIA back to the duplicity of the Governor-General and the then Opposition leader, whom he called 'Kerr's cur'.

I now believe that Whitlam's reticence in discussing the part played by the intelligence organisations had to do with his extraordinary sense of propriety. After the dismissal he told a Labor caucus that, because he would never breach confidential information that came to him while he was Prime Minister, 'my place in history will bring no discredit on me, my country or on my family'.[99] According to Clyde Cameron, one of his Ministers, 'He knows a great deal, but will not tell

... He was duped over Pine Gap, but he is not prepared to make admissions that will confirm this.'[100]

However, the same sense of propriety which inspired his compulsion to respect Government secrets sharpened his resentment at the suggestion that he had been deceived. Christopher Boyce's revelations in May 1977, that the CIA had de-stabilised his Government, produced vintage Whitlam. 'There is profoundly increasing evidence', he told Parliament, 'that foreign espionage and intelligence activities are being practised in Australia on a wide scale ... I believe the evidence is so grave in its detail and so alarming in its implications that it demands the fullest explanation. The deception over the CIA and the activities of foreign installations on our soil all affect Australia's independence.'[101] Later, in a television interview, he described the CIA's actions as 'an onslaught on Australia's sovereignty'.[102]

Yet it was typical of Whitlam that he should bury the most damning confirmation of this 'onslaught' in a large, dry book not published until 1985. In *The Whitlam Government, 1972 –75*, he revealed that, in the wake of the Boyce disclosures in 1977, President Carter had sent a personal emissary to meet him over a private breakfast in the VIP lounge at Sydney airport. The envoy, Deputy Secretary of State Warren Christopher, was on his way to an ANZUS meeting in New Zealand. 'He made it clear', wrote Whitlam, 'that he had made a special detour in his itinerary for the sole purpose of speaking to me.' The crux of Carter's message was 'that he respected the democratic rights of the allies of the US, and that the US administration would *never again* interfere in the domestic political processes of Australia'.[103] (Emphasis added.)

There remains an exquisite irony to all this. On August 21, 1975, Whitlam, in a parliamentary reply, said that his Government had no intention of terminating the Pine Gap agreement. Moreover, those close to him say that he meant it; that he sought only the respect of 'our great ally' not its indifference to and veiled contempt for the rights of small nations; his warnings and strictures about the bases were proper, if unfamiliar, responses to the arrogance of American imperial assumptions; and that the CIA's paranoia, the histrionics of Shackley, Angleton, Wright and others and the web of sub-contracted plots, were wholly unnecessary. That is beside the point now; *how* an elected Australian Government fell is the point.

The established wisdom is that the Whitlam Government disintegrated as a result of its own incompetence and that the CIA and its accessories merely watched with satisfaction 'from the sidelines'. In public discussion 'conspiracy' was made into a pejorative word, so that those who dared to mention it were themselves 'paranoid' or 'left wing', the contributors of 'theories' and 'scuttlebutt'. This was an odd attitude. That conspiracies by definition provide predominantly circumstantial evidence and are difficult to prove in a legal sense does not make them less true, or less likely to happen. As Denis Freney has pointed out, 'conspiracies are in fact an everyday part of political, economic and social life. Politicians conspire to win power by fair means or foul; organised crime figures conspire naturally to corrupt and influence police and politicians . . . And intelligence services conspire to de-stabilise Governments, sabotage, murder, or what you will.'[104]

But could this happen in *Australia*?

During 1987 the 'Iran/Contragate' hearings at the US Senate in Washington were shown live on Australian television and preoccupied much of the Australian press. The list of conspirators appearing before or named in the hearings read like a *Who's Who* of the Nugan Hand Bank of Sydney; but this was barely acknowledged and only by those journalists who understood Nugan Hand's links with international crime, the CIA and the overthrow of Whitlam; and they are a diminishing few and in uncertain employment.

An editorial in the Adelaide *Advertiser* pronounced that if the CIA had conspired to bring down the Australian Government, 'it could succeed only in the *unthinkable situation* that Australia had in positions of power people who were utterly unscrupulous and misguided in their conception of the responsibilities of their office'.[105] Shoring up a myth of 'national innocence', in a society of established venality, remains a quaint pastime of Australian editorial writers.

When Bill Hayden, a senior Minister in the Whitlam Government, succeeded Whitlam as Leader of the Opposition, he addressed the question of conspiracy. Hayden then had a reputation for speaking his mind. 'It's always a dangerous thing', he said, 'for Labor Party people to talk about conspiracies and certainly international conspiracies [but] I'm quite convinced that there was an international conspiracy that contributed to the undermining of the Government of the day.' Moreover, he said he had evidence of 'a well-orchestrated effort stretching beyond this country's shores' in copies of 'documentation still securely stashed away'. He declined to say more, except that the conspirators had operated 'in a lurid and inexcusable way'.[106]

In June 1988 I sent Hayden the transcript of a 1981 radio interview in which he made his damning remarks. I asked him for details, on or off the record, of the 'documentation' he had 'stashed away'. He was then Minister for Foreign Affairs in the Hawke Labor Government. He replied that 'with the benefit of a further seven years' reflection', he had come to the view that the problems of the Whitlam Government 'were of our own making and were not the product of an international conspiracy'.[107] I replied that I fully understood that opinions and conviction could change, but that I was enquiring about a clear statement of fact which he had made. I added, 'With great respect, either these documents exist or they don't.'[108] He did not reply.

The Whitlam Government left in its wake many secrets which, until they are made known, leave Australian politics disfigured and national independence as remote as ever. Some individuals and groups understandably fear that, with the passage of time, more pieces will fit the puzzle and the whole truth will emerge. Their concern was made evident early in the Bicentenary year when, in my television documentary series, *The Last Dream*, I raised questions about Whitlam's demise: questions which were not new, but which remain unpalatable and unanswered.

When the series was shown in Australia it drew a positive popular response described by the Australian Broadcasting Corporation as 'unprecedented'. This contrasted with attacks mostly by those who had not seen the series. One whose indignation became ubiquitous was Gerard Henderson, described as 'Director of the Institute of Public Affairs, NSW'. This title gave Henderson a certain legitimacy in media interviews, although few journalists could say who exactly he was or what his 'institute' represented. Henderson wrote a weekly column in Rupert Murdoch's *Australian*, in which he described a 'breast-beating left-wing intelligentsia [giving] vent to their frustrations and self hatred' in the Bicentenary year. He named expatriates as among the worst culprits: Robert Hughes, Germaine Greer and myself. I was bracketed with Pol Pot, which seemed harsh. (The logic was that, although I had helped to expose Pol Pot, I had been a closet supporter of his.) Worse, I was a propagator of 'a brand-new conspiracy theory' about the Whitlam Government: the sort of conspiracy theory which caused some Australians to 'salivate with glee'.[109]

Henderson's apparently unconscious sense of comic irony became a regular treat. In one column he bemoaned my 'tactic' of accusing critics of not having seen my documentary. In order to overcome this 'debating trick' of mine he told his readers, in who-dunnit tones, how he got into his office at five in the morning to receive a purloined copy of the transcript overnight from London. 'I have never read anything so full of self-loathing and so complete with conspiracy theories,' he wrote. He then took the transcript to Sir John Kerr, who told him that he 'resented this Pilger nonsense' because he had never had 'any direct or indirect association with the CIA or with British intelligence organisations' or indeed 'any intelligence contacts whatsoever'.[110]

I have already dealt with this denial of Kerr's; suffice to say here that the record is rich with his intelligence connections. In issuing blanket denials through an ideological messenger such as Henderson, Kerr was merely maintaining his silence. But who is Gerard Henderson and what is his 'Institute'?

Henderson is part of Australia's established extreme right. He was an adviser to the former conservative Opposition leader, John Howard, and worked with B. A. Santamaria, the ideologue of the era of McCarthyism in Australia. Certainly, his views are heard widely, often as a result of a phone call to a radio or television station from Henderson himself, demanding 'equal time'. The 'Institute of Public Affairs', long associated with conservatism in Australia, has become a shop front for the far right. Since renamed the 'Sydney Institute' in New South Wales, it is similar to the ultra-right 'think tanks' which devoted themselves during the Reagan years to monitoring and 'naming' American liberal politicians and journalists and to exploring methods and avenues of propaganda*. While campaigning for 'greater accountability' in the media, Henderson has consistently refused to reveal the sources of his funding. In 1987 Henderson attended a seminar in Washington entitled 'The Red Orchestra in the South-West Pacific'. Speakers described 'the left network and the Australian media' and Moscow's 'penetration' of the Australian press (most of which is controlled by Rupert Murdoch). Henderson spoke on the subject, 'How Fertile the Ground?' The conference was organised by the Russians-are-coming Hoover Institution with the help of Owen Harries of the Association for Cultural Freedom, which, wrote Jonathan Kwitny, 'was exposed in the US Congress as founded, funded and generally run by the CIA'.[111]

With Henderson's attacks on my films came a shower of denials. Almost everybody, it seemed, who had been involved in or had profited from the overthrow of the Whitlam Government, issued or was asked for a denial. Malcolm

---

* The Sydney Institute is given dubious respectability by the ruling Labor Party's right-wing establishment. Its speakers have included Federal cabinet ministers, notably the Minister for Foreign Affairs, Gareth Evans. One of Henderson's numerous smear campaigns has been against the internationally-renowned Australian Khmer scholar, Ben Kiernan, author of *How Pol Pot Came to Power* and now Associate Professor of South East Asian History at Yale University in the US. Henderson has accused Kiernan of failing to oppose Pol Pot before the tyrant's overthrow and of 'visiting' Pol Pot's closed regime during the terror. Kiernan never made such a visit, and on the contrary, has devoted most of his work to exposing Pol Pot's crimes, which include the killing of many of his Cambodian wife's relatives.

Fraser denied that foreign intelligence organisations had assisted him to power. 'Absurd,' he said. He failed to remember that, as Prime Minister, he was sufficiently nervous about what the CIA might do to *his* Government to seek reassurance from President Carter.[112] Denials also came from the former head of ASIO, Sir Charles Spry ('utter drivel and rubbish') and the US Consul-General in Sydney, John C. Dorrance, who complained that my report had omitted the denial of CIA complicity by the Director of the CIA in 1975, George Bush, as well as various 'Royal Commission findings'.[113] William Colby, not Bush, was Director of the CIA at the time, and there has been no Royal Commission into the dismissal of Whitlam or CIA activities in Australia. The US Ambassador during most of the Whitlam time, Marshall Green, happened to arrive in Australia as my series was about to be broadcast. 'NO CIA PLOT IN 1975, SAYS FORMER US AMBASSADOR' ran the headline in the *Sydney Morning Herald*. 'Our people weren't operating behind your back,' Green was quoted as saying. As Ambassador he had 'believed in knowing everything [that was] going on'.[114] A few months earlier, in a recorded interview in Washington, Green had told me the very opposite: that as Ambassador he had not known 'the CIA contact points'.[115]

The last 'denial' came from Bob Hawke, who described the very notion of foreign involvement in Whitlam's demise as 'ridiculous'. In 1977 a front-page headline in the Sydney *Sun* read, HAWKE SUSPECTS CIA OF SACKING, and beneath it Hawke called for an urgent public enquiry into 'foreign interference into the domestic processes of Australia'. What had made Hawke change his mind? He did not say.[116]

History is hosed down with official denials. Of course they are worthless unless they are subjected to scrutiny. Journalism is not about accepting the glib assurances of politicians and intelligence bosses. One has only to read Edwin R. Bayley's *Joe McCarthy and the Press* to appreciate how easily lies become enshrined as 'objective facts' simply because they are invested with specious authority.[117] This process was in evidence during and immediately following the Whitlam *coup*.

Journalists on Murdoch's *Australian* walked out, demanding that the paper cease systematic censorship and distortion that amounted to a vendetta against the Whitlam Government. Newspapers paid large sums for dubious documents, a number of them forgeries; these were published as if their validity was never in doubt.

The spirit of that campaign survives, ensuring that the public memory remains short and the truth obsolete. In this way, historical amnesia is induced. Facts already on the record are omitted or obscured; vital connections are not made because of ignorance and idleness, and only sensational snippets are published. Analysis suggesting the culpability, even criminality of established forces is denigrated or ignored; and professional propagandists, or 'lobbyists', are allowed to fill a vacuum where there ought to be real and challenging journalism.

'WHERE IS THE EVIDENCE?' demanded a headline in Murdoch's Melbourne *Herald* in 1988, while ignoring the wealth of *prima facie* documented evidence. The same question can be asked of almost every political *expose´*, which relies on leaks and the anonymity of primary sources. As one of Australia's finest journalists, William Pinwill, pointed out, 'The bulk of better reporting consists of information that does not meet the courtroom standards of proof. Journalism is not a court of law; it is a process of weaving together, often from necessarily anonymous sources, the strands of history. If legal standards were applied to news reporting, the public would have learned nothing of the Watergate scandal and President Nixon would not have resigned in disgrace.'[118]

When Christopher Boyce spoke out in a Los Angeles courtroom, in 1977, his revelations about Australia made big news in the United States. In Australia, only three journalists, Brian Toohey of the *Financial Review*, Bill D'Arcy of the Sydney *Sun* and Ray Martin of the ABC's bureau in New York, pursued the story with original research and information. The significance of Whitlam's response to Boyce's allegations, in a speech in which he effectively broke his silence about the *coup*, was little understood. Instead, the evidence now on the record was denigrated. In a long editorial headed 'THE CIA BOGY', the *Sydney Morning Herald* commented:

> The furore is childish. Why do the Left and perhaps a few other misguided Australians pursue it? Is it not a kind of McCarthyism in reverse – an undermining of public confidence in government and the probity and good sense of officials of all kinds, from trade-unions upwards? Does it not promote anti-Americanism by troubling Australian minds with dark insinuations that we are the helpless puppets of a vast but impalpable conspiracy?[119]

Absurdity is always close at hand in these matters. Shortly before *The Last Dream* was broadcast in Australia, with more evidence to 'trouble Australian minds', it was promoted by the ABC as 'the conscience of the Bicentenary'. On the night of transmission, however, a disclaimer was added, disassociating the ABC from the 'opinions' expressed in the films. A voice intoned the words of the disclaimer in case the viewers missed them. Not only was the 'conscience of the Bicentenary' disavowed, it was also censored. A line in an interview which referred to Sir John Kerr's sacking of Whitlam as 'not necessarily in the interests of Australia' was cut – for 'legal reasons', even though the film had been cleared by two Australian barristers.

The day after the last film was shown, Gough Whitlam was to be interviewed on the ABC's main current affairs programme, *The 7.30 Report*. The interview was cancelled. 'They thought interest had declined in the issue,' Whitlam said, 'which seemed to me a remarkable judgment . . . They seem to be running scared [as if they] are being stood over.'[120] In the only interview he gave subsequently, Whitlam said he had no doubt that the CIA had been involved in Australia in 1975 and there had been contact between the CIA and MI6. None of this, he said, was 'scuttlebutt' or 'loose talk'. He repeated that President Carter had sent an envoy to assure him that the United States would 'never again' intervene in Australian affairs. However, he believed that Sir John Kerr 'needed no encouragement from outside forces to do what he did'.[121]

Australian Associated Press, the agency which services almost all the Australian media, put this on its wires under the headline, 'WHITLAM DOESN'T SEE CIA/MI6 HAND IN EVENTS IN 1975' and reported that the former Prime Minister 'rejected theories of foreign intelligence service involvement in his downfall'.[122] With the exception of the Melbourne *Age*, this interpretation was used in all the principal newspapers of Australia. Thereafter the story died.

'The struggle of people [against power]', wrote the Czech author Milan Kundera, 'is the struggle of memory against forgetting.'[123]

From the Melbourne *Age*, February 23, 1988

No doubt over CIA part in 1970s politics, says Whitlam

By ANNETTE YOUNG,
Sydney

Mr Gough Whitlam said last night he had no doubt that the CIA had been involved in Australian political events while the Whitlam Government was in power.

6

MATES

The Rise and Rise of the Silver Bodgie,
Sir Peter and the Dirty Digger, Goanna and Nifty,
Bondy and Others

The billions lost in taxation revenue from shonky deals by those who can most afford to pay tax; the price paid by society for heroin-related crime; the cynical secret deals between Governments and big business over the carving up of cities . . . have all been shameful features of Australian life over the past ten years and more.

Robert Milliken, journalist

If I see my mates attacked without justification, my mates will find me shoulder to shoulder with them.

Bob Hawke, Prime Minister

If this was South America, a people's liberation movement would be under way . . .

Australian Financial Review

FITZROY GARDENS ARE in the centre of Melbourne, Australia's most English city. They are green and gentle and landscaped around imperial statues; on days when the Melbourne rain is fine and steady the setting could be Kew or St James's Park in London.

Melbourne is where Australia's establishment used to reside, and its powerful men would gather at the nearby Melbourne Club, an uneasy blend of White's in London and the Calcutta Club in the days of the Raj. They were the proconsuls of English interests in the Antipodes: men of the 'squattocracy' whose forebears had acquired the best of the land, having 'squatted' on it and claimed it, or stolen it outright; mercantile men in wool and shipping; men of the judiciary who sweltered in imported wigs of English horsehair; and men of politics, who were Whigs of a sort but for the most part regarded politics as the pursuit of commerce by other means. This last group were the heirs of Sir Robert Menzies, who was above all a Melbourne man. But this was 1976, Menzies was long retired and for most of the previous three years there had been political disruption of an especially unsettling kind. Thankfully, that dark episode was now past.

I had arranged to meet Bob Hawke – the Silver Bodgie – in Fitzroy Gardens at three. On the same day I had been invited by my father-in-law to have lunch at the 'gentlemen only' Melbourne Club. He was a mischievous Scot who had managed the Orient Line in Australia, and he wanted me, he said, 'to observe the beached whales of the Australian establishment at close quarters'.

Entering the Melbourne Club, we were greeted by a huge moose head and a tiger head with skin. Presumably these were to give the impression of Lord Delamere's Kenya or Lord Cromer's India; there are no big-game hunters in Australia. The assistant secretary, a colonel from out of the pages of pre-war *Punch*, shook my father-in-law's hand and led us through Doric columns to the Lawn Room, where members were drinking gin and brandy and reading old copies of *Punch*, from whose pages they, too, appeared to have stepped.

'Ah, little boys,' the cry suddenly went up, 'my favourite!'

'Little boys', at the Melbourne Club, are cocktail sausages dipped in tomato sauce. The grandfather clock had just chimed noon, and those in the leather chairs rose and funeral-marched to the dining-room where, beneath chandeliers, the members eat off monogrammed plates in the atmosphere of a minor English public school common room. The food is what the English upper classes call 'nursery food' — sausages, beans, boiled potatoes, jam tart.

Etiquette dictates that you join a table and your 'leader', who sits at the head, takes your order and gives it to the waitresses. But first our leader called us to attention. 'Gentlemen, the Queen!' he said, and those who were able to, stood. All but two at our table were Australian born, but their accents were a puzzling blend of swallowed consonants and rounded vowels, brayed rather than shouted; and the word 'actually' was deployed frequently. But as more was drunk the familiar nasal pitch of the Australian voice asserted itself in statements such as: 'That socialist bastard, Whitlam.'

Here, as almost everywhere in Australia at that time, the talk was about the demise of Gough Whitlam's government three months earlier and its replacement by the forces of established order, led by the black-hatted Sir John Kerr and Malcolm Fraser, the squatter who was now Prime Minister and, of course, a member of the Melbourne Club. It was agreed at our table that Whitlam and 'those commos around him' had presented an intolerable risk to national stability, but all was well now that 'the right people' were again in charge.

At this, I decided to dissent and proposed a toast to Gough Whitlam as 'Australia's first truly independent national leader'. Mouths opened and eyes squinted, fingernails and Adam's apples were inspected and excuses made; the port clearly would be taken in company other than mine. 'Up 'em,' said my father-in-law as we sat alone.

The 'right people' were back in power, if only for the time being. The paternalism cast by Menzies would be adhered to by Fraser; but beyond Canberra power was shifting in unexpected directions, as if those like Fraser, who were beneficiaries of the *coup* against Whitlam, were themselves being overtaken by others slicker than they: men not of the Melbourne Club but of the main chance, men from the 'big end of town' and their political suppliants, who were forming a new Australian establishment. This would be known as the Order of Mates.

Unlike the Melbourne men, Bob Hawke, who came from faraway Western Australia, wore suits that shone, wide bottomed trousers and shirts with the buttons undone. A 'bodgie' was a 1950s Australian Teddy Boy and 'Hawkie', with his thick, grey-black *coiffure*, was the Silver Bodgie. He also talked out of the corner of his mouth in an accent which was said to be 'ocker', or working class, although Hawke himself was of the middle class and Oxford educated. Indeed, while he was President of the Australian Council of Trade Unions, much of Hawke's popularity rested on his reputation as a 'larrikin': an Australian sobriquet as good as a bestowed title in another society. A larrikin is admired because he likes a beer and gets into trouble and does not mind the consequences. Most of all a larrikin never forgets his Mates.

Australia has an historic reverence for booze, having been 'on the grog' since rum was the accredited anaesthetic for the cruelties visited upon the convict nation. What was remarkable about Hawke – and perhaps this could happen only in Australia – was that during much of his ascendancy to power he was one, two or three parts cut; and that regardless of this, or perhaps because of this, his popularity as a public figure grew. The following incident, recounted by journalist

Brian Toohey, is not untypical. Toohey describes Hawke's first meeting with the Sydney publishing scion, Sir Warwick Fairfax and his wife, Lady Mary.

Hawke was in his 100-drinks-a-day phase ... The occasion was a Parliament House reception in Canberra where the guests had spilled into the courtyard outside the non-members' bar. While Sir Warwick and I conducted the usual, polite *tour de l'horizon*, the putative PM was most solicitous of Lady Mary's sexual welfare (nodding to Sir Warwick), 'I bet this old bastard doesn't give your cunt much use.' Considerable effort was then devoted to explaining in florid detail that, fortunately, a remedy was available in the form of R. L. J. Hawke himself.

Lady Mary was too much of a lady, naturally, to respond in other than the most graciously off-hand manner. The flattery was somewhat undercut, however, by Hawke's attention being diverted intermittently to a young journalist in the group, Jo Hawke. 'Your name's Hawke, eh, then you'd have to be a good fuck.'

These initiatives were temporarily interrupted when a friend of mine, then a Labor Party staffer, poured a cooling glass of beer over Hawke's head. However, as Toohey recalled,

this minor lapse aside, Sir Warwick and Lady Mary were sufficiently impressed to invite the future statesman to Fairwater, their harbourside pile in Sydney. From there the relationship grew, until Hawke felt free to call Sir Warwick whenever he felt some slight upon his good name had sullied the pages of the Fairfax papers.[1]

As a trade-union lawyer Hawke understood well the complexities of the arbitration and 'awards' system which govern Australian working conditions; and although his public image was that of an aggressive, often belligerent man – 'Hawke by name and by nature' – he did more to 'cool' strikes (his word) than to back them. He did this with the maximum flamboyance, by skilful use of the media, especially television, through which he would castigate 'the bosses' (and the television interviewers if they probed too deeply) while appealing for 'common sense' among workers who 'you can bet will do the right thing as good Australians'. Precisely what this meant, and whose interests 'the right thing' favoured was never entirely clear. At the end of his ACTU presidency in 1979, the average weekly wage in Australia was a modest $A216.

On his progress through committee rooms, television studios and bars, Bob Hawke grasped the hands of many Mates, but none so warmly as those more influential than him. Abroad he was welcomed as a fervent Zionist and anti communist, and he cultivated many ties with powerful groups and individuals in Israel and the United States. George Shultz, who held several Cabinet posts under Presidents Nixon and Reagan, developed what he called 'a fine partnership' with Hawke. The two first met when Shultz was head of the huge Bechtel Corporation, which has worldwide interests in construction and energy and was then linked to the political extreme right in the United States and later to the Reagan administration.

During the Whitlam years in the early 1970s Hawke pursued these ties in his dual capacity as union boss and President of the Australian Labor Party in office. The American Ambassador at the time, Marshall Green, told me he found Hawke so amenable to 'our common cause' that 'Bob gave me his private telephone number and said if anything ever comes up that desperately needs some action, this is the number to call'.[2]

In the 1970s the trade-union movement of Australia had long been infiltrated by American intelligence: the Australian Council of Trade Unions was based in Melbourne, and the US labour attaché had his office nearby. 'It was generally accepted in the trade-union movement', said John Grenville, assistant secretary of the Victorian Trades Hall, 'that the labour attaché was the station agent for the CIA.'[3] In a secret speech, the former Chief of the CIA's Clandestine Services, Richard Bissell, described the two main activities of these agents. The first was that which could be 'initiated through CIA channels because they could be started more quickly and informally but do not inherently have to be secret. An example might be certain exchange of persons [in] programs designed to identify potential political leaders and give them some exposure to the United States.'[4]

This 'exchange' is usually in the form of 'study' or 'scholarship' trips which are offered to trade-union officials as they rise through the hierarchy of their unions. In 1950 the US 'labour attaché', Herbert Weiner, handed out the first of what were known as 'Leader Grants', which, funded by the US Information Service, sought to influence prominent figures in politics and the trade unions and incidentally to provide subject material for the CIA to survey and occasionally choose 'agents of influence'.[5]

Thus, the General Secretary of the powerful Australian Workers' Union, Tom Dougherty, was fêted across Cold War America and returned to boast that he could always arrange a Leader Grant for a 'worthy' person. The CIA later admitted giving money to Dougherty to 'fight communism in the AWU'.[6] Four years later the National Secretary of the Federated Ironworkers' Association, Laurie Short, made the first of many sponsored visits to the United States long before the disclosure of CIA funding made both sponsors and recipients more cautious. Short met President Eisenhower and Vice-President Nixon and was lauded as a crusader against communism. 'Somebody should strike a medal for Laurie Short,' wrote New York columnist Victor Riesel.[7] On his return a Brisbane newspaper noted that, 'in 97 days in the United States as a State Department grant holder, Laurie Short travelled 16,300 miles . . . all on a travel allowance of 12 dollars a day, and the generosity of people all round the country'.[8] Most Australian iron workers were then getting less than $A30 a week. Washington's largesse, not surprisingly, was much sought after in those austere times.

Richard Bissell described the essence of the CIA's influence in a country's 'internal power balance' as 'the identification of allies who can be rendered more effective, more powerful, and perhaps wiser through covert assistance'.[9] The effect of 'study trips' on right-wing union officials could be quite dramatic. Laurie Short returned to Australia determined to get rid of 'the Commies and their friends' from the Labor Party and the unions. He also delivered the clear message that 'in America, the trade-union movement looked to Australian unionists to help counteract the spread of Communism in the Far East'.[10]

One of the Australians' most important mentors in Washington was Arthur J. ('Harry') Goldberg, a senior official of the Free Trade Union Committee of the American Federation of Labor, which was later exposed in Congress as CIA-funded. In 1960 Goldberg visited Australia to draw up a secret report for the CIA on Australian unions. 'In regard to Communist influence,' he wrote, 'I find the situation is even more serious than I thought it to be ... The vermin have infiltrated more extensively into the Labor Movement than I had thought.' But Goldberg found the 'situation far from hopeless' and noted that 'the Labor [union] boys ... who are fighting an uphill battle versus the commies ... are looking to us and only us'. He added that 'all these groups are more or less loosely in touch with each other'.[11]

Few rank-and-file trade unionists have heard of the 'Australian Trade Union Training Program at Harvard Foundation'. Set up in 1976 by the American Chamber of Commerce in Australia, the seventeen-week course provides 'training' for senior union officials. Its aim is to prevent 'counter-productive disruptions' (strikes) and to create 'union leaders who are reliable professionals'. The 'training' includes a month-long tour of the United States to 'see the Harvard-learned principles in action'. Meetings with leading union and Government officials are arranged and paid for by the US Government. However, as Richard Bissell pointed out, such schemes 'are more effective if carried out by private auspices than if supported officially by the United States Government'.[12] The Harvard Training Program is funded mostly by the American Chamber of Commerce and American-based multi-national companies. Its original trustees included two of the then most powerful figures in the right-wing machine which runs the Labor Party in New South Wales, Neville Wran and Barrie Unsworth. The year the Harvard scheme was set up Wran was elected State Premier; ten years later Unsworth succeeded him.

Together with 'study trips', Bissell identified the most important activity of CIA 'attache´s' as the process of cultivation. He said, 'Many of the "penetrations" don't take the form of "hiring" but of establishing a close or friendly relationship which may or may not be furthered by the provision of money from time to time.'[13] The US labour attache´s in Melbourne are invariably gregarious, even 'larrikins', have an apparently inexhaustible expense account and throw memorable parties for the Mates they cultivate in the Australian trade-union establishment. That it was 'generally accepted' they were CIA agents did not deter the forging of close friendships with important trade-union officials. For example, Bob Hawke was considered a Mate by three of the best-known labour attache's: Robert Walkinshaw, Emil Lindahl and Edward McHale.

Robert Walkinshaw was labour attache' from 1962 to 1964. During his time in Melbourne, a trade-union publication, *Spotlight*, was set up, funded and run by the CIA. *Spotlight* was so well informed that in 1964 it predicted the outcome of the ballot for positions in the South Australian branch of the Australian Workers' Union, as well as the action the union's federal executive took the following year to dismiss those elected in the 'ballot'!

Walkinshaw was named in Parliament as a CIA agent by Clyde Cameron, who later became Minister of Labour in the Whitlam Government.[14] Cameron told me:

> Some weeks later I was invited to have dinner at the US Embassy where Walkinshaw challenged me to repeat my charge in the presence of our host. The host commented, 'Well this is a pretty serious charge, Mr Cameron.' I replied, 'Well, it *is* serious; and what I'm saying to you is that now that the mask has been torn from Walkinshaw's face and we know what he is, I don't think he will be very effective in carrying out his mission in Australia much longer.' My host feigned deep shock and [denied] that US Embassies anywhere employed CIA agents and that it was part of the Soviet's propaganda against the US.[15]

Walkinshaw's next CIA posting was Indonesia during the military *coup*, in which hundreds of thousands of alleged communists and communist sympathisers were murdered. Walkinshaw worked with the head of the army-approved trade-union movement, Agus Sudono, who was accused of pointing out communist trade unionists for 'elimination'.[16] Sudono visited Australia in 1977 and, in spite of demonstrations pointing out his complicity in the massacres, he was met by the President of the Australian Council of Trade Unions, Bob Hawke.

Walkinshaw renewed his contact with Australia in 1970 when he was posted as CIA adviser in Phuoc Tuy, Vietnam, where the Australian army and Australian CIA advisers were based. Over lunch in Giadinh province with the journalist William Pinwill, Walkinshaw asked after 'my good friend' Bob Hawke. 'Hawke stays in my apartment in New York when he's in town,' he said.[17]

Emil Lindahl also found his way from the US labour attaché's office in Melbourne to Vietnam. Known among Australian trade-union officials as 'the Big Swede', Lindahl was a popular and influential figure when Bob Hawke began his campaign for the ACTU Presidency in 1969. John Grenville

recalled:It was around about this time there was a visit by some American officials to Melbourne and a reception was held for them at the Downtowner Motel. Bob Hawke was there and a number of other trade-union officials, myself included. The Labour Attaché, Emil Lindahl, got Bob Hawke aside and he and Lindahl and Harry Goldberg and Gerry O'Keefe left the room for some period and then they came back. Bob Hawke seemed rather pleased and the message I got loud and clear was that the Americans would be supporting Bob Hawke.[18]

The three Americans closeted with and 'supporting' Bob Hawke all worked for or with the CIA. Gerry O'Keefe was filmed by Granada Television in Chile in 1973 and exposed as a major CIA operator in right-wing Chilean unions which helped to overthrow the Allende Government. He was later named as a CIA agent during the hearings of the Church Committee of the US Senate.[19]

Ed McHale was labour attaché in the early 1970s when Hawke, as ACTU President, was one of the most powerful union bosses Australia had ever had. He was a guest at Hawke's Melbourne home and, according to former US Ambassador Marshall Green, 'spent a great deal of time with Bob Hawke and knew him extremely well ... they had a close personal relationship'.[20] McHale was internationally known as a senior CIA officer, having long been Assistant Director of Radio Free Europe, which had been set up, financed and run by the CIA.

Hawke denied he knew that the three attachés worked for the CIA. When told by Pinwill about Walkinshaw, he expressed surprise and said that it was normal practice for a trade-union official to have close contact with the labour attachés of a friend and ally. He also explained to the *Nation Review*:

> I've never known them to try in any way to traduce people. I've met them all the way back to Walkinshaw and I've never been aware of any sort of activity that would make me identify them as CIA agents. That proves nothing of course. You could think of them asking more specific questions which would make you wonder. But they have never done anything other than ask questions which one would associate with a sensible and lively interest in the labour movement.[21]

Clyde Cameron told me that the Americans actually opposed Hawke's candidacy for ACTU President, as Hawke was known as the 'darling of the Left'.[22] Certainly, Hawke wooed the vote of the left and was judged more militant than his opponent, who was an uninspiring leftover of the traditional trade-union leadership. But if Hawke's aggressive image was confused with left-wing militancy, he himself would correct this by his subsequent actions.

In 1977 Gough Whitlam told Parliament he believed the American Christopher Boyce, convicted that year of spying for the Russians, was 'a man in the know' about CIA activities in Australia. Whitlam referred specifically to 'the manipulation of unions'.[23] In an interview following his trial Boyce had described one instance when his company, a CIA contractor, had 'hardware, software and personnel' to ship out to the CIA base at Pine Gap near Alice Springs. He said there was concern about strikes at Australian airports that 'could wreck our schedule' and referred to a telex from CIA headquarters which said, 'CIA will continue to suppress the strikes. Continue shipment on schedule.' Boyce said he concluded that 'either the CIA directly, or through intermediaries, would have to have infiltrated the hierarchy of [Australian] trade unions'.[24]

Business International is a worldwide American organisation of 'consultants' which represents the top multi-national companies in Australia, including those concerned with 'strategic materials', such as the formidable mining companies. It dispenses information, corporate strategies and informed assessments such as 'corporate risks in the Australian political environment'. In December 1977 the *New York Times* exposed Business International's clandestine links with the CIA.[25]

In April 1981 senior executives of nineteen corporations assembled in Melbourne's Noah's Hotel for a 'forecasting round table' organised by Business International. More than five years after the overthrow of Whitlam, 'the big end of town' (as corporate business is known in Australia) was concerned about the resurgence of the Labor Party under Bill

Hayden, who had held senior portfolios in the Whitlam Government and who described himself as a republican and a democratic socialist. The nineteen had come to hear American-trained economist Alan Carroll, of Business International, 'forecast' the future of the Labor Party and its leader.

Carroll got quickly to his subject – the rise of Bob Hawke. At that time Hawke, having completed his term as ACTU President, was a newly elected Labor member of Parliament. Carroll said he knew Hawke 'pretty well' and 'basically Hawke will be [Labor Party] leader by the middle of next year; and that's my business, and we won't go into that in any great depth. But he will be there. It's all under way. The game plan is totally under way, and I forecast 3 to 5 on a Hawke Government in '83!'

He did not say how he knew this, and added that 'basically Hawkie wants to be Prime Minister for ten years, not for three . . . No Labor Party has ever held power, other than in wartime, for more than one term . . . We [Business International] had a meeting with him about one month ago and we're meeting with him every six months from now. It's terribly important.'[26]

It was not only Alan Carroll's forecast that was correct in almost every detail. Shortly after the *coup* against Whitlam, a top-secret CIA briefing document for the President described Hawke as the 'best qualified' to succeed Whitlam as Labor leader.[27] The CIA's judgment on what was best for Australia came true in February 1983. Three weeks before an election was due, Hawke and others on the party's right wing mounted a successful *putsch* against Hayden. With the slogan, 'Bob Hawke, Bringing Australia Together', the Silver Bodgie became Prime Minister.

To Bob Hawke the future lay not in Whitlam's 'dream', but in the world of 'consensus', a word which was to pepper his speeches. But what he meant was not immediately clear. Whose consensus was he referring to? Indeed, what consensus was there between the rich suburbanites of Toorak and Bellevue Hill and Aboriginal Australians who possessed not even running water; between those who sailed luxurious cruisers in Sydney Harbour and those who sweated for a dollar an hour over a sewing machine in a tin shed in their backyard; between those who dominated the Australian property markets and the elderly who peered from behind lace curtains in rented slums? Labor's great post-war reformers, Ben Chifley and Gough Whitlam, subscribed to no such 'consensus', rather to modest application of white Australia's egalitarian dream: a 'fair go for all'. The beneficiaries of Hawke's 'consensus' would not be the same people.

Those who ran the 'big end of town' would build this consensus. They would provide the money and the power. Their values would be the values of the consensus; and, of course, their own wealth and power would be reinforced by it. Without such Mates, Hawke would argue, he, the 'best qualified' of his party, might never have come to office.

The principal Mate in this reconstruction was, and remains, Sir Peter Abeles. 'Bob and I', said Abeles, 'dreamed dreams together.'[28] Abeles is mightily rich. He is head of the multi-national trucking and shipping corporation, Thomas National Transport (TNT), which operates in some eighty countries and employs more than 50,000 people. With Rupert Murdoch, he controls Ansett Airlines and most of the Australian airline industry. Abeles, who came to Australia from Hungary in 1949, understood 'influence'. From gifts of perfume and whisky to favoured journalists, trips and other 'facilities' to politicians and trade-union officials, the urbane Abeles became, according to the National Times, 'the godhead of an extraordinary network of power, patronage and influence'.[29]

For example, one of Abeles's oldest Mates was the Liberal Party Premier of New South Wales, Robert Askin. Abeles and Askin played poker together; and Askin saw that his Mate was knighted by the Queen in 1972 for 'services to transport, charities and universities' (Askin had himself knighted on the same day). When Askin retired as State Premier in 1975, he joined the board of Abeles's TNT. Four years later an independent member of the New South Wales Parliament, John Hatton, alleged that 'under the Askin Government in the 1960s, the real penetration of organised crime by overseas gangsters, mobsters and the Mafia took place. I have no doubt that ex-Premier Askin knew and may have encouraged these activities.'[30] In 1981, on Askin's death, David Hickie wrote in the *National Times*:

When Sir Robert Askin was in power, organised crime became institutionalised in New South Wales for the first time. Sydney was, and has remained, the crime capital of Australia.

Askin was central to this. His links with three major crime figures . . . allowed the transformation of Sydney's baccarat clubs into fully-fledged casinos . . . According to a reliable source very high in the old Galea [crime] empire, Askin and [Police Commissioner] Hanson were paid approximately $100,000 each a year from the end of Sydney's gang wars in 1967/8 until Askin's retirement. The source is impeccable.[31]

Abeles sought out Hawke almost immediately after Hawke became President of the ACTU. On the day of their appointment Hawke fell ill and Abeles took a gift to his sick bed. The two men soon developed a close relationship that was not so much one of Mates, rather of mentor and student. According to Hawke's biographer, Blanche d'Alpuget, Abeles would sit up through the night with Hawke, listening to his problems, which often had to do with the fate of his manoeuvres in the trade-union world; and the mentor would calm him when he cried. 'Bob shows his emotions,' said

Abeles, 'I find that most attractive about him . . . when I've had personal problems, I cry. If I've had problems with my children, Bob will listen to me. And I will do that for him.'[32] Abeles became omnipresent in Hawke's life. He intervened during a domestic crisis and reportedly helped to 'save' the family. He gave one of Hawke's daughters, Ros, a Citroën car for her seventeenth birthday; he also gave her a public relations job with Ansett Airlines. And it was the Abeles's white Rolls-Royce which Hawke drove with such evident joy.

Abeles is an international figure, and whenever Hawke travelled to the United States he entered an important sphere of the 'empire of influence'. In 1978, when he arrived in San Francisco on his way to a Socialist International meeting in Vancouver, Hawke was Abeles's guest. He and his travelling companion, David Combe, were met at the airport by a TNT manager, who drove them to a luxury hotel where accommodation had been 'taken care of' by TNT. (At the time TNT and the ACTU had a joint travel company, of which Hawke was a director.) 'The entertainment', the TNT man informed them, 'has been taken care of by Rudy Tham of the Teamsters' Union.'

Both Rudy Tham and the venue for the 'entertainment', Sal's Bar, were notorious. Sal was a minor Mafia figure who specialised in 'private parties' and his bar was under constant surveillance by a special intelligence unit of the San Francisco police. Rudy Tham was also an important Mafia 'associate', who later went to prison for embezzlement. Tham ran Local 856, the second largest Teamsters' branch in San Francisco. Without the co-operation of Local 856, whose members included freight checkers, TNT could not function in the United States.

During the 1970s TNT's American operation had been beset by a series of strikes, shootings and bombings. These stopped when Rudy Tham became what TNT's Australian manager in the United States described as a 'co-ordinator/ intermediary in the industrial scene'. Abeles later denied that Tham held such a position. Whatever the truth, the Teamsters' unexpected accommodation of TNT proved critical to the establishment of Abeles's interests in the United States. When TNT first acquired an American freight-forwarding company, a loss of $US3 million was expected; with the Teamsters' co-operation the company made a profit in its first year.

During this time – the early 1970s – Tham visited Australia and, according to the *National Times*, 'contacted New South Wales organised crime figures. Thus began a series of visits to Tham on the US west coast by Sydney businessman Bela Csidei and ex-policeman Murray Riley.'[33] Csidei, who with Riley was later convicted of major drug trafficking, was a friend of Abeles. Riley had purported to represent the interests of Abeles as a prospective buyer of a Las Vegas casino; Abeles denied this.

According to court testimony, Tham introduced Abeles to Jimmy 'the Weasel' Fratianno, the famous Mafia 'hit man', and to 'Benny Eggs' Mangano, who was associated with Frank Tieri, the boss of the New York Genovese family.[34] In 1981 Tieri became the first mobster to be convicted of running a Mafia crime family, largely on Fratianno's evidence. Abeles vigorously denied that he knew about their Mafia connections; but he did acknowledge that he had paid Mangano and another a 'consultancy fee' of $US300,000 for 'advice' on how to acquire an east coast shipping line, Seatrain, and other matters related to the New York waterfront.

Fratianno testified that he had several meetings with Abeles; again, Abeles denied this. In 1977 the Crime Intelligence Division of the San Francisco police got in touch with the New South Wales police seeking information on three Australians associated with Fratianno; one of them was Abeles. A San Francisco police official said, 'Money has been exchanged between Abeles and Tham.' Abeles denied he had paid any money to Tham, Fratianno or the Teamsters' Union. In 1981 US Senate hearings on waterfront corruption heard evidence that Seatrain, Abeles's shipping line, was paying kickbacks to organised crime.[35]

The Abeles's home overlooks Sydney Harbour, and the butler wears gloves and, when required, knee breeches. Lady 'Kitty' Abeles has a private fortune and was featured on the cover of the *Bulletin* magazine under the headline HOW THE RICH LIVE. She compared the splendid position of her Sydney home with Monte Carlo, which she and Sir Peter visit often. They both like to gamble large sums and when they travel, Lady Abeles prefers to carry 'a separate safe' from Sir Peter.[36]

Among the Abeles's frequent guests is Neville Wran, also known as 'Nifty Neville'.

Wran played a critical part in the founding of Australia's new Order of Mates and in the rise and rise of Bob Hawke. It was Wran who brought the Labor Party back to power in Australia's most populous State less than a year after Whitlam's dismissal and the crushing of the Federal party. New South Wales is the home of Labor's right-wing machine and Wran, as Premier, was arguably its most talented product. Like Hawke, Wran saw himself as a 'realist', a 'pragmatist' and a future Prime Minister of Australia. Like Hawke, he saw as a means to this end the cultivation of the rich and powerful, especially those who controlled the media and were Labor's traditional enemies.

Shortly after he was elected Premier, Wran and his wife, Jill, were flown free by Sir Peter Abeles to a holiday in tropical New Caledonia. It was a happy beginning to a long Mateship. One of Wran's first actions on becoming Premier was to ask Abeles's advice on who should run an enquiry into the troubled New South Wales docks. Abeles nominated his codirector and Mate, Alex Carmichael, whom Wran appointed deputy chairman of the State dockyard. The first major contracts at the dockyard went to Carmichael's and Abeles's company, TNT. When the opposition Liberal Party complained about Carmichael's conflict of interest, the State Auditor-General made the surprising announcement that only minimal information about the TNT contract had been made available to him.[37] Shortly afterwards Carmichael was appointed chairman of the State Rail Authority. In 1983, reported the *National Times*, 'the Railways Union asked for an enquiry into why the SRA had paid $4·2 million to buy back a lease of railway land from TNT subsidiary Seatainers Ltd'.[38]

Perhaps the most significant bonding of new Mates was Wran's granting of the lucrative Lotto (lottery) licence to a consortium dominated by the media proprietors Kerry Packer, also known as 'the Goanna' (a primeval Australian lizard) and Rupert Murdoch, also known as 'the Dirty Digger'.

Murdoch is one of Abeles's oldest Mates. Between them they have dominated the Australian airline industry. It was Abeles's TNT trucks which broke the siege of Murdoch's printing operation at Wapping in London in 1986, allowing Murdoch the profits he needed to extend his television empire in the United States and ensuring that the 5,000 print workers, sacked by Murdoch, would never regain their jobs.

Wran's decision to give the Lotto licence to Murdoch and Packer caused a furore among those of his Labor colleagues who recalled the lengths to which the two proprietors had gone to keep Labor from office, especially the orchestrated distortions in the Murdoch press before the 1975 *coup*. Wran ignored these complaints and appointed the ubiquitous Abeles man, Alex Carmichael, as the chairman of the Lotto Control Board. Carmichael remained in that post in spite of his subsequent appointment to the board of Ansett Airlines, owned by Murdoch and Abeles. (Ansett was already employing Wran's wife, Jill, as a consultant.)

Wran's 'pragmatism' did not go unrecognised; during his decade as political boss of New South Wales he was often supported by the Packer and Murdoch media, and this may well have helped to sustain him in office in times of acute political and personal stress. During the Wran years more than a dozen major enquiries, including Royal Commissions, were held into political corruption and organised crime in New South Wales. Several of these involved Wran's predecessor, Sir Robert Askin, who was in the pay of organised crime, and a previous Labor Justice Minister, N. J. Mannix, who on being informed that his name appeared in the 'black book' of Sydney's most powerful criminal, Richard Reilly, said, 'I knew he was a criminal, but I saw nothing wrong in having him for a friend while I was Minister of Justice.'[39]

During the Wran years corruption seemed at times to be pervasive and to justify the description of Sydney as the most corrupt city in the Western world after Newark, New Jersey and Brisbane, Queensland. Politicians, judges and senior policemen and their various 'associates' were, and remain, the subject of official investigation and criminal charges. The New South Wales Minister for Prisons was jailed for seven and a half years for taking bribes to bring about the early release of prisoners. He did this apparently because he owed hundreds of thousands of dollars in gambling debts. The State's former Chief Stipendiary Magistrate was given four years for perverting the course of justice. (He served just ten months.) Neville Wran himself was fined for contempt of court and subjected to relentless questions and allegations about his knowledge of corruption, but was exonerated by a Royal Commission.

The 'Botany case', a relatively small affair, was not untypical of the times. Shortly before the Wran Government was elected in 1976, senior executives at Rupert Murdoch's News Limited headquarters expressed their concern about News Limited land in the Sydney suburb of Botany, which was due to be re-zoned as residential land and on which the company wanted to build a factory. The local Labor member, Laurie Brereton, was later charged with conspiring to bribe two local aldermen, who gave evidence that Brereton had told them that, if they deferred the zoning, the Labor Party would get $A20,000 and that this would include $A5,000 of 'personal campaign funds'. Brereton allegedly told the aldermen that the Labor Party owed Murdoch a favour because he had supported Labor in 1974.

The case was heard by Chief Stipendiary Magistrate Murray Farquhar, who dismissed it on a legal technicality. (Farquhar subsequently received a four-year prison sentence on another matter.) The Solicitor-General decided to indict

Brereton; but the election which brought Wran to power in 1976 intervened and the case was dropped. Brereton continued with his political career and became a Cabinet Minister.

In spite of living in a hot-house atmosphere of innuendo, Neville Wran not only survived, but retired as something of an elder statesman of a 'new' Australian Labor Party, now the party of Bob Hawke, based on the 'Wran model'. However, not even a eulogistic send off by Rupert Murdoch's newspapers could compensate for the reward he wanted above all others; the Silver Bodgie had beaten him to that. When I met Bob Hawke in Fitzroy Gardens in February 1976 he did not look like a bodgie. He was dishevelled, drawn and wore what seemed to be a permanent scowl. As the novelist Howard Jacobson later wrote of a lost-property clerk he encountered in Darwin, 'He possessed that twinkling callousness which passes in Australia for calm.'[40] He reminded me of Richard Nixon. He had Nixon's half-smile, with the top lip drawn in, Nixon's habit of 'strap-hanging' on an ear lobe and Nixon's darting eyes. When passers-by recognised him – 'Gidday, Bob. Howyergoin?' – he would reply in what was becoming known then as an 'ocker accent': full nasal with vowels spread-eagle. However, this would change remarkably for other occasions: the vowels would be rounded and some French would be added: *on dit* was a favourite.

Three weeks earlier Hawke had held a secret meeting with Rupert Murdoch, who was then well on the way to becoming the most influential press proprietor in the world. Murdoch had demonstrated this influence with his vendetta against Whitlam; and many in the Labor Party felt great bitterness towards him. 'Is this country', asked a Labor Senator in Parliament, 'to continue to be run with Governments being made and broken, and men being made and broken, by snide, slick innuendoes of a lying, perjuring pimp – Rupert Murdoch?'[41]

When word of the Hawke/Murdoch meeting slipped out, and Hawke, then Federal President of the Labor Party, was observed slapping Murdoch's back, many people were angry and felt betrayed. However, others who claimed they knew Hawke well saw no inconsistency; he was 'building bridges', or, in Hawke's words, 'a consensus for the future'. There were other secret meetings with Murdoch, as the two men constructed a 'bridge' that stands today as a monument to their mutual, accrued benefits.

I was making a documentary film for British television about Australia in the immediate aftermath of the Whitlam *coup*. With a film cameraman walking ahead of us, Hawke and I strolled the length of Fitzroy Gardens. A 'new Australia' was emerging, he said, out of the 'mistakes' of the Whitlam period; Whitlam was naïve to expect people to 'keep up their rage'; Labor had to 'move forward'. When I asked him what he and Murdoch had talked about at their secret meeting, his face became florid and his eyes rolled back into his head. I had not seen this done before, not even by Nixon; interviewing someone whose eyes disappear is disconcerting.

'You bloody Poms come out here', he said, still eyeless, 'and think you know exactly how things are done in Australia . . .'

'I'm an Australian,' I interjected.

His accent changed to wind-tunnel ocker and he waved the camera aside. 'Bloody Poms are everywhere,' he half-joked. 'John, take some advice: get off the Murdoch line. We've got to bring this country back together again and we can only do it by reaching out to everybody.'

'How will reaching out to Murdoch help?'

'At heart he's a good Australian.'

'Many in your party regard him as an amoral bastard.'

'Bastards can change.'

'Shouldn't they also be opposed?'

'John, you don't seem to understand certain facts about Australian politics. You can't move forward without the bloody media. That's a bloody fact.'

'Are you frightened of Murdoch?'

'That's an unworthy question.'

'Are you?'

'Let's wind this up.'

In his fine book, *Guilty Secrets*, the journalist Robert Pullan wrote that in Australia the very notion of free speech had to struggle 'against the idea that Australian experience did not count because it was the experience of convicts. Free speech ... had no foothold at all in the law and institutions the British brought to Australia. It survived precariously in the minds of dreamers and democrats.'[42]

Nothing in the Australian Constitution or any statute of law guarantees the public's right to know. Australian politicians have seldom supported this right or that of an honest editor to publish. These have remained, at best, nebulous features of Australian political life, considerably less important than the protection of public reputation; yet, in spite of this and in the face of entrenched and frequently vicious opposition, 'dreamers and democrats' laid down the fragile roots of an inquisitive press which owed no sectarian favours and was to play a pivotal role in the establishment of Australian democracy. Like so much else in our secret past, the struggles and achievements of the dreamers are little known.

The enduring assumption in Australia is that the institutions of 'freedom' were imported wholly from England, a notion of exquisite perversity when one considers the nature of white origins in Australia. For most Australians the name Edward Smith Hall will mean nothing; yet this one journalist did more than any individual to plant three basic liberties in Australia: freedom of the press, representative government and trial by jury.[43]

Edward Smith Hall launched his weekly, eight-page, eight-penny Sydney *Monitor* on May 18, 1826. In the first issue he declared himself. 'For an editor in New South Wales', he wrote 'to withhold his opinions on colonial politics argues either no fixed principles at all, or a distrust of their truth.'[44] A month later he left no doubts in the minds of his readers as to the direction of the *Monitor* by giving prominence to a letter from a reader who described the function of a newspaper as 'an inveterate opposer [rather] than a staunch parasite of government'.[45]

The measure of Hall's principled audacity can be judged

by the times. He had launched his newspaper not in a new Britannia flowering with Georgian liberalism, but in a brutal military dictatorship run with white slave labour. The strong man was General Ralph Darling; and Hall's defiance of Darling's authority was effectively that of a revolutionary; and he, and other independent editors, were to suffer accordingly.

Hall's campaigns for the rights of convicts and freed prisoners and his exposure of the corruption of officials, magistrates and the Governor's hangers-on made him a target of the draconian laws of criminal libel (which, in essence, have not changed in Australia). He was routinely convicted of criminal libel by military juries, whose members were selected personally by General Darling. He spent more than a year in prison where, from a small cell lit through a single grate and beset by mosquitoes, he continued to edit the *Monitor* and to campaign against public venality. In spite of his privations, his journalism was primarily responsible for Darling's recall to London in 1831 and for the beginning of free speech in the colony.

When Hall died in 1861 there were some fifty independent newspaper titles in New South Wales alone. Within twenty years this had risen to 143 papers, many of which had a campaigning style and editors who regarded their newspapers as 'the voice of the people' and not of the 'trade of authority' or of vested mercantile interests. By the beginning of the twentieth century there were twenty-one metropolitan newspapers in Australia owned by seventeen different proprietors. By 1950 this had been reduced to fifteen dailies owned by ten proprietors. By 1988, of Australia's sixteen principal newspapers, ten were owned by Rupert Murdoch, four by the Fairfax organisation and one each by Alan Bond and Kerry Packer. If Australian journalism could be described at the time of Edward Smith Hall as 'a medley of competing voices',[46] it has since become an echo chamber. With 63 per cent of national and metropolitan daily newspaper circulation controlled by Rupert Murdoch, Australia has the distinction of the most concentrated press ownership, and the least independent newspapers, of any Western democracy. Most of the media is now the exclusive preserve of a few immensely powerful Mates. Next to the rejection of Aboriginal land rights, this erosion of such a hard-won liberty was the outstanding tragedy of the Bicentenary year.

Bob Hawke's victory in the 1983 election was hailed by Rupert Murdoch as 'a brilliant start'.[47] Murdoch's *Australian* newspaper made Hawke 'Australian of the Year' and poured columns of praise upon him. On the following Australia Day Murdoch received the Companion of the Order of Australia, considered by many the country's highest award, 'for services to the media'.

Murdoch's relationship with Hawke is part of a much wider strategy. Murdoch's brilliance has been to understand the relationship between governments and the movement of capital. Without the co-operation or patronage of one, the other can be cumbersome and extremely expensive. To Murdoch, politicians are merely the purgatives in this process. During the 1980s Murdoch began to realise his ambition to establish a world media empire – a 'world newspaper' as Phillip Knightley has called it. In Britain Murdoch's mass circulation *Sun* supported Margaret Thatcher with a vociferousness seldom seen even in Fleet Street. Thatcher duly knighted the editor of the *Sun*, Sir Larry Lamb, 'for services to journalism'. (Sir Larry described Murdoch as 'being on the side of the side of the angels'.)[48]

In 1981 Murdoch announced his intention of buying *The Times* and the *Sunday Times*, a deal which the Board of Trade was expected automatically to refer to the Monopolies Commission. Since its inception the Commission had examined every major takeover of British newspapers by companies already holding interests in the British press. After discussion at Cabinet level and with the support of Thatcher herself, Murdoch became the exception. In his biography of Murdoch, Thomas Kiernan quotes Charles Douglas-Home, the then editor of *The Times*, as saying, 'Rupert and Mrs Thatcher consult regularly on every important matter of policy, especially as they relate to his economic and political interests. Around here he's often jokingly referred to as Mr Prime Minister.'[49] Murdoch's alliance with Thatcher – which both have been at pains to keep secret – deepened following his 'victory' over the print unions at Wapping in 1986. 'Wapping' had been crucial to Thatcher's strategy to destroy the trade unions. Three years later he was rewarded when the Government's de-regulation of broadcasting allowed him to launch Britain's first satellite television network, Sky Channel.

In demonstrating the 'cross-over' power of his media, Murdoch for years had used his newspapers' editorial pages to attack and undermine those, such as the BBC and Independent Television, who had stood in the way of his broadcasting plans. This was consistent practice for Murdoch. During the weeks leading to the start of his Sky Channel, his journalists were used to promote the new venture; and when the great day arrived, *The Times*, long faded, published a celebratory picture of its proprietor.

This concentration of power did not seem to concern the Government, nor did the Prime Minister see any contradiction between her support for Murdoch and her regular lectures to the nation, notably to broadcasters, on the need for higher moral standards. This was understandable, as her own standards are entirely compatible with Murdoch's. His *Sun*, far from being a mere comic as many on the left have argued, presents a coherent, ideological view of a society shaped by the Thatcher revolution. It is a society in which you look after yourself and trust nobody, except Lady Luck. It is a society in which money is all that matters, not to mention the fun of looking on at misfortune, sex and violence, especially violence. And those who oppose this society are, of course, 'loony'; Mrs Thatcher has said as much.

Moreover, Murdoch's standards are on most vivid display when his papers are supporting the Prime Minister's actions. Their unbridled backing for the Falklands War led the *Sun* to gloat over the drowning of hundreds of conscripted Argentinian sailors, and to invent an interview with the widow of a British soldier. Similarly in 1988 the *Sun* described a Gibraltar woman as a prostitute involved with drug dealing after she had given evidence about the killing of an unarmed IRA squad by British soldiers in Gibraltar – evidence that conflicted with the Thatcher Government's, and the Murdoch papers', version of events. The *Sun* paid the woman £50,000 in damages, the day after it had paid the singer Elton John £1 million, having fabricated a report about his private life.

During the week of the Australian Bicentenary, the *Sun* published an editorial which described Aborigines as 'treacherous and brutal', a people without skills, arts or graces who would have wiped themselves out if left alone. There was an illustration of the stereotype of a savage. The British Press Council described the article as 'offensive, misleading and unacceptably racist'. Murdoch was quoted as saying it went 'ten per cent too far'.[50]

On the day he launched his Sky Channel Murdoch was asked about standards, why almost everything he touched went 'downmarket'. He seemed puzzled. 'I don't know what you mean by downmarket and upmarket,' he said. 'That is so English, class-ridden, snobbery-ridden . . . I'm an Australian. I believe in equality.'[51] But even this was not quite right. Murdoch is an American citizen.

Murdoch's heart, it is said, lies in the United States, where his strategy has been especially bold and his own politics have been sharpened.

In July 1980 the New York State Democratic primary was crucial for candidate Jimmy Carter. His main opponent, Senator Edward Kennedy, was an acknowledged supporter of the Israeli cause, while Carter's quest for de´tente between Israel and Egypt cast him in many Jewish eyes as pro-Arab. Murdoch's *New York Post* had found a woman who agreed to speak about an affair with Kennedy. At the same time, with the aid of public relations men retained by Murdoch, a meeting with President Carter at the White House was arranged for February 19, 1980. The same morning Murdoch met the Chairman of the Export-Import Bank (Eximbank), John Moore, an old friend and political supporter of Carter. The subject was the sale of Boeing aircraft to Ansett, the Australian airline owned by Murdoch and Sir Peter Abeles. Murdoch demanded a loan of 656 million $US at 8 per cent interest.

On February 22 Murdoch's *Post* published an editorial

headed, THE DEMOCRATIC PRIMARIES: THE POST
ENDORSES CARTER. An Eximbank loan of such size usually
took three weeks to develop; and the bank's current interest
rate was well above 8 per cent, rising to 13 per cent in March.
Murdoch reduced the loan figure to $US290 million and
announced that the deal had been settled at 8 per cent. US
Treasury officials expressed their concern; the *New York
Times* published a story about the low interest rate, the lunch
with Carter on the same day as the bank meeting, the *Post*'s
endorsement of Carter and Moore's political background.
The US Senate committee on banking called for the documents and Murdoch testified before a hearing. The White
House lunch, he said, was unconnected with the Boeing sale.
The committee reported that the Ansett loan had been
handled 'sloppily' and that lending rates several points below
costs amounted to an extraordinary subsidy of Rupert Murdoch's business fortunes. But the loan went ahead.

Later that year Murdoch switched allegiance to Ronald
Reagan, whom he embraced as he had done Thatcher. 'Rupert
Murdoch', said New York Representative Jack Kemp, 'used
the editorial page, the front page and every other page necessary to elect Ronald Reagan.' After his inauguration the new
President paid generous tribute to his Australian supporter.
'Nancy and I', he said, 'want you to know you will always
have our deepest appreciation.'[52] Reagan's de-regulation
policies meant that Murdoch could now begin to expand.
But in order to circumvent laws preventing foreign nationals
owning US television stations, he first had to renounce his
Australian citizenship and become an American. This he did
speedily.

In January 1984 Murdoch was appointed to the board of
United Technologies, the United States' fifth largest manufac-
turing corporation and part of the 'military-industrial com-
plex'. The media magnate was now an arms dealer. Why
Murdoch chose to be a director of a company in which he
had only minimal stock holding was not clear. According to
Thomas Kiernan, the chairman of United Technologies,
Harry Gray recruited Murdoch partly because 'the Australian

Government was about to make a major investment in military helicopters and Gray wanted United Sikorsky Helicopters Division to get the contract'.[53] The Australian Defence Department subsequently agreed to pay Sikorsky $A570 million for sixteen Seahawk and fourteen Blackhawk helicopters.

Kiernan also claimed that 'Murdoch's footprints were all over the Westland affair' in Britain. In 1985 the Thatcher Government agreed to allow partial foreign ownership of the Westland helicopter company and the Defence Secretary Michael Heseltine announced that a European consortium had the Cabinet's and the Prime Minister's approval. Then Thatcher appeared to change her mind and the contract finally was awarded to a partnership dominated by Sikorsky. Heseltine resigned. According to Kiernan, Murdoch was involved. He wrote, 'If anyone benefited from [the deal], he did . . . a major American corporation in which he had a significant interest had achieved an advantageous position in a multi-billion dollar market that until then had eluded it.'[54]

Kiernan's evidence of Murdoch's influence is circumstantial; what is not in doubt is Murdoch's commitment to American strategic aims, reaffirmed during the Reagan years, and of which corporations like United Technologies are the beneficiaries. Indeed, imperial America, according to Murdoch, is 'the richest, freest and happiest country in the world'.[55] Such is his devotion that he even admonished Margaret Thatcher for her refusal to support President Reagan's invasion of Grenada. 'She waged a war in the Falklands over property rights', he told Kiernan, 'and she bloody well botched it up, if you ask me. Reagan's Grenada action has to do with the freedom of the Western World, including Thatcher's England. She had no business opening her mouth. I'll see she pays for it.'[56]

Murdoch's ideological advisers have included Charles Z. Wick, whose 'Project Truth' and numerous other paranoid campaigns converted the US Information Agency to an instrument of black propaganda abroad. Wick subsequently joined the board of Murdoch's News Corporation. The 'world view' of those like Wick and others on the American far right is ever present in Murdoch's papers, regardless of where they are published. This can be explicit, as in the prominence given to columnists who are little more than sectarian lobbyists, and in the willingness of some Murdoch papers to act as cyphers of Government disinformation.

In 1979 Murdoch's syndication network took its lead from his newly acquired *New York Post*, which (along with non-Murdoch papers) accused the Russians and Vietnamese of plotting to starve Cambodia in the aftermath of the expulsion of Pol Pot: an assertion derived principally from a bogus CIA report.[57] In 1983, quoting 'unnamed intelligence reports', the Murdoch press reported the presence of Soviet troops in Grenada. There were none. In 1986, following the American bombing of Libya, the *Post* published a picture of Colonel Qadafi which had been altered to make him appear as a transvestite. The headline read, GADAFFI GOES DAFFY – HE'S TURNED INTO A TRANSVESTITE DRUGGIE. This had come from the same 'US intelligence sources' and was recycled through Murdoch's newspapers around the world. The front page of the Sydney *Daily Mirror* of June 18 was headlined, LIBYAN LEADER 'ON DRUGS AND MENTALLY DISTURBED'. The *Mirror* quoted two sources: the 'influential' *New York Post* and 'unnamed US intelligence sources'.

More than any corner of the Murdoch empire, the Australian press is the compliant recipient of the Washington/Murdoch view. Wherever there is a choice between the national interests of the United States and those of Australia, as perceived by the administration in Washington, Murdoch's Australian newspapers generally can be relied upon to confuse American and Australian interests as the same. When in 1985 the Labor Cabinet took the unusual step of forcing Hawke to reverse an agreement he had made secretly with Washington to allow the testing of the MX missile in Australian waters, Murdoch's *Australian*, the country's only national newspaper, was beside itself. Australia's foreign policy was 'falling into chaos'; the 'basic values of our society' were at stake; a 'strong treaty' with the United States was urgently needed.[58] Beneath the headline 'The Americans Give Us a Second Chance' was this memorable editorial:

> The Australian Government should feel grateful to the Reagan administration . . . for the tolerance shown by our friends in Washington towards Mr Hawke's handling of the MX missile incident. It would, however, be reckless to expect that another such lapse would be treated with similar forbearance.[59]

Australia's new economic order is the child of Paul Keating who, long before he deposed Bob Hawke as Prime Minister in 1991, was described by Hawke as 'the world's greatest Treasurer'. Indeed, Keating's policies, according to the Silver Bodgie, had brought about an 'historic transformation' of Australian society. Keating himself has described his economic policies as the beginning of 'a golden age for Australia' and 'a unique model' for the rest of the world. The media agreed; Alan Ramsey, a seasoned political commentator, called him 'the Van Gogh of treasurers'. Only in 1989, when the 'historic transformation' and the 'golden age' turned out to be the worst recession in living memory, did the press review its idolatry of this Very Important Mate.

Keating's de-regulation of the fragile Australian economy, with its small manufacturing base and traditional reliance on agriculture and wool, has been swift, unsparing and disastrous. As farm, commodity and mineral prices began to fall in 1983, Keating suddenly lifted all banking controls and floated the currency in a highly unstable speculators' market. This has left a deeply wounded Australian dollar – sometimes known contemptuously as the 'Pacific peso' – and world record interest rates, as testified by the frequent evictions of small farmers unable to pay up to 34 per cent on their loans.

Since Keating abandoned exchange controls, more than

$A7,000 million has fled Australia every year. A major industrial economy, like Britain's, can sustain bleeding of this magnitude for some time. A small economy cannot; and unless the flight of capital is stemmed, Australia will be left with an insoluble balance-of-payments' deficit and is likely to join the ranks of Latin American states in permanent hock and bereft of their sovereignty. Indeed, in surrendering one of the few weapons with which a small country can defend its economic sovereignty, Keating has given away almost all that the Labor Government in the 1940s fought to preserve against extreme American pressure. No Australian Government now can afford to stand up to the power of the international money markets or to major foreign investors. If, for example, the Government wants to improve rather than further reduce its welfare provisions, the international banks almost certainly will 'sell down' the Australian dollar, and bring intolerable pressure to forestall such a measure. Brokers in New York have said as much when consulted by Australian politicians and by those Australian commentators who constantly seek Wall Street's approval of Australian policies.

This is reminiscent of the Great Depression when Sir Otto Niemeyer, on behalf of the British banks, insisted that ordinary Australians accept reduced wages and a lower standard of living so that their Government might continue paying interest on the nation's overseas debt. Then, as now, the call was for 'tightening of belts'. Australia's new entrepreneurs have had their own response to what Keating has called 'this emergency for all of us to bear'.

In the late 1980s the official company tax rate stood at 49 cents in the dollar. In 1987 Rupert Murdoch's News Corporation paid less than 13 cents and Alan Bond's Bond Corporation paid less than 9 cents.[60] By 1988 Bond had got his tax down to even less than that, of which more later. In 1989/90 Kerry Packer's Consolidated Press Holdings also paid only nine cents in the dollar.[61] The huge Elder's IXL company (Foster's lager), which paid less than 11 cents, was run during the 1980s by John Elliott, an outspoken character who has had gold buckles installed in his private jet. Elliott has threatened to move his business empire to England, saying 'Australia would be the last place you would want to invest.' His ingratitude remains a mystery. Australia's newly de-regulated banks granted entrepreneurs like Elliott access to virtually unlimited funds. And when Elliott left Elders in 1990, with the company crippled with debt, he walked away with \$A20 million in 'free' shares.[62]

'A new establishment is in the making,' rejoiced Sydney's *Business Review Weekly* in 1986, 'its fortunes growing with a rapidity not seen since the word "millionaire" first entered the English language. Entrepreneurs are breaking down the boardroom doors.' In the following years, a 'billion dollar club' was established and the magazine published a 'gold edition' celebrating the 200 richest Australians. Of those, it was said that only one made his fortune out of pure brain power – inventing a computerised betting system for horse-racing.

The Australian Labor Party has always had its conservatives and dreamers, even radicals, but for the most part their differences have been reconciled by a shared belief that, under Labor, the rich should not grow richer while the poor become poorer. When Hawke and Keating came to power in 1983 the combined wealth of the top 200 was less than five billion dollars. In 1989 it was twenty-five billion dollars and still climbing. Before the recession got under way, Australia had an estimated thirty-one thousand millionaires, compared with seven million wage earners, whose wages are falling in real terms, and two million people living in poverty, including one Australian child in five. Put another way: at the beginning of the 1980s the top one per cent of the population owned as much as the bottom 10 per cent. Now that one per cent owns as much as the bottom 20 per cent.[63] Such is Keating's 'historic transformation'.

Keating is an egocentric and pugnacious man, self taught in economics, antiques dealing and neo-classical art, subjects upon which he pronounces a great deal. For example: 'You couldn't get any better [than neo-classical art]. There hasn't been any better since; and, since deco, there have been only fag packets and bottletops.'[64] His descriptions of the Opposition and others opposed to his economic policies include the following: harlots, sleazebags, frauds, immoral cheats, boxheads, brain damaged, loopy crims, stupid foul-mouthed grubs, pieces of criminal garbage, rustbuckets, scumbags, dimwits, dummies, perfumed gigolos, piss-ants, gutless spivs, stunned mullets, ghouls and barnyard bullies. Inexplicably, Keating is described by his supporters as 'eloquent'. According to Alan Ramsey, if you probe too deeply into the man himself, 'he's as likely to tell you to piss off and mind your own business. He is, and always has been, very much his own man.'[65]

Keating has spoken a great deal about Australians' need for sacrifice, although he does not mention those exempt from his strictures, notably himself. Up until 1987 Keating listed his 'principal place of residence' as Sydney. This allowed him to claim more than $A17,000 a year as tax-free living-away-from-home allowance, designed to compensate him for separation from his family. In fact, he and his family lived together virtually full-time in a rented house in Canberra. A Remuneration Tribunal has now 'regularised' Keating's expenses for a home he seldom visits. In response, Keating has boasted openly that he could make $A17,000 in a day, an hour, even a minute, on the Stock Exchange. Such is the contemporary voice of the Australian Labor movement.[66]

One of Keating's closest Mates is the multi-millionaire property developer, Warren Anderson. Keating has been a frequent house guest in all of Anderson's five luxury homes, which are worth some $A50 million. Anderson was ordered to pay $A1·2 million in back taxes by the Perth office of the Tax Department, while the Sydney office wanted several million more, although the final figure was reduced after negotiations. When Keating was blaming the nation's housing crisis on the greed of Australians who own a quarter of an acre of suburban land, his best Mate was knocking over six surrounding mansions to provide a five-acre garden for his residence in Perth. Anderson's other homes include an imitation eighteenth-century English 'stately home' in the Northern

Territory. Called Tipperary, it has an $A800,000 chandelier and a real hippopotamus in the grounds. Anderson's interest in animals came to light when he paid $A30,000 to Eskimos for the right to shoot a polar bear, which he stuffed. He gave his wife a $A2 million diamond-studded choker for her fortieth birthday. His collection of antiques represents a passion which he shares with his Mate, Paul Keating, who is often transported by Anderson helicopter to one of Anderson's five estates.

In 1986 Anderson was convicted of bringing a loaded .38 revolver into the country on a private jet that had flown in from Papua-New Guinea. The Treasurer wrote him a reference for presentation to the court hearing the charges. Keating, a minor union official before entering parliament, has amassed a small fortune in antiques, especially French empire clocks and eighteenth-century European silver. He has dealt in clocks with Anderson but refuses to disclose the details.[67]

Anderson is also renowned for hiring strong men with criminal records whose jobs include visiting those opposed to his many property development schemes. They are known as 'enforcers'. One of them, Tom Domican, is a much feared individual who has talked about 'stacking' and 'rigging' Labor Party pre-selections in Sydney on behalf of right-wing candidates. Tax records show that Anderson has paid more than $A20,000 to Domican, who was given fourteen years in prison for shooting with intent to murder a fellow hit man, his wife and child. He was subsequently acquitted on appeal.[68] Speaking on television about his admiration for Warren Anderson, Treasurer Keating said, 'I haven't got much time for the wimps, and there are lots of wimps around. As far as I am concerned, wimps are out.'[69]

As part of his de-regulation policies, Keating abolished the Federal Reserve Bank's power to monitor money leaving the country, which allowed the very rich to practise 'tax avoidance' on a previously unheard of scale. Moreover, the interest incurred on the huge amounts borrowed on world money markets in order to finance takeovers is tax deductible in Australia. This has helped to give Australia a foreign debt which, under Keating's stewardship, rose from $A25 billion in the early 1980s to $A114 billion in 1990 and is behind only that of Mexico and Brazil.

The scandal of this is that Australia, with one of the smallest *public* debts in the world in relation to Gross National Product, has had to bear two-thirds of the overall debt because of the private borrowing of corporations, banks and individuals like Rupert Murdoch, Sir Peter Abeles and Alan Bond.[70] In 1990 the Bond empire alone owed between $A8 billion and $A14 billion. This meant that the company, which was unaccountable to the Australian Government and the Australian people, was responsible for at least 10 per cent of the national debt – a debt that the nation as a whole has to reduce by earning export income. In one year, 1986, Sir Peter Abeles's company, TNT, had foreign loans which accounted for almost half its assets. While Abeles reaped tax relief on the interest on his loans, Australia's balance of payments suffered proportionately, particularly as almost all foreign loans are in US dollars, which have steadily appreciated against the Australian dollar. During the same period almost 40 per cent of Murdoch's News Corporation's assets were funded by foreign loans; and this was to increase sharply in January 1987 when Murdoch paid $A2·3 billion for the Herald and Weekly Times publishing group.[71]

Buying the Herald and Weekly Times group was Murdoch's dream. The Melbourne *Herald* had been his father's paper; Keith Murdoch, its most famous editor, had been something of an Australian Lord Northcliffe. Although the paper was never owned by the family, the Murdochs considered it theirs, and the son's ambition was to buy it and to honour his father's memory by restoring it to its albeit exaggerated former glory. Another factor, entirely unrelated to filial sentiment, was that the Herald group was the largest newspaper empire in Australia and its acquisition would give Murdoch unprecedented dominance of the Australian press.

Apart from having to borrow to pay an inflated share price,

Murdoch faced a trickier problem. The Foreign Takeovers Act stood between him and his dream; for he was now an American citizen. The Government's foreign investment guidelines were unambiguous: 'Foreign investment in mass circulation newspapers is restricted.'[72] Moreover, Section 51 of the constitution gives Parliament power to prevent concentrated ownership of any section of the economy. Clearly, Murdoch needed a Mate.

On November 13, 1986, three weeks before Murdoch flew to Melbourne from Los Angeles to make his bid for the group, his *Australian* published a surprising editorial beneath the headline, 'Opposition flounder around aimlessly'. The conservative coalition was described as 'an opportunistic rabble ... looking less and less like an alternative Government'. Although the Murdoch press had given Hawke the gentlest ride of any Labor leader, it had endorsed the 'new right' policies of the Opposition leader, John Howard. The shift was sudden and unexplained.

Shortly before the editorial appeared, Murdoch met Keating in the United States, where they discussed proposed changes in government policy towards the media. On their return to Australia, they met again, this time with Hawke present. It was a jocular, first-names encounter. They discussed 'putting the Herald and Weekly Times into play' (jargon for making a company vulnerable to takeover). Within days of the meeting, Murdoch's senior executives were left in no doubt that his papers now supported the Federal Labor Government.[73]

Murdoch flew to Melbourne on December 2 and offered $A1·8 billion for the Herald and Weekly Times Group. The Minister for Communications, Michael Duffy, whose portfolio covered the press, described Murdoch as 'the prodigal son returned'. The Murdoch papers could barely contain their obsequiousness. On December 4 the front page of the Sydney *Daily Mirror* carried a half-page picture of Murdoch in running shorts, jogging 'before the battle'. Beneath the headline MURDOCH HAS THEM ON THE RUN! the *Mirror* informed its readers that 'Mr Murdoch had a peaceful night's sleep' and had said that 'journalists should do this every day' (jog). 'Mr Murdoch said he was pleased with the morning newspapers which splashed headlines of his lightning move for Australia's biggest media company.' When it was pointed out to him that the chairman of the Trade Practices Commission had said that the takeover might contravene the law, Murdoch said, 'That is not an insurmountable problem': just as the Foreign Takeovers Act and the constitutional safeguard were no longer 'problems'.

The only remaining 'problem' was a law which prevented Murdoch from owning television and radio stations that were part of the Herald and Weekly Times empire. Murdoch dealt with this problem by vanishing. His company, News Limited, announced his disappearance thus:

1 Although Mr Murdoch was formerly a director of News Ltd he is no longer a director and he holds no office in the company.

2 Mr Murdoch has no authority to speak on behalf of or to bind News Ltd . . .

The ruse beckoned endless court action, so Murdoch tried another. Now in *de facto* control of the Herald and Weekly Times Group, he arranged the sale of its television and radio interests *before* he took it over officially. That one worked. The Australian Broadcasting Tribunal, although pressed by the Australian Journalists' Association and other groups to investigate the deal, was outmanoeuvred and, with no encouragement from the Government to do otherwise, simply gave up.[74]

Bob Hawke had only to remain silent to acquiesce. The Minister of Foreign Affairs, Bill Hayden, and the Opposition spokesman on communications, Ian Macphee, called for an urgent public enquiry into the Murdoch bid, to no avail. Hayden was silenced by the Cabinet and Macphee was visited on a Sunday morning by his frantic leader, John Howard, who had interrupted a holiday to tell him that under no circumstances was Murdoch to be offended. On both sides of the Australian Parliament the silence was contagious. One MP told me, 'The hostility of Murdoch would mean my political death. So I shut up and I'm not proud of it.' Another, in seeking to justify his silence, recounted a famous Murdoch ultimatum to a politician in the 1960s, 'Look, you can have a headline a day or a bucket of shit a day. What's it to be?'[75] That the public trust had been breached behind veils of political expediency, fear and cowardice was one more Australian secret.

Few other dogs barked. Coverage by the non-Murdoch media of such an historic shift in power was primarily of the gee-whizz-isn't-Rupert-clever school. Financial journalists allowed the spectacle of Murdoch's cunning to obscure the critical issue of ownership of a national resource. That freedom of expression was in trouble, that censorship now could be conducted across a majority of the press, by commission and omission, was not an issue.

One young journalist, Paul Chadwick, resigned from the Melbourne *Sun*, a Herald and Weekly Times paper, in protest and helped to set up the 'Free the Media' organisation. As Chadwick put it, journalism in Australia was now distinguished by 'a kind of feudal service to one's proprietor'. 'Many of my colleagues', he told me, 'believe that their professional identity derives from being a Murdoch journalist or a Fairfax journalist rather than from any set of principles which are not appropriated by any owner.'

The Australian Press Council, the 'watchdog' of the press, all but disintegrated as a result of the Murdoch takeover. Of its fifteen members, seven represent the newspaper proprietors, and all of them closed their ranks behind Murdoch and voted unanimously against a proposal for an enquiry into the takeover. The chairman, Hal Wootten, a Queen's Counsel and former judge, resigned in protest, saying with bitterness that the Government had made a 'mockery of the Foreign Takeovers Act'. He said,

> Allowing Murdoch to assume control of Australian newspapers was unparalleled outside totalitarian countries. The Federal Treasurer could stop the takeover if he wanted to ... in this case it is a man who has renounced his citizenship to further his worldwide media power, and who makes no secret of the fact that he intends to make personal use of his control of newspapers.[76]

When Hawke finally spoke out about the Murdoch sale, he and Keating had been entertained by Murdoch on his estate at Yass, a short drive from Canberra. The episode was then declared over. 'If we are going to be a free market economy based on the operation of market forces,' said Hawke, 'then I think [the sale to Murdoch] has to work its way through.' He made no mention of the law, which is above market forces and which a Prime Minister is meant to uphold and protect. Nor was the Australian public made aware of Keating's boasting that he had helped Murdoch. In a meeting with a senior executive of the Fairfax group, Max Suich, Keating made clear his support for 'our crowd'. In a Fairfax internal document, Suich wrote, 'The Treasurer is a product of the New South Wales right wing (of the Labor Party) and his conversation is littered with threats, references to getting even, doing deals and assisting "our crowd" in business, the press and within the (Labor Party). He is very blunt about the fact that the right are "deal-makers" and that they provide favours for "our crowd" in return for favours given'.[77]

Ian Macphee refused to accept the Government's silence on the Herald and Weekly Times and pursued his own investigation. Under the Freedom of Information Act, he requisitioned from Keating's office documents relating to the takeover and especially the Foreign Investment Review Board's recommendations. Six of the eight pages he received were blacked out and stamped 'commercial in confidence'. One paragraph, released almost two years after the sale, indicated that the Board had opposed the takeover. In 1989 Hawke told Parliament the opposite. When pressed by Ian Macphee, Keating still refused to release the Board's report.[78]

To Murdoch's other Mates on the right wing of the Labor Party, the deal Hawkie had done was worth rejoicing about. Neville Wran, who as Premier of New South Wales had given Murdoch a licence to print lottery tickets, remarked that he 'wished Rupert owned 95 per cent of the Australian press'.

As Murdoch began his bid for the Herald and Weekly Times Group, Hawke and Keating launched an attack on the *National Times on Sunday*, owned by the Fairfax family. The Australian Journalists' Association newspaper described this as an 'extraordinary campaign' in which 'Hawke and Keating decided to go in boots and all [and which was] significant because of the timing. Speculation about the future of the *National Times on Sunday* was rife, making the paper more vulnerable to a concerted political attack.'[79]

Two stories the paper had published were singled out by Hawke and Keating. On September 10, 1986 a front-page report headlined, URANIUM: HAWKE WANTS PARK MINED, quoted a letter Hawke had written to his Environment Minister, in which he objected to the absence of a provision for mining in the draft management plan for Kakadu National Park in the Northern Territory, the world's biggest and richest uranium province. The story was true, and no facts were disputed. On December 7 the paper's front page reported that the Government had decided to contribute to a World Bank loan to the Pinochet regime in Chile, and that Bill Hayden had opposed the decision. Hayden denied his opposition, but the story essentially was true. Nevertheless, on December 8 Keating denounced it as 'a complete fabrication' and said that other stories the paper had published, such as the Kakadu uranium story, were 'wrong and squalid'. He made no attempt to justify this and dismissed journalists' questions about the Chile connection. 'The *National Times*', he said, 'is a flagging, desperate newspaper which is going out of sight at a rate of knots and the quicker the better.' The next day Hawke described the paper as 'totally dishonest . . . a total disgrace to journalism' and added, 'They will not learn.' He, too, offered nothing to substantiate this.

The *National Times on Sunday*, a broadsheet, had grown out of a remarkable 'stretched tabloid', the *National Times*, whose strength had been that indeed it had not 'learned' to subvert its journalism to the ambitions and manipulations of politicians and their Mates. The paper had been given a degree of independence which was as rare as it was provisional. This was due to the paternalism and idiosyncrasies of the Fairfax organisation and specially the support of its libertarian chairman, James Fairfax.

This degree of independence seemed genuinely to baffle Hawke, who, like so many public figures in Australia, regards his secret and contradictory activities as beyond the limits of free enquiry and comment.[80] The *National Times*, wrote David Bowman, who had been editor in chief of its sister paper, the *Sydney Morning Herald*, 'was a unique paper with an extraordinary history of tough, independent enquiry bent on exposing secrets, showing up social ills, and going over the high and mighty, for the health of the nation and the benefit of ordinary people. The trouble was that it lost money continually and made an army of enemies for Fairfax.'[81]

For twelve years, the *National Times* presented a catalogue of some of Australia's darkest, contemporary secrets. The paper's small editorial team posed the first serious threat to political corruption and organised crime in Australia. Certainly, I cannot think of a newspaper anywhere in the world quite as tenacious and fearless and which, at its best, employed so many journalists of distinction: Max Suich, Evan Whitton, Brian Toohey, Wendy Bacon, Marian Wilkinson, Colleen Ryan, Adele Horin, David Hickie and others.

Between them they attracted 'an army of enemies' and attempts were made to frame and discredit several of them, even to threaten their lives. Their enemies ranged from street thugs to thugs of another kind, among them the most powerful individuals in Australia. When Hawke was asked on television to confirm or deny that he had ordered the Australian security organisation, ASIO, to tap Brian Toohey's phone, he refused to say. Toohey was the paper's most famous editor and the recipient of more official 'leaks' than any journalist I know. He had so many leaked documents that he left them in suitcases at secret addresses all over Sydney. Politicians hated him, mostly for reasons of which a journalist ought to be proud.

But when a Prime Minister and his senior Cabinet Minister make such a vehement public attack on a newspaper that is in financial difficulties, something has to happen. In March 1987, Brian Toohey, by now relieved of the editorship, wrote a long polemic which analysed the new establishment. Entitled 'The Death of Labor', it was illustrated by the brilliant Sydney artist Michael Fitzjames and showed two black horses with mourning plumes drawing a Victorian hearse and coffin. Astride one horse was Keating, in formal suit and topper, raising a glass of champagne on high. Similarly attired on the other horse was Bob Hawke, waving a big cigar. They were gazing at each other with looks of sublime satisfaction. Toohey described 'a new Australia forged by a new type of entrepreneur [whose] fortunes are built on deals where nobbling official watchdogs or bribing union bosses eliminates much of the risk ... [where] tax cheats become nation builders'. Hawke and Keating, he wrote 'do more than enjoy the company of the new tycoons: they share their values [while] the sacrifices are being made by the battlers for whom Labor once fought'.[82]

Toohey's article was withdrawn by the Fairfax management several days before publication. As a result, the editor, Robert Haupt, resigned. Toohey did the same, and launched, virtually single handed, a magazine called The Eye, which promised 'the stories the big boys won't print'.

On Friday, February 13, shortly after he had wrested control of the Herald and Weekly Times group, Rupert Murdoch

flew to Queensland. It was St Valentine's Day – the day that
a coterie of Chicago's Mafia bosses were assembled in a garage and dealt with in the customary way by their Mates –
and the editors of Murdoch's papers in Australia were
assembled in a Gold Coast hotel and dealt with in the customary way. This was the Class of '87, thirty-five in all, including
the new boys from the Herald and Weekly Times group.
They were billeted at the luxurious or hideous Gold Coast
International Hotel, where Rupert and Anna Murdoch held
a reception to welcome their guests. 'They have a marvellous
way of putting people at their ease,' said one of the editors.[83]

The next morning, sharp at nine, the editors gathered in
the hotel's Penthouse club, where the atmosphere was very
different. 'Each of us had to sing for our supper,' one of them
told me. 'It was like I always imagined the Moonies behaved.
Each of us had to reaffirm the Murdoch ethos: the kind of
newspapers *he* wants, *he* gets and *he* controls; the kind of
newspapers most Australians will read into the next century.

I went home shaken and humiliated. But I still had my job.'

David Bowman once described the Murdoch papers as 'that augmented team of well-broken horses'. Two days after the augmented team had returned to their desks from the Gold Coast, they were writing headlines like these:

MURDOCH A TRUE BLUE AUSSIE, SAYS PM

HAWKE PRAISES MURDOCH COMMITMENT.

The story was about a lavish dinner to celebrate Murdoch's mother's favourite charity, although, of course, there was more to it than that. Eighteen members of the Murdoch family were assembled to hear the guest of honour, Prime Minister Hawke, praise the 'Australianness' of Rupert Murdoch (who had not long renounced his Australian nationality in order to pursue his American commercial interests). 'The crucial test of "Rupert's national loyalties"', said Hawke, 'came during the America's Cup challenge when he barracked for an Australian victory!'

Knowing, temperate laughter lapped the smiling Labor leader and the smiling proprietor as a string quartet played, 'For he's a jolly good fellow'. The two men turned towards each other and raised their glasses in mutual approval; their Mateship now consecrated. During the first four years of the Hawke Government, the Murdoch family's fortune increased from $A250 million to $A2,500 million.[84]

'In other countries', said Paul Chadwick, 'it is a small group of generals who sit above the main institutions. In Australia we also have a junta, for it seems that a small group of media owners can now cause politicians of all persuasions to desert their responsibilities to the public. The fear that politicians are showing is evidence of the danger it imposes.'[85]

In November 1986, Treasurer Keating unexpectedly announced a new policy for the 're-structuring' of commercial television. Under the old regulations no one could own more than two television stations. Now the Government proposed that any one owner could command an 'audience reach' of 75 per cent of the population. This would mean that a single operator could control stations in every capital city. It would also mean that the nation's fifty television stations, which had been spread among twenty-five owners, would be taken over by a handful of conglomerates, notably those with numerous and often conflicting commercial interests. Not since the dawn of the television age had there been such a contraction of ownership. Not since the cry of 'Gold!' had sent diggers to Eureka had such a bonanza beckoned to so few. The Government's announcement alone caused the share trading value of television stock to soar. And this time the diggers had only to reach for their phones.

Keating said his concern was that those who owned newspapers ought not to own television stations. This was bad for democracy, he said. Some would have to sell and some would have to buy. Three Mates, Rupert Murdoch, Kerry Packer and Alan Bond, reached for their phones. In the words of the Sydney financial analysts, County Securities Australia:

> The Federal Government allowed the two most powerful print media proprietors next to Fairfax to gain substantial returns for their TV interests by way of allowing aggregation of TV licences under the 75 per cent rule. Mr Kerry Packer and News Corporation have received approximately 1·8 billion dollars in income, whereas the valuation pre the rules would have been in the vicinity of 800 million dollars – a one billion dollar gift.

> And it was a gift entirely free of tax.

Kerry Packer is known as 'Australia's richest man'. This is probably true. Certainly, the years of the Hawke Labor government have seen his fortune rise from $A100 million to more than $2 billion[86]. In many ways he is like his father, Sir Frank Packer, a former boxer who owned Consolidated Press, whose power was respected, if not feared. Sir Frank was one of a group of newspaper proprietors known as the 'wild men of Sydney'. I worked on his *Telegraph* newspapers during my tender years as a journalist. As a sub-editor on the *Sunday Telegraph*, I was sacked along with all my colleagues late one Saturday night after Sir Frank had stormed back from the races and disapproved of the front page. After an hour or so in the pub, we were re-instated when it was pointed out to the proprietor that he would have no paper the next day without us. The chief sub-editor knew him as 'Gorgo', which was a 1950s Hollywood beast.

Kerry Packer had mild polio as a child and was apparently called 'boofhead' at school. Yet he excelled at sport. He was never the heir apparent and had to live two paces behind his elder brother, Clyde, who was regarded as brighter. They were, and remain massive men, like sumo wrestlers or of the kind you see in the southern states of America. In my second year on the Sydney *Daily Telegraph* I mistakenly rode in a lift with both of them and feared for the progress of our elevation. Kerry has a Lizard-like head: thus he is known as 'The Goanna'.

When Sir Frank died it was Kerry, not Clyde, who emulated their father's manipulative skills; Clyde was paid off and went to live in Los Angeles. When he sold the unprofitable *Daily Telegraph* to Rupert Murdoch, Kerry did the deal in a car parked outside Murdoch's hotel after a boxing match. When Packer escorted his daughter Gretel down the aisle at her wedding, it was Murdoch's hand he grasped on the way.

Packer's personal passions are gambling, polo and cricket; he is said to gamble a million dollars at a time. He is widely admired for challenging the English cricket establishment and establishing 'world series cricket'. He is also a serious fan of Genghis Khan, whose life he has studied. From time to time he goes into the bush of the Hunter Valley and, dressed in army fatigues and armed with a pellet rifle, plays war games with cronies; he has re-fought the Falklands War. He has been a secret backer of the South African Zulu leader Chief Buthelezi, giving the *Inkatha* movement several millions of dollars. His conservatism is as ingrained as his father's; he sees no contradiction in supporting a Labor prime Minister who complies with his own ethos.

The Packer 'empire' covers vast tracts of the Northern Territory and 170 companies around the world. He owns most of the magazines Australians read and the only national commercial television network. Although he is a corporate 'deal maker', he has made much of his wealth by currency trading, moving money from country to country and minimising tax; the Bahamas is his favourite tax haven. His most famous *coup* was in selling the Channel 9 Network to Alan Bond for a billion dollars, then buying it back from Bond for less than half that amount.[87]

The original Channel 9 deal meant that Australia had, in Alan Bond, a brand-new media magnate. Bond was already famous as the man who had backed Australia's successful America's Cup challenger; and what Murdoch had done for the press, Bond had done for beer. Australians, who drink a lot of beer, used to have a wide choice. Today they drink beer owned mostly by John Elliott (Foster's) and Alan Bond (XXXX, Toohey's and Swan). Perhaps only 'Bondy' could make a fortune selling Swan lager to teetotal muslims by renaming it Long Nose Goose and taking the alcohol out. 'There is an old Irish saying,' said John Hogan of the West Australian Development Corporation, '"Stop shaking the rat, it's dead." In getting the best from a deal, Alan Bond doesn't know when the rat is dead.' A Texan banker, who knew Bond, said, 'Doing business with Alan Bond is like wrestling with a pig. You both get sprayed with shit and the pig loves it.'[88]

Indeed, Bond has almost gone bust and risen again. 'He has been declared dead more times than Dracula', said the business journalist Trevor Sykes in 1991, 'However, I'd say he's down to the last nails in the coffin this time. It's amazing he's survived for so long'.[89] Apart from breweries and TV stations, Bond in his heyday owned satellites, hotels, world-wide property interests, oil fields, gold fields, and airships, much of it on borrowed capital. Bond still exudes a devotion to his adopted country; he came from England as a boy and believes the dry warmth of Western Australia saved his asthmatic father's life. When he told me he would sell 'anything' except his Australian nationality, as Murdoch has done, he seemed sincere. He began as a signwriter and is partly responsible for a huge red dingo painted on the side of a building in Fremantle, near Perth. It used to be said he had an 'edifice complex'. He liked to buy or construct great phalluses and call them after himself, such as the Bond Centre in Hong Kong. His fifty-first floor office in Perth was decorated with the works of Gauguin, Renoir, Toulouse-Lautrec and Van Gogh, whose 'Irises' cost him $A58 million, a world record. He is married to Eileen, who has been described as a legend in her own lunchtime and is seen about Perth either in her white Rolls-Royce, with cocktail cabinet, fridge and picnic table, or in her pale blue Mercedes sports with leopard-skin seat covers. 'Alan', she said, 'calls it my pooftah car.'[90]

Bondy's first 'personal yacht' was built to his specifications in Japan for $A30 million. It had a helicopter pad and a grand piano and a guest list which included his Mates, Paul Keating and Bob Hawke. During the first four years of the Hawke Government, Bondy's personal fortune rose from $A25 million to $A400 million.[91] When Bondy planned his daughter Suzanne's wedding reception, he told Eileen she could spend what she liked, and she spent at least half a million dollars. She had a church completely re-fitted and she built a tented city and filled it with guests flown in from around Australia and the world, including Princess Diana's dressmaker and a dress costing $A170,000. She had the table napkins woven with gold thread and she paid $A10,000 for a pair of Michael Jackson's diamanté socks, suspended in a plastic tube and authenticated by his own hand. The cake was said to 'The biggest in the Southern Hemisphere'. At dawn the Krug '79 was still flowing. Bob Hawke sent his best wishes. Suzanne has since filed for divorce.

In December 1986 the *Sydney Morning Herald* disclosed that the Western Australian Corporate Affairs Commission was investigating two deals in which Bond had allegedly made more than $A16 million in tax-free profits. A Bond family company was said to have made $A8 million for a cash outlay of just $A100.[92] The paper put a list of detailed questions to Bond concerning the allegations, but he refused to answer them; and when the story appeared he issued a writ for defamation and cancelled all Bond Group advertising with the Fairfax group. Two months later the Corporate Affairs Commission announced that it had cleared Bond of the allegations; surprisingly, it published no report. Bond subsequently dropped his libel action against the *Sydney Morning Herald*, just as the 'discovery' stage in the action was reached: that is, when the *Herald* lawyers would have had access to the records of the Bond family company, Dallhold. The newspaper published no apology and its advertising account with the Bond group was restored.

In 1989 the Australian Broadcasting Corporation's *Four Corners* programme acquired a copy of Dallhold's accounts, which are normally not published. These showed that in 1988 the Bond family company made a profit of $A48 million, but paid not one cent of tax. *Four Corners* also revealed that the tax authorities had found that Bond and three of his senior directors had set up a 'two dollar company' through which each of them had made a profit of $A900,000 on developing the site for the Bond Building in Perth, without telling shareholders of the Bond public company that owns the building. At the time of writing in 1989, the Bond group was claiming to be $A36 million in tax *credit*.[93]

I met Bond in his Sydney headquarters, in offices trimmed with fake walnut and ebony. The oppressiveness of the surroundings seemed at odds with Bond's ebullience. In one corner was a model of his proposed Sydney Bond Tower.

'Ugly isn't it?' he said. That afternoon he had bought Sydney's Hilton Hotel. 'I only got the building,' he said with a laugh, 'not the people in it.'

The Hilton did not long remain Bond property. It was sold shortly afterwards for a clear profit of $A480 million – all of it untaxed. The Hilton deal, according to *Four Corners*, had been done through a web of companies, ending up with one based in the Cook Islands, a volcanic pile in the middle of the Pacific. Bond executives described the sale as an 'international transaction' and claimed that no Australian tax was payable. But, whatever the subterfuge, here was a major Australian corporation selling an Australian asset to an undisclosed buyer and, on the face of it, owing the Australian people around $A40 million in tax, of which not a cent had been paid.[94]

The Hilton deal was not unusual. In 1988 the Bond Corporation made 90 per cent of its profits – or $A250 million – in the Cook Islands, where it does not sell a single can of XXXX. 'This Government', Treasurer Keating said, 'will not tolerate any action by companies which rips off the rest of the community.'[95]

According to a report by the Australian Tax Office, Bond Corporation and Rupert Murdoch's News Corporation made their profits for 1987–8, a total of $A673 million, in tax havens like the Cook Islands. The report said that they and thousands of other Australian companies had cost ordinary tax payers $A1·2 billion in lost revenue in just one year.[96]

I asked Alan Bond how, with so many potentially conflicting commercial interests, he could run an honest media. 'How would you respond', I said, 'if one of your TV journalists found out something untoward in a corner of your empire and exposed it?'

'The instructions to our journalistic staff', said Bond, 'is that if you find something you release it first and be *seen* to release it first.'[97]

This was interesting in the light of a finding by the Australian Broadcasting Tribunal that Bond had made an 'unprecedented' payment of $A400,000 to the Premier of Queensland, Sir Johannes Bjelke-Petersen, 'in order to maintain good relations between the Premier and the Bond group of companies'. The payment, said the Tribunal, 'could have compromised the independence' of one of Bond's Queensland TV stations and 'led the beneficiary to believe that the station will bow to pressure in future'. Bjelke-Petersen had brought a libel action against the Brisbane station, QTQ, after a current affairs programme had alleged that he had used his official position for private advantage on a trip to Japan. When Bond bought the station he was told by its insurance advisers that the Premier's claim was unlikely to succeed, that although the station had technically libelled the Premier, its defence was 'strongly arguable'. Still, Bond rejected this and paid up.[98] Bond has mining, brewing and hotel interests in Queensland, all of them highly dependent for their profitability on Government decisions.

In 1989, the Broadcasting Tribunal decided that Alan Bond was not a 'fit and proper' person to run a television service: a decision which is still being contested in the courts. Prior to this judgment, the Minister for Communications announced that the Hawke Government might change the Broadcasting Act to ensure that the Australian public was not deprived of Bond's broadcasting services. Such has been the essence of the Order of Mates.

By 1990, however, Bondy's empire was crumbling under the weight of its IOUs. Banks and investors sought the immediate repayment of $A1.4 billion and his beer interests were threatened with the receiver. Edifices were sold. His television network was put on the market, prompting Kerry Packer, who sold it to him, to reach for his chequebook: mateship, after all, has its limits. And yet for all the disclosures of practices more akin to an unlicensed gambling den than a great international corporation, Bondy did not sink. Indeed, in full-page newspaper advertisements he pleaded his case direct to 'my dear fellow Australians'; and as if to underline 'my patriotism above all' he pledged Bond Corporation to build a $A12 million replica of Captain

Cook's ship, the *Endeavour*, as a gift to 'this greatest of nations'.

However, by 1992 the saga of Australia's most glamorous Mate had become a farce. Owing billions, Bond stood before bankers at his Tricontinental Corporation and said that he had only one asset to his name: a gold Rolex watch. 'So the bankers asked for it', reported the *Asian Wall Street Journal*. 'Broke but not beaten, Mr. Bond refused to turn over the timepiece . . .

> It is a long way from the hero's welcome Mr Bond received from the nation when he won the coveted America's Cup away from the Americans in 1983. On the eighth anniversary of his famous yachting victory, Mr Bond woke to an ignominious day that began with a high-speed car chase witnessed by his neighbours in Perth's swank Dalkeith suburb.
>
> With television crews in hot pursuit filming the chase for the nation's nightly news, a harried Mr Bond sought refuge at a local police station where he told reporters that a stranger in a big red truck with big bumper bars on it tail-gated him and tried to run him off the road . . . The stranger turned out to be an agent hired by the banks to track down Mr Bond. One witness reported a skirmish in the police parking lot during which Mr Bond was served with the papers.[99]

A judge ruled that the bankruptcy order served on Bond was deficient on technical grounds. He was served with another at Sydney Airport; at the time of writing, he is fighting this in the courts. Indeed, courts are where Bondy spends much of his time these days. He has been given bail of $A100,000 on charges related to his part in the collapse of the Perth merchant bank, Rothwells Limited. If convicted, he may face a prison term. When the 'sirens began to wail' in 1989, Bondy explained it all like this: 'Maybe it's because I'm out there like any entrepreneur should be, breaking new ground, taking risks, doing things that other, more conservative people only dream about'.[100]

Christopher Skase embodied the Hawke/Keating years. Skase was the bankers' and journalists' Mate. He would fly them almost anywhere and pay their bills for almost anything. He was, after all, once a journalist himself; he understood the value placed on patronage and comfort by certain of his former colleagues. The very best mates would find themselves on Mirage III, which Skase bought for $A6 million and which featured baby blue carpets and Chinese antiques. These mates would be flown to its Brisbane mooring in Skase's jet, with its big leather seats and a bed. Even a visit to Skase's office was an occasion high above a reception of marble and Egyptian antiques. 'Skase was probably Australia's greatest salesman', said a bankers mate. 'Better than Bondy. Very smooth . . . yeah, we liked him'.[101] Skase and his wife Pixie were almost always photographed smiling, often wearing their twin T-shirts which declared, TOO GOOD TO BE TRUE.[102]

It was Skase's Quintex company, which owned Channel 7 and resorts, that could not bear the fees Skase and his directors paid themselves; in one year Skase took $A12.6 million from his management company. When two independent directors resigned in 1989, after refusing to approve the company's accounts, yet another siren wailed. Among the disclosures was the fact that $A44.7 million had been paid by Quintex for 'management services and expenses' to a company controlled by a number of Quintex directors. When Quintex finally collapsed, Skase was trying to take over the Hollywood studios of MGM in a deal involving more than $A2 billion – which was the sum of the company's debts and for which 'prospects for recovery are slim', according to the receiver.[103]

Skase was declared bankrupt in June, 1991 and three days later he and Pixie left Australia to continue their good life in La Noria, a luxurious estate on the Spanish island of Majorca. At the time of writing he has been summonsed to appear before a Federal Court to answer questions about his financial affairs, but has yet to turn up. The Justice Minister, Michael Tate, says he believes Australians 'are sick to death and quite angry at the spectacle of high-living bankrupts . . .'[104] 'Still, you have to admire Skase's gall', mused an investigative team in the *Sydney Morning Herald*, 'After Quintex went into receivership, Skase claimed $A634,000 in holiday pay and long-service leave'[105]

For many Australians the ABC is the last redoubt of honest news and current affairs, 'an oasis of public service broadcasting in a desert of commercialism', according to a friend of mine who once took elocution lessons before applying for a job in what used to be the ABC Talks Department. Unfortunately, vowel transplants did him no good; he was 'too Australian'. 'You really should go to London for a year or two,' he was advised at the ABC, which had digested the shibboleths of Lord Reith's BBC, including a view of itself as a temple of impartiality. Like the BBC at its best, the ABC has been run with high professionalism and flair. Like the BBC at its worst, the ABC has looked upon impartiality as a principle to be suspended when the established order is threatened. Unlike the BBC, the ABC is dependent upon direct Government funding. This has meant that Governments in Canberra have been able to 'reward' and 'punish' the public broadcasting service.

The real importance of the ABC is its national character. In a continent as vast as the United States and with a fraction of the population, the ABC alone broadcasts almost everywhere: from Tasmania in the far Antipodes to Pilbara in the north-west and to the islands that brush Asia.

In the 1980s the ABC began to discard its BBC 'blanket'. The automatic purchase of BBC television programmes ceased, and a variety of other sources were sought at home and overseas. Under a new Director of Television, Richard Thomas, ironically a former BBC man, the nature of much of ABC television began to change. Unlike many of his colleagues, Thomas believed that the sacred lore of 'balance' in practice too often served to disguise a system biased in favour of the prevailing establishment wisdom and against a genuine diversity of viewpoint. The latter is known in much of the Australian media as 'controversy'. In 1985, on Thomas's initiative, the ABC broadcast a documentary film I made with Alan Lowery which examined distortions in white Australia's history of the Aborigines. I was subsequently contracted to make a series of short reports for the current affairs programme, *The 7.30 Report*. I proposed an interview with the Silver Bodgie.

In 1986 Richard Thomas suffered a heart attack and was forced into a long convalescence. It was during this time that David Hill, a Mate of the New South Wales Labor Party machine, became the Chairman of the ABC, after being interviewed for the job by Bob Hawke. Shortly afterwards he took over the chief executive's job, even though he has no background in broadcasting. He was briefly a financial journalist on Rupert Murdoch's *Australian*, then a lecturer in economics, then an assistant to Premier Neville Wran. Wran sent him to the United States to negotiate the Lotto licence with Murdoch, then gave him the State railways to run.

At the State Rail Authority, Hill's own runner was Tony Ferguson, a former ABC producer and Labor Party fixer who had been a prominent member of the Hawke Government's 'liaison service', or propaganda unit. He is a confidant of Hawke and a guest at the Prime Minister's home in Canberra. It was Ferguson who had offered valuable support to Hill's prospects at the ABC and it was Ferguson who, as Hill's political sherpa, joined him as 'executive assistant' at the ABC.

On the day Richard Thomas returned to his office, he was summoned to see Hill, told he had been removed from his job, offered a 'consultancy' and, when he refused this, was sacked. This was the way the Labor machine had run New

South Wales, and it was to be David Hill's way at the ABC. Hill was a 'ratings man'. Thomas had tried to change the format of the nightly news programme and had failed to increase the viewing audience; he was not a ratings man. Hill would do almost anything for ratings. He dressed up as a chauffeur and drove a veteran entertainer called Mike Walsh to a press conference where he announced Walsh's acquisition by the ABC; to Hill, Walsh was a 'ratings asset'. *EastEnders* became the ABC's first foreign soap opera to be shown in prime time. It failed. Hill commissioned a thirty-episode soap opera set in a Bondi hotel and aptly called *The Last Resort*. It achieved unusually low ratings. When new programmes were presented to him, Hill enquired, 'Listen mate, is there any rootin' or shootin' in it?'[106] Rootin', in Australia, is fucking.

My ABC interview with Bob Hawke for *The 7.30 Report* was set for March 4, 1987, the eve of his fourth year as Prime Minister. My request had gone originally to Paul Ellercamp, who subsequently resigned as Hawke's press secretary. This was not surprising, as Hawke reportedly had a habit of clicking his fingers at Ellercamp and yelling 'Cigars!'[107] His replacement was Barrie Cassidy, who a few weeks earlier had been the ABC's chief political correspondent in Canberra. This sudden shift from journalism to parliamentary 'public relations' is common practice in Australia; journalists slip in and out of political service with such ease that an inner circle of politicians and members of the Canberra Press Gallery are often indistinguishable in their machinations. The level of this incest is such that a vice president of the Australian Journalists' Association, Gary Scully, can claim to be defending his members' professional independence while he is part of the Prime Minister's propaganda unit. The language of Mates is used by all: Hawke is 'Hawkie', Murdoch is 'Rupert', Packer is 'Kerry'.

Cassidy appeared deeply anxious about the interview, if not terrified. 'It's important the PM is relaxed,' he said. 'I want to see you both *really* relaxed. I want it to be a conversation.' He and I had several phone conversations about the art of relaxation during a political interview. He called me once to say he was re-arranging the furniture in the Prime Minister's outer office so that we would have the most comfortable chairs and be '*really* relaxed'.

Early on the day of the interview I went for a run around Lake Burley Griffin, the artificial lake in the centre of Canberra named after the American architect who designed the city. To its admirers, Canberra is one of the most perfectly planned cities of the twentieth century; to its detractors, it is the Ulan Bator of the southern hemisphere. With the lake as its focus, the streets radiate out in ever-increasing circles: a design said to reflect the indecisiveness and bloody mindedness of politicians in Melbourne and Sydney, who could not agree which city would host the Federal Parliament. The compromise was a cow pasture between the two State capitals, a site of inconvenience and isolation, broiling in summer and freezing in winter.

For years the airport building at Canberra, the gateway to the capital of Australia, had the architectural charm of a shearers' shed; and foreign diplomats returning to their Australian posts could be observed thumbing forlornly through the coy Australian version of *Playboy* while waiting for their luggage to arrive on a conveyance resembling a small stage-coach. Foreign Governments built odd buildings in Canberra, apparently in defiance of the locale. The Thais erected what appears to be a huge, ornate massage parlour; the Americans put up a pile of mock Georgian Disneyland. Only the squat, banal shape of the Australian Parliament House seemed to fit the landscape; in the Bicentenary year this was replaced by a structure resembling a shopping mall with a rocket launch pad.

All this belied the fact that 10 per cent of Canberra's inhabitants lived in poverty, and more than a quarter of Canberra's young people were unemployed.[108] You seldom saw these rejected people from your car. Running back to my hotel, I passed three dishevelled teenagers asleep under a bridge, where they had spent the night. 'Gidday,' said the one awake, 'gissadollar.'

When I arrived at Parliament House there were numerous Russians and police in the forecourt and on the steps. I bumped into Bill Hayden, the Minister for Foreign Affairs, who was showing his Soviet opposite number around King's Hall, which is lined with gilt-framed oils of Australia's past leaders and assorted colonial worthies. 'Gidday,' said Bill, 'Howyergoin?' At the reception counter I joined the Chinese Ambassador, who was waiting for an appointment. 'Russians are coming! Russians are coming!' he said, apparently as a joke. This was accompanied by maniacal cackle. All of us at the reception desk, an Indian, a Yugoslav and a refrigeration engineer, were infected by the Ambassador's cackle. 'How can I help you, Mr Ambassador?' said the man behind the desk, now pink from trying not to laugh. 'Gidday,' said the Ambassador, who began to laugh at himself. I had not seen a Chinese Ambassador behave that way before, nor had I heard one say, 'Gidday.' A friend in the parliamentary press gallery describes the condition as 'Canberra release'.

Barrie Cassidy looked hunted. He said the Prime Minister was running late and I would have to settle for an abbreviated interview. Yes, but what about the 'relaxed conversation'? 'Sorry, not on,' said Cassidy.

Bob Hawke arrived at ten past eleven and Cassidy said I had exactly twenty minutes. Hawke seemed to have shrunk in the eleven years since our last meeting, the result perhaps of the Pritikin diet to which he had devoted himself since giving up the booze. Indeed, his face appeared to be so small that his hair, which had swollen to a silver Thatcher-like bloom, appeared precariously balanced. Flanked by aides, he was no longer reminiscent of Nixon, but of Jimmy Cagney in one of his affected tough guy roles. I held out my hand. 'Get on with it,' he said.

I began by asking him why the rich had grown richer and the poor poorer under his Government and why he did not tax the interest on overseas borrowings which had helped to make those like Rupert Murdoch and Alan Bond extremely rich. He replied that this was a view of 'Johnnie-come-latelys' like myself; that he had incurred the wrath of the wealthy

Queensland 'white shoe brigade' by bringing in a capital gains tax; and that when he came to office he had been confronted with an economy that had been brought to its knees and since then he had de-regulated the financial sector and brought in the foreign banks and, as a result, Australia was off its knees. 'There is no virtue', he said, 'in saying that existing enterprises are sacrosanct; that is the essence of conservatism. The essence of change is that you allow the processes to take place which allows takeovers, which allows existing management to be bought out and taken over.'

This was all very well, but he had not answered the question, and it was plain he was becoming increasingly agitated as I urged him to answer it. When I asked him why he had not used the law to stop Rupert Murdoch gaining control of most of the Australian press, he replied that the press had never been more diversified. He was now angry, indeed approaching incandescence. Suddenly his eyes rolled upwards into his head and failed to return. I remembered this from our meeting in Fitzroy Gardens. It was a successful tactic, for it rendered me speechless before a surreal visage not unlike a small Grecian statue in a silver wig.

I asked him about Aboriginal land rights, and there I lost him. He got up and walked off, 'You've had your time!' he shouted from across the room. 'You took up a lot of time on an issue on which you were obviously wrong' – Murdoch's dominance of the press – 'You asked the wrong questions on the wrong issues. You should *learn*!'

I phoned the ABC and asked the executive producer, John Turner, to transmit all twenty-two minutes of the interview, but Turner insisted that it should have only eight minutes. 'Hawkie is Valium,' he said. During the course of editing I negotiated another minute of air time and sought to retain the essence of each of the answers to my questions.

The interview drew a remarkable public response. A minority complained to the ABC that I had been 'biased' and 'disrespectful'. Others felt that the interview had confronted Hawke with, as Ian Davis wrote in the *Canberra Times*, 'that tiny grain of truth, that kernel of self realisation, which threatens a public figure with exposure with something less than he has successfully persuaded others he is'.[109] The next day Cassidy issued a statement which described the interview as 'slanted' and 'heavily edited'. The transcript of the interview, he said, 'does not record the admonishment referred to by Pilger, nor does it record the question concerning Aborigines mentioned by Pilger, nor Mr Hawke replying that he couldn't answer the question.' All of this was false.

On the transcript the beginning of Hawke's admonishment of me was clear, my question about Aborigines was clear and Hawke's expressed unwillingness to stay and answer the question was clear. Cassidy also complained about 're-filmed questions'. The separate filming of 'reverse' or 'cutaway' questions is standard television practice when there is only one camera. Otherwise editing is virtually impossible. Each of my 'cutaways' as recorded was no different in substance or meaning from the original question.

The ABC's Controller of News and Current Affairs, Bob Kearsley, immediately mounted an enquiry. He compared the edited and unedited tapes and interviewed the programme's executive producer, the camera crew and me. He then phoned me to say that the accusation 'is plainly ridiculous on the evidence. As far as ABC current affairs is concerned the complaint is rejected and that's the end of it.' Kearsley wrote a report for the ABC's acting managing director, Stuart Revill – David Hill was overseas – in which he left no doubt that the charge of misrepresentation 'is not justified . . . the Prime Minister appears to have approached the interview in a way which made confrontation inevitable'. He recommended 'no apology or correction'.[110] The response of viewers left little doubt that Hawke had angered many by his hostility to questions about fundamental issues, and that had the ABC shown all twenty-two minutes of the interview, his populist image would have been at some risk. The response of the Mates was prompt.

Hawke's confidant, Tony Ferguson, was in touch with Cassidy and with Neville Wran. Wran was incensed by the interview and agreed to handle the matter in Sydney. This led the former Premier of the State to demand time on Sydney radio in which to read an extraordinary prepared statement. Wran attacked the interview as 'deeply disrespectful' to awke and called on his former aide and protegé, David Hill, to take action. Hill had been informed in New York and on his return to Sydney on March 13 he went straight from the airport to a closed meeting with Ferguson about the episode. On the same day I asked Bob Kearsley for a copy of his report; Kearsley agreed, then changed his mind and wrote me a note saying that the report could not be given out because it was now an 'internal ABC document'. The next day Hill flew to Canberra, and without consulting his own head of news and current affairs or anyone else associated with the production of the Hawke interview, myself included, made a speech in which he effectively apologised to Hawke for the interview. He also refused to confirm whether or not I would again be allowed to work for the ABC.

Hill's remarks were widely reported. They could not be justified in any way by the results of the ABC's own enquiry, nor did he attempt to justify them. I called on him to show the unedited interview and allow people to judge for themselves. He refused. Two newspapers, the *Australian* and the *Sydney Morning Herald*, planned to publish my response on March 16. As both papers were about to publish their first edition, they received calls at the behest of the ABC's Controller of Corporate Affairs, Keith Jackson, himself a member of the Labor Party's right wing and a Mate of Hawke. Under New South Wales libel laws, claimed Jackson, my reply was 'potentially defamatory'. Both papers heeded the warning and dropped the story.

On the same night Jackson and an ABC legal officer were busy warning ABC journalists that if they interviewed me, or even got in touch with me, they could be sued by their own managing director. The acting Chief of Staff of ABC radio phoned me to read me the bulletin she proposed to put on the air. She said she had been instructed to delete all mention of my reply. Two ABC current affairs producers phoned me with similar stories and to say there was nothing they could do about it. The presenter of the ABC's *AM* programme, John Highfield, a respected broadcaster, phoned to apologise for the 'embarrassment' he felt about having to take me off his programme. 'It's come from above', he said, 'and no one is prepared to put their job on the line. The pressure has been crude; I feel very bad about it and I'm very sorry.' Highfield, however, felt deeply about the matter and talked to the *Sydney Morning Herald*. When a report appeared quoting him, he was phoned by a superior at six in the morning and told, 'You're in deep shit, son.' In this way David Hill gagged Australia's public broadcasting body for almost two days.

High farce now ensued. Hill and I were invited to appear on the *Midday Show*, a popular 'chat show' broadcast live on the commercial Channel 9 network. But when Hill arrived at the studios with Ferguson, he refused to debate with me face to face; and when told that I would have the last word, they began to walk out, bellowing expletives at the presenter, Ray Martin. This took place during a commercial break and behind a precariously mounted screen which separated Hill and Ferguson, Martin and his producers from a studio audience of mostly suburban matrons. As the refrain of 'What a load of bullshit!' and 'You unethical bastards!' drifted over them, the ladies appeared at once perplexed and entertained in a manner they had not anticipated. And when the man who did the 'warming up' came and told them a joke, hoping to deflect their interest, he was told by a formidable woman to 'piss off'. After spirited negotiations, Hill agreed to say his say separately from mine, but refused to allow a clip of the Hawke interview to be shown.

On March 28 a letter appeared in the *Sydney Morning Herald* signed by sixteen distinguished Australians, including the historian Manning Clark, the writers Dorothy Hewett, John Hepworth, Faith Bandler and the former Labor Minister and judge James McClelland. 'The recent controversy over John Pilger's interview with the Prime Minister', it read:

raises serious questions about the independence of the ABC ... The heart of the matter is that this was an important interview, in which Pilger raised issues of a nature and in a way not usually seen on TV. The Prime Minister's office promptly complained to the ABC about alleged misrepresentation and distortion on Pilger's part. Those charges were explicitly rejected by the ABC's controller of news and current affairs ... Doubts that ABC employees were subject to political pressure could be resolved by the publication of the relevant documents.

Two months passed, during which I made several applications under Australia's Freedom of Information Act for the 'relevant documents' to be released. The report of Bob Kearsley's enquiry was not included in the first batch. However, other documents were revealing. On March 9, five days after the interview with Hawke, the ABC's acting Director of Television, Grahame Reynolds, wrote a confidential memo to Kearsley, in which he instructed that any future 'major political interview' should be referred to David Hill before being broadcast. This, he wrote, 'used to be the practice'. In his reply, Kearsley wrote that such a 'practice' had never existed and added that he would have 'some difficulty with such a system, both philosophical and practical'. Kearsley was writing as a journalist who understood that such a system equalled the most insidious form of censorship and control. It is a pity the Australian people, who own the ABC, were not made aware of this important development; but by the time ABC management had complied with the law and released more papers it was too late; the story was 'dead'. No newspaper would publish the documented evidence, which appeared finally in *The Journalist*, the union paper. 'Intimidation, black bans and other forms of pressure', Mike Steketee, a leading political journalist, once wrote, 'have all been part of the attempts to coerce unco-operative journalists. After all, politics is a tough game and, in New South Wales, they play it for keeps.'[111]

In April 1987, the ABC appointed a new chairman, Rob Somervaille who, with David Hill, was to run public broadcasting in Australia. Somervaille is a Mate of Bob Hawke and Rupert Murdoch. As a director of a Murdoch 'shelf company', Somervaille played a principal role in Murdoch's takeover of the Herald and Weekly Times group and he did this while a member of the ABC board. Once confirmed as chairman, Somervaille announced his intention to prevent 'unfortunate incidents' at the ABC. He nominated my interview with Hawke as one such 'incident'. During the Bicentenary year political control was further secured at the ABC. Wendy Bacon, one of Australia's leading investigative reporters, was hired by the producer of a new ABC current affairs show, *The World Tonight*, only to be told subsequently that the Director of Television, Grahame Reynolds, considered her 'unsuitable' and had withdrawn her appointment. Wendy Bacon's numerous investigations for the *National Times* had revealed deep corruption in the Labor Party machine. David Hill refused to say in what way she was 'unsuitable', only that he would not have her 'at any price'.[112]

Indeed, under Hill some of the best people in Australian broadcasting have been refused entry, or have got out or have been forced out. One of the finest journalists in Australia was warned off because his politics were 'wrong' and he was 'too good' at his job. Among others, a subtle McCarthyism ensures silence, only occasionally broken. When John Beeston, a radio current affairs producer, complained about crude political interference by management, he spoke for many of his colleagues who fear losing their livelihood. Beeston's programme had lodged a Freedom of Information request for the tape of a talk given by Paul Keating, who did not want it made public. The request was being considered, said Beeston, when David Hill inexplicably told the ABC's legal department to drop the request. Beeston has now left the ABC.[113]

The precariousness of the ABC's independence was vividly demonstrated during the 1991 Gulf War. Bob Hawke had dispatched two warships to the Gulf long before the 'coalition' attacked Iraq. Hawke's unquestioning support for

Israel ensured that this was 'Bob's war' almost as much as it was 'George's war'.

The ABC reported the war little differently from most western media organisations. Saddam Hussein was identified as a universal enemy and the United Nations the defender of the rights of small nations. However, the ABC did allow several dissenting voices to be heard, notably that of Dr Robert Springborg of Macquarie University, Sydney, whose work on the Middle East is standard text in many countries. Springborg suggested the war was wrong and cynically motivated: that the United Nations was not experiencing its finest hour and Australia had no reason to be involved. Hawke exploded. 'I find it difficult to summon the language', he said 'to describe my contempt for the analysis by so-called experts. They are loaded . . . and disgraceful'.[114]

A familiar process of intimidation began. Hawke was fed by two minor Mates on the far right: Michael Danby, who runs Australia Israel Publications and Gerard Henderson, of the Sydney Institute, who writes a column in the *Sydney Morning Herald*. Danby sent Hawke a 'dossier' which purported to show Springborg's sympathy for the Iraqi regime; it failed to mention that he was banned from Iraq. For his part, Henderson wrote preposterous articles that relied on sophistry in an apparent attempt to prove that the ABC was an Israel-hating, subversive organisation. Here is an example:

Yesterday, on ABC 3LO in Melbourne Ramona Koval interviewed Manning Clark, a Ranbow Alliance activist, Belinda Probert and the expatriate journalist John Pilger (who related how he 'laughed' at the 'farce' of Israeli residents putting on gas masks). Some joke . . .[115]

In fact, I had merely referred to the famous black comedy staged by journalists in the CNN office in Jerusalem which was carried 'live' around the world and exemplified so much of the instant media coverage of the war. There was no suggestion of laughing at the plight of Israelis.

At first the ABC's managing Director, David Hill, defended the ABC, then in a repeat of events already described in this chapter, he flew to Canberra and effectively apologised to Hawke. Having listened to a reportedly 'two-hour rant' by Hawke, he returned to Sydney and attacked the ABC's Head of TV News and Current Affairs, Peter Manning, along the same lines. Manning, a former editor of the excellent *Four Corners* investigative series and one of the ABC's independent spirits, rejected Hill's pressure.[116]

When the Silver Bodgie opened his third election campaign, he chose the splendour of the Sydney Opera House. Striking a commanding stance, he was ferried across the world's finest natural harbour on a naval barge. It was pure Hollywood-in-Oz, staged by none other than the director of *Crocodile Dundee*. When the queen of croneyism, Imelda Marcos, paid a visit to Sydney, she demanded a similar nautical display of her worth. The comparison is not remote.

One of Hawke's principal image-makers in the late 1980s was the Sydney advertising 'tycoon' John Singleton. To some in the Labor Party, this was a curious choice. During Whitlam's second election campaign in 1974, Singleton had made a television commercial for the conservative coalition which showed a frightened Estonian woman warning that Labor 'is disguised communism'. In the same year he founded the extreme right-wing Workers Party, later renamed the Progress Party, with a platform calling for a 20 per cent flat rate tax and the virtual destruction of trade unionism. He was also an associate of Frank Nugan, co-founder of the Nugan Hand bank. Before he took on Hawke, Singleton was advertising agent for the Pope on his tour of Australia. He was clearly proud of this campaign, as he told *Woman's Day* magazine, 'If Jesus Christ was around, he'd have commissioned something like that for Himself. Now that's a product I'd like to handle. The consumer would never know for sure whether you'd misrepresented the product until he died!'[117]

In the week he called the election, Hawke rushed a Media Bill through Parliament. This confirmed the 're-structuring' of Australian commercial television, which had reduced the ownership of most of the industry to a few very rich Mates and given Murdoch and Packer a billion dollars in tax-free profit. When a leading commentator, Max Walsh, suggested to Hawke on television that on the one hand he was exhorting ordinary Australians to make sacrifices while, on the other, helping Kerry Packer pay off his million-dollar losses at the races, Hawke became florid with rage and, once again, his eyes rolled upwards in his head. He is seldom challenged in this way. On another programme the level of political discourse was undisturbed. 'I love the Australian people', said Hawke, 'because I think they are, in the end, dinkum.' And to his quiescent interviewers: 'Laurie and George, it's been a pleasure.'[118]

At that time – 1987 – Alan Bond had bought up so many gold mines that he became one of the biggest owners of gold on the planet. During the election campaign Hawke made a special point of pledging that gold would not be taxed. No reporter asked or dared to ask why; Hawke had demonstrated his power of humiliation and his Mates now employed most of those who might ask such questions. Moreover, here was the phenomenon of the world's first Thatcherite Labor Party and there was no one to write the story. Instead, readers were expected to 'wade through thickets of monetarist mystification', to quote the former ABC journalist Allan Ashbolt. 'Where', lamented Ashbolt, 'are the commentators and analysts with a sense of history, a vision of the future, with even a vocabulary of social progress, justice and enlightenment?'[119]

They exist, of course, however few in number; and their names have distinguished these pages. And of course the same question could be asked in other countries: Britain, certainly, also the United States. The critical difference remains the unique concentration of ownership which both underpins and depends upon the new political order. 'The world is divided into two types of journalist,' said Barry Porter, Federal President of the Australian Journalists' Association, 'those who have worked for Rupert Murdoch and those who are about to.'[120] But Murdoch's dominance is not the only obstacle to free journalism. As many of the best and most troublesome Australian journalists have been forced into the margins, muted by under-employment or, in some cases, by commercial success, a group of commentators has assumed a dominant place. In tombstones of column inches they echo the invocations of a pseudo-economic and political deity, imported whole from New York and the City of London by so-called Labor politicians and business economists. Together they have succeeded in dressing up stale conservative ideology as economic necessity and, as a consequence, are accessories to the present recession. They have – rather, had – a confident style, inclining to start their tracts whimsically, perhaps with reference to a jolly meeting they once had with a 'financially literate' politician (i.e. a *believer*). This expression is much used by Ross Gittins, economics editor of the *Sydney Morning Herald*. In one memorable report, Gittins told of a visit to Britain, which was paid for by the Thatcher Government: or as he put it, 'flying business class all the way courtesy of the long-suffering Pommy taxpayer':

As a guest of Her Majesty (Mrs Thatcher, I mean) I was amazed to be supplied with a Minder (female), who held my hand, hailed taxis and even searched for laddies' loos.

I trust my judgement wasn't too badly affected by the red carpet, but I did come to the conclusion that things are much improved in Britain . . . People on the street in London seemed better dressed, for example. I noted the absence of the formerly ubiquitous dirty yellow anorak. And my nose told me that the use of deodorant is spreading.

Not only was the use of deodorant on the increase, so were company profits and house prices, but 'best of all', unemployment was falling. In his rejoicing, Gittins paid tribute to 'the discipline imposed by high unemployment'.[121] This, of course, was not journalism, but a victory for the Thatcher propaganda machine.

What Gittins failed to tell his readers was that the affluence he saw was restricted to where his minder led him; that unemployment was 'falling' because the Government was doctoring the figures – simply leaving people off; that the homeless had been effectively abandoned; that Dickens's debtors' prisons were returning; that millions of Britons were living in poverty, and so on. The article was a crude but accurate representation of a form of pamphleteering which has helped to narrow the agenda for public discussion in Australia to that set by the new order.

Overshadowing and at times intimidating those journalists who fail to see their job as the promotion of doctrine are some of the most punitive libel statutes in the world. 'The politicians', wrote Evan Whitton, a distinguished journalist, 'have never surrendered the weapon of the libel laws which are concerned with what is publicly known about their reputations, not what is privately known about their character and activities.'[122] One of Australia's best columnists, James McClelland (ironically, a former judge), described this as 'the great defamation rort [i.e. scam] which has flourished under our antiquated laws [and] protected corrupt people in high places from exposure and fostered a language of double-speak about "well-known identities" etc., leaving it to the inevitable scuttlebutt to fill in the names.' McClelland wrote that this 'rort' had long been 'a useful source of tax-free capital for many members of what passes for an elite in this country, notably politicians'.[123]

One beneficiary of this system has been Prime Minister Hawke, who used to delight in showing off the fruits of his successful libel actions, including the swimming pool and sauna in his Melbourne home.[124] In one action Hawke's lawyers managed to persuade a Sydney television company and a newspaper to pay him untold dollars in an out-of-court settlement after it had been satirically reported that he had said he would be prepared to use nuclear weapons against the Arab hordes if he were a wartime Israeli Prime Minister. Hawke's biographer, Blanche d'Alpuget, recalls that Hawke did indeed make remarks to this effect.[125]

For many journalists, the most disastrous consequence of the Government's Media Bill was that it left the Fairfax organisation, the only rival to Murdoch, in chaos. The principal Fairfax papers were then the *Sydney Morning Herald*, the *Age*, the *Times on Sunday* and the *Canberra Times*. The new rules had set in train a process of lucrative deal-making which deepened an already bitter feud within the Fairfax family, forcing out the chairman, James Fairfax. He was replaced by his twenty-six-year old American-educated half-brother, Warwick, known as 'Young Wokka', and a new board of Mates. The new managing director was Martin Dougherty, publicist to the powerful, a Mate of Murdoch, Hawke, Abeles, Wran, and so on. Also on the new board was Laurie 'Last Resort' Connell, a moneylender and gambler who had been warned off the Kalgoorlie racetrack in Western Australia. Connell is a Mate of Hawke, whom he has entertained on a deep-sea cruiser. With these Mates behind him, Young Wokka, a religious recluse with no experience of newspapers, turned a huge, profitable business into a much-reduced debt-burdened one and in the process closed down two newspapers with the loss of 500 jobs.

In February 1988 there was rebellion at the *Herald*. The editor-in-chief, editor and other senior executives resigned, protesting management interference. The paper's journalists supported them and went on strike, forcing Young Wokka to appoint a new board. But the company's debt had increased in the aftermath of the stock-market crash, and major assets had to go, including its other principal newspaper, the Melbourne *Age*.

A few weeks earlier Paul Keating had met Robert Maxwell in London. Keating and Hawke had been impressed by the support given by Maxwell's Mirror Group of newspapers to the British Labour Party, or rather to its right wing. And Maxwell was interested in confronting Murdoch on his home territory. In his subsequent bid for the *Age*, Maxwell even gave a public guarantee of the paper's future political leaning. 'As I understand it', he said, 'Mr Keating, according to newspapers, is alleged to have told the caucus of his party that he would prefer Mr Maxwell to own the *Age* because I have never reneged on my political promise.'[126] A new, large Mate was on the way.

The *Age* journalists decided to fight. A defence committee was formed, backed by the editor, Creighton Burns. A 'Charter of Independence' was drawn up as the basis for any future sale. It is a concise document, which insists that a potential owner be bound to the principle that journalists 'must record the affairs of the city, state, nation and the world fairly, fully and regardless of any commercial, political or personal interests, including those of any proprietors, shareholders or board members . . . that the editor shall not sit on the board of the owning company . . . and shall not be directly responsible to the board'.

Leaflets were distributed asking people to sign a pledge to cease buying the *Age* if its editorial integrity was lost. More than 15,000 were returned. The Labor Premier of the State of Victoria, John Cain, backed the campaign; as did many others in and outside the Labor movement. The issue quickly became foreign ownership and the onus once again fell to the Hawke Government. Having given Murdoch his way, Hawke now had little choice but to stop the Maxwell bid.

At the end of 1990, with Fairfax in receivership, the Canadian newspaper prorpietor Conrad Black began his bid. Black's fight against two others – the Irish entrepreneur Tony O'Reilly and a Melbourne consortium – awakened many Australians to the prospects for their press. Black, owner of the

London *Daily Telegraph* and backer of the Tory Party, joined up with Kerry Packer to form the Tourang Consortium. As Gough Whitlam pointed out, a Tourang takeover would mean that '95 per cent of newspapers in Australia could be run by two men living in North America, Murdoch and Black'[127] Whitlam and his arch foe, Malcolm Fraser, stood on a platform together to declare, 'We share a common concern about the future of the Australian media and about the concentration of its ownership and control, now without parallel in the democratic world'[128] Packer allegedly told a financial adviser that he and Murdoch had a 'game plan' for the Australian newspaper industry.[129]

As was the case during Murdoch's takeover of the Herald and Weekly Times, the Hawke government remained silent; Packer was one of Hawke's most valued Mates. But this time public pressure could not be ignored. A Parliamentary enquiry into the press was announced and Packer was summoned. His appearance was one of Australian democracy's most demeaning moments. His arrogant behaviour before a Parliamentary committee said to be 'interviewing' him, merely demonstrated his power. The event was a Packer triumph.

However, another enquiry was announced, this time by the Australian Broadcasting Tribunal. On November 28, 1991 the eve of the enquiry, Packer withdrew from the Tourang bid. 'History will ask', wrote Tom Burton in the *Sydney Morning Herald*, 'what, if anything, did Mr Packer have to hide?'[130] The Chairman of the Tribunal, Peter Westerway, announced that 'important information', which prompted the enquiry, would not be released.

With Packer out of it, Tourang was in difficulty. In December the Black bid was rejected by the Federal Treasurer, John Kerin, on grounds of 'national economic interest'. Less than a week later Kerin was replaced by Ralph Willis, who immediately announced that Black could go ahead. On December 16 Fairfax was effectively his. There was no gratitude, alas. Black described his suspension from bidding as 'sleazy, venal and despicable' and himself as 'the victim of sleazy political lobbying'.[131] Although Australian institutions would own 80 per cent of Tourang, and Black's *Daily Telegraph* 15 per cent, there was no doubt who was in charge of Australia's oldest and second biggest newspaper group. The following, written by Conrad Black for one of his Canadian papers, is said to express his world view:

If Moscow has provided the requiem for communism, Toronto and Ottawa are witnessing the Gotterdammerung of the soft left. Sweden has electorally repudiated six pretentious decades of socialism to the self-conscious silence of all those Canadians of the drivelling left who keened after Nordic socialism . . . New Zealand has repealed and is rooting out the socialist encrustations of generations. Only in Ontaria in the entire democratic world, is the cant and hypocricy of union-dominated soak-the-rich, anti-productivity politics of envy official, approved and po-facedly presented as 'caring and compassion'[132]

Murdoch has said as much. Together, with Packer, who owns most of the magazines, they now control Australia's 'free press'.

The Fairfax débâcle has left Rupert Murdoch with unparalleled power in a country whose citizenship he has forsworn. It is a power greater than he has acknowledged, a power not always visible. When Murdoch took over the Herald and Weekly Times group, he was forced to divest those of his interests that would have given him a press monopoly in Adelaide and Brisbane. This was a sop to an enfeebled watchdog, the Trade Practices Commission. However, as Colleen Ryan and Andrew Keenan have revealed, 'negotiations with the Commission to remove this dominance have led to the extraordinary situation whereby two former [Murdoch] News Corporation employees now own papers which are effectively underwritten by their only competitors, News Corporation'.[133] Through a web of indemnities and 'put options' Murdoch has guaranteed that the two owners do not lose a cent for four years, an arrangement which mocks the spirit of freely competing newspapers. All involved deny back-door control and motives untoward. But it is clear that a man who can 'disappear' from his own company records is a man who can run newspapers without actually owning them.

In his fine book *The Captive Press*, David Bowman, one of Australia's most experienced journalists, chronicles Rupert Murdoch's rise to power, then compares it implicitly with the ascendancy of Alfred Hugenberg in Germany in the 1920s and 1930s. 'Hugenberg is reliably estimated to have enjoyed control or influence over nearly half the German press by 1930,' wrote Bowman.

His philosophy was right-wing nationalist, and accordingly he helped block the spread of democratic ideas in Germany, to that extent weakening the Weimar republic and paving the way for the triumph of the Nazis. This may seem an extreme case to hold up to innocent, laid-back Australia, but it is a fair warning that a concentrated press can contribute to political and social evils.[134]

At the other end of the spectrum from Murdoch was *The Eye*, published by Brian Toohey on a desk-top computer from his home. Until resources finally ran out in 1991, *The Eye* continued the disclosure tradition of Toohey's old paper, the deceased *National Times*. Documents were leaked to it, and the issues of corruption, duplicity and hypocrisy in high places were kept alive in it. When Senator Gareth Evans, also known as the 'Minister for Mates', took over at Foreign Affairs in 1988, one of his first tasks was to arrange a High Court injunction against *The Eye*. According to Evans, an article in the magazine threatened national security. The article was said to be about the operations abroad of the Australian Secret Intelligence Service, ASIS. No such article existed, nor had Toohey intended to publish one. Yet Evans had persuaded the highest court in the country to convene at night on the basis, as it turned out, of speculation and gossip.

Although farcical, the incident demonstrated the Government's resolve to punish and intimidate, using a favourite legal weapon against those journalists who tell the public what politicians and their Mates prefer they should not know. This is not to suggest that investigative journalism – the vogue term for good reporting – ought to be beyond the law or can rely on public support. The press is not regarded highly by its readers; and even the most honourable muckrakers find their motives regarded with hostility by a readership grown dangerously cynical about all journalism, even about its own 'right to know'. Cynicism of this order has increased as the diversity of both the media and politics has diminished; and this situation is not unique to Australia, but perhaps it is only in Australia that the media is so diminished. In his book, David Bowman proposed a way out. What the good journalist must have, he wrote,

is a sense of commitment. Moral courage goes with it. Who is to tell the world what's going on, if the journalist doesn't? Someone has to represent those hundreds of thousands of innocent readers who without the selfless journalist to inform them would be at the mercy of malign forces in society. In time the selfless journalist learns what ingrates these innocent readers can be. How many of them give a damn? The good journalist's response is not to take refuge in cynicism but to try to persuade the readers to give a damn.[135]

'Australia in the first half of the 1980s', wrote Supreme Court judge Athol Moffitt, 'has seen rise before its eyes the spectre of organised crime and corruption, highlighted by allegations, revelations and associated political turmoil beyond any prior experience in Australia.'[136]

While Prime Minister Bob Hawke said that his Mates could count on him being 'shoulder to shoulder' with them. He also said he would protect no persons, whoever they might be and whatever his associations with them, if evidence emerged that they were corrupt. When Hawke came to power in 1983 he endorsed a Royal Commission which already had been assigned to enquire into crime and corruption, under a tough Melbourne lawyer, Frank Costigan. The Commission had access to police files on 70,000 individuals – roughly one in every 200 Australians. Graft, extortion, blackmail and the elimination of awkward witnesses were found to touch on almost every corner of Australian life. More than 600 charges were laid. There was promise of bigger fish.

Hawke announced abruptly that the Commission must be wound up. His then Attorney-General, Gareth Evans, accused Costigan of being 'a gung-ho commissioner' with an inadequate concern for people's civil rights. However, reported Robert Milliken, 'not all Australians are convinced that a sincere concern for civil rights explains all the opposition that Costigan has aroused. The opposition leader, [Andrew] Peacock, for one, hints that the increasing closeness of the investigation to the Government and its friends provides a more convincing explanation.'[137] What the Costigan Commission had done was to penetrate a wall of secrecy. Until then, many of the corrupt and criminal in Australia could project a publicly unsullied reputation, secured behind the laws of libel.

When Hawke received Costigan's final report in November 1984 he said, 'As far as my Government is concerned, we will be taking a very positive approach to [all] his recommendations.' Thereafter, his Government rejected Costigan's model for a National Crime Authority and his recommendation for the removal of a Government veto over the Authority's powers and for the appointment of a tax crime investigator. Costigan also called for further Royal Commissions to enquire into his unfinished work; but this, too, was rejected.

The Hawke/Keating government has refused to release some 1,200 documents on the Nugan Hand Bank, the front for international crime and CIA operations in Australia. The Government has repeatedly refused to find out why the CIA bars the release, under the US Freedom of Information Act, of fourteen intelligence reports on Commerce International, the CIA-front company that played a central role in the destruction of the Whitlam Government.[138] In 1989 a committee headed by a former Chief Justice of the High Court recommended rigorous Government secrecy in order to prevent disclosures about the actions of the security services, such as the CIA, and MI5/6, in the internal affairs of Australia.

The recession of the 1990s has not been kind to the Order of the Mates. The principal Mates are no longer public heroes, or rather, heroes of those who so assiduously promoted them in the financial pages. Their new public image was reflected in a series of damning articles in the *Sydney Morning Herald* entitled 'Greed Inc.'.[139] Even Murdoch has seen his shares fall dramatically and his debts rise to almost £5 billion.[140] He is selling, not buying now, though the family silver seems safe for the moment.

So the Order survives. For example, the Australian transport industry is being de-regulated. This means that much of it will be handed over to Sir Peter Abeles and Rupert Murdoch, who already own most of the Australian airline industry. The first 'independent', Compass Airlines, has already collapsed, and the Government-owned Australian Airlines has been denied revenue to buy aircraft which it needs to compete with Abeles's Ansett airline; the reason given is the drain on foreign reserves. However, Abeles's borrowing against the national debt to buy new aircraft is seen as beneficial to the tourist industry.

Abeles, with whom Bob Hawke 'dreamed dreams', has become a close Mate of Treasurer Keating. On Keating's recommendation, Abeles was appointed to the board of the Federal Reserve Bank, a post of great prestige and value. As the *National Times* pointed out, it is 'a position that allows an intimate insight into the conduct of the country's monetary policies, briefings from the Bank's highly regarded research department and, perhaps most significant of all, ready access to most of the key figures in the financial community'. Soon after Keating saw Abeles on to the board of the Reserve Bank, his closest staff adviser, Barbara Ward, left to join the private sector. She later went to work for Abeles.[141]

When 'Nifty' Neville Wran retired as Premier of New South Wales his Mateship with Abeles did not end. Nifty went into the cleaning business and his company, Allcorp Cleaning Services, immediately won a million-dollar contract to clean Abeles's Sydney air terminal. Asked to explain Allcorp's spectacular success in winning forty contracts so quickly – several of them contracts abruptly cancelled with other cleaning companies – a spokesman for Allcorp said, 'Mr Wran has an enormous understanding of the cleaning industry. He has occupied offices himself and has seen what good cleaning is and what bad cleaning is.'[142] Wran's wife, Jill, was appointed to the board of Ansett New Zealand, owned by Abeles, and Wran's former press secretary, David Hurley, advises Abeles on how to deal with the press. When he was Premier, Wran gave Rupert Murdoch and Kerry Packer the licence to run the State's 'Lotto' lottery. Wran is now on the board of an investment bank which was partly owned by Packer at the time of his appointment, and his Allcorp company won a contract to clean the television studios of Channel 9, then owned by Packer.

On the other side of the continent, the Mates run 'the Dallas of Australia', as Perth was optimistically known in the 1980s. Until recently, Bondy still owned much of the best land, a daily newspaper, a brewery, and most of the State's gold mines. He was the central figure in 'WA Inc', a Mates' arrangement under which the Western Australian Government entered into 'partnerships' with very rich financiers in order to give the taxpayers 'a slice of the action'. An estimated $A500 million of public money was lost as a result of such liaisons: notably one with Rothwell's Limited, a bankrupt moneylending organisation owned by Laurie 'Last Resort' Connell, the well-known Mate and confidant of Bob Hawke.

Connell, together with Bond and others, is awaiting trial on charges relating to a network of deals that involved land which was never developed, a petro-chemical plant that was never built, millions of taxpayers' dollars and the State Labor Government. Giving evidence before yet another Royal Commission enquiry into corruption – this one set up to look into WA Inc and described by Jim McClelland as 'undoubtedly the most revealing striptease show currently running anywhere in Australia'[143] – Connell talked, and talked.

He recounted a lunch he and Bob Hawke attended during the 1987 election campaign at which, he claimed, Hawke promised not to introduce a gold tax. Connell, who then had majority holdings in gold mines, subsequently gave $A250,000 to Hawke's election campaign. Hawke's response to this was to deny making any public commitment on a gold tax. He then had to apologise to Parliament when the record was checked. Connell said his interest in seeing Hawke re-elected had been 'heightened' by Hawke's private assurances to him. Such an 'imputation', countered Hawke, was 'unfounded'.[144]

Connell said he is 'pretty well broke'[145]. Yet he and his wife, Elizabeth, enjoy beautiful things. Their silver collection alone was valued at $A3 million. The family jewellery collection included one necklace that had 58 carats of diamonds and was valued at $A1.2 million. Connell had no difficulty

34.

35. Mates. US Secretary of State George Shultz and Bob Hawke, 1987

36. The top-secret American base at Nurrungar, South Australia, where 'Star Wars' is developed

37. Jack Platt, the Bondi Beach shark catcher, 1952

38. An Australian icon: 'The Sunbaker' by Max Dupain

39. Bronte Beach, Sydney 1985

40. *Above:* Thelma Thompson,
nurse, Broken Hill, 1920

41. *Left:* Harry King, wheat farmer,
Mollerin, 1987

42. Working at home on poverty rates, Melbourne 1987

43. King's Cross, Sydney, 1986

44/45. The 'new surburbia', western Sydney, 1987

46. John Pilger with the parrot that won't drink Bondy's XXXX beer, Silverton, 1986

47. With Sam Pilger, Ayers Rock, 1987

paying for these; his personal drawings from his business amounted to $A44 million in five years. He also owned more than 400 racehorses and four thoroughbred studs.[146] In January, 1992 he was charged with fixing a horse race and conspiring to defeat or pervert the course of justice[147].

Others named in the Perth 'striptease' include Hawke's successor, Paul Keating, whose advice was said to have been sought on the rescue of Connell's bank, Rothwells. Keating has denied this.[148] The former Premier of Western Australia, Brian Burke, one of Hawke's inner circle, was said to have arranged for his ruling Labor Party to avoid paying tax on millions of dollars which he invested.[149] Burke told the Royal Commission he had 'no idea' as to the source of $A207,000 cash that went into gold investments he initiated as Premier.[150] He also admitted secretly investing $A87,000 of Party funds in 'about 100' rare stamps[151]; and he revealed that money given as Party donations was used to pay for the defence of two senior Party men charged with offences relating to WA Inc.[152]

In Queensland, until recently, the local Mates ran a game park of corruption that at times was reminiscent of Nicaragua under General Somoza. The Royal Commission into police corruption in Queensland gave the impression of a police force used as an instrument of the ruling ultra-conservative National Party, which has long been manipulated by international criminals and political thugs. Opponents of Sir Johannes Bjelke-Petersen, State Premier for seventeen years, were constantly harassed by the Queensland Special Branch, which regarded non-National Party members as fair game, together with homosexuals, environmentalists and 'uppity Christians'. Queensland probably has more tax dodgers and other assorted hucksters than any other State. It certainly has more knighthoods than any other former British colony. Knighthoods are currency in Queensland, where all but the cane toads seem to have them and the term 'patronage' had a meaning and dynamism not known elsewhere. During the reign of Sir Johannes Bjelke-Petersen, half the 55 knighthoods recommended to the Queen by Sir Johannes were bestowed upon Mates linked to his Government. The Queensland Police Commissioner was knighted Sir Terence Lewis in 1986, following an astonishing rise from country inspector, jumping ahead of 106 officers of equal rank and 16 superiors. Sir Terence was described in evidence before the Fitzgerald enquiry as 'Big Daddy' and a 'bribes shark'. At his subsequent trial he was found guilty of 15 corruption charges and sentenced to 14 years prison.[153]

During his enquiry, the Royal Commissioner, Tony Fitzgerald, said he was 'appalled' by the information held by the Commission, 'which I suspect is merely the tip of an enormous iceberg'.[154] The Fitzgerald hearings became a litany of leading names in Queensland politics, business, crime and law enforcement. Sir Johannes himself was a star witness. Knighted on his own recommendation for his 'mission-like zeal and dedication to his role', Sir Johannes was questioned about a total of $A560,000 in 'political donations', most of them delivered in cash when the Queensland Government was awarding contracts to the donors. In 1986 a total of $A210,000 found its way to the Premier's office in suitcases and packages of cash. Sir Johannes agreed that $A100,000 of this had come from a Hong Kong businessman wishing to invest in the State's hotel industry and cocoa plantations. He said he could not recall who had delivered the rest of the money; anyway, he explained, packages of cash normally would have been handed to his secretary.

Commissioner Fitzgerald asked, 'Would one of your secretaries come up and say: "We've just had someone drop in and leave fifty thousand dollars in cash and we don't know who he is?"' To which Sir Johannes replied, 'People don't talk like that . . . I didn't know who did it. I didn't want to know . . . I always tried to stay as far away from that sort of thing as possible.'[155] Sir Johannes eventually stood trial on charges of corruption and perjury relating to the $A100,000 wrapped in brown paper, left at his office. This was reduced to perjury. In October 1991, the trial jury was dismissed after failing to reach a verdict. The Queensland Attorney-General said he had decided not to proceed with a second trial, partly because of Sir Johannes's age.[156] Sir Johannes is 81.

The former Queensland Minister for Transport named fourteen Cabinet Ministers who, he said, had misused public money for private expenses. The ruddy-necked Buddha-shaped figure of Russ Hinze, the former Police Minister, was asked about a total of $A2·09 million in loans paid into his family companies by property developers and other entrepreneurs. Among those named was one Eddie Kornhauser who, according to evidence before the Commission, paid Hinze $A250,000 in loans within days of the Cabinet approving legislation designed to help his property interests on the Gold Coast. Eddie Kornhauser is an old Mate of Bob Hawke; they like to gamble together. In 1982 Hawke defended Kornhauser against what he described as 'totally improper attacks'. At that time Kornhauser was an applicant for a casino licence on the Gold Coast.[157] In 1988 Hawke said that he was 'absolutely confident that any connection I have had with Mr Kornhauser over the years has been entirely proper'.[158] Hinze was subsequently found guilty of corruption and perjury, and died. Four Cabinet ministers are in prison at the time of writing.

In 1989, the people of Queensland voted resoundingly against corruption and, in spite of the gerrymandered electoral boundaries, threw out the National Party. But that was not the end of it. In 1992, the new, 'squeaky clean' Labor government in Queensland disclosed that 14 serving and former Labor MPs were being investigated by the Criminal Justice Commission. Four Cabinet ministers may also be investigated.[159] In the meantime, Sir Johannes has founded a merchant bank, to be based in a Pacific island tax haven. He denies this is to avoid paying taxes. 'Business is cracking that fast we can't cope with it all', he said.[160]

During the 1990 election campaign Bob Hawke offered his fellow Australians a vision 'not of a lucky country but a *clever* country'. The word 'clever' seemed to hang in the air, unexplained and with contradictory implications. 'Lucky country', after all, is an ironic term; and 'clever bastard' on the streets means sharp operator. For most Australians the Hawke years had brought diminished living standards and for many, once again, the prospect of unemployment. Voters were given the choice of two main parties devoted to an Antipodean version of Thatcherism. On polling day, independents and so-called 'centre' parties received unprecedented support; and although Labor received little more than a third of primary votes, under Australia's preferential system, the Hawke Government was able to hold on to office by eight seats.

In December 1991, after a failed earlier attempt, Bob Hawke was dumped as party leader and Paul Keating became Prime Minister. Keating's 'personal approval rating' in the polls stood at 25 per cent, the lowest ever recorded for an incoming Prime Minister.[161] 'It's a very humbling experience', said Keating. 'I feel the poignancy of the moment'.[162] Said Hawke, 'I hope they think of me as the Bob Hawke they got to know ... a dinky-di Australian'.[163]

Everyone has their favourite snapshots from an album. Mine are from a gala evening staged by Kerry 'The Goanna' Packer in Sydney's vast Regent Hotel shortly before the 1987 election. This was the 'Businessman of the Year' awards ceremony, both a get-together and a celebration of the Mates.

Bob Hawke was the guest of honour.

'I am pleased as Prime Minister of this country', said Hawke, 'to count as a close personal friend and to measure as a very great Australian, Kerry Packer ... and when you talk of Kerry you almost inevitably lead to Alan Bond ... to you, Alan, congrats for all your achievements and may I thank you for your generous comments about the Government.' Hawke embraced Bondy and drew Packer with him in front of the television cameras. A Jaguar car was raffled for a charity that looks after the poor. The irony shouted; here was a Labor Prime Minister, whose predecessors have pioneered some of democracy's most enduring reforms, massaging the quick-rich at an event ostensibly in aid of the poor.

Packer remarked that he was proud 'the Prime Minister refers to me as a friend'. During most of the evening Hawke remained at Packer's side. Packer at times seemed uneasy, and as he was leaving he whispered to a friend that he wished Hawkie had not been so damned deferential in public; after all, that kind of thing should be done in private.

This was remedied a few weeks later when Packer threw a twenty-first birthday party for his daughter, Gretel, at the family mansion in Sydney's Bellevue Hill. Gretel wore her father's gift, an $A290,000 Cartier diamond choker and ear-rings, flown in from Hong Kong. Members of the New South Wales police force ensured the privacy of the 350 guests, whose combined wealth, according to the *Sydney Morning Herald*, was more than four billion dollars. Almost all the Mates were there: the Goanna, the Dirty Digger, Nifty, the

Silver Bodgie and even minor mates like David Hill. And when everybody departed they were made just that bit richer, with gold necklaces for the ladies and gold cufflinks for the Mates.

7

BATTLERS

To the operative classes, Australia is a veritable land of promise.

Victorian Review (1881)

I used to think I was poor. Then they told me I wasn't poor, I was needy. Then they told me it was self-defeating to think of myself as being needy, I was deprived. Then they told me deprived was a bad image. I was underprivileged. Then they told me underprivileged was overused. I was disadvantaged. I still don't have a cent. But I have a great vocabulary.

Jules Feiffer

WHEN THE AUSTRALIAN journalist Geraldine Brooks returned home in the 1980s after living in the United States, she described a tour of Sydney she liked to give American friends who visited her. She wrote:

I'd always take them for a ferry ride into the city, because it's the best way to show off Sydney's beautiful harbour, its bridge and its Opera House. But there's another building that gives me even more pride: the funny-looking concrete ziggurat by the bridge with the big picture windows and the balcony gardens. It's a block of New South Wales Housing Department flats, built in the late 1970s to keep low-income earners from being pushed out of the Rocks [on the harbourside].

That, I'd tell my American friends, is where poor people live. Of course, I know that particular apartment building isn't typical – that most low-income earners are braving punishing waiting lists to get into far less salubrious accommodations with views of the Great Western Highway rather than the harbour.

But to me those flats are a symbol of the best of Australia: a generosity of spirit that has never equated people's worth with their wealth. So far, Australia has always managed to afford a share of society's good things for those who couldn't possibly purchase them.[1]

I have shown those same flats to visitors from other countries and have also felt pride. I remember reading as a youngster Mark Twain's description of Australia as 'an entire continent peopled by the lower orders', and I was proud of that, too; I quite liked the notion that we were the poor who got away; that ours was the People's Country 'that has never equated people's worth with their wealth'.

The truth, as Geraldine Brooks went on to say, is sadly different. A great many of the poor did not escape poverty, which sank its roots deep into a society begun as a 'living hell', then maintained as a fragile economic colony: a status unchanged today. The poor were known by a variety of euphemisms, of which 'battlers' was the most popular. 'Battlers' could expect the nation's sympathy, if not its support. In Australian literature the poets Henry Lawson and 'Banjo' Patterson romanticised battlers as brash, rugged, sardonic combatants against nature in a harsh land. Women did not exist; or they coped stoically. It is a perfect irony in a society renowned for its cult of the male that those who have so often told the truth about a nation built on the blood, sweat and tears of ordinary men and women, are women.

Writers like Miles Franklin, Dymphna Cusack, Kylie Tennant, Jean Devanney and Marjorie Barnard not only wrote about people enduring drought, flood, fire, loneliness and fear; they also described active, energetic women in revolt against the poverty and privations imposed on them by the arbiters of class and gender. A few were forced to assume men's names so that their work might be published. As recently as the 1970s students reading English at Australian universities were told little about these secret chroniclers of Australia.

In 1959 the Australasian Book Society boldly published Dorothy Hewett's *Bobbin Up*, an unsentimental account of Australian working-class life in a Sydney I knew well:

Riley's Lane . . . a running sore, littered with orange peel, empty milk bottles and old papers. A damp dead-end lined with two-storey weatherboards, built straight onto the road, hump-backed, sagging with time and rot and cynical neglect. The crazy, toppling balconies hung over the lane, defying the laws of gravity. The incredible patched fences of corrugated iron were kept partially upright with paling cross pieces. A puff of wind in the night sent the loose, rusty iron flapping and scraping in a mournful music. On washing day each back yard accommodated one double sheet at a time. And over it all swung the limpid Australian sky, cotton-woolled with cloud. It was hard to raise your eyes above the level of the toppling balconies of Riley's Lane, better to mix a bottle of pinkie and drown your sorrows in the dry, yellow grass behind the bottle factory.[2]

The inheritors of the 'living hell', the children of the Chartists and Fenians and those who simply survived, wanted no Riley's Lanes. They wanted 'Utopia under the Southern Cross'; and their achievements were considerable. Long before Europe and North America, Australia had a legal basic wage, an eight-hour working day, pensions, maternity allowance, child benefits and the vote for women. The secret ballot was invented in the State of Victoria in 1856 and became known as 'the Australian ballot'. The world's first labour government was formed in Queensland; and the Australian Labor Party formed governments twenty years before any comparable socialist or social democratic party took office in Europe.[3] 'To Europeans', wrote the historian Jill Roe, 'the state in Australia appeared to be a boldly experimental agent.'[4]

In Britain Australia became known as the 'Workers' Paradise', although this was also patronising. In France, extensive literature credited Australia with being a 'social laboratory' where 'socialism without doctrines' was practised.[5] Among German social scientists and trade-union leaders the Australian labour movement was considered 'the most advanced in the world'.[6] Indeed, to many in Europe, Australia was proof that Karl Marx's prediction of bloody revolution was wrong; and in 1913 Lenin was moved to refute such heresy and to ask, 'What sort of peculiar capitalist country is this, in which the workers' representatives predominate in the *Upper House*?'[7]

The truth was complex and very different from the distant idolatry. In Australia, as in South Africa, the white labour movement was founded not on ideals of international brotherhood, but on fear and the bigotry of white supremacy. The reason Australian politicians supported child endowment legislation was not necessarily visionary; many were obsessed by racist theories of 'populate or perish'.

When the English Fabians Beatrice and Sidney Webb travelled to Australia, they were shocked by the harshness of ordinary life in the 'Workers' Paradise'. Poverty seemed intractable in the tenement slums of the cities and in the extreme isolation of the bush. Utterly dependent on imperial markets and immersed in debt, Australia suffered disproportionately during every world depression. There had been historic gains, but these had yet to be balanced against continuing losses.

This began to change dramatically in the years following the Second World War when the Labor Government of Ben Chifley enacted an ambitious programme of economic planning. The results were great public works, new industries, a remarkable immigration programme and full employment. By the end of the 1960s Australians could claim to live in a country where the spread of personal income was the most equitable in the world. The egalitarian myth of 'fair go for all' appeared safe at last.

Today this is no longer true. Indeed, the opposite is true. The new order of the 1980s, the Order of Mates, has redistributed the national wealth with such alacrity that many Australians, especially those comforted by nostalgic certainties, have yet to appreciate that their sunny society is changing beyond recognition.

The most profound effects of these changes are seen in demography and people's self-image. In the post-war years 'middle Australia' was not perceived in the popular middle-class terms of Western societies. A successful Australian was 'a battler who made it'. 'He wears a blue collar', wrote the journalist Deirdre Macken, 'and lives under those red-tiled roofs smeared across suburbia. He left school early, got a trade and joined a union. He rented a house and married a woman who wanted to stay at home and look after the kids. He thinks of himself as middle Australia and his spirit is celebrated in commercials on the telly.' However, this embodiment of the nation 'now represents only one per cent of the Australian population. In just twenty years, his dominance of the Australian economy, culture and society has disappeared.'[8]

As middle Australia has disappeared, so the Bonanza Class has risen. Until the 1980s there were few millionaires. 'To protect its well being,' wrote the English reformer Robert Schachner, 'Australia has refuted big wealth.'[9] The rich were mainly of the 'old money' and, in the tradition of a European gentry, they maintained a discreet subterfuge. Indeed, in 1969 only 12 per cent of households were considered 'well off'. By 1984 this group had grown to 30 per cent and controlled more than half the nation's income.[10] Today there are some 31,000 millionaires, multi-millionaires and billionaires who are the antithesis of gentry and whose conspicuous frolics have already been described.

In striking contrast, the numbers of the 'less well off' have risen sharply from 17 per cent of households in 1969 to almost a third of the population commanding only 10 per cent of incomes in 1987.[11] Since the Hawke Government came to power in 1983 the rich have grown richer, wages have been effectively cut and poverty has deepened.

This has been caused in part by a 'consensus' which Hawke and Keating established between big business, Government and the Australian Council of Trade Unions. The aim of this arrangement was to 'restrain' wages. This meant that union campaigns 'outside the guidelines' – for wage increases that might compensate for inflation – were defeated; that tax cuts for higher income earners were approved; and that by the late 1980s more than $A30 billion had been shifted from wages to profits.[12] In the countryside, the new order has meant de-regulated markets, interest rates of up to 34 per cent on farm debts, with rates of unemployment treble and poverty double the national average.[13]

While the Australian Bonanza Class are now wealthier than the rich in most advanced industrial nations, the poor are worse off. The phenomenal growth of poverty is one of Australia's contemporary secrets. Indeed, modern Australian poverty is distinguished by its concealment. The word itself carries a stigma not known in other countries; and poor people will go to lengths to hide the deprivation of their lives and others to deny that poverty exists at all. Rather than dispel the myth of an egalitarian, one class society, with a 'fair go for all', people are encouraged by politicians and some commentators to regard the growing number of poor no longer as 'battlers', rather as 'slackers', 'dole bludgers', even 'loose women'. Of course, when it comes to children, this argument is difficult to maintain. 'Australia's record for the treatment of its children', wrote the journalist Ade`le Horin, 'is, in fact, shocking.'[14]

One in five Australians born during the Bicentenary year faces the prospect of long-term poverty. A higher proportion of Australian children live in poverty than do children in Britain, Germany, Canada, Sweden, Norway and Switzerland. Australia's child poverty rate is 16·5 per cent. Only the United States is marginally worse.[15] Moreover, provision of support for the poor is less than in any other advanced society.[16]

Daisy and Chikka live on the streets around King's Cross in Sydney. Daisy's face is pitted and skeined grey, her blonde hair matted to her waist. Chikka is the shape of a pipe cleaner, his forearm bandaged, his hand extended. They are both seventeen. Tourists cruising 'The Cross', with its nefarious reputation, see them. Foreign journalists, scratching beneath the Paul Hogan gloss, occasionally speak to them. 'Other than that,' said Daisy 'we're not noticed, really, not even by the cops. We're embarrassing.'

There are about 200,000 children living in poverty in Sydney alone. The Human Rights Commission has found that between 20,000 and 25,000 Australian children are homeless. 'Not only are their human rights not being observed,' said the Commissioner's report, 'but in some cases these children are actually dying.'[17]

The day before I met her, Daisy's friend, Pip, was found in Darlinghurst Road with a needle in her arm. 'She's in St Vincent's,' said Daisy. 'They got her in time.' Chikka has had his own experience with the needle. 'I got into it up on the Gold Coast', he said, '. . . mucking around up there.'

Daisy and Chikka are 'Westies' from Campbelltown and Minto, which are suburbs more than thirty miles down the western line. The last she heard, Daisy's mother was working in a bottling factory. She and her two sisters had been brought up by whomever 'kept an eye on us'. 'Mum didn't have the time,' she said. 'She had to work. I knew from when I was small I'd be off as soon as I could.'

Up to a third of young 'Westies' are unemployed. Daisy and Chikka have never had jobs. Without skills, there are no 'real jobs' for them. Their homes vary from 'friendly floors' and refuges to beaches and parks. Daisy was living in a launderette when I met her. After two days the owner spotted her and seemed kind, and gave her food and money. 'But the greasy bastard wanted to screw,' she said. 'I might have done it to stay there, but he was . . . yuk.'

Chikka lived in a clothing charity bin next to a church in Manly, across the harbour. 'There was a system,' he said. 'If it was already occupied, the person inside left an empty cigarette packet on the edge of the hole you crawled in. It held three of us. I lived there on and off for six months.' He has also lived in a tunnel near Palm Beach, and under the bridge over Cook's River, and on the floor of a block of lavatories. Daisy's longest stretch was in an abandoned car. 'I used to have a little boy,' she revealed, 'but they took him off me.'

'She's bullshitting,' said Chikka.

'No I'm not!' said Daisy. 'How would you know anyway? Yeah, what have you ever done? You can't even remember *anything*.'

In the inner city the battlers used to be old and acceptable: the 'wino', the bent old woman with a string bag. Today a decorous veil is drawn over the new poor, for the young as derelicts are incongruous and unacceptable in a 'young country'. It was not long ago that the young were at the beach, or joyously hitting a tennis ball against a playground wall, or in cricketing whites or uniforms of some sort. Then they were spruce and 'keen'. The family was said to be universal and alternatives were aberrations. This was not true, but it was believed and believed in.

There is an added confusion. Those like Daisy and Chikka do not look like battlers, or the needy, disadvantaged or underprivileged. On a sparkling Sydney day few look poor in the way the iconography says the poor should look. Australia, more than most developed countries, is where poverty has been 'modernised'. A consumerist 'skin' is readily available here: a cheap copy of designer jeans and running shoes, a fashionable haircut, even a tan. In an age of mass-marketed expectations, real poverty is internalised as hope is denied. 'What have *you* done with your life?' Daisy asked Chikka in a cruel aside.

Home ownership in Australia is a national ethos. About 70 per cent of Australians are home owners or mortgage holders, one of the highest rates in the world. This leaves the bottom third with few choices. Australia invests a lower proportion of its Gross National Product in public housing than many developed countries; and as home ownership has risen the public housing programme has become, in effect, a welfare housing programme.[18] This has helped to create colonies of the new poor far from the low-rent flats with the big picture windows overlooking the harbour, the symbols of our pride.

Western Sydney is seen by few outsiders. If you do not live

here, there is every reason not to come. One and a half million people, almost half the population of Sydney, live here. But the Sydney of beaches and views and tree-lined, undulating streets, with Thai restaurants and Italian delis, does not reach here. Western Sydney is a void between Arcadia and 'the back of beyond'.

Campbelltown and Minto are in western Sydney. The white African notion of 'township' has an echo here. This is a fringe place, at once dependent upon and estranged from the 'advantaged' world. It is also the fastest 'growth area' in Australia. Since 1971 the population has trebled. The reason for this is to be found in newspaper headlines such as: THE PRICE OF A HOME: NO KIDS FOR TEN YEARS. People unable to repay mortgages at interest rates of up to 17 per cent, or rents that have doubled overnight, have no choice. Aborigines, new immigrants, single women and unemployed teenagers have no choice. As many as sixty new residents arrive in western Sydney every day, and this is expected to continue into the twenty-first century.[19]

Some arrivals have even less choice and must remain outside in caravans, 'mobile homes', old cars and structures that look like shipping containers. These are plywood boxes and are known as 'modular homes'. They are waterproof and come with sewerage. Eighteen-year-olds, those with jobs, rent them for $A141 a week.

Much of Campbelltown was built rapidly by the New South Wales Ministry of Housing for the new poor. Its houses are set against a flat horizon, relieved by tracts bulldozed as common recreational ground, which were later found to be swamp. There are no corner shops and few bus routes. For young people casual work exists in the fast-food chains, which employ those aged between fifteen and eighteen, then dismiss them rather than pay the higher rate required by law.

In their health Westies are another nation. Campbelltown people are 30 per cent more likely to die from heart attack, cancer and respiratory diseases than other Australians. Women are 30 per cent more likely to die from diabetes. Among the highest rates of death from all preventable diseases are here, along with the highest rates of low birthweight babies and congenital birth defects.[20]

Conditions in this other Australia are occasionally revealed by a few diligent journalists, notably Graham Williams of the *Sydney Morning Herald*. A study on 'human service provision' in the Campbelltown region was not widely reported. It described 'profound stress arising from social isolation', 'inadequate basic services . . . public transport, public telephone, child care and neighbourhood centres', 'the highest rate of juvenile crime' (adding that 'only desperate teachers will come to Campbelltown'), 'relatively easy availability of heroin', 'the highest number of referrals of children at risk'.

The young of western Sydney, said the study, 'will shortly be reproducing another generation born to inherited disadvantage . . . Australia's future well-being will rely to a major extent on how well we service young families, for it is they who will provide the nation's wealth in the 1990s and early next century.'[21]

The television soap, *Neighbours*, which represents Australian suburbia to much of the world, ought to be set in Campbelltown, for it is the real 'Neighbours'. Campbelltown might have been painted by an Antipodean L. S. Lowry. It is dotted with inanimate figures, young women walking aimlessly, with prams and children. One of them is Julie, aged thirty-three. Her six-year relationship broke up when she was pregnant with her second child. When the baby was two months old, she was given a Housing Commission home in Campbelltown, for which nothing in her life had prepared her. In 1989 she and her two children had $A176 a week to live on. This included less than $A35 support for each of her two children. If she is able to find a job paying more than $A160, she would have to give back two-thirds of every dollar she earned, or she would lose her pension. Either way her dependence on an inadequate and punitive welfare system was ensured.

'I had worked in an office and a boutique,' she said, 'but here there was nothing. The local supermarket would only employ teenagers. Going into the city meant travelling as much as four hours a day; and, anyway, employers don't like taking on Westies because the trains are unreliable and, I suppose, because of everything else they are told about us.'

She gave the impression of being under house arrest. She had no family of her own. She could not join the local netball team because she could not afford the twenty dollars for a babysitter. Yet she is neatly dressed, bright and pleasant. Poverty for her is an almost complete lack of control over her life. 'I think that among the women here I'm one of the strongest,' she said. 'We know we're dumped, and that leaves us not knowing what sort of lives we're meant to lead.'

When the dust came, it was like a ball of fire, rolling toward the town. There was a silence in its path, and no breeze. Then the blood red dissolved to the colour of sand and earth, and the dust was both walls and ceiling, as if the world had turned upside down. Once it reached Sulphide Street, it eclipsed the sun.

'The air was full of the same zinc and lead that rotted the miners' lungs,' said Thelma Thompson, 'we knew it would do the same to us. Whenever we saw that thing coming we ran and ran; and when we got home we shut everything and nailed down everything that moved: tables, chairs and chooks. Then we hung on as it shook our souls. And when it was over there was dirt and sand inches thick on everything: food, everything. We didn't get rid of it for weeks, that damn poison.'

Thelma survived the 'storms over the lode'. She was eighty-nine when I visited her in her weatherboard and iron house in Broken Hill, five hundred miles from Sydney in the far west of New South Wales. 'The memory', she said, 'is so important. If we forget why we fought to gain what we gained, if we don't pass that on, or just put it back into pages of a history no one will read, we'll be caught short again. It doesn't matter if there's videos and that sort of thing; progress is what men and women are prepared to suffer for.'

Thelma was born shortly after Broken Hill was established in a wilderness. The annual rainfall seldom reached seven inches and all water and food came overland from South Australia. In winter the earth froze; in summer the temperature seldom fell below the century fahrenheit. These unconsoling conditions were well understood by the Wilyalo people, who had lived here for 30,000 years. They were few and they survived with a rhythm that exploited the plains in winter while conserving the resources of the Barrier Range for the long, dry summers. Their land included a jagged, humpbacked ridge, the tip of an orebody containing the world's largest deposit of silver, zinc and lead. A boundary rider, Charles Rasp, had named it Broken Hill.

Believing the extraordinary shape was rich with minerals, Rasp formed a syndicate with seven sheep-station workers and pegged out a claim. But they were inexperienced and their initial exploration yielded little; Broken Hill was sold to a group of wealthy pastoralists who formed the Broken Hill Proprietory Company (BHP). 'By 1890 the mines were conservatively valued at £8,000,000,' wrote Edward Stokes in his history, *United We Stand*,

but little of their wealth found its way back to improve the community. By 1897 all the original syndicate had left the area to pursue lives of luxurious ease, and distant ownership exacerbated the town's neglect. If some of the syndicate had actually lived in Broken Hill – or even re-visited their mine – conditions might have been better. However, none ever did. Not one extravagant mansion ever graced the town, despite the orebody's vast wealth. Similarly, few Broken Hill shareholders had any notion of the town's drab existence. A few mine managers took an interest in their men's lives, but most were transients who contributed little to the town. Others displayed an almost contemptuous disinterest. W. H. Patton, BHP's manager, rarely donated any of his opulent salary to local causes and in 1889 he refused to open the new hospital.[22]

With no fresh food and mostly contaminated water, epidemics decimated the very young and old. Typhoid took 123 lives in one year. Safety in the mines was non-existent; Broken Hill's death rate was twice the national average. Thelma Thompson was a trainee nurse in Broken Hill hospital when the Great Strike began in 1919. 'The men and the town had had enough,' she said. 'There were twenty-one different kinds of lung disease and all the men had them. One after the other they'd be brought to the hospital, dead or half-dead, often from cave-ins on the night shift, between two and four in the morning. The attitude of the company was summed up by one of the managers who said, "No working man should have butter on his table; margarine is good enough." Well, margarine in those days was worse than dripping!'

Broken Hill's will to fight had been forged partly by its isolation from the rest of Australia. The New South Wales State Government in Sydney cared little about its distant outpost, and the indifference was mutual. With a population of 30,000, fifty-five hotels, brewery, Theatre Royal, two roller-skating rinks, two newspapers, the *Barrier Miner* and the *Barrier Truth*, and a brass band, Broken Hill regarded itself, justifiably, as an industrial principality with only a passing acquaintance with the nation emerging around it. When the States federated in 1901 in what was said to be the birth of the Commonwealth of Australia, Broken Hill was unmoved. The mayor, Jabez Wright, refused to attend the patriotic celebrations in Sydney and instead sent a cryptic telegram: 'I have something more important to do than attend the National Drunk.' In the same year Queen Victoria finally expired, and appeals were launched throughout Australia for public subscription to raise monuments to her in every centre, including Broken Hill. A derisory £29 9s was contributed by the Silver

City, where no memorial was raised. The money instead was given to the widows of twenty miners who had been killed that year.[23]

In 1908−9 wages were cut to below subsistence level. Ordered by the new Arbitration Court to pay 'a living wage', the company responded by closing down production for two years.[24] By the end of the First World War the miners were determined to 'win the future'. They struck and for nineteen months bore what Thelma Thompson describes as 'a kind of retribution'. 'The hospital was like a relief station in wartime,' she said. 'The wives would drag themselves to us, after miscarriages brought on by malnutrition. The children were close to starving. No one had anything, but everyone stayed together: the shopkeepers: everyone. They'd parade every day, the miners, the women and kids, behind Bartley's Barrier Band. Troops were sent, as if this was a revolution; and in some ways it was.'

The miners won because Broken Hill was theirs and only they would work the lode and suffer its misery. However, they won conditions of work up to half a century ahead of the rest of the world. These included the first thirty-five hour week. Night shifts, when most accidents occurred, were banned. Controlling the dust underground, and other safety measures, were given priority. For this, the owners were allowed to make bonanza profits.

When the strike was over, the unions formed the Barrier Industrial Council, for sixty years Broken Hill's effective government. As well as determining who could or could not work in the mines, the BIC controlled prices in shops, published one of the two local newspapers, allowed and regulated illegal gambling and set the hours for trading in pubs. (The sale of bottled beer was banned on Sundays 'to preserve family life'.) Trades Hall, with its stolid, rusticated stone façade facing on to Sulphide Street, was the most confident building in the town. It was here, every three years, that the miners' representatives and the companies (there are now three), re-negotiated the 'living wage'. As for the work and safety practices won in 1920, these were inviolable, sacrosanct. Today almost every mining family can name a grand-father, father, uncle or brother who has died beneath the 'line of lode' or from a disease of 'the dust'.

Had Shorty O'Neil been a boxer, he would have struggled to reach featherweight. The impression is left, however, that he would have taken on and beaten big men. The deep scar on his face is part of the crust of his working life. As the longest-serving President of the Barrier Industrial Council, Shorty was 'King of Broken Hill'. He is a voluble, irascible and sardonic man, as possessed of prejudice as he is of wilful courage. I met him standing among the stone gnomes in his small front garden. He had just turned eighty-three. 'Some things are simple, mate,' he said. 'If you don't kick, you get kicked.'

Like Thelma Thompson, he extolled the importance of memory, of 'not writing off the past simply because it all *looks* different now'. 'I watched a cage going down the shaft with four men in it,' he said, 'and I heard it crash to the ground, and I heard those blokes cry. Three of them were left crippled for life. The manager told the driver to be a bit careful next time. Three weeks later, the same driver dropped the cage on a horse and killed it. They sacked him for that. The same *attitude* remains.'

I asked Shorty how his family survived during the Great Strike. 'We lived next to the gaol,' he said, 'and I knew this warder who'd call me Billy. Mate, that gaol had the best garden in Broken Hill and this warder would say, "Billy, you better come over the wall tonight." That's how we kept going: by stealing from a bloody gaol ... As for clothes, well we had this heavy brown material, thousands of yards of it which someone had donated. The women organised a sewing circle in the Socialist Hall and after that, you could pick every miner's kid because they all had brown: brown dresses, brown shirts and brown trousers. I was a teenager and already in the mines. I wore the brown, mate. I was proud to be marked. You see, what was gained was phenomenal. There are workers in this country *still* fighting for a thirty-five hour week, and for the *peace* that working people crave. We got that peace, mate; we got agreements that allowed men to work out their lives, to build a home.'

I asked him, 'Is Broken Hill a closed place where the men, and only the men, count?'

'In my time', he said, 'I never let married women work. We've paid in blood for these jobs, mate. You have to understand the feeling here. I walked into a pub once and this bloke said, "Come and have a beer, Shorty." Well, I had a beer with him, but then this mate of mine called me over and said, "What are you doing? He's no bloody good; he's got his wife working."

'There's a law in Australia that says that any man that lives off the immoral earnings of a woman should be sent to gaol; and I say that a man that's working, that's taking money off his wife, he should be in bloody gaol, too. Look at it from the girl's point of view. If a young girl marries a bloke who can't earn enough to keep her, then she shouldn't have married the bugger in the first place. We never stopped any woman on her own with a child; we never stopped any divorced woman. But if we ever found out that the husband and wife were both working, we'd give the woman three months to give it up.'

The Barrier Industrial Council amended this policy only under pressure from the New South Wales Government through its anti-discrimination laws. But one of Shorty's rules remains. 'You've got to be born, educated or have lived here for the last ten years before you get a job in the mines,' he said. 'That means, mate, we're the only white city in Australia. You don't see any Vietnamese and that sort wandering around the streets here.'

I mentioned that modern Australia had been built with the labour of immigrants from all over the world. 'Not here, mate,' said Shorty. 'Before the Great Strike we had a lot of Yugoslavs. They were part of Austria in those days. My father used to say, "Bill, never do anything to the Austrians because there's never been an Austrian scab in Broken Hill." They're all right, mate.'

By the early 1980s the 'peace' was in danger. Apprenticeships, the life blood of mining, were terminated. A recession debilitated the town's commercial life; more than 4,000 people, or a third of the workforce, were retrenched or unable to find jobs. In 1986 the mining companies sought an end to many of the gains of sixty years earlier. Mineral prices had fallen, they argued, and Broken Hill was no longer 'viable'. This was in contrast to the companies' persistent lobby that Australia could solve its economic problems only by developing its mineral resources, regardless of fluctuating prices. The companies announced they would no longer help to pay for the regeneration of the surrounding parks and countryside, where the great dust storms used to gather. Their contribution to this had taken forty years' persuasion.

For two months the men were locked out. Their wives put on their husband's work clothes, blackened their faces and marched down Sulphide Street with their children behind a brass band. Shorty O'Neil held the banner with Heather Thomas; he cried and said the women's support was 'the best thing that has ever happened in the history of this town'. I told one of the wives that Shorty had said that women would never be equal to men in Broken Hill. 'Oh, he did, did he?' she said. 'The poor old bugger must be confused in his dotage. He should have learned that, without us, he would never have won a duck in a raffle, let alone a strike.'

When the men returned to work in the winter of 1986, to await the decision of an Arbitration Court judge, there was the usual defiant talk to mask their anxiety. Pam Byron, whose husband Dennis had been a miner for fifteen years, said, 'Because we're isolated the fear is different in Broken Hill. When the work goes, where do we go?'

Within days of their return to work, a familiar black flag was raised over Trades Hall. Ray Bloomfield, aged thirty-four, had fallen 100 feet down a shaft. The next shift stopped and the town filled for his funeral procession, which passed the length of the line of lode. In the church, men struggled to control their coughing.

I joined a shift and walked downhill through a fog of dust, judging the man in front from the beam of his lamp. 'Wait!'

said a voice. Ahead, silhouettes tapped the roof with crow-bars. A crack appeared and another blow with a bar brought down a raft of stone, only inches from its tormentors. The company had no quarrel with this 'work practice'.

The shaft narrowed. The noise of drilling was now constant, and the ricochet of water and dust stung exposed skin. Those ahead gently moved the timber supports, as heavy as cannons, that propped up the roof. They reminded me of troops bringing up artillery under fire, with their lives depending upon how each man worked; and in every sense – the clipped commands, the tense, planned assault on a stubborn adversary, the degradation of a filthy wet trench and the spirit of comradeship, of watching out for each other – this was mining's universal front line.

In February 1987 the *Sydney Morning Herald* reported:

A meeting of mine workers at Broken Hill yesterday voted to accept the introduction of new work practices underground . . . The decision marks the end of a year-long dispute [and] spells the end of work practices which have remained virtually unchanged since the 1920s . . .

The changes to be introduced include the firing of explosives while men remain underground on their meal break . . . Firings have occurred at the end of each shift for more than 60 years, with the next shift waiting an hour for dust and fumes to clear before going underground.

The President of the Mining Managers' Association, Mr Craig Bermingham, said the rest of the world was moving a bit faster than the Broken Hill mines.

At the annual Broken Hill Eisteddfod in the R. K. Sanderson Basketball Stadium the 'Gnomes Dance' was being performed in the 'Piano Solo Ten Years and Under' category. This was followed by 'Highland Dancing, Ballet, Tap and Modern'. Mothers wore taffeta and fathers long white socks. The applause was sparse. Unlike previous years, there were empty seats. People were leaving Broken Hill. At the 'Bachelors' and Spinsters' Ball' held in a large iron shed with a concrete floor, the 'belle of the ball' wore a leopard-skin hat, gloves and shoes and a large rose behind her ear. The 'beau of the ball' wore a baggy suit and left town the next day to look for work. The young leave mostly on Sundays in old Holden cars, Valiants and Datsuns, usually in convoy. Pam Byron said, 'Both my son and daughter have been unemployed for nearly three years after leaving school. My daughter was put off during the disputes. My son has never had a job. They'll have to go eventually. I can't remember so many young people leaving, just driving out.'

As in other parts of Australia, tourism is regarded as a possible solution. People from Adelaide and Sydney have opened restaurants serving expensive and pretentious food. One of the main tourist attractions is at nearby Silverton, once a prosperous town of 25,000 people until the mining companies decided that Broken Hill offered greater profit. Silverton retains the empty shells of two-storey stone hotels, banks, the *Silver Age* newspaper office and the brewery. An occasional tourist bus comes through and people are taken to the Silverton pub, where television commercials for Castlemaine beer are made. ('Australians wouldn't give a XXXX for anything else.') The parrot that appears in these commercials resides in the pub. The tour guide explains that although the parrot is depicted drinking a can of XXXX, the parrot hates beer. The can contains raspberry juice, which the parrot likes.

On their return to Broken Hill the buses pass the cemetery on Rakow Road, but they do not stop. There is no regeneration here; no grass grows in the dry and dusty earth between the plots. Row upon row of the gravestones are those of miners who died on the line of lode. Dominating them is an obelisk commemorating the death of Percy Brookfield, an independent socialist who was elected to represent Broken

Hill early in the century and held the balance of power in the New South Wales Parliament during the Great Strike.

After the strike had been won, Percy Brookfield was killed as he tried to disarm a Russian who had fired on a train filled with passengers. His death was believed by many of his supporters to have been a political assassination, although it was not. He was a brave and principled man who fought hard for the miners when others in the labour movement saw their cause as lost. On his obelisk are inscribed the words, 'Workers of the World Unite!' Every day, for almost seventy years, fresh red flowers have been placed here, in the dust.

Running east from Perth is C. Y. O'Connor's Great Pipe. Like an iron worm beside the highway, it carries water from the coastal dams of the Darling Range to a wheat belt surrounded by salt bed and sand. C. Y. O'Connor, an Irish engineer, shot himself dead at South Beach near Perth on March 10, 1902 after a campaign of vilification in which he was accused of building a pipe that would not work. His farewell note to his wife and seven children included instructions for the completion of his dream, which was later described as 'an engineering wonder of the world'. It is a peculiarly Australian story of vision, farce and tragedy.

The State of Western Australia, into which Europe would fit with room to spare, occupies a third of the continent. Less than 9 per cent of the Australian population live here, about 1,407,000 people, a million of whom live in Perth, the most isolated city in the world. Perth, the home of Alan Bond and other Mates, is said to have the highest concentration of millionaires in Australia.

When C. Y. O'Connor's Great Pipe reaches Goomaling, there are no millionaires. There are prefabricated houses, and a garage that puts back together old cars; and a shop with a Billabong ice-cream sign and a large hole in its flyscreen door. The first abandoned farmhouse is here. Beyond the railway line at Wyalkatchem there is another, and another.

Near Koorda on a straight empty road, a patrol car

appeared and a cop silently handed out a speeding ticket. The owner of the Koorda Hotel, Mike Kelly, said, 'You must've run into Al Boyer. Al likes to hand out parking tickets in places where there's more space to park than on the moon. What gets up people's noses is that Al won half a million bucks on Lotto, *and* he wants to stay being a cop!'

Land around Koorda was cleared only in the 1950s. The atmosphere is of a town half born, a community half formed in a country half won. Koorda was the site of one of the ill-fated 'soldier settler schemes', in which returning veterans of the Second World War were sent to struggle, unskilled, with the bush from which eventually they fled in despair. There is more than an echo of this today. In the local paper a page is given over to the 'rural facilitator' explaining his mission. 'My name is Francis,' he wrote. 'I have been recently appointed by Mount Marshall Shire to help people see more objectively their financial and personal situations . . . In times of crisis we all experience stress or pressure and tend to feel isolated and alone with our problems . . . so it is essential to have someone who in the strictest confidence is interested in listening.'[25]

There is an apprehensive edge to local pride. Bert Street was named 'Street of the Year' in 1986, the year the Homestead Store closed down and the population dropped to 350. Hazel Jones, the local historian, has placed a sign over her one-room museum: 'Patrons – in the event of earth tremors please vacate premises quickly for mutual safety.' This is said to stimulate 'the Japanese tourists', although only one has been sighted.

North from Koorda the earth moves. Sand scuds across the road and the horizon shimmers with the silver and gold of salt bed, desert and, miraculously, wheat. Harry and Kath King live here, on a farm optimistically called Golden Acres. Their address is Mollerin North Road, Mollerin North. But there is no Mollerin, north or south. Their farm is the last one; the town itself died in May 1984. Harry's father came here in 1930 from the gold fields at Kalgoorlie. 'He had an axe and a big heart,' said Harry, of whom the same ought to be said. Harry and Kath married young and cleared their own land in 1959, nurtured it and became, against all sensible odds, successful wheat farmers.

The Kings borrowed money in the late 1970s when wheat prices were up and interest rates down. After constant drought, a contracting market for Australian wheat and interest rates of more than 20 per cent, they fell into serious debt for the first time. To keep up his repayments Harry has had to lease more and more land and so increase the area of his wheat crop. 'At the moment I'm putting in about 7,500 acres at a cost of around 130,000 dollars,' he said. 'I've no guarantee I'll even get that money back, let alone make any profit. If it doesn't rain, the desert will take it; and it's got to be the sort of rain that doesn't disappear the moment it hits the ground.'

C. Y. O'Connor's Great Pipe does not reach here. There is no running water. Water has to be trucked in, or caught on the rare occasions it falls from the sky. Harry turned off the engine of his tractor and switched on the ABC's rural news. The first item reported a 30 per cent drop in rainfall throughout Australia during the previous ten years. Harry shook his head and got back into his tractor. He has no help; there is just him and Kath and their son-in-law, Rob. Their eldest son, Greg, was killed on his motor-bike in 1985. 'We had a fifteen-year plan to hand everything over to Greg,' said Harry. 'Now it'll be Rob.'

At dusk Harry and Kath drove me the fifteen miles to Mollerin. We passed two abandoned homesteads. A desiccated shrub rolled the length of a leaning picket fence and the front yard was ablaze with wild flowers: the red velvet stems of kangaroo paws and the fiery cylinders of bottle brush. A child 's pinny flapped stiffly on a clothes' line. The bush had already claimed one of the rear bedrooms, and sand coated the floors. 'Doesn't take long,' said Kath. 'There was a family in that one last Christmas. They came to our barbecue, then just drove away.'

We turned past the sign warning motorists about kangaroos and into Mollerin's main street. At first our voices and reflections in shop windows held promise, as if people would emerge in their own time. We leaned on the bonnet of a parked car which had no tyres, and watched nothing move on a windless day.

In the general store and post office, beneath a sign, 'Just say Golden West and choose your flavour!' the door was open, caught by a pair of slippers. On the counter was a tax declaration for the financial year 1983–4. A newspaper's TV guide for the first week of April 1984 lay on an ancient 'Admiral' television set. Then a muffled scream filled the next room, shocking us all. I opened the door with caution, and a cockatoo hurled itself past us, plumage up, feathers flying, circling, thudding into the ceiling, screeching. It eventually found the front door and soared and dived against the fading light, before perching on a telephone box. The light in the box had come on; there is no other light in Mollerin.

Inside the community hall a banner announced 'Merry Xmas Everyone'; another congratulated Doug Parker on having been elected captain of the Mollerin badminton team. The petrified face of a woman peered from behind the tea and biscuits counter. It was a cut-out, left perhaps as a surreal joke, to nod and smile at nothing. 'The last New Year's Eve cabaret we had over 200 people,' said Harry. 'You couldn't get a parking place, could you, Kath?'

Mollerin Public School had two teachers and up to fifty children and was one of the first in the State to have its own computer. It is modern, yet endearing, as the best Australian country schools are, with its tuck-shop rotas ('Anne King to cook the pies in June . . . Pam Clarke to do the hot dogs'), a mural entitled 'Wow, am I growing!' and bushland as an infinite playground. Now it is empty, the small sports ground is all but overgrown and the cricket pitch is woven with cracks and the nests of large ants.

In the great depressions of the 1890s and 1930s the only choice for most rural Australians was to wait out the difficult times in the hope that prosperity would be restored. In the 1990s this seems unlikely. Fifty per cent of Australian farmers earn less than $A11,800 a year and almost a third have no incomes at all; or they have 'minus incomes', which means they are heavily in debt.[26] Many pay interest on their interest. Evictions are common and television crews lie in wait to film them for the evening news. As families leave and take away the young, country trades are lost and, in the end, there is nothing to restore. Other towns in the West Australian wheat belt, Bonnie Rock, Cleary and Beacon, are vanishing. People know it is happening when the authorities remove the hospital, the post office and, finally, the school.

In summer 1989 I phoned Harry and Kath King. It was two years since I had last spoken to them and I did not expect them to answer the phone. 'Yeah, we're here, we're hanging on!' said Harry. 'The rain finally came two years late, and we've had to sell off most of our machinery: the heavy stuff, the tractors and heavy trucks. This has given us just enough to satisfy the bank for a while. No one is going to throw us off! When we bail out, we'll hand over to Rob in proper, dignified style. The way you go is important.'

In February 1992, I phoned again; this time there was no answer. I finally found Harry and Kath in Jurien Bay, on the wild and beautiful coast north of Perth. 'We tried', said Harry, 'but the debt was too much and we sold off everything to pay it. We just left the house, took the truck and headed here'.

'How are you living?' I asked.

'We're mowing lawns, the two of us. I know it sounds funny; but we don't have a choice. Anyway, we've worked all our lives. The thing is, we're not down'.

8

BREAKING FREE

This is the greatest coming of age of Australia. This is the golden age of economic change.

Paul Keating, Federal Treasurer

Australia is the big one, the jewel of south-east Asia. Looking down the road, Australia is going to be increasingly important to the United States, and so long as Australians keep on electing the right people then there'll be a stable relationship between the two countries.

Victor Marchetti, CIA officer

We won't let you down. And we will stay involved right up to the very end of eternity because we know it's fundamentally in our interests and hope like hell it's in yours.

President Bush, visiting Australia

ON JANUARY 26, 1988 the 'dignitaries' assembled on the foreshore of Sydney Harbour to view the spectacle of the Bicentenary sailing ships included a familiar snowy head and florid face, dressed in familiar morning suit and holding a familiar glass of vintage champagne. It was Sir John Kerr, the former Queen's Man who had conspired successfully to get rid of an elected Australian Government.

Until his death in 1991, Kerr's position as national pariah was assured. Bob Hawke did not agree and expressed little patience for those who 'dwell upon the past'.[1] Such forgiving sentiment was shared by lesser *duces* of the Labor Party machine, who on the great day demonstrated their generosity by queueing to greet 'Sir John' and even to embrace him, causing his Bollinger to splash his shoes and a waiter to be summoned to replenish 'Sir John's glass'.

Several months later an election was held in New South Wales, the State run almost as a political fiefdom by the Labor machine and its Mates. Labor was beaten; and the significance of its defeat was expressed in the party's heartland, the Hunter Valley, in towns of coal-mines and steel works and weatherboard houses, where my parents had grown up and their parents before them, where the miners had fought the Basher Gang and one colonial Government after the other for the right to a decent life, which they now lived precariously. For the first time since the colonies federated in 1901, a Labor member was not returned here. The miners, the people in the foundries, the factories, on the wharves, in the K-Mart, who represent the majority of Australians, voted with anger and bitterness for an independent to represent them in the State Parliament. The 'workers' party', which had buttressed Hawke, Keating, Wran and their Mates, was disavowed.

Every assessment showed that Labor had lost a bloodline of support because people resented its 'silvertails' and 'spivs' and the new economic and political order, which excluded them. One analysis, which did not receive the attention it deserved, was that the old Labor Party was extinct and that, in national politics, a series of 'hung Parliaments' was now likely, with the minority parties and independents holding the balance, and the final result determined by the Governor-General and those who backed him.[2]

If this is so, then in the 1990s Australian democracy will be dependent again on the caprice of one unelected, unaccountable man and on the degree of his malleability. This may not be apparent to many, because the precedent of the part played by the Governor-General in the Whitlam *coup* has been distorted, consistently and painstakingly, by its beneficiaries and apologists, so that the probability of a repetition of the events of November 11, 1975 is no longer a public issue. In 1975 no political commentator warned of what was coming. And there are no warnings now. Next time the form will be different, of course, but the dynamics, the sources of support and collaboration, are likely to be the same. Most important, the powers of the Governor-General remain unchanged. Gough Whitlam has listed them:

He can sack the Government. He can appoint and sack individual Ministers. He can dissolve the House of Representatives. He can call or prorogue both Houses. He need not grant a double dissolution although the Government asks for it. He need not assent to a Bill. He need not submit a Bill to alter the Constitution which has twice been passed by one House, even if he is advised to do so by the Government.

He need not assent to a Bill to alter the Constitution

even if it's been approved by the electors. And he need not assent to any Bills which are passed by both Houses.

Whitlam added that the Australian constitution made the Governor-General, as the Queen's representative, commander of all military forces. 'A lot of people have said: 'Why didn't I defy him? Why didn't I tear up his letter? The answer is that this man would have called out the armed forces . . . There would have been chaos in this country.'[3]

Few Australians, I believe, are aware of the existence of such despotic reserve powers, which are unheard of in any other advanced democracy, and which are dangerous. To break free from them is imperative if Australia is ever to achieve independence from its imperial legacy and from the colonial state of mind that permeates its political life.

The sad story of Bill Hayden is instructive. Hayden is the present Governor-General. A former Whitlam Minister, Hayden was leader of the Labor Party until Bob Hawke and his faction pushed him aside in 1983. Long regarded by his supporters as the keeper of the nation's political conscience and its egalitarian spirit, Hayden was an avowed republican who spoke out often and passionately against the position and power of the Governor-General. In 1988 Hayden underwent a swift conversion. The job of Governor-General fell vacant and he applied, explaining that his past criticism and support for republicanism had been made in the heat of the moment. 'I don't find the idea of the role repugnant,' he said. 'It is a role with considerable public prestige and respect.'[4]

The more Hayden spoke about 'the role' and its 'prestige and respect', the more it became clear that he yearned for it, and had yearned for it for some time. He said, 'If you allow for my background from infancy at south Brisbane [a working-class area], where we never saw the Governor-General and rarely saw a politician, let alone ever expected that someone from that area would ever assume such a respected office, then the more I look at it, the more I find it a very exciting role . . . I think there's a case for very ordinary Australians to have a share of the action . . . It would allow, I hope, my wife and our children, and maybe one day our grandchildren, the opportunity for them to say, "Well, the old chap came from south Brisbane without much hope, and look where he ended up." '[5]

When he finally ended up in the vice-regal mansion, with the butler and the Rolls-Royces, the portrait of Sir John Kerr and the numerous 'perks' paid for by people's taxes, a newspaper headline said, 'Dream finally comes true for the poor boy from Mabel Street.'[6] On his first official visit to Sydney, the new Governor-General spoke about 'the dignity and stature of this high public office'. He referred to 'dignity' three times; and women in large floral hats curtsied to him, apparently unaware that you curtsy only to the Queen.

The colonial state of mind is not always obvious. The politicians and public servants of the new order, who guide and advise on the nation's economic life and see themselves, even during a recession, as ultra-modern 'economic rationalists', or 'econocrats', have a colonial mentality disciplined to serve overseas interests. The 'world view', to which they are wedded, requires nothing less. Australia has long been the most foreign-owned country in the world, apart from Canada; but since Paul Keating dismantled the last major protective barriers, Australia has become the economic 'banana republic' Keating himself once described: a 'First World' country with a 'Third World' economy. As in the Third World, transnational companies are denuding Australia's finite resources while the national debt grows and grows. That Australia no longer is able to trade its way out of debt is part of a pattern familiar in Latin America. Like his Brazilian counterpart, the Australian Treasurer must pay regular visits to Wall Street and Washington to sing for his country's credit rating.

Like most small and vulnerable countries, Australia has become trapped in the world of 'money power', which has brought about the economic harshness of the 1990s. The Australian political economist Ted Wheelwright has described money power as 'a force quite divorced from production and the real world, but by its gyrations it determines whether industries live or die. Its activities are now parasitical and quite undemocratic; it is the source of the main immediate danger to the system, of a financial collapse.' In Australia's 'transnational economy' money is free to flow to the points of highest return anywhere in the world, and wages forgone become profit which can flow out of the country or into money market speculation rather than be invested in employment-creating industries.[7] Few Australians reading their daily newspapers are made aware of this. Dissenters from the orthodoxy, such as Professor Wheelwright, are seldom heard or read by the public. Instead, the 'econocrats' and soothsayers wait passively in front of their electronic screens to be told about the next 'world crisis' on the stock market or in banking, property speculation, commodity prices and oil prices.

Unless Australia breaks free from this trap, Australians will pay a price in permanent high unemployment (in 1992 it touched 11 per cent), in sharply reduced wages and living standards, and intractable poverty. Sydney and Melbourne do not have the scale of sub-life of New York and Detroit; not yet. Australia is not the property of the great Japanese *zaibatsu* companies; not yet; and Australians are not the 'poor white trash' of an Asia whose promotional model is go-getting, repressive Singapore; not yet. But Japan already operates a veto over much of the Australian economy, and by the end of the 1990s Australian skilled workers will earn less than their counterparts in Japan, Singapore, Taiwan and Korea.

The solution surely is not to build an isolationist, 'Fortress Australia'. It is to manage fairly the natural resources of which Australia has more per head of population than any other nation. It is first to provide the necessities of food, clothing, shelter and transport for *all* the people of Australia. It is to assault child poverty, a national shame, by ending the gross inequities and waste in the tax system and shifting financial power back to the majority. And it is to unravel the ties with the catastrophic, debt-ridden American economy, and it is to trade with the peoples of the Pacific and Asia on a planned basis: buying that which Australia cannot economically produce – not free trade, but *fair* trade.

If Australians are serious about living fairly in their own region, rather than as occupants of an antiquated imperial lighthouse, the issue is even wider. No other developed country is such a geographical part of the 'developing world' – that is the majority of humanity – than Australia. There is a war currently being waged against this majority by forces representing the new 'transnational' order. It is a war of rich against poor; and it is a cost effective war. Indeed, the profits to date have surpassed all expectations. In the period 1983–90, the poor countries paid £98,000 to the rich countries in interest payments on debt that may well be impossible to pay back. That is a net figure, after taking into account new loans and all new aid.[8] The international banks such as the International Monetary Fund and the World Bank, which are based in Washington and manipulated by US governments, say there is no way forward other than that of 'growth' and 'structurally adjusted' economics in which export production and foreign investment have every priority and health care, education and decent employment have none. Australians, with their debt-laden colonial economy, are on the sidelines of this war. But they can hear the gunfire, which is not so distant now.

Like Ted Wheelwright, Ted Trainer is an Australian thinker whose views are not widely known. Trainer says that if the present growth rates were to double, only seven poor countries would reach the level of the rich majority in 100 years and only nine more would do so in the next 1000 years. In the meantime all the gains of 'growth' go to the few; one-fifth of the world consumes four-fifths of its resources, while child malnutrition increases, with 43,000 deaths every day. The majority cannot feed themselves often because they are compelled by their foreign creditors to grow luxury crops for the rich – such as coffee and carnations. This is the real meaning of 'international market forces at work' and the unspoken price of 'growth'. It is a truth that deserves to be printed as a health warning in the financial sections of newspapers.

What is interesting about Australia is that, although 'developed', it is also a victim of indebtedness and of 'market forces at work'. This gives Australians a shared vulnerability with their closest neighbours – and with the majority of humanity. Those Australians who understand this, and are able to act upon their understanding, will promote both the independence of their country and of their region.[9]

The opponents of real independence are formidable, as Gough Whitlam learned. Australia's place in the world community, its relations with its own region, continue to be defined by the strategic interests of the dominant great power. Public discussion about this is 'tricky', as Australians say; yet few would want a return to the silence and ignorance of the 1950s and 1960s, when a mendacious Menzies allowed one great power to drop nuclear bombs on his country and committed young Australians to die in the cause of another. Few would want this, but perhaps few realise that the aims and machinations of the 1990s are different only in form.

'Australia is the big one, the jewel of south-east Asia,' the former CIA strategist, Victor Marchetti, told me. 'What with the way things are going in the Philippines, what may happen in Formosa . . . looking down the road Australia is going to be increasingly important to the United States, and so long as Australians keep electing the right people, then there'll be a stable relationship between the two countries.'

I asked Marchetti what the CIA had learned from Whitlam. 'Oh, I think we learned a lot,' he replied. 'When Hawke came along we didn't panic to begin with, and then Hawke immediately sent signals that he knew how the game was played and who was buttering his bread. He became *very* co-operative, and even obsequious in some fashion.'[10]

After coming to power in 1983 one of Prime Minister Hawke's first 'signals' was to agree secretly to test the American first-strike MX missile in Australian coastal waters, a move considered so rash that it was turned down by his own Cabinet. In the same year the Hawke Government issued a policy statement which effectively welcomed foreign nuclear-armed ships into Australia's ports and dry docks. The statement was dictated, virtually word for word, by the American Secretary of State, George Shultz. 'Now there are not many countries in the world', said Bob Hawke, 'where a Prime Minister can just say to his Foreign Minister to ring George Shultz, knowing that, if we ring, we'll be listened to immediately.'[11]

Prime Minister Hawke went regularly to Washington, where he had many 'old Mates'. During one visit he announced he had been given an 'unqualified assurance' that none of the American bases in Australia were being used for 'Star Wars' research.[12] The veracity of this is challenged by the head of strategic and defence studies at the Australian

National University, Desmond Ball. Using American sources, Ball has established that the data drawn from the monitoring of Soviet missile and satellite launches at the most secret of the bases, Nurrungar, has been passed on to the Star Wars organisation. This has enabled American scientists to conclude that 'a space-based infra-red sensor system can be developed . . .': in other words, a Star Wars system.[13] In 1988 Hawke announced that his Government had signed a new agreement with Washington to continue operations at Nurrungar and nearby Pine Gap for ten years. He described Nurrungar as a warning station and Pine Gap as 'vital for verification of arms control'. He made no mention of their other purpose.[14] During the Gulf War in 1991, both Nurrungar and Pine Gap were used by Washington to gather intelligence and further its war aims against Iraq.

There is limitless promise and tragedy in the American perception of Australia as 'the jewel' of south-east Asia. When the New Zealand Labor Government of David Lange was elected in 1984, it banned nuclear weapons and nuclear-armed ships from New Zealand's waters and promoted the idea of a truly nuclear-free zone in the south Pacific. For this, it was expelled from the ANZUS Pact by the United States, with the zealous backing of the Australian Government.

New Zealand's stand was shared by most governments of the south Pacific. It was warmly supported by the new Labour Government of Fiji. When, in 1987, Colonel Rabuka marched into the Fijian Parliament with a gun and put an end to Fijian democracy, his actions were greeted in Washington. 'We're kinda delighted,' said a Pentagon official. 'All of a sudden our [nuclear armed] ships couldn't go to Fiji and now all of a sudden they can. We got a little chuckle outta the news.'[15]

The reaction in Canberra was not quite as direct. Australian commercial interests, such as those of the BHP mining corporation, owner of gold mines, had long controlled the Fijian economy. The Australian Government eventually recognised the illegal and racially motivated Rabuka regime. No attempt was made to use Australia's considerable economic influence. The deposed Prime Minister, Dr Timoci Bavandra, told me, not long before he died, that he had tried to speak to Bob Hawke on the phone for almost a year. 'He was always unavailable,' he said. 'It hurt me a bit, I must say.'[16]

According to Dr Alfred McCoy, whose studies on foreign intervention in Asia have earned wide respect, Australia's actions over Fiji 'could well be the turning point where it surrenders all influence in the Pacific and an era begins of healthy democracies being replaced by banana republics that are weak, divided client states of the US.' He pointed to the Caribbean experience, which demonstrated how the US interest lay in 'bumping off' island democracies and subjugating them.[17]

A similar 'bumping off' process is under way in the subjugation of trade unions throughout the Pacific, using Australia as a base. In 1983 the CIA-linked Labor Committee for Pacific Affairs held its first major conference in Sydney. The LCPA was set up by the Georgetown International Labor Program with a grant of $US300,000 from the United States Information Agency, the propaganda arm of the US Government.[18] The Georgetown International Labor Program was itself established with the help of an extreme right-wing 'think tank', the Centre of Strategic and International Studies. The New Zealand *Times*, in exposing the LCPA, described one of its 'backroom boys', Gerry O'Keefe, as 'a CIA agent with considerable clout'.[19] O'Keefe was one of three CIA officers closeted with Bob Hawke shortly before his election as President of the Australian Council of Trade Unions in 1969. Four years later he was exposed as a CIA agent operating inside the trade unions in Chile shortly before the Allende Government was overthrown.[20]

One of the aims of the LCPA has been to counter the anti-nuclear policies of the New Zealand and other Pacific governments. Trade unionists in the region are given all-expenses-paid 'study trips' to the United States. Their itinerary has included lectures by CIA agent Gerry O'Keefe on the Soviet 'threat' to the south Pacific. The organising secretary of the LCPA, Michael Easson, was appointed Secretary of the powerful New South Wales Labor Council. He has strongly denied these CIA links and says the people involved are 'all liberal Democrats'.[21] In a letter to Easson, dated December 16, 1983 and signed by his private secretary, Prime Minister Hawke expressed his 'sincere regrets' that he could not accept an invitation to open the first LCPA conference. The letter concluded that 'Mr Hawke was pleased to see the formation of this organisation ... and sends his best wishes for the success of the conference.'[22]

The Treaty of Raratonga, signed by the small island nations of the south Pacific, is a bold and imaginative attempt to abolish nuclear weapons from a vast area of the southern world, much of it defiled by American and French nuclear testing. To most of its signatories, the treaty is an article of faith in the peaceful future of their region and in their own independence. Although Australia has signed the treaty, Australian diplomats have worked hard to minimise its provisions so that American nuclear-powered and armed ships are allowed into the zone. Only in this way, the Australians have argued, will Washington join in and sign. This has proven a forlorn hope. The Pentagon, not surprisingly, wants nothing to do with it.

In 1986 the Australian Labor Party reaffirmed its opposition to selling the principal ingredient of nuclear weapons, uranium, to France while the French continue to test nuclear weapons in the Pacific. In 1988 secret documents leaked from the European regulatory body, Euratom, disclosed that Australian uranium was being 're-flagged', or re-labelled, so that it appeared to originate in other countries. There was nothing to prevent it ending up in French bombs.[23] In 1988 the Hawke Government sold $A66 million worth of Government-held uranium stock to France, clearing the way for uranium sales eventually to go ahead.

Australia's promise and tragedy are no more acute than in south-east Asia, where generations of Australians have been sent to fight. In Cambodia the return of Pol Pot's genocidal Khmer Rouge is a real possibility. For several years Bill Hayden distinguished himself as the only Western diplomat working to bring about a regional settlement. In March 1985 he met the then Cambodian Foreign Minister, Hun Sen, in

Saigon, and was attacked by the Australian press for his initiative. Senior Vietnamese officials have told me that had Hayden been allowed to proceed, he might have helped to start negotiations for the first real peace in Indo-China for more than a generation.

Today Pol Pot and his murderous gang are being wheeled back to power in Cambodia in a Trojan Horse built by China and Western governments, notably the Australian Government. This is not what Australians have been told. The Government's version of the present United Nations 'peace plan' for Cambodia is that it is the only hope for a 'comprehensive settlement', as well as a triumph for the so-called 'Evans Plan', upon which it is based. The Evans Plan came to light in November, 1989 as the direct result of public concern in Australia that the Hawke Government was selling out Cambodia as part of Washington's continuing war of attrition and revenge against Vietnam.

At the Paris conference on Cambodia in August of that year none had been more zealous than the Australian Minister for Foreign Affairs, Gareth Evans, in supporting US and Chinese plans to bring the Khmer Rouge into the 'peace process' – itself a striking contradiction in terms. Evans supported American and Chinese demands that all reference to 'genocide' should be excluded from official statements. In a briefing document bearing Evans' hand-writing, a 'specific stumbling block' is 'identified' as 'whether it is appropriate or not to refer specifically to the genocidal practices of the past . . .' Nowhere in the 153 pages of the Australian Government's 'working paper' prepared for a subsequent conference in Djakarta, and effectively a draft of the Evans Plan, is there mention of Khmer Rouge atrocities. These are dismissed as 'human rights abuses of a recent past': a euphemism agreed between Washington and Peking.

Like so much Australian foreign policy, the Evans 'initiative' complied with Washington's plan for Cambodia – guided, promoted and defended by Congressman Stephen Solarz, the influential Chairman of the House Committee on Asian and Pacific Affairs and the architect of much of US policy in the region. A pugnacious personality with cold war views, Solarz has long lobbied for the Khmer Rouge to be accepted in the 'peace process' as 'necessary *realpolitic*': in truth, as a means of ensuring an anti-Vietnamese regime in Phnom Penh and that pressure remains on Hanoi. When Evans briefly departed from the Solarz line and proposed that Cambodia's seat at the UN should be declared vacant, he was told the Bush administration would never agree to it. The proposal was dropped. Thus, the Khmer Rouge, as members of a 'Supreme National Council', have maintained their diplomatic network and effective veto over the 'peace process', and two of Pol Pot's most trusted henchmen, one of them directly complicit in mass murder, are currently ensconced in Phnom Penh, protected by the United Nations. Solarz has recommended Evans for the Nobel Peace Prize.

The upheavals of Indo-China, especially the Vietnam war remain deep in the Australian memory and psyche. Many Australians, like many Americans, have found that excising the war without understanding its atrocious nature, is impossible; and that sublimating it is destructive. They say that coming to terms with what was done must be a gradual process, and helping the people of Vietnam is an essential part of that process. In February 1983, a few weeks before the election of the Labor Government, Hayden said, 'Without any hesitation at all we will re-establish aid programmes to Vietnam and seek to encourage other countries to provide aid.'[24] It was a popular commitment because it provided the first opportunity to help the Vietnamese and to express a common decency unrelated to the Cold War requirements of Australia's great ally. It was also seen by some as a modest expression of Australian independence.

Within a few weeks of his election, Bob Hawke received two phone calls from his Mate, George Shultz, who raised the question of Australia's assistance to Vietnam in the context of Hawke's first visit to Washington. As a result, the Cabinet deferred the decision on aid until after the visit in June 1983. When Hawke returned from Washington, the matter became a 'non-issue'. In 1989 the Vietnamese army withdrew from

Cambodia, taking with it a pretext of the Hawke Government to deny aid to Vietnam. In the same year the *Sydney Morning Herald* published a one-paragraph item saying that a million Vietnamese were suffering from famine.[25]

In 1987 Australians who had fought in Vietnam were given a long-awaited parade through the streets of Sydney. The marching, limping boys of the 1960s got cheers and tears, but no public apology. Today, Australian schoolchildren are taught little about why their fathers were sent on false pretences to join in the destruction of a small, impoverished country. The Hollywood version, of movies that celebrate and pity the invader, has become the popular history.

This is not to suggest that Australian governments have simply gone along with American designs for the region and expected nothing for themselves, apart from American 'protection'. The tragedy of East Timor is illustrative of Australia not only backing an important American client-regime, but of taking its cut of the spoils. There is, of course, no Evans 'peace plan' for East Timor, which lies considerably closer to Australia than Cambodia and has been illegally occupied by Indonesia since 1975. In December of that year the UN Security Council unanimously called on 'the Government of Indonesia to withdraw without delay all its forces from the territory' and 'all states to respect the territorial integrity of East Timor as well as the inalienable right of its people to self-determination . . .'[26]

The similarity of East Timor's plight with that of Kuwait under Saddam Hussein is striking, yet no international force, led by the United States, has gone to the aid of the Timorese – in spite of the fact that some 200,000 people or about a third of the population, have died during the years of Indonesian oppression and terror. On the contrary, the American Ambassador to the UN, Daniel Patrick Moynihan, has described implementing State Department directives to render the UN 'utterly ineffective in whatever measures it undertook' in response to Indonesia's invasion, because 'the United States wished things to turn out as they did and worked to bring this about'.[27]

For the Hawke government, the invasion of Kuwait was

quite different. Explaining why Australian warships were being sent to the Gulf, Hawke invoked the 'commanding moral authority of the UN' 33 times in one speech, concluding: 'So now we must fight!'[28] Driving home the point, Hawke declared, 'Big countries cannot invade small countries and get away with it'.[29] Contrast that with Hawke's reaction to the latest known Indonesian massacre in East Timor: that of at least 100 mourners at a funeral in 1991. In what was considered a strong statement, Hawke *asked* Indonesia for 'genuine contrition, a dinkum enquiry and an intention to punish those responsible'.[30] The equivalence of this would have been the Australian Prime Minister asking Saddam Hussein for 'genuine contrition' following a massacre of Kuwaitis, while knowing that the prize for Australia was a share of Kuwaiti oil.

Five months before the Indonesian invasion in 1975, Australia's Ambassador in Djakarta, Richard Woolcott (who became head of the Department of Foreign Affairs) sent this message to Canberra:

> (We) might well have an interest in closing the present gap in the agreed sea border and this could be much more readily negotiated with Indonesia than with Portugal or independent Portuguese Timor. I know I am recommending a pragmatic rather than a principled stand but that is what national interest and foreign policy is all about.[31]

Two years later Australia gave *de jure* recognition to Indonesia's integration of East Timor as the preliminary to finalising a sea-bed accord and exploiting the off-shore oil. A 1977 study forecast production of between one and seven billion barrels of oil. In December 1989 Australia and Indonesia signed the Timor Gap Treaty assuring lucrative expansion of petroleum resources[32]. At the time Foreign Affairs Minister Evans said, 'There is no binding legal obligation not to recognise aquisition of territory that was acquired by force'.[33] Earlier he had put it more succinctly: 'The world', he said, 'is a pretty unfair place'.[34]

I count myself among the many Australians who have not forgotten the vision, if not the turmoil, of the Evatt and Whitlam years, however flawed. We were briefly, tenuously, almost an independent community with the hope of a future not pre-empted by a war of attrition between nuclear giants and by a discredited piety known as 'anti-communism'. The regression has been sketched in this book. That Australia, a nation of Asia and the Pacific, which did much to establish the independent voting rights of small countries at the United Nations, should now vote predominantly with what is known as the 'Western European and Other Group', is a measure of that regression. That the Australian Prime Minister on his Bicentenary visit to the United States should feel the need to describe himself as Crocodile Dundee, then to eulogise 'American leadership', only to be told that the Senate Majority Leader did not have the time to see him, is also a measure of that regression. That Hawke in the Gulf War should do precisely as Menzies did in Vietnam – that is, ask the American President to 'request' Australian military assistance – is a measure of the obsequiousness that is still with us. That members of both houses of the Federal Parliament should be flown back to Canberra during the Christmas recess just to hear George Bush utter inanities about Australia and America together 'until the end of eternity' is more of the same. That Australia remains literally a second-class monarchy overseen by a viceroy who once was proud of his republicanism, is the vision lost.

This need not be so. Across the Tasman Sea in New Zealand there is, among the majority of the people, a compelling example. When I first went to New Zealand in 1973, New Zealanders led the opposition to France's nuclear testing in the Pacific. I found a society much like Australia's on the surface, yet quite different. This is especially true of the regard people have for the land, whose beauty is invested almost with sanctity. In that year the Government declared almost 10 per cent of the land surface to be a national park, a move not considered at all radical. A few years earlier New Zealanders had demonstrated their deep and emotional opposition to the establishment of an American Omega communications base in the South Island; as a result, the base was moved to Australia. An argument that might have held sway in Australia – that American 'protection' was needed against the gravitational threat of the Red and Yellow Perils – was irrelevant in a country relatively unblighted by such phobia.

During the early 1980s significant changes began to take place in the lives of New Zealanders. People began to declare their homes 'nuclear free'. Churches and schools followed, then whole streets and local councils. Derided as trivial by some members of New Zealand's peace movement, the trend soon became a national act of faith. People said they were taking charge of their lives and reclaiming their future; and the strength of their feeling led to Government policy banning nuclear-armed ships, indeed all things nuclear from New Zealand and its waters. What was unique about this was that it became, in effect, a bi-partisan policy. As Mary-Louise O'Callaghan has pointed out, 'To be anti-nuclear in New Zealand is not to be cast as a radical, but as a patriot.'[35]

'A great power protects itself', wrote the Australian historian Gavan McCormack, 'by securing allies that may be sacrificed when necessary to gain some advantage or provide intermediate targets (and so make war "winnable") without inviting an all-out attack on its own territory.'[36] What remains exciting about New Zealand is that the subtlety of this argument is understood by a broad band of the population, and that endless debate about the efficacy of nuclear deterrence was long ago replaced by national and rational self-interest.

In Washington New Zealand's anti-nuclear stand used to

371

be known as the 'New Zealand disease'. Sceptics who regarded the New Zealand precedent as hopelessly idealistic and of little consequence now might note that much of the world has since caught this 'disease'. President Bush's announcement in 1991 that US ships will no longer carry nuclear arms in vindication of the campaigning of New Zealand's peace and environmental groups, and the stand of the government of David Lange. Neither has the commitment faded; and the apparent eagerness of the present New Zealand government to amend the anti-nuclear legislation may turn out to be its undoing.

Worrying symptoms of the New Zealand disease have long appeared in Australia; and today the energy, optimism and idealism of so many Australians – qualities which excite outsiders – ought not to be politically disaffected. The description 'lucky country' ought not to be ironic. Among young Australians there is little of the sterile, one-dimensional conservatism that marks so many of the dullards in power, who are products of the Menzies years of the Great Australian Silence. Instead, I detect a hunger for movements of change that accurately reflect the social, racial and sexual complexion of an extraordinary society. One has only to look to the overwhelming support among the young for Aboriginal land rights and for a whole range of politically independent groups.

For many of these Australians it is an entirely feasible proposition that, united with New Zealand and the other Pacific nations, Australia would add a compelling voice of sanity in its vast region, one that no intruding power could ignore. This would then become the 'Australasian disease' and in all likelihood lead to the creation of other nuclear-free zones, in which all nuclear weapons testing – still the scourge of the Pacific, its people and environment – would be banned. Perhaps these developments could be the beginning of a morally-based way of dealing with international problems that would not only continue the dismantling of the enmities of the old Cold War, but provide the next stage of mobilising people against the refurbished imperialism of the so-called 'new world order'. This is not a fanciful 'dream'. The process has been started by the entirely pragmatic initiatives of Mikhail Gorbachev. Now it could be the turn of 'small big' countries, like Australia. A truism is that people are never still, and only political will is required. At the very least we Australians would begin to break free from our imperial past; and for us, like everyone, breaking free is the only future.

NOTES

Chapter One
ON THE BEACH

1 Cited in Meg Stewart, *Bondi* (James Fraser, Sydney, 1984), p. 39.
2 *Sun* (October 11, 1958), cited in ibid.
3 'Beachstuck on Bondi', ibid., p. 28.
4 Ian Moffit, *Sydney Morning Herald* (July 7, 1972).
5 Stewart, *Bondi*, p. 14.
6 Ibid., p. 32.
7 Ibid., p. 82.

Chapter Two
A WHISPERING IN OUR HEARTS

1 Russel Ward, *Man Makes History: World History from the Earliest Times to the Renaissance – for Boys and Girls in the First Year of Secondary School Courses* (Shakespeare Head Press, Sydney, 1952), p. 9, cited by Bill Cope in research notes, 1987.
2 *The Australian School Atlas* (Oxford University Press, Melbourne, 1939), pp. vii, 51–62, cited by Cope.
3 Cited by Andrée Wright in *Australian Racism: One People, One Prejudice*, research for *Island of Dreams*, Channel 7, Sydney, 1981.
4 *Triumph in the Tropics*, p. 179, cited in Ross Fitzgerald, *A History of Queensland from 1915 to the 1980s* (University of Queensland Press, 1984), p. 552.

5   Cited in Jan Roberts, *Massacres to Mining – the Colonisation of Aboriginal Australia* (Dove Communications, Melbourne, 1981), p. 68.

6   See Peter Conrad, 'A Treasure-house of Godzone Lingo', *Observer* (March 19, 1989).

7   For part of this information I am indebted to Dr Rhys Jones (*Sydney Morning Herald*, July 30 and August 1, 1988) and the Information Department of the National Parks and Wildlife Service. The fragment of a human skull, believed to be 60,000 years old, was found in Lake Eyre in May 1988 (*Sydney Morning Herald*, November 10, 1988).

8   This 'silence' was broken in large part by the publication in 1969 of D. J. Mulvaney's landmark work, *The Prehistory of Australia* (Thames & Hudson, London, 1969).

9   D. Gillespie, *The Rock Art Sites of Kakadu National Park – Some Preliminary Research Findings for their Conservation and Management*, Australian National Parks and Wildlife Service Special Publications 10 (1983), pp. 3–5.

10 Henry Reynolds, *The Other Side of the Frontier* (James Cook University of North Queensland, 1981), p. 163.

11 *Sydney Morning Herald* (July 23, 1988).

12 Keith D. Suter and Kaye Stearman, *Aboriginal Australians*, Minority Rights Group, Report no. 35 (London, July 1988), p. 5.

13 Keith Willy, *When the Sky Fell Down: the Destruction of the Tribes of the Sydney Region, 1788–1850s* (Collins, Sydney, 1979), cited in Roberts, *Massacres to Mining*, p. 14. I am indebted to Jan Roberts for her research and insights.

14 Ibid.

15 Ibid.

16 Cited in ibid., p. 16.

17 Fergus Robinson and Barry York, *The Black Resistance* (Widescope, Camberwell [Victoria], 1977), cited in ibid.

18 *Sydney Monitor* (December 24, 1838).

19 *Exploitation and Extermination: Race Relations in Colonial Queensland* (ANZ Books, Sydney, 1935), p. 49, cited in Roberts, *Massacres to Mining*, p. 21.

20 Raymond Evans, '"The Owl and the Eagle": the Significance of Race in Colonial Queensland', *Social Alternatives*, vol. 5, no. 4 (1986).

21 Ibid.

22 *Sydney Morning Herald* (January 3, 1987).
23 *A Demographic Survey of the Aboriginal Population of the Northern Territory*, Occasional Paper No. 1 (Australian Institute of Aboriginal Studies, Canberra, 1963).
24 For information about Namatjira's life, I am indebted to the authors of *Albert Namatjira, the Life and Work of an Australian Painter*, ed. Nadine Amadio (Macmillan, Australia, 1986).
25 *Tribune* (December 4, 1985); *Land and Justice: Aborigines Today*, a report on Australian Aborigines by the Anti-Slavery Society (London, June 1987), p. 2; Henry Reynolds, article in *Times on Sunday* (January 16, 1988).
26 Frank Hardy, *The Unlucky Australians* (Nelarn, Melbourne, 1968).
27 This summary of the Woodward report is from *Land and Justice: Aborigines Today*, pp. 17, 18.
28 *Sydney Morning Herald* (May 10, 1986).
29 This summary of the Land Rights Act is from *Land and Justice: Aborigines Today*, pp. 18, 19.
30 *Courier-Mail* Brisbane (April 19, 1983).
31 *Guardian* (February 24, 1982).
32 See *Land and Justice: Aborigines Today*, p. 34.
33 *Sydney Morning Herald* (March 30, 1985).
34 *Australian Society* (May 1986).
35 Ibid.
36 *National Times* (March 29–April 4, 1985).
37 *National Times*, letter from Sylvia Lawson and others (April 4, 1986).
38 *Australian Society* (May 1986).
39 Ibid.
40 Cited in Harry Gordon, *An Eyewitness History of Australia* (John Currey, O'Neil, Melbourne, 1976), p. 43.
41 Ibid., p. 44.
42 *Bingara Advocate* (January 20, 1965).
43 *Land and Justice: Aborigines Today*, p. 11.
44 N. S. Kirkman, *The Palmer River Gold Fields, 1873–1883*, B.A. Hons thesis (James Cook University of North Queensland, 1981).
45 Estimate by Justice James Muirhead, Royal Commission into Aboriginal deaths in custody: 'Down Under and Dying', *World in Action*, Granada Television, Britain, December 12, 1988.

46 Estimate by Dr Edgar Freed, former psychiatrist-in-charge at Bargwanath Hospital in Soweto, South Africa; *Sydney Morning Herald* (August 31, 1987). See also 'Down Under and Dying', *World in Action*.

47 *Land and Justice: Aborigines Today*, pp. 51, 53.

48 Ibid., p. 53.

49 David Wilson, 'Australia's Death Cells', *Good Weekend*, supplement to *Sydney Morning Herald* and Melbourne *Age* (November 19, 1988).

50 *Land and Justice: Aborigines Today*, p. 63.

51 Interviewed by the author, Sydney, June 1987.

52 *Sydney Morning Herald* (March 10, 1988).

53 Summarised in a letter from Attorney-General Terry Sheahan, May 26, 1986.

54 Interviewed by the author, Sydney, June 1987.

55 Interviewed by Tony Hewett, *Sydney Morning Herald* (November 7, 1987).

56 Interviewed by the author. See also *Sydney Morning Herald* (August 12, 1988).

57 Reporting by Tony Hewett and Michael Cordell, *Sydney Morning Herald* (August 10 and 17, 1987).

58 *Sydney Morning Herald* (May 10, 1991).

59 *Daily Telegraph Mirror* (May 10, 1991).

60 *Sydney Morning Herald* (May 8, 1991).

61 *Australia News* (May 31, 1991), Australia House, London.

62 *Sydney Morning Herald* (October 18, 1991).

63 *Sydney Morning Herald* (May 8, 1991).

64 *Sydney Morning Herald* (November 19, 1988).

65 Suter and Stearman, *Aboriginal Australians*, p. 4. I am indebted to the authors of *Aboriginal Australians* for their analysis of Aboriginal differences.

66 *Sydney Morning Herald* (May 19, 1985).

67 Interviewed by the author, Alice Springs, June 1987.

68 Interviewed by the author, Worowa, February 1987.

69 Cited in the documentary film *Lousy Little Sixpence*, directed by Alec Morgan.

70 Cited in a discussion guide for *Lousy Little Sixpence*, by Chikka Dixon.

71 *Sydney Morning Herald* (November 3, 1988).

72 Interviewed by the author, October 1986, and correspondence November 1988.

73 Kevin Gilbert, *Because a White Man'll Never Do It* (Angus & Robertson, Sydney, 1973).

74 *Sydney Morning Herald* (December 21, 1988).

75 Cited in *Times on Sunday* (October 18, 1987).

76 *Sydney Morning Herald* (April 23, 1986).

77 I am indebted to Lyndall Crisp for her reporting and analysis of Imparja's prospects; *Times on Sunday* (October 18, 1987).

78 Leo Schofield, *Sydney Morning Herald* (January 27, 1988).

79 *Times on Sunday* (January 24, 1988). I am indebted to Sarah Walls for her fine article on 'freedom rides' to Sydney.

80 Ibid.

81 Cinesound/Movietone archives, Australia.

82 Cited by Martin Thomas in the *Age*, monthly review (December/January 1987/1988).

83 Ibid.

84 *Sydney Morning Herald* (January 27, 1988).

85 *Land and Justice: Aborigines Today*, pp. 90, 91.

86 *Sydney Morning Herald* (August 5, 1988).

87 See Michael Barnard, *Northern Territory News* (February 13, 1988); Hamish McDonald, *Far Eastern Economic Review* (March 10, 1988).

88 *Sydney Morning Herald* (February 25, 1987).

89 *Illawarra Mercury* (October 31, 1987).

90 *Sydney Morning Herald* (February 27, 1988).

91 Ibid. (March 3 and 9, 1988).

92 Interviewed by the author, Alice Springs, June 1987.

93 *Sydney Morning Herald* (June 10, 1987).

94 *Independent* (December 21, 1991).

Chapter Three
HEROES UNSUNG

1 David Day, *The Great Betrayal: Britain, Australia and the Onset of the Pacific War* (Angus & Robertson, Sydney, 1988).

2 Jeremy Bentham, *Panoptican Versus New South Wales*, p. 7, cited in Robert Hughes, *The Fatal Shore* (Collins Granville, London, 1987), p. 2.

3 Edmund Burke, cited by Hughes, *The Fatal Shore*, p. 19.

4 I am indebted to my cousin, Ken Marheine, the 'family

source'. Ken's scholarly research into our antecedents allowed me to correct and add to the 1992 edition.

5   Hughes, *The Fatal Shore*, pp. 252, 253.

6   Ibid., p. 354.

7   Cited in Graham A. Edwards, *Factory to Asylum*, privately published, p. 23.

8   Cited by Michael Cannon, *Who's Master? Who's Man? Australia in the Victorian Age* (Nelson, Melbourne, 1971), p. 56, originally published in *Reminiscences of Thirty Years of Residence* (London, 1863).

9   Cited by Cannon, *Who's Master? Who's Man?*, p. 56.

10 Cited in John Pilger, *Heroes* (Jonathan Cape, London, 1986), p. 9.

11 Cited in *Sydney Morning Herald* (July 6, 1988).

12 A. A. Calwell, *Be Just and Fear Not* (Lloyd O'Neill, Hawthorn, Australia, 1972), pp. 109, 126.

13 *Australian Society* (July 1987). I am indebted to Ken Inglis's research for *People of Australia* (Penguin, Sydney, 1987).

14 Ibid.

15 Ibid. I am indebted to Andrew Markus's research for his article in *Labour History* (November 1984).

16 Ibid.

17 Ibid.

18 See Jock Collins, *Migrant Hands in a Distant Land* (Pluto Press, Sydney and London, 1988), pp. 53–9, 140.

19 Ibid., p. 229.

20 Ibid., p. 207.

21 Morag Loh (ed.), *With Courage in their Cases: the Experiences of Thirty-five Italian Immigrant Workers and Their Families in Australia* (FILEF, Australia, 1980), pp. 47–50.

22 *Sydney Morning Herald* (April 10, 1987).

23 Ibid. (September 11, 1987).

24 Evidence of Rukiye Savigil, a Turkish woman.

25 *Sydney Morning Herald* (April 4, 1987).

26 *Yass Courier* (March 3, 1881). I am indebted to Andrée Wright's research for *Island of Dreams*, Channel 7, Sydney, 1981.

27 Research by Andrée Wright.

28 *Bulletin* (November 1898).

29 Research by Andrée Wright.

30 Collins, *Migrant Hands*, p. 60.

31   Cited in Nancy Viviani, 'Australian Government Policy on the Entry of Vietnamese Refugees in 1975', CSAAR Research Paper No. 1 (Centre for the Study of Australian and Asian Relations, Griffith University, February 1980), p. 11.

32   *Far Eastern Economic Review* (May 10, 1984).

33   Geoffrey Blainey, *All for Australia*, cited by Collins, *Migrant Hands*, pp. 212–22.

34   Collins, *Migrant Hands*, p. 220.

35   *DIEA Migrants Attitudes Survey* (Dept of Immigration and Ethnic Affairs, Canberra, 1986).

36   Research School of Social Sciences, Australian National University, cited in *Sydney Morning Herald* (January 1, 1989).

37   This poem (edited) 'Leaving Homeland' was published in *In a Strange Land I Live*, a 1982 collection by Ken Cruickshank for the Materials Production Project, Sydney.

38   Interviewed by the author in 1980. He wishes to remain anonymous.

39   *Sydney Morning Herald* (April 19, 1991).

40   *Sydney Morning Herald* (March 10, 1988).

41   Ibid. (February 4, 1988).

42   Ibid. (March 3, 1988).

43   Ibid. (July 20, 1988).

44   Ibid. (January 1, 1989).

45   See *New Statesman* (August 26, 1988); also *Sydney Morning Herald* (August 6, 18 and 20, 1988).

46   *Time* (February 13, 1989).

47   *Sydney Morning Herald* (August 8, 1988; December 12, 1988).

48   *Sydney Morning Herald* (January 18, 1992).

49   *Far Eastern Economic Review* (May 10, 1984).

50   *Sydney Morning Herald* (August 3, 1987).

51   Ibid. (July 20, 1988).

52   *Times on Sunday* (March 8, 1987).

Chapter Four

THE STRUGGLE FOR INDEPENDENCE

1   Manning Clark, *The Quest for an Australian Identity*, James Duhig Memorial Lecture delivered at the University of

Queensland in 1979 (published by University of Queensland Press, St Lucia, 1980), p. 18.

2 I am indebted to Donald Horne for this and other quotations. See Donald Horne, *The Story of the Australian People*, (Reader's Digest, Sydney, 1985).

3 Geoff Page, 'Inscription at Villers-Bretonneux', in *Shadows from Wire: Poems and Photographs of Australia in the Great War*, ed. Geoff Page (Penguin, Sydney, 1983), p. 94.

4 Horne, *The Story of the Australian People*, p. 199.

5 Ibid., p. 200.

6 Ibid., p. 207.

7 My grandfather wrote his seafaring autobiography, *With Folly on My Lips*, unpublished.

8 John 'Togs' Tognolini, 'Red Anzacs', *Newswit* (May 25, 1988).

9 Interviewed by the author, June 1987.

10 A. G. L. Shaw, *A Story of Australia* (Faber, London, 1955), p. 243.

11 See Miriam Dickson, 'Stubborn Resistance', *Strikes: Studies in Twentieth-Century Social History* (Angus & Robertson, Sydney, 1973). See also Robin Gollan, *The Coalminers of New South Wales, A History of the Union, 1860–1960* (Melbourne University Press, in association with the Australian National University, 1963).

12 Cinesound newsreel cited in *The Last Dream*, Central Television, January 1988.

13 *Sydney Morning Herald* (January 27, 1988).

14 *Daily Telegraph* (Sydney, December 12, 1938).

15 *Hansard* (Australia, April 22, 1940).

16 *Sydney Morning Herald* (October 11, 1986).

17 Ibid. (January 27, 1988).

18 Humphrey McQueen, 'The Sustenance of Silence: Racism in the 20th Century', *Meanjin Quarterly* (June, 1971).

19 David Day, *The Great Betrayal: Britain, Australia and the Onset of the Pacific War* (Angus & Robertson, Sydney, 1988), p. 287.

20 *Sydney Morning Herald* (June 18, 1988).

21 McQueen, 'The Sustenance of Silence'.

22 Denis Freney, *The CIA's Australian Connection* (published by Freney, Sydney, 1977), p. 35.

23 I am indebted to Bruce McFarlane's insights in *Australia's*

First Cold War, 1945–53 (Allen & Unwin, Sydney, 1984), pp. 23, 37.

24 *The Australian* (February 19, 1972).

25 Ibid.

26 Ibid.

27 Dennis H. Phillips, *Cold War Two and Australia* (Allen & Unwin, Sydney, 1983), p. 30.

28 McFarlane, *Australia's First Cold War*, p. 27; *Sydney Morning Herald* (November 25, 1949).

29 Interviewed by the author, Sydney, January 1988.

30 *Argus* (Melbourne, March 24, 1950).

31 Gavan McCormack, 'The Korean War: Comments on "Review Article"' (1986).

32 Ibid.

33 Phillips, *Cold War Two and Australia*, p. 28.

34 Ibid., pp. 28–9.

35 Interviewed by the author, Sydney, October 1986.

36 Phillips, *Cold War Two and Australia*, p. 43.

37 Ibid., p. 44.

38 I am indebted to Allan Fox for his description of central Australian fauna in the brochure 'Welcome to Aboriginal Land', produced with the Department of Aboriginal Affairs, Canberra.

39 Interviewed by the author, Sydney, January 1988.

40 Joan Smith, *Clouds of Deceit* (Faber & Faber, London, 1985), p. 33.

41 Robert Milliken, *No Conceivable Injury* (Penguin, Sydney and London, 1986), pp. 104–5.

42 I am indebted to the author of the *Uluru* tourist brochure for this outline of *Tjukurpa*.

43 Adrian Tame, 'Maralinga: Britain's Atomic Legacy', *Penthouse* (November, 1980).

44 Jan Roberts, *Massacres to Mining: the Colonisation of Aboriginal Australia* (Dove Communications, Melbourne, 1981), p. 47.

45 Milliken, *No Conceivable Injury*, p. 116.

46 *Sydney Morning Herald* (May 22, 1991).

47 Ibid.

48 Melbourne *Age* (April 11, 1987).

49 *Sydney Morning Herald* (April 28, 1987).

50 Dwight D. Eisenhower, *The White House Years: Mandate for*

Change 1953–1956 (Doubleday, New York, 1963), p. 372.

51 Michael Sexton, *War for the Asking: Australia's Vietnam Secrets* (Penguin, Sydney, 1981), p. 41.

52 *Sydney Morning Herald* (January 18, 1986).

53 Noam Chomsky, 'The Vietnam War in the Age of Orwell', *Race and Class* (Spring 1984), p. 46.

54 Ian McNeill, *The Team: Australian Army Advisers in Vietnam*, Australian War Memorial (Canberra, 1984).

55 *Time Australia* (August 10, 1987).

56 Ibid.

57 *National Times* (April 20–6, 1984). See also *Time Australia* (August 10, 1987).

58 *Allies*, documentary film directed by Marian Wilkinson, produced by Sylvie Chezio, Cinema Enterprises Property Ltd, Australia, 1981.

59 Interviewed by the author, January 1988.

60 *Time Australia* (August 10, 1987).

61 Ibid.

62 Greg Pemberton, *All the Way* (Allen & Unwin, Sydney, 1987), pp. 197, 198.

63 Greg Lockhart, 'Fear and Dependence, Australia's Vietnam Policy, 1965–1985', a paper (1987).

64 Neville Meaney, *Australia and the World: A Documentary History from the 1870s to the 1970s* (Longman, Melbourne, 1985), p. 679.

65 Don Chipp and John Larkin, *Don Chipp: the Third Man* (Rigby, Adelaide, 1978), p. 50.

66 *Sydney Morning Herald* (May 7, 1987).

67 Sexton, *War for the Asking*, p. 94.

68 *Allies*.

69 Alan Renouf, *The Frightened Country* (Macmillan, Melbourne, 1979), p. 279.

70 *Allies*; also quoted to the author by former US Ambassador Marshall Green, August 1987.

Chapter Five
THE *COUP*

1 Joan Coxsedge, Gerry Harant and Ken Coldicutt, *Rooted in Secrecy* (CAPP, Melbourne, 1982), p. 6.

2 Ibid., p. 8.

3 Cited in James A. Nathan, 'Dateline Australia: America's Foreign Watergate', *Foreign Policy*, no. 49 (Washington, Winter 1982–3).

4 Cited in Coxsedge et al., *Rooted in Secrecy*, p. 22.

5 Cited by William Pinwill in *The Last Dream*, Central Television, January 1988.

6 Acting Justice White, *Special Branch Security Records Report* (Government Printer, Adelaide, 1977).

7 *The Bulletin* (June 22, 1974).

8 My own experience of ASIO was instructive. In 1982 I was in contact with a person who had access to files at the Australian High Commission in London. This person said he wanted to warn me that an ASIO officer, who he named, had recently travelled to London to 'do a job on Pilger'. He said that the ASIO officer was based at the Australian Embassy in Rome, ostensibly as an immigration officer. (It is common practice for ASIO to use the Australian Department of Immigration as a cover for its officers abroad.)

My informant said that the ASIO officer had deposited in my file a document in Arabic allegedly published in Libya, which described my support for Aboriginal 'freedom fighters' and implied that I had visited Libya to help these 'freedom fighters' buy arms in preparation for their 'struggle' against the Queensland authorities during the forthcoming Commonwealth Games in Brisbane. My collaborator in this venture, according to the document, was Charles Perkins, a former Aboriginal activist, then an officer of the Department of Aboriginal Affairs in Canberra. According to my informant, the document was illustrated by a photograph of Perkins and me 'taken in Libya'. (The photograph was taken near Alice Springs in 1976. Perkins has never been to Libya. I was there once, in 1973, on my way to the Middle East war.)

My informant gave me a number in Rome, which I rang. I asked for the ASIO officer, who came to the phone and was clearly in a state of some apprehension. I told him something of what I knew. He was hesitant, but expressed no surprise and offered no denial. He replied that I should 'forget the whole thing'. 'Are you ASIO?' I asked him. 'And have you been concerned with me?' He replied, 'I can't tell you anything. You have nothing to be worried about. Whatever you know isn't going to happen. I give you my word, Mr Pilger.

I'm sorry you're upset. Can't we just forget it?'

The ASIO officer called me back twice to reinforce these assurances. Some time later I was phoned by a person who said he had worked for the ASIO officer in Italy and Libya. He knew about the document. He said he no longer worked for the ASIO officer, who had treated him badly. He said the ASIO officer was 'furious about the tip-off' I had received because it had 'blown his cover'.

9   *National Times* (May 6, 1983).
10 Cited in Nathan, 'Dateline Australia'.
11 *Correspondents Report*, ABC radio, June 12, 1977.
12 Ibid.
13 *National Times* (December 2–8, 1983; originally published August 1983).
14 Desmond Ball, *A Suitable Piece of Real Estate* (Hale & Iremonger, Sydney, 1980), p. 153.
15 *National Times* (May 23–8, 1977).
16 From the forthcoming memoirs of an Australian diplomat (anonymous) cited by William Pinwill, *The Eye*, March quarter, 1990.
17 Department of Foreign Affairs Minute, cited in *The Eye* (July 1987).
18 I am indebted to Adèle Horin for this description in the *National Times* (May 24, 1985).
19 *Tribune* (Australia, August 24, 1988).
20 *Broadband*, ABC radio interview by Ray Martin, June 12, 1977.
21 See Ball, *A Suitable Piece of Real Estate*, p. 138; Melbourne *Age* (November 22, 1984).
22 Interviewed by the author, Washington, October 1988.
23 Interviewed by the author, Washington, August 1987.
24 *National Times* (December 30, 1978).
25 *Sydney Morning Herald* (May 16, 1977).
26 *Hansard* (Australia, April 29, 1969).
27 Ibid.
28 Greg Lockhart, 'Fear and Dependence: Australia's Vietnam Policy, 1965–1985', a paper (1987), p. 13.
29 Nathan, 'Dateline Australia'.
30 Interviewed by the author, Washington, October 1988.
31 *Canberra Times* (May 11, 1977). I am indebted to Desmond Ball for this and other references.

32 Ball, *A Suitable Piece of Real Estate*, p. 50.

33 *Daily Mirror* (Sydney, May 1, 1963).

34 Cited in *The Last Dream*.

35 *Hansard* (Australia, February 28, 1973).

36 *The Age* (March 29, 1973).

37 Denis Freney, *The CIA's Australian Connection* (Freney, Sydney, 1977), p. 31.

38 John Pilger, *Heroes* (Jonathan Cape, London, 1986), p. 377.

39 Gil Scrine, *Home on the Range*, a documentary film for the Association for International Co-operation and Disarmament, 1981.

40 Freney, *The CIA's Australian Connection*, p. 17.

41 Coxsedge et al., *Rooted in Secrecy*, p. 24.

42 Interviewed by the author, Washington, August 1987.

43 Cited in an ABC transcript of Kep Enderby's remarks, US Consulate, Sydney, February 1988.

44 *Bulletin* (June 22, 1974).

45 Ibid. (July 13, 1974).

46 See Philip Frazer, *Mother Jones* (March 1984).

47 *National Times* (August 30–September 9, 1981).

48 Denis Freney, *Get Gough! & Dr Jim & Rex & Lionel & All*, (Freney, Sydney, 1985), p. 13. (Jim Cairns supported this in parliamentary statements at the time.)

49 *Daily Mirror* (Sydney, July 8, 1975).

50 *Wall Street Journal* (February 17, 1981).

51 Brian Toohey and Marian Wilkinson, *The Book of Leaks* (Angus & Robertson, Sydney, 1987), p. 107.

52 *Bulletin* (June 5, 1976).

53 *National Times* (August 16–22, 1981).

54 *Sunday Times* (London, September 7, 1980); *National Times* (January 4–10, 1981).

55 Coxsedge et al., *Rooted in Secrecy*, p. 197.

56 Melbourne *Age* (February 16, 1981).

57 Nathan, 'Dateline Australia'.

58 The Schuller story first was reported by Nancy Grodin in *Covert Action* (March 1982); the Marchetti story appeared in the *Sun* (Sydney, May 4, 1977).

59 Brian Toohey and Nancy Grodin made the Freedom of Information requests, cited in *Covert Action*.

60 Nathan, 'Dateline Australia'.

61 Toohey and Wilkinson, *The Book of Leaks*, p. 216.

62 Nathan, 'Dateline Australia'.
63 Freney, *The CIA's Australian Connection*, pp. 22, 23; also William Pinwill, *Secret Partners* (unpublished).
64 Court records, cited by Pinwill in *Secret Partners*.
65 Assessment by Pinwill in ibid.
66 Interview by Ray Martin, *60 Minutes*, Channel 9, Sydney, 1982.
67 Interviewed by William Pinwill, *National Times* (1978).
68 Jonathan Kwitny, *The Crimes of Patriots* (Norton, New York, 1987), p. 140.
69 Ibid., pp. 140–1.
70 Ibid., p. 141.
71 Richard Hall, *The Real John Kerr: His Brilliant Career* (Angus & Robertson, Sydney, 1978), p. 116.
72 Ibid., pp. 119, 120.
73 Ibid., p. 140.
74 Interviewed by the author, Washington, August 1987.
75 I am indebted to Joseph Trento and William Pinwill for much of this research.
76 *National Times* (December 13, 1985).
77 Jeffrey T. Richelson and Desmond Ball, *The Ties that Bind* (Allen & Unwin, Sydney, 1985), pp. 153, 154, 161.
78 Ibid., p. 154.
79 Interview with David Leigh by Bruce Phillips, *The World Today*, ABC Radio, October 19, 1988.
80 Diaries of Clyde Cameron, cited in *Times on Sunday* (February 21, 1988).
81 Freney, *Get Gough!*, p. 59.
82 This was told to the author by a former Government official, who must remain anonymous.
83 Toohey and Wilkinson, *The Book of Leaks*, p. 97.
84 Pinwill, *Secret Partners*.
85 *Weekend Australian* (January 30–1, 1988).
86 *Times of Sunday* cites reporting by Mungo McCallum (February 21, 1988).
87 *Hansard* (Australia, May 3, 1977).
88 Melbourne *Age* (November 12, 1975).
89 Interviewed by Ray Martin for ABC Radio, May 13, 1977.
90 Freney, *The CIA's Australian Connection*, p. 49.
91 Interviewed by David Langsam, *Sydney Morning Herald* (February 9, 1988).

92 Cameron, diaries; see also Coxsedge et al., *Rooted in Secrecy*, p. 38.
93 *Sydney Morning Herald* (November 12, 1975).
94 Coxsedge et al., *Rooted in Secrecy*, p. 38.
95 *Daily Mirror* (Sydney), cited in Freney, *Get Gough!*, p. 33.
96 Ibid.
97 *Nucleonics Week* (November 6, 1987).
98 Hall, *The Real John Kerr*, p. 144.
99 Cameron, diaries.
100 Ibid., also Cameron interviewed by the author, February 1988.
101 *Hansard* (Australia, May 4, 1977).
102 *A Current Affair*, Channel 9, Sydney, May 4, 1977.
103 Gough Whitlam, *The Whitlam Government 1972–75* (Viking, London, and Penguin, Sydney, 1985), p. 52.
104 Freney, *Get Gough!*, p. 2.
105 *Advertiser* (Adelaide, January 30, 1988).
106 *PM*, ABC Radio, October 16, 1981; Melbourne *Age* (October 17, 1981); Melbourne *Age*, letters (February 16, 1988).
107 Letter to the author from Bill Hayden, June 21, 1988.
108 Letter to Bill Hayden from the author, July 26, 1988.
109 *Australian* (January 18, 1988; January 29, 1988).
110 *Weekend Australian* (January 30–1, 1988).
111 Kwitny, *The Crimes of Patriots*, p. 140.
112 *Times on Sunday* (February 21, 1988).
113 *Australian* (February 26, 1988).
114 *Sydney Morning Herald* (February 23, 1988).
115 Interviewed by the author, Washington, August 1987.
116 *Sydney Morning Herald* (January 26, 1988); *Times on Sunday* (February 21, 1988).
117 Edwin P. Bayley, *Joe McCarthy and the Press* (University of Wisconsin Press, 1981).
118 *Times on Sunday* (February 21, 1988).
119 *Sydney Morning Herald* (May 5, 1977).
120 Interviewed by Brian White, Radio 2UE Sydney, February 22, 1988.
121 Ibid.
122 *AAP News Report* (February 23, 1988).
123 Milan Kundera, *The Book of Laughter and Forgetting* (Penguin, London, 1983), p. 5.

Chapter Six
MATES

1   *The Eye* (Sydney, October 1987).
2   Interview with Marshall Green by the author, August 1987.
3   *Allies*, a documentary film directed by Marian Wilkinson and produced by Cinema Enterprises Property Ltd, Sydney, 1981.
4   Bissell was addressing the US Council for Foreign Relations in 1968: cited in Denis Freney, *The CIA's Australian Connection* (Freney, Sydney, 1977), pp. 52–3.
5   In a letter to the author, Clyde Cameron, Minister of Labor in the Whitlam Government, described Leader Grants as 'a CIA operation' (March 10, 1988).
6   Letter to the author from Clyde Cameron, June 17, 1988. (Robert Walkinshaw, US labour attaché from 1962 to 1964, admitted to Cameron that he had funded the AWU.)
7   New York *Daily Mirror*, cited in Freney, *The CIA's Australian Connection*, p. 53.
8   *Courier Mail* (Brisbane, May 13, 1954).
9   Bissell, cited in Freney, *The CIA's Australian Connection*, p. 49.
10 Cited in Freney, *The CIA's Australian Connection*, p. 54. See also *Sydney Morning Herald* (May 13, 1954).
11 Letter from Clyde Cameron to the author, March 10, 1988. For Arthur Goldberg's CIA connections see also *Counterspy*, vol. 2, no. 1 (Fall 1974).
12 Bissell, cited in Freney, *The CIA's Australian Connection*, pp. 53, 54.
13 Ibid., p. 67.
14 *Hansard* (Australia, May 4, 1977), p. 1525.
15 Letter from Clyde Cameron to the author, March 10, 1988.
16 ABC interview with Harry Goldberg, cited in Freney, *The CIA's Australian Connection*, p. 18.
17 *National Times* (April 20–6, 1984).
18 *Allies*.
19 Cited in Freney, *The CIA's Australian Connection*, p. 61.
20 *Allies*.
21 *National Review* (May 5–11, 1977).
22 Letter to the author, March 10, 1988.
23 *Hansard* (Australia, May 4, 1977).
24 Interview with Ray Martin for *Sixty Minutes*, Channel 9, Sydney.

25 The Business International/CIA link was exposed as part of three articles on CIA penetration of the American media by Carl Bernstein, of Watergate fame. *New York Times* (December 25, 26 and 27, 1977).

26 Carroll's speech, cited in Joan Coxsedge's Evatt Memorial speech, *What Price Socialism?* delivered at the University of Adelaide, July 21, 1982.

27 Brian Toohey and Marian Wilkinson, *The Book of Leaks* (Angus & Robertson, Sydney, 1987), pp. 102–3.

28 Blanche d'Alpuget, *Robert J. Hawke* (Swartz/Penguin, Sydney, 1982), p. 183.

29 *National Times* (September 20, 1987).

30 Evan Whitton, *Can of Worms* (Fairfax Library, Sydney, 1986), p. 18.

31 Cited in ibid., pp. 18–19.

32 D'Alpuget, *Robert J. Hawke*, pp. 236–7.

33 *National Times* (September 9, 1987).

34 Fratianno stated this under oath in his testimony to the US District Court, Southern District of New York, case of US *vs* Mangano and Gavarenti of July 1982. He stated Tham had introduced him to five or six Australians, including Abeles, Bela Csidei and Ross Cribb. In the same case Ross Cribb, the TNT general manager, said, 'We met Mangano and Gavarenti in early 1975 . . . Abeles was present at the meeting.'

35 Waterfront Corruption Hearings before Permanent Senate Sub-Committee on Investigations, February 1981. Testimony of Ralph Picardo, Mafia informant: 'The Teamsters were receiving payoffs from Seatrain' (p. 275 of hearings). Testimony of Michael Devorkan, former US Attorney, New York: 'Picardo was partly responsible for receiving labor payments in the past from Seatrain for the Teamsters' (p. 307).

36 *National Times* (December 12, 1982).

37 Ibid. (September 20, 1985).

38 Ibid.

39 Whitton, *Can of Worms*, p. 14.

40 Howard Jacobson, *In the Land of Oz* (Hamish Hamilton, London, 1987).

41 George Munster, *A Paper Prince* (Viking Penguin, Sydney, 1985), p. 2.

42 Robert Pullan, *Guilty Secrets: Free Speech in Australia* (Methuen, Australia, 1984), pp. 38–9.

43 See Harry Gordon, *An Eye Witness History of Australia* (John Currey, O'Neil Publishers, Melbourne, 1986), pp. 42–4.

44 Pullan, *Guilty Secrets*, p. 63.

45 Ibid.

46 Ibid., p. 62.

47 Munster, *A Paper Prince*, p. 252.

48 *Clarion* (December 1986).

49 Thomas Kiernan, *Citizen Murdoch* (Dodd, Mead, New York, 1986), p. 311.

50 *Sun* editorial (January 20, 1988). David Langsam successfully reported the *Sun* to the Press Council. See the *Independent* (July 20, 1988).

51 *Guardian* (February 6, 1989).

52 Both Kemp and Reagan quotations appeared in the *Clarion* (December 1986).

53 Kiernan, *Citizen Murdoch*, p. 285.

54 Ibid., p. 320.

55 *New Society* (March 1985).

56 Kiernan, *Citizen Murdoch*, p. 287.

57 The report was *Kampuchea: A Demographic Catastrophe*, National Foreign Assessment Center, Central Intelligence Agency, May 1980.

58 *Australian* (March 12, February 28, March 6, 1985).

59 Ibid. (February 2, 1985). This analysis of the *Australian* is by David Bowman.

60 Statex – *Sydney Morning Herald* study (October 31, 1987).

61 *Sun-Herald* (September 15, 1991).

62 'Greed Inc. Australia's missing millions', *Sydney Morning Herald* (July 28, 1990).

63 *Sun-Herald* (December 15, 1991)

64 Quoted by James McClelland in the *Sydney Morning Herald* (September 10, 1987).

65 *Sydney Morning Herald* (April 23, 1988).

66 Allan Ashbolt, 'In Praise of Heresy: the Role for Political Economy', *Arena*, 78 (1987).

67 See Brian Toohey, 'Life Styles of the Rich and Famous', *Listener* (New Zealand, November 14, 1987).

68 *Sydney Morning Herald* (March 24, 1989; June 15, 1989; July 8, 1989; August 11, 1991).

69 *Four Corners*, ABC TV, August 18, 1986.

70 *Australian Society* (August 1988).

71 Analysis by Frank Walker, *Sun Herald* (February 15,1987).

72 *Sydney Morning Herald* (December 17, 1986).

73 The original account of the meeting appeared in the *Clarion* (December 1986), and has been substantiated by the author from sources within News Limited. See also Gavin Souter, *Heralds and Angels*, cited by Brian Toohey, *Sun-Herald* (February 24, 1991).

74 See David Bowman, *The Captive Press* (Penguin, Sydney, 1988), pp. 13–14.

75 *Australian Financial Review* (July 30, 1981). See also Robert Duffield, *Rogue Bull*, a biography of Lang Hangcock (Collins, Sydney, 1979), p. 173.

76 *Sydney Morning Herald* (December 17, 1986) and *Inside Media* (December 1986).

77 Gavin Souter, cited *Sun-Herald* (February 24, 1991).

78 Letter to the author from Ian Macphee, October 31, 1988. *See also* Australian *Hansard*, December 21, 1989

79 *Clarion* (December 1986).

80 See interview with Paul Kelly, *Australian* (September 20, 1986).

81 *Australian Society* (June 1987).

82 *The Eye* (Sydney, July 1987).

83 *Times on Sunday* (February 15, 1987).

84 *Business Review Weekly*, Gold Edition (August 14, 1987).

85 Melbourne *Age* (February 2, 1987).

86 *Guardian* (November 30, 1991).

87 *Sun-Herald* (September 15, 1991).

88 Quoted by Tony Stephens and Paul McGeough, *Good Weekend* (December 6, 1986).

89 *Sun-Herald* (July 7, 1991).

90 Ibid.

91 *Business Review Weekly*, Gold Edition (August 14, 1987).

92 *Sydney Morning Herald* (December 6, 1986).

93 'Bondy's Bounty', *Four Corners*, reported by Paul Barry, ABC, March 13, 1989.

94 Ibid.

95 Ibid.

96 *Sydney Morning Herald* (April 27, 1989).

97 Interviewed by the author, June 1987.

98   See the *West Australian* (June 2, 1987) and *Australian Society*
     (July 1987).
99   *Asian Wall Street Journal* (October 16, 1991).
100 *Sydney Morning Herald* (July 28, 1990).
101 Ibid.
102 Ibid.
103 *Asian Wall Street Journal* (October 16, 1991).
104 *Sydney Morning Herald* (July 28, 1990).
105 Ibid.
106 *Sydney Morning Herald* (December 26, 1987).
107 *Weekend Australian* (June 11–12, 1988).
108 *Sydney Morning Herald* (April 10, 1988).
109 *Canberra Times* (April 13, 1987).
110 ABC memorandum from Bob Kearsley to Acting Director of
     Television, March 4, 1987.
111 *Sydney Morning Herald* (December 14, 1985).
112 Ibid. (February 13, 1988).
113 *Herald*, Melbourne (January 23, 1988).
114 *Sun-Herald* (January 24, 1991).
115 *Sydney Morning Herald* (January 22, 1991).
116 *Tribune* (February 13, 1991).
117 Quoted in *Sydney Morning Herald* (March 8, 1988).
118 *Sunday*, Channel 9, Sydney, March 22, 1987.
119 *Arena 78* (1987), pp. 20–1.
120 *Sydney Morning Herald* (March 30, 1989).
121 Ibid. (March 23, 1988).
122 Ibid. (September 28, 1987).
123 Ibid. (July 7, 1988).
124 D'Alpuget, *Robert J. Hawke*, p. 117.
125 Brian Toohey gave this example in his speech to the AAP
     Edcon 1987 Conference, Broadbeach, Queensland, June
     1987. See also d'Alpuget, *Robert J. Hawke*, pp. 268–9.
126 *Australian Society* (May 1988).
127 Cited in the *Morning Star* (January 28, 1992). I am indebted
     to John Cryer for his summary of the Fairfax bids.
128 Ibid.
129 *Sydney Morning Herald* (June 5, 1991).
130 Cited in the *Morning Star* (January 28, 1992).
131 Ibid.
132 From the *Financial Post*: 'Conrad Black Guest Column', cited
     in *Hard Facts for Hard Times*, (November 1991).

133 *Sydney Morning Herald* (July 30, 1988).

134 Bowman, *The Captive Press*, pp. 226–7.

135 Ibid., p. 193.

136 Athol Moffitt, *A Quarter to Midnight* (Angus & Robertson, Sydney, 1985), p. 3.

137 *Sunday Times* (September 30, 1984).

138 Toohey and Wilkinson, *The Book of Leaks*, pp. 80, 196, 197.

139 *Sydney Morning Herald* (Series beginning July 28, 1990).

140 *Guardian* (November 4, 1991).

141 *National Times* (September 20, 1985).

142 *Observer* (February 14, 1988).

143 *Sydney Morning Herald* (May 22, 1991).

144 *Sydney Morning Herald* (April 9 & 10, 1991); *The Age* (April 12, 1991).

145 *Sydney Morning Herald* (January 11, 1992).

146 Ibid.

147 Ibid. (January 20, 1992).

148 Ibid. (September 4, 1991).

149 Ibid. (May 2, 1991).

150 Ibid. (May 7, 1991).

151 Ibid. (May 9, 1991).

152 Ibid. (April 29, 1991).

153 Ibid. (August 6, 1991).

154 *Sydney Morning Herald* (November 12, 1988).

155 Ibid. (December 6, 1988).

156 Ibid. (November 1, 1991).

157 Ibid. (December 1, 1988).

158 Ibid. (November 30, 1988).

159 Ibid. (January 21, 1992).

160 Ibid. (January 29, 1992).

161 *Morning Star* (January 30, 1992).

162 *Sydney Morning Herald* (December 28, 1991).

163 Ibid.

Chapter Seven
BATTLERS

1 *The Eye* (September 1987).

2 Dorothy Hewett, *Bobbin Up* (Virago, London, 1985), p. 63.

3 The ALP was formed in Queensland in 1891, took office in Queensland briefly in 1899 and in five other States between

1904 and 1913. The first Federal Labor Government was formed in 1904.

4   Jill Roe, *Social Policy in Australia* (Cassell, Stanmore, NSW, 1976), p. 5.

5   Ibid., p. 4.

6   Jurgen Tampke, *Pace Setter or Quiet Backwater? German Literature on Australia's Labour Movement and Social Policies, 1890–1914*, cited in *Labour History*, no. 36 (November 1978), pp. 3–17. (I am indebted to Colin Griffiths for this and other references.)

7   *Pravda*, no. 134 (June 13, 1913).

8   Deirdre Macken, 'Vanishing Middle Class', *Sydney Morning Herald* (August 8, 1987).

9   Roe, *Social Policy in Australia*, p. 5.

10 Research by IBIS, cited by Macken, 'Vanishing Middle Class'.

11 Macken, 'Vanishing Middle Class'.

12 *Direct Action* (November 29, 1988).

13 *Weekend Australian* (February 28–March 1, 1987).

14 *Sydney Morning Herald* (May 7, 1988).

15 Report of the Institute of Applied Economic and Social Research, University of Melbourne, June 1988. See also Luxembourg Income Study, cited in *Sydney Morning Herald* (May 7, 1988). On November 21, 1990 the *Sydney Morning Herald* reported: 'Current estimates of poverty indicate that . . . between 30 and 35 per cent of children are below the poverty line'.

16 1986 OECD figures researched by Carole Sklan for *The Last Dream*, Central Television, January 1988.

17 *Sydney Morning Herald* (February 28, 1989).

18 Patrick Troy, 'Is Australia a Just Society?', in 'Social Justice in Australia', supplement to *Australian Society* (December 1988/January 1989).

19 Working Paper 5, Human Services Macarthur Regional Environmental Study, prepared by Meredith Smith, consultant town planner for Dept of Environment and Planning (Sydney, 1986).

20 Western Sydney Health Task Force Report, cited in *Sydney Morning Herald* (November 14, 1988). On November 12, 1990 the *Sydney Morning Herald* reported that helath services were so bad in Liverpool, Western Suburbs, that the situation was 'akin to passive euthanasia'.

21 Working Paper 5, Macarthur.

22 Edward Stokes, *United We Stand* (Five Mile Press, Australia, 1983), pp. 10, 11. (I am indebted to Edward Stokes for his rare and forthright background to life and conditions at Broken Hill.)

23 Ibid., p. 14.

24 See Graeme Osborne, 'Town and Country', in *Strikes: Studies in Twentieth-Century Australian Social History*, ed. J. Iremonger, J. Merritt and G. Osborne (Angus & Robertson, Sydney, 1973).

25 'Narkal Notes', *Koorda and District News* (May 6, 1987).

26 Nigel Hall and Martin Backhouse, 'Performance of the Farm Sector', *Farms' Surveys Report* (Rural Production Economics Board, 1987), pp. 7, 15.

Chapter Eight
BREAKING FREE

1 Blanche d'Alpuget, *Robert J. Hawke* (Swartz/Penguin, Sydney, 1982), p. 302.

2 Emeritus Professor A. L. Burns, letter to *Sydney Morning Herald* (May 9, 1988).

3 *Sydney Morning Herald* (November 13, 1978).

4 *Independent* (July 27, 1988).

5 *The 7.30 Report*, ABC Television, July 26, 1988.

6 *Sydney Morning Herald* (August 18, 1988).

7 *Socialist Labour* (June–July 1986).

8 World Bank figures, cited *New Statesman* (October 18, 1991).

9 Ted Trainer, a sociologist at the University of New South Wales, is author of *Developed to Death: Rethinking Third World Development* (Marshall Pickering, London, 1989).

10 Interviewed by the author, Washington, August 1987.

11 *The Eye* (September 1988).

12 *Australian* (February 15, 1985).

13 Desmond Ball, *A Base for Debate* (Allen & Unwin, Sydney, 1987), p. 76.

14 *Sydney Morning Herald* (November 23, 1988).

15 Ibid. (May 16, 1987).

16 Interview with the author, Radio 2GB Sydney, March 23, 1988.

17 *Sydney Morning Herald* (May 19, 1988).

18   Honolulu *Star Bulletin* (December 1, 1983).
19   Cited in *Tribune* (November 16, 1983).
20   Ibid.
21   *Sydney Morning Herald* (February 14, 1984).
22   Cited in *Tribune* (February 29, 1984).
23   *Sydney Morning Herald* (April 16, 1988).
24   Bill Hayden, February 22, 1983, cited by William Pinwill, despatch to *National Times* dated April 13, 1983.
25   *Sydney Morning Herald* (March 13, 1989).
26   General Assembly Resolution 1514, XV, and Security Council Resolution 384 (1975).
27   Moynihan's memoir cited by Noam Chomsky, *Guardian* (January 10, 1991).
28   Cited by Catherine Lumby, *Sydney Morning Herald* (January 9, 1992).
29   Cited by Chomsky.
30   Cited by Lumby.
31   Cited in *Backgrounder* published by Tapol, the Indonesian Human Rights Campaign. London (February, 1991).
32   Ibid.
33   Australian *Hansard* (November 1, 1989).
34   Cited by Chomsky.
35   Ibid. (November 18, 1987). I am indebted to Mary-Louise O'Callaghan for her perceptive reporting of New Zealand.
36   Gavan McCormack, 'Korea and the Cold War: Towards a World Historical Perspective', a paper presented at a conference at Yokohama, Japan, July 6–8, 1985.

INDEX

Abarcia, Sonja, 117
Abbott, Barry, 63
ABC (Australian Broadcasting
  Corporation), 65, 233, 237, 290,
  295–307
Abeles, Lady 'Kitty', 258
Abeles, Sir Peter, 254–9, 267, 276,
  318–19
Aboriginal Advancement Council, 58
Aboriginal National Theatre Trust,
  73
Aborigines, 21–82; artists, 36–40,
  62–3, 72–3; and Ayers Rock, 170;
  birth rate, 64; at Bondi beach,
  19–20; cemeteries, 45, 67;
  children, 23–4, 67–73; deaths and
  illnesses, 32, 34–5, 38–9, 45–6,
  83; deaths in police custody,
  54–62, 73; early civilisation,
  27–30; killing of, 31–5, 50–4; at
  La Perouse, 23–5; land rights
  movement, 42–51, 63–4, 84–5;
  life expectancy, 45–6; population
  figures, 64, 78; settlements near
  nuclear test site, 169–74; *Sun*
  article on, 267; in textbooks, 25–7
Aborigines Progressive Association,
  78
Aborigines Protection Board, 68, 69
Aborigines Protection Society, 31
abortions, 16
Age: see Melbourne *Age*
airline industry, 267, 318–19
Alabama (United States), 46
Alice Springs, 36–9, 44–5, 197
All Quiet on the Western Front, 147
Allcorp Cleaning Services, 319
Allende, Salvador, 194, 204, 212
Alpuget, Blanche d', 255, 311

Anderson, Warren, 274–5
Angleton, James Jesus, 192, 198, 220,
  231
Ansett airline, 256, 259, 267–8, 319
Anthony, Doug, 221
Anthony Hordens (department store),
  89
Anti-Slavery Society, 54, 79
ANU (Australian National
  University), 125, 131
Anzac Day, 142
ANZUS Pact, 165, 196, 363
Arena, Franca, 135–6
Argus (newspaper), 142
artists, Aboriginal, 36–40, 62–3,
  72–3
Ashbolt, Alan, 308
Asian immigrants, 119–38
ASIO (Australian Security and
  Intelligence Organisation), 160,
  166, 190–4, 204–5, 207, 209, 218,
  220–1, 222, 228, 283
ASIS (Australian Secret Intelligence
  Service), 193–4, 220, 316
Askin, Sir Robert, 254–5, 259
assimilation policy, 107
Assisted Passage Scheme, 111–12
Association for Cultural Freedom,
  234
Atorino, Ed, 5
Attlee, Clement, 168
Australian, 49, 125, 233, 236, 265,
  270, 302
Australian Arbitration Commission,
  118
Australian Commission for Cultural
  Freedom, 215
Australian Broadcasting Corporation:
  see ABC

Australian Broadcasting Tribunal, 129, 278, 291
Australian Journalists' Association, 278, 281, 309
Australian National Dictionary, 27
Australian Press Council, 279
Ayers Rock, 169–70

Bacon, Wendy, 282, 305
balance of payments, 276
Ball, Desmond, 194–5, 201, 363
'Balts' (immigrants from Baltic states), 104–7, 130
Bandler, Faith, 166, 303
Barak (Yarra Yarra elder), 68
Barbour, Peter, 220
Barnard, Lance, 188, 202
Barnard, Marjorie, 330
Barrington, George, 99
Basher Gang, 150, 355
Battarbee, Rex, 39
Bavandra, Dr Timoci, 363
Bayley, Edwin R., 235
Because a White Man'll Never Do It (Gilbert), 73
Beeston, John, 305
Bendigo, 119, 123
Bennelong Point, Sydney, 101, 115
Bentham, Jeremy, 92
Bermingham, Craig, 346
Bernays, Edward, 5
Bicentenary celebrations, 76–80
Bingara: Myall Creek massacre at, 51–4
Bissell, Richard, 225, 246–8
Bjelke-Petersen, Sir Johannes, 1, 46, 227–8, 292, 321–3
Black, Conrad, 312–14
Black, Edwin, 210
Blainey, Geoffrey, 124–5, 131, 133
Blakemore, Michael, 18
Bloomfield, Ray, 145
'boat people', 123
Bobbin Up (Hewett), 330
Bonanza Class, 333–4
Bond, Alan, 4, 264, 272, 276, 286–94, 308, 320–5
Bond, Eileen, 289
Bondi beach, 9–20
Bonegilla migrant camp, 112–14, 135
Boney, Lloyd, 59–60

Booker, Malcolm, 154, 155
'Botany case', 260
Bowman, David, 282, 285, 315–17
Boyce, Christopher, 212–15, 230, 236, 252
Boyer, Al, 349
Bradley, Lieutenant, 32
Brandt, Willy, 220
Brereton, Laurie, 260
Briggs, Geraldine, 67
Britain, 331; immigrants from, 102–3, 111; immigrants in, 128–9; and the Second World War, 154–5, 156; and the Thatcher Government, 309–10
Brogan, Sir Mervyn, 179
Broken Hill, 4, 340–8
Brookfield, Percy, 347–8
Brooks, Geraldine, 329–30
Brown, Norman, 150
Bundy, William, 182
Burger, Dr Julian, 54
Burgmann, Verity, 3
Burke, Brian, 47, 321
Burns, Creighton, 312
Burton, Dr John, 158, 159, 160
Burton, Tom, 313
Bush, George, 211, 235, 353, 370
Business International, 252–3
Butlin, Noel, 80
Byron, Pam, 345, 347

Cain, John, 312
Cairns, Dr Jim, 189, 191, 204, 206–7, 218
Calcagno, Carlo and Maria, 115–16, 136
Calwell, Arthur, 87, 102, 104, 111, 130
Cambodia, 194, 202, 270, 365
Cameron, Clyde, 203, 229, 249, 251
Cameron, James, 164
Campbelltown, Sydney, 335, 337–9
Canberra, 297–8; Aboriginal rally in, 64–5
Canberra Times, 300, 311
Captive Press, The (Bowman), 315–17
Carey, Alex, 181
Carmichael, Alex, 258, 259
Carroll, Alan, 253

Carter, Jimmy, 230, 238, 267–8
Casey, Lord, 165
Casey, Ron, 129, 131, 133
Casey, William, 190
Cassidy, Barrie, 297, 299, 301
Castellorizia (Greek island), 114
Catholics: in Bondi, 12
Caulfield's Lagoon: massacre of
    Aborigines at, 52–3
Chadwick, Paul, 279, 285
Chifley, Ben, 104, 157, 160, 161,
    166, 254, 332
children: Aboriginal, 23, 65–73; in
    poverty, 5, 334–6
Chile: Allende Government,
    overthrow of, 194, 204, 212–13,
    222, 251, 364; investment in, 4;
    refugees from, 117, 190
China, 176, 180; Boxer Rebellion,
    142
Chinese immigrants, 119–23
Choong, Mrs, 138
Christopher, Warren, 230
Christopherson, John, 77
Chulung, Frank, 77
Churchill, Winston, 91, 154, 156
CIA (Central Intelligence Agency),
    175, 176, 177, 178, 179, 185,
    187–238, 362–5; Australian trade
    unions, 246–51; and Bob Hawke,
    251–2; and the LCPA, 364–5; and
    the loans affair, 207–12; and
    Vietnam, 175
Cilento, Sir Raphael, 26
citizenship, 134–6; ceremonies,
    136–8
Clark, Ed, 201
Clark, Manning, 141, 182, 303, 306
Clark, Reg, 16–17
Cline, Dr Ray, 222
Coates, George, 147
Coe, Paul, 63
Colby, William, 185, 210, 211, 219,
    235
Cold War Two and Australia
    (Phillips), 160
Coldicutt, Ken, 188, 227
Collins, Jock, 123, 125
Combe, David, 256
Comerford, Jim, 150
Commerce International, 206, 318

Communist Party of Australia:
    referendum on, 166
Connell, Laurie 'Last Resort', 311,
    320
Connolly, Patrick, 172
Connor, Rex, 205, 218
conscription: ending of, 189; and the
    Vietnam War, 180; women's
    campaign against (1916), 145–6
convicts, 90–101; women, 93–101
Cook, Mrs Esme, 9–10
Cootamundra Training Home for
    Aboriginal Girls, 69
Cope, Bill, 127
Corbett, Helen, 65
Cordell, Michael, 81
Corson, William, 200
Costigan Commission, 317–18
County Securities Australia, 286
Cousins, Leila, 126
Coxsedge, Joan, 188, 227
Crimes of Patriots, The (Kwitny),
    215–16
Crocodile Dundee (film), 100, 307
Crowley, Robert, 198
CSD (Combined Studies Division),
    177
Csidei, Bela, 257
Cuba, 207, 210
Cullen, Peter, 81–2
Curlewis, Jean, 13
currawongs: on Bondi, 9–10
Curtin, John, 156, 157, 158, 159,
    188
Cusack, Dymphna, 330

D'Arcy, Bill, 236
Daily Mirror (Sydney), 217, 270, 277
Daily Telegraph (Sydney), 101
Dampier, William, 31
Danby, Michael, 306
Darling, Ralph, 264
Davey, Des, 174
Davis, Ian, 300
Dawe, Bruce, 34
Day, Brian, 177–8
Day, David, 156
'Death in Custody' (painting), 73
Democratic Labor Party (DLP), 167,
    215
Depression (1930s), 152, 161, 272, 351

Devanney, Jean, 330
Displaced Persons programme, 104–111, 129
doctors: immigrant, 129
Dodson, Pat, 66–7, 83
Domican, Tom, 275
Dorrance, John C., 235
Dougherty, Martin, 311
Dougherty, Tom, 247
Douglas-Home, Charles, 265
'dreaming tracks' (Aboriginal), 29
DSD (Defence Signals Directorate), 194–5, 223
Duffy, Michael, 277
Dulles, John Foster, 164
Dunstan, Don, 190–1
Dupain, Max, 19

Easson, Michael, 364
economic policies: and the Great Depression, 152; Government, 271–2, 275–6, 333–4, 359–61; New Zealand Government, 370–2
Eisenhower, Dwight D., 175, 247
Eldridge, J. C., 152
Elizabeth II, Queen, 39, 161, 229, 254; oath of allegiance to, 135–7
Ellercamp, Paul, 297
Elliott, John, 131, 272, 288
Encyclopaedia Britannica, 26
Enderby, Kep, 204
Evans, Gareth, 48, 133, 316, 317, 366, 370
Evans, Neil, 209
Evatt, Dr Herbert Vere, 156, 157, 159, 163, 166, 370
Eye, The, 283, 315

Fairfax, James, 282, 311
Fairfax, Sir Warwick and Lady Mary, 244
Fairfax, Warwick 'Young Wokka', 311
Fairfax organisation, 264, 281, 290, 311–14
Fairhall, Alan, 199
Falklands War, 266, 269
Family Reunion Programme, 126, 130
Fancher, Henry Wiley, 1, 228
Farquhar, Murray, 260
Farrell, 'Bumper', 16

Fatal Shore, The (Hughes), 2, 93
Feiffer, Jules, 327
Female Eunuch, The (Greer), 183
Female Factory, 94
Ferguson, Bill, 78
Ferguson, Tony, 296, 301, 303
Fesl, Eve, 50, 75
Fiji, 363
'Fiona' (car), 15–16
First World War, 142–7, 149
Fishlock, Trevor, 7
Fitzgerald, Ross, 80
Fitzgerald, Tony, 322
FitzGerald Report, 130, 133
Fitzjames, Michael, 283
Flynn, Joseph, 208
Flynn, Sonny, 52
Fokkema, Gerrit, 170
Foley, Gary, 65
Foreign Takeovers Act, 277, 278, 279–80
Four Corners (TV programme), 281, 290, 307
France, 331; fascism in, 131; testing of nuclear weapons, 365, 366
Franklin, Miles, 330
Fraser, Malcolm, 44, 124, 131, 208, 218, 223, 227, 228, 234–5, 242–3, 313
Fratianno, Jimmy 'the Weasel', 257
Freney, Denis, 231
Frontier (Reynolds), 80

Game, Sir Philip, 153
Gander, Bob, 137
Georgetown International Labor Programme, 364
Germany, 131, 331
Gilbert, Kevin, 73
Gittins, Ross, 309–10
Glynn, Freda, 74, 75
gold diggers: Chinese, 119, 121–3
Goldberg, Arthur J. ('Harry'), 187, 247–8, 250
Gorbachev, Mikhail, 374
Gorton, John, 139, 179, 199
Governor-General: office of, 356–9
Gray, Harry, 268
Greek immigrants, 112
Green, Marshall, 139, 203, 218, 235, 246, 251

Greer, Germaine, 183, 233
Grenada, US invasion of, 269
Grenville, John, 246, 250
Grodin, Nancy, 210
Guilty Secrets (Pullan), 263
Gurindji people, 43, 44, 65

Haildary, Zalmai, 129
Hall, Edward Smith, 51, 263–4
Hall, Richard, 190, 216, 217, 229
Hand, Michael, 208, 209
Harant, Gerry, 188, 227
Harries, Owen, 234
Harris, George, 206, 207
Harris, Stewart, 64–5, 81
Harrison, Joe, 215
Harvard Training Programme, 248
Hasluck, Sir Paul, 216
Hatton, John, 255
Haupt, Robert, 81, 283
Hawke, Bob, 79, 83, 130, 133, 227, 239, 241–5, 250–326; and Aboriginal land rights, 46, 47, 48, 49; becomes Prime Minister, 253; campaign for ACTU presidency, 250–2; and Eddie Kornhauser, 323; J.P.'s Melbourne meeting with, 241, 262; J.P.'s televison interview with (1987), 297–304; and Kerry Packer, 313; and the LCPA, 364–5; libel actions, 311; meeting with Fairfaxes, 244; and the MX missile incident, 271, 362; and Rupert Murdoch, 261–2, 265, 276–88; third election campaign, 307–8; as trade-union lawyer, 243; and the United States, 362; and Whitlam, 227
Hawke Government: and Aboriginal deaths in custody, 58–60; economic policies, 271–2, 275–81, 333–4, 359–61; and immigration, 130–8
Hawkesbury (river), 32
Hayden, Bill, 87, 134, 232, 253, 278, 281, 299, 365, 367; as Governor-General, 358–9
Helliwell, Paul, 207
Henderson, Gerard, 233–4, 306
Hepworth, John, 303
Herald: see Melbourne *Herald*

Herman, Mayor Lew, 137–8
Heseltine, Michael, 269
Hewett, Dorothy, 162, 303, 330
Hewett, Tony, 60, 81
Hickie, David, 255, 282
Highfield, John, 303
Hill, David, 296–7, 301–5, 307, 326
Hilton Hotel deal, 291
Hinze, Russ, 228, 323
history: Australian, 2–4, 24–7, 53–4, 84
History of Australia (Clark), 182
History of Australian Land Settlement (Roberts), 27
Hitler, Adolf, 33, 46, 154
Ho Chi Minh, 175
Hogan, John, 288
Hogan, Paul, 11, 335
Holding, Clyde, 46, 48, 49, 50
Holt, Harold, 179, 199, 201
Holten, H. R., 199
home ownership, 336
homeless children, 5, 334–6
Hopetoun, Earl of, 141, 147
Horin, Adele, 282, 334
Horne, Donald, 146, 182
Houghton, Bernie, 209
House of Commons Select Committee (1838), 42, 87, 95–6
housing, 329–31, 336–7
Howard, John, 132, 234, 277, 278
Hugenberg, Aldred, 315
Hughes, Billy, 145, 146
Hughes, Robert, 2, 93, 94, 233
Hughes, Wilfred Kent, 164
Hungarian refugees, 105
Hunter Valley, 150, 288, 355
Hurley, David, 319
Hussein, Saddam, 306, 368, 369
Hutton, John, 173
Huxley, Aldous, 5

Illawara Mercury, 81
immigrants: Asian, 119–38; at Bondi beach, 14; British, 102, 103, 111; at Broken Hill, 344; Chilean, 117, 190; Chinese, 119–23; Italian, 111, 116–17; Turkish, 1–2, 118, 128; Vietnamese, 118, 124, 125, 126

immigration: post-war policies, 103–138
Imparja Television, 74–6
Indonesia, 31, 190, 203, 223, 249, 368–70
infant mortality rates: central Australia, 38
Inmam, Bobby, 212
'Institute of Public Affairs', 233, 234
intelligence services: see ASIO; ASIS; CIA; DSD; JIO
International Monetary Fund, 158, 361
Italian immigrants, 111–16, 117

Jackson, Keith, 302
Jacobson, Howard, 261
James, Henry, 6
Japan, 155, 156, 157, 202, 360
Japanese tourists, 170, 349
Jay Creek: visit to, 40–2
'Jay Creek Country' (painting), 37, 40
Jews, 12, 119; and immigration policies, 104–5
JIO (Joint Intelligence Organisation), 195
Jockel, Gordon, 176
Joe McCarthy and the Press (Bayley), 235
John, Elton, 266
John Barry (convict ship), 92, 93
Johnson, Lyndon B., 139, 181, 182, 199, 201
Jones, Hazel, 349

Kalantzis, Mary, 127
Kalkadoons: extermination of, 33–4
Kampuchea: see Cambodia
kangaroos: red, 168
Kealy, P. L., 200
Kearsley, Bob, 301, 302, 304
Keating, Paul, 271, 273–6, 277, 280–2, 286, 289, 305, 312, 321, 324, 333, 353, 356, 359; and Abeles, 319
Keenan, Andrew, 314
Kelly, Mike, 349
Kemp, Jack, 268
Kennedy, Edward, 267
Kennedy, John F., 175
Kent, Bruce, 6

Kerin, John, 313
Kerr, Sir John, 44, 215–18, 222–4, 228, 229, 233, 237, 238, 242, 355
Khemlani, Tirath, 205, 207, 208, 218
Kiernan, Thomas, 265, 268
Kinchella Home for Aboriginal Boys, 69
King, Harry and Kath, 349–52
Kirk, Jim, 135
Kissinger, Henry, 222
Knightley, Phillip, 265
Korean War, 111, 164, 166
Kornhauser, Eddie, 323
Kundera, Milan, 238
Kurri Kurri, 147, 150–2
Kwitny, Jonathan, 215–16, 234

La Perouse, 23–4
labour movement, 331–2
Lack, Glem, 26
Lamb, Sir Larry, 265
Lambert, George, 147
Lambing Flat gold field, 121–2
land rights movement, 42–50, 63, 83–4, 370
Landsdale, Edward, 175
Lang, Jack, 107, 152–3
Lange, David, 363, 372
Langton, Marcia, 65
Last Dream, The (film), 3, 80, 232, 237
Law of the Land, The (Reynolds), 80
Lawson, Henry, 122, 330
LCPA (Labor Committee for Pacific Affairs), 364–5
League of Rights, 125
Lee, Andrew Daulton, 213–14
Lee, Jenny, 3
Leigh, David, 220
Lenin, V. I., 332
Lewis, Sir Terence, 322
Libya, 270
Lindahl, Emil, 249–50
Lingiari, Victor, 65
Lingiari, Vincent, 44
Lippmann, Walter, 175
Llana, Peter, 129
Lockhart, Greg, 199
Lodge, Henry Cabot, 179
Loomis, Patry, 210

Lousy Little Sixpence (film), 69
Lowery, Alan, 3, 62, 296
Lowry, L. S., 11
Lucky Country, The (Horne), 183
Lynch, Phillip, 206

MacArthur, General Douglas, 155, 164
McCarthy, Francis (ancestor of J.P.), 91–3, 96
McClelland, James, 168, 303, 310, 320
McCormack, Gavan, 371
McCoy, Dr Alfred, 364
McElroy, Lynne, 127
McHale, Edward, 249, 251
Macken, Deirdre, 333
McMahon, William, 187, 199
McNeill, Ian, 177
Macphee, Ian, 278, 280
Macquarie, Governor Lachlan, 32
McQueen, Humphrey, 158
Mahoney, Frank, 221
Makeev, Michael and Valentina, 109–11
Man Makes History: World History from the Earliest Times to the Renaissance (Ward), 25
Mangano, 'Benny Eggs', 257
Manning, Peter, 307
Mannix, N. J., 259
Manor, General LeRoy, 210
Mansell, Michael, 65
Maralinga: nuclear test site at, 170–4
Marchetti, Victor, 185, 197, 198, 210, 216, 225, 353, 362
Marcos, Imelda, 307
Maréchal Suchet (ship), 148
Maris, Hyllus, 29–30, 67
Marks, John, 216
Markus, Andrew, 33, 50
marriage: of J.P.'s great-great grandparents, 96; of immigrants, by proxy, 115, 116; marriage market for convicts, 96
Marston, Dr Hedley, 172
Martin, Ray, 236, 303
Marx, Karl, 332
Materials Production Project, 127
Mates, 3, 239–326
Mathews, 'Matchstick', 52

Maxwell, Robert, 312
Mayman, Jan, 81
Melbourne *Age*, 125, 225, 238, 311, 312
Melbourne Club, 241–2
Melbourne *Herald*, 236, 276
Menzies, Robert (later Sir Robert), 111, 139, 154–5, 161–7, 168–9, 174, 180, 187, 206, 362, 370; and American bases, 201; and Melbourne, 241; and Vietnam, 180, 181
'middle Australia': concept of, 333
Middle East War, 202, 205, 219
Migrant Hands in a Distant Land (Collins), 123
Miles, Bea, 17
Miller, Mick, 65
Milliken, Robert, 173, 239, 317
millionaires, 4, 273, 333–4
mineworkers: at Broken Hill, 340–8; in the Hunter Valley, 150, 288
mining companies: and Aboriginal land rights, 46–50; and Chinese gold diggers, 121–3
Moffit, Athol, 317
Mollerin, 350–1
Monash, John, 143
Moore, John, 267
Morgan, Alec, 3, 62, 69
Moynihan, Daniel Patrick, 368
multi-cultural: in Australia, 102–4, 127–38
Mulvaney, D. J., 80
Mungo, Lake, 27–8
Murdoch, Keith, 276
Murdoch, Rupert, 5, 49, 121, 254, 259–62, 272, 276–80; and the airline industry, 318; and Bob Hawke, 261–2, 265, 276–88; News Corporation, 269; newspapers, 264–71; takeover of Herald and Weekly Times group, 276–81, 308–9; and the United States, 267–71
Murphy, Lionel, 190, 192, 228
Murray, Arthur, 55, 57–8, 60
Murray, Eddie, 55–8, 59, 60
Myall Creek massacre, 51

Nader, Ralph, 46
Nagy, Leslie, 206

Namatjira, Albert, 37, 38–40, 45, 62
Namatjira, Oscar, 37, 38, 45, 62
Namatjira, Reg, 62, 63
Namatjira, Rubina, 37, 40, 45
National Action, 125
National Times, 48, 191, 206, 254, 255, 259, 281–2, 305, 315
Neighbours (television programme), 338
New Guard, 153
'New World' policies, 157, 158
New York Post, 270
New York Times, 214, 252, 268
New Zealand, 142, 363, 370–2
newspapers: on multi-culturalism, 127–8; ownership of, 5, 264, 276–81, 311–13. *See also* individual newspapers
Ngo Dinh Diem, 175
Niemeyer, Sir Otto, 152, 272
Nixon, Richard M., 189, 192, 196, 202, 212, 236, 246, 247, 261, 262
NLF (National Liberation Front, Vietcong), 176, 180
Non-aligned Movement, 190
Non-European Policy, 105
North West Cape base, 201–3
Northern Territory: Aborigines in, 43–4, 62–3, 77
NSA (American National Security Agency), 194–5
nuclear weapons: Australian attitudes to, 365; British testing of, in Australia, 168, 171–4; and the Hawke Government, 362, 363, 365; and New Zealand, 363, 370–2
Nugan, Frank, 209, 210–12, 307
Nugan Hand Bank, 208, 209–12, 231, 307, 318
Nurrungar: American base at, 199, 200–1, 202, 363

O'Callaghan, Mary-Louise, 371
O'Connor, C. Y.: Great Pipe, 348, 350
O'Hoy, Denis, 119, 122–3
O'Hoy, Louey, 123
O'Hoy, Que, 123
O'Keefe, Gerry, 250, 364
O'Neil, Shorty, 343–5

O'Reilly, Tony, 312
Oak Valley, 173–4
Obiri paintings, 28–9
Oldfield, Maurice, 219
ONA (National Assessments), 195
One Australia Policy, 132
Order of Mates, 4, 239–326
Osborne, Barton, 177
Other Side of the Frontier, The (Reynolds), 30, 80
outstation movement, 61
outworkers, 117–19

Packer, Frank, 160, 287
Packer, Kerry, 74, 259, 264, 272, 286, 308, 313, 319, 325
Palm Island: cemetery on, 45
Palm Valley (painting), 37
Palmer, Mary (ancestor of J.P.), 91, 93–5, 96
Papunya people, 36
Parker, Doug, 351
Pat, John, 59, 61
Patten, Jack, 78–9
Patterson, 'Banjo', 330
Patton, W. H., 340
peace movement, 165–6; New Zealand, 370–2
Peacock, Andrew, 223–4, 317
Peacock, Matt, 81
Penny, Sir William, 172
People's History of Australia, A (Burgmann and Lee), 3
Perkins, Charlie, 40–1, 42, 65
Perkins, Hetti, 40, 41, 42
Perron, Marshall, 132
Personal History of the Australian Surf, A (Blakemore), 18
Perth, 321, 348
Petrov, Vladimir (Petrov affair), 167
Phillip, Captain Arthur, 24, 77
Phillips, Dennis, 160, 165
'Phoenix Programme' in Vietnam, 177, 179, 208, 210
Pilger, Alice (grandmother of J.P.), 148
Pilger, Elsie (mother of J.P.), 17, 89–90, 146, 147, 150
Pilger, John: at Bondi beach, 9–20; meets Bob Hawke in Melbourne, 241, 262; parents and

grandparents, 147–9; schooling, 162–3; television interview with Bob Hawke, 297–304

Pilger, Richard (grandfather of J.P.), 146

Pilger, Sam (son of J.P.), 170

Pine Gap (American base), 197–200, 201, 202, 204, 212, 213–14, 219, 221–3, 228, 230, 252, 363

Pinwill, William, 214, 236, 250

Platt, Jack, 17, 18, 19

Plimsoll, James, 164

poetry: Aboriginal, 21, 29–30

Pol Pot, 127, 194, 233, 270, 365

police: and Aborigines, 53–60, 66, 67–8

porpoises: at Bondi beach, 19

Porter, Barry, 309

poverty, 272, 327, 329–39; in Sydney, 11–12, 329–39

Powell, Enoch, 133

Powell, Webster, 159

Price, Dr Charles, 134

Prichard, Katharine Susannah, 149

Probert, Belinda, 306

Proctor, Dr John, 219

Progress Party, 307

Pullan, Robert, 263

Qadafi, Colonel, 270

Quat, Dr Phan Huy, 180

Queensland, 321–3; Aborigines in, 33, 45–6, 48, 52

Rabuka, Colonel, 363

racism, 129–34

radio broadcasting: Aboriginal station, 74–6

Ramsey, Alan, 271, 274

Raratonga, Treaty of, 365

Rasp, Charles, 340

Raynor, Hayden, 159

Razak, Tun Abdul, 193

Reagan, Ronald, 240, 268–9

Reilly, Richard, 260

Renouf, Alan, 179

Returned Soldiers and Sailors Imperial League, 147

Revill, Stuart, 301

Reynolds, Grahame, 304–5

Reynolds, Henry, 2, 30, 80

Rice, Walter, 196

Riesel, Victor, 247

Riley, Bob, 65

Riley, Murray, 257

Roberts, Jan, 81

Roberts, Rhoda, 73

Roberts, Stephen, 27

Roe, Jill, 331

Roosevelt, Franklin D., 156

Rose, Murray, 17

Rothwell's Bank, 294, 321

Ryan, Colleen, 282, 314

Samuels, Peter, 205

Saunders, Justine, 73

Saunders, Woli, 3

Savigil, Rukiye, 118

Schachner, Robert, 333

Schlesinger, James, 202

schools: multi-racial, 127

Schuller, Karl, 210

Scully, Gary, 297

Second World War, 146, 154–6

secret ballot, 4, 331

Secret State, The (Hall), 190

segregation, racial: in New South Wales, 41

Sen, Hun, 365

Serong, Ted, 177, 179

'sesquicententary' celebrations, 76–8

Sgro, Giovanni, 112–14

Shackley, Theodore, 221–2

Shaw, A. G. L., 152

Short, Laurie, 247

Shultz, George, 246, 362, 367

Sihanouk, Prince (Cambodia), 194

Silverton, 347

Singapore, 132, 360

Singleton, John, 81, 307, 314

Skase, Christopher, 294–5

Smith, Joan, 169

Smith, Lawrence, H., 167

Snepp, Frank, 190

Snowy Mountains Scheme, 108–10, 114, 157

Solarz, Stephen, 366–7

Somervaille, Rob, 305

South Africa, 35–6, 80, 100, 133, 142

Spender, Percy, 164, 165

Spooner, Eric, 14
Springborg, Robert, 306
Spry, Sir Charles, 235
squatters, 99, 163
Squatting Age in Australia, The
  (Roberts), 27
'Stain, The', 90, 99, 162
Stallings, Richard, 198–9, 221, 222
Steketee, Mike, 304
Stevenson, Adlai, 176
Stewart, Meg, 7, 14
Stokes, Edward, 340
Stratton, Tom, 105–7, 130
strikes: Great Strike at Broken Hill
  (1919), 341–8; Gurindji people,
  42–3; Hunter Valley mines, 150
Strong, James, 48
Sudono, Agus, 250
Suich, Max, 282
suicide rates in Australia, 5
Sukarno, Achmed (President of
  Indonesia), 203
Sun (British newspaper), 265, 266
Sun (Sydney), 235, 236
'Sunbaker, The' (photograph), 19
sweatshops, clothing, 118
Sydney: corruption in, 255, 260;
  poverty in, 11–12, 330, 334–9
'Sydney Institute': *see* 'Institute of
  Public Affairs'
Sydney Mail, 78
Sydney Monitor, 33, 51, 263
Sydney Morning Herald, 5, 68, 80,
  82, 107, 121, 125, 126, 225, 235,
  237, 282, 290, 302, 303, 306, 309,
  311, 313, 318, 325, 338, 346, 368
Sydney Surfing (Curlewis), 13
Sykes, Roberta, 69

Taiwan, 360
Tange, Sir Arthur, 221
Tasmania: Aborigines in, 33, 48
Tate, Michael, 295
Taylor, Elizabeth, 1
Teamsters' Union, 255, 257
television broadcasting: Imparja
  Television, 74–6; 'restructuring'
  under the Hawke Government,
  286, 308; Sky Channel, 266,
  267
Tennant, Kylie, 330

terra nullius: concept of, 25, 42
Terry, Roger, 95
Tham, Rudy, 256–7
Thatcher, Margaret, 265, 266, 269;
  Britain under, 130, 309–10
Thomas, Heather, 345
Thomas, Richard, 296, 297
Thompson, Thelma, 339–41, 342,
  343
Throssell, Jim, 149
Tieri, Frank, 257
Times, The, 265, 266
Times on Sunday, 311
Tjukurpa culture, 170
TNT (Thomas National Transport),
  254, 255, 256, 258, 276
Tolpuddle, Martyrs, 92
Toohey, Brian, 191–2, 208, 222,
  236, 244, 282; and *The Eye*, 283,
  315; on Warren Anderson, 274–5
Tourang Consortium, 313–14
tourism, 44, 347
trachoma (eye disease), 35
trade unions: and the CIA, 246–52;
  and the Gurindji people, 42–3; and
  the Hawke Government, 333; and
  outworkers, 118–19; racial
  exclusion from, 103
Trainer, Ted, 361
Trento, Joseph, 225
Triumph in the Tropics (Cilento and
  Lack), 26
Turkish immigrants, 1–2, 118, 128
Turnbull, Malcolm, 74
Turner, John, 300
Twain, Mark, 330

UKUSA Co-operative Intelligence
  Agreement, 160, 191, 194–5
unemployment, 298, 310
United Nations, 163–4; study of
  Aborigines, 80
United States, 139, 156, 353,
  362–70; and Australia under
  Menzies, 163–83; Australian
  attitudes to, 100; and communist
  influence in Australia, 160–1;
  military installations in Australia,
  197–204; and New Zealand, 372;
  and Rupert Murdoch, 267–71. *See
  also* CIA

United Technologies, 268
United We Stand (Stokes), 340
Unsworth, Barrie, 248

Vann, John Paul, 176
Vestey, Lord, 43
Victoria, Queen, 92, 341
Vidal, Gore, 6
Vietnam War, 123, 145, 175–82,
  189–200, 208–9, 210, 367–8
Vietnamese immigrants, 18, 123, 124,
  125, 126, 128
Villers-Bretonneux (French village),
  143–5

Walker, John, 209
Walkinshaw, Robert, 249, 250, 251
Wallace, George, 46
Waller, Ruth, 73
Walsh, Max, 133, 308
Walsh, Mike, 297
Ward, Barbara, 319
Ward, Russel, 25
Waugh, Auberon, 82
Wearne, J. T., 52
Webb, Beatrice and Sidney, 332
Weiner, Herbert, 246
welfare benefits, 4, 152–3, 336, 338;
  and immigrants, 130; under
  Whitlam, 189
Westbridge Migrant Hostel, Sydney,
  126
Western Australia: towns in, 348–52
Westerway, Peter, 313
Westland affair, 269
Weston, Hunter, 142
Wheelwright, Ted, 359, 361
White, Dr Peter, 80

White Australia Policy, 105, 132, 157
Whitlam, Edward Gough, 43–4,
  46–7, 123–4, 187–8, 307, 356;
  Government of, 159, 187–92, 193,
  194, 195, 201–31; and the
  Governor-General, 356–7; reasons
  for fall of, 224–8; sacking of,
  220–4; television interviews,
  237–8; on trade unions and the
  CIA, 252
Whitton, Evan, 282, 310
Wick, Charles Z., 269
Wilkes, Owen, 198
Wilkinson, Marian, 206, 282
Williams, Graham, 81, 338
Williams, Joy, 70–3
Willis, Ralph, 313
Wilson, Edwin, 209
Wilson, Harold, 220
Wilson Plot, The (Leigh), 220
women: at Broken Hill, 339–40;
  campaign against conscription
  (1916), 145–6; convicts, 93–101;
  post-war immigrants, 114–18;
  poverty, 329–30, 336–9
Women of the Sun (Maris), 65
Woodward Commission, 43
Woolcott, Richard, 369
Wootten, Hal, 279
World Bank, 361
Wran, Jill, 258, 259, 319
Wran, Neville, 248, 258–61, 281,
  296, 301, 319, 356
Wright, Jabez, 341
Wright, Peter, 220, 231

Yates, Earl, 210
Yunupingu, Galarrwuy, 65